Alaska Northwest Books™
Anchorage • Seattle

Copyright © 1989 by GTE Discovery Publications, Inc. All rights reserved. No part of this book may be reproduced or transmitted in any form or by any means, electronic or mechanical, including photocopying, recording or by any information storage and retrieval system, without written permission of the publisher.

Thirteenth edition 1990

ISBN 0-88240-246-3
ISSN 0270-5370
Key title: The Alaska Almanac

From the editors of
The MILEPOST®, THE ALASKA WILDERNESS MILEPOST®
and NORTHWEST MILEPOSTS®

Cover illustration by Mark Zingarelli

Alaska Northwest Books™
A division of GTE Discovery Publications, Inc.
22026 20th Avenue S.E.
Bothell, Washington 98021

Printed in U.S.A.

Contents

Agriculture	1
Air Travel	2
Alaska Highway	4
Alaska Northwest Library	197
Alcoholic Beverages	6
Alyeska	6
Amphibians	6
Arctic Circle	7
Arctic Winter Games	7
Aurora Borealis	8
Baleen	9
Barabara	9
Baseball	9
Baskets	10
Beadwork	11
Berries	11
Billiken	12
Birds	12
Blanket Toss	13
Boating	14
Bore Tide	15
Breakup	15
Bunny Boots	15
Bus Lines	16
Bush	16
Cabin Fever	16
Cabins	17
Cache	18
Calendar of Events	18
Camping	21
Canada-Alaska Boundary	22
Chambers of Commerce	23
Cheechako	24
Chilkat Blankets	24
Chilkoot Trail	24
Chill Factor	24
Chitons	25
Climate	25
Coal	28
Conk	29
Constitution of Alaska	29
Continental Divide	40
Convention and Visitors Bureaus	41
Coppers	41
Cost of Living	41
Courts	42
Cruises	44
Dalton Highway	45
Daylight Hours	46
Diamond Willow	46
Dog Mushing	46
Earthquakes	48
Education	49
Employment	50
End of the Trail[e]	51
Energy and Power	62
Eskimo Ice Cream	63
Ferries	63
Fires on Wild Lands	65
Fish Wheel	66
Fishing	66
Furs and Trapping	69
Glaciers and Ice Fields	70
Gold	71
Gold Strikes and Rushes	72
Government	73
Highways	74
Hiking	75
History	76
Holidays	78
Hooligan	78
Hospitals and Health Facilities	78
Hostels	79
Hot Springs	80
Hunting	81
Hypothermia	82
Ice	83
Icebergs	83
Ice Fog	84
Iceworm	84
Iditarod Trail Sled Dog Race	84
Igloo	86
Imports and Exports	86
Income	87
Industry	87
Information Sources	87
Islands	88
Ivory	89
Jade	90
Kuspuk	90
Labor and Employer Organizations	91
Lakes	93
Land	93
Languages	96
Mammals	97
Masks	100
Medal of Heroism	102
Metric Conversions	103
Mileage Chart	104
Military	104
Minerals and Mining	107
Miscellaneous Facts	108
Miss Alaska	110
Mosquitoes	110
Mountains	111
Mount McKinley	112
Mukluks	113
Muktuk	113
Museums, Cultural Centers and Repositories	113
Mushrooms	115
Musk Ox	116
Muskeg	116
National Forests	117

National Guard	118
National Historic Places	120
National Parks, Preserves and Monuments	124
National Petroleum Reserve	126
National Wild and Scenic Rivers	127
National Wilderness Areas	130
National Wildlife Refuges	131
Native People	132
Nenana Ice Classic	136
Newspapers and Periodicals	137
No-see-ums	140
Nuchalawoya	140
Officials	140
Oil and Gas	143
Parka	145
Permafrost	146
Permanent Fund	147
Pioneers' Homes	147
Pipeline	148
Place Names	149
Poisonous Plants	150
Populations and Zip Codes	150
Potlatch	157
Radio Stations	157
Railroads	159
Regions of Alaska	160
Religion	163
Reptiles	164
Rivers	164
Roadhouses	165
Rocks and Gems	166
School Districts	166
Shipping	167
Sitka Slippers	168
Skiing	168
Skin Sewing	170
Skookum	170
Soapstone	170
Sourdough	170
Speed Limits	171
Squaw Candy	171
State Park System	171
State Symbols	176
Subsistence	178
Sundog	178
Taiga	178
Telecommunications	178
Telephone Numbers in the Bush	180
Television Stations	180
Tides	181
Timber	181
Time Zones	182
Totems	183
Tourism	184
Trees and Shrubs	184
Tundra	185
Ulu	185
Umiak	185
Universities and Colleges	185
Volcanoes	186
Waves	188
Whales and Whaling	188
Wild Flowers	191
Winds	191
World Eskimo-Indian Olympics	192
Yearly Highlights—1989	193
Zip Codes	150

Agriculture

Agricultural production in Alaska is still confined to a relatively small percentage of the state's total acreage. In 1987, approximately 1.4 million acres in Alaska — less than one-half of 1 percent of the state — was considered land in farms. In 1987, crops covered 29,134 acres; the balance was idle in pasture or uncleared land. Since 1978, state land sales have placed more than 151,000 acres of potential agricultural land into private ownership. Most of this acreage is in the Delta Junction area, where tracts of land ranging up to 3,200 acres were sold by lottery for grain farming.

In 1988, the total value of Alaska's agricultural products was $30,000,000 ($527,000 higher than in 1987); crops accounted for $19.5 million of the total, livestock and poultry for $10.5 million. Broken down by region, the Matanuska Valley contributed 70 percent of the total value; the Tanana Valley, 22 percent; the Kenai Peninsula, 6 percent; and southwestern Alaska, 2 percent.

According to the state Division of Agriculture, the value and volume of principal crops in 1988 were:

	Sales Value (in thousands)
Milk (34,800 lbs.)*	$7,044
Potatoes (204 cwt)*	3,305
Hay (24.7 tons)*	3,458
Barley (228 bu.)* (for grain)	775
Eggs (550 doz.)*	NA
Vegetables (49.7 cwt.)* (except potatoes)	817
Pork (240 lbs.)*	223
Silage (12.8 tons)*	576
Beef and Veal (1,318 lbs.)*	1,687
Oats (36.6 bu.)*	90

*Volume in thousands

Sales of reindeer meat and by-products in 1988 were valued at $1,474,000.

Most of the state's reindeer are located on the Seward Peninsula and Nunivak Island. About 33,000 reindeer roam freely across much of western Alaska.

The number of small farms has grown through state sales of smaller tracts and the use of farming as a supplement to other income.

In 1987, there were 660 farms with annual sales of $1,000 or more.

The Matanuska Valley sells primarily to Anchorage and military markets. Dairy farming, including feed crops for cows, is the dominant income source.

The valley has a 120-day growing season with up to 19 hours of sunlight daily (occasionally producing giant-sized vegetables), warm temperatures and moderate rainfall. During some years, supplemental irrigation is required. Residential development in the Matanuska Valley has contributed to a decline in the amount of agricultural land.

In September 1982, 13,780 acres of state land in the Point MacKenzie Agricultural Project, across Knik Arm from Anchorage, were sold by lottery. Of the 29 parcels sold, 19 were designed for development as dairy farms. New dairies have begun operation, and land clearing and dairy barn construction are continuing on other tracts. Officials anticipate that the nondairy parcels will be used to raise crops for livestock feed.

In the Tanana Valley the growing season is shorter than the Matanuska Valley, with 90 frost-free days and low precipitation levels making irrigation necessary for some crops. However, the area has the greatest agricultural potential, with warmer temperatures during the growing season and the presence of large tracts of reasonably flat land with brush rather than forest growth. Barley, oats and wheat are raised for grain and hay. (Most Alaska-grown grain is used for domestic livestock feed.) Almost all are spring varieties as few winter varieties survive the cold and produce lower yields when they do.

The promotion of grain farming in the Tanana Valley has been a major effort by the state. In 1978, the Delta Agricultural Project sold 65,000 acres of land in the Delta Junction area by lottery, with 22 buyers getting roughly 3,000 acres each. By early 1983, one-third of the land had been cleared and planted. The primary crop is barley, which has proven to be the grain most adaptable to the valley's growing conditions. The Delta II land auction in March 1982 sold an additional 24,000 acres in 15 parcels for agricultural development. The Tanana Valley produces 83 percent of all grain grown in Alaska.

The Kenai Peninsula produces beef, hay, eggs and potatoes. Kodiak Island produces more beef than any other area in the state. Umnak and Unalaska islands provide grazing area for 2,000 sheep, the smallest number in many years — down from 3,900 in 1980 and 27,000 in 1970.

Based on Soil Conservation Service information, there are at least 15 million acres of potential farmland in Alaska suitable for raising crops, plus 118 million acres of range for livestock grazing, and 100 million acres suitable only for reindeer and musk oxen. State policy currently emphasizes farm development on agricultural parcels sold by the state in past years. Possible sales of additional land for agricultural development, such as in the Nenana area, will be re-evaluated in the coming years.

More information is available from the Alaska Department of Natural Resources, Division of Agriculture, P.O. Box 949, Palmer 99645.

Air Travel

Alaska is the "flyingest" state in the Union; the only practical way to reach many areas of rural Alaska is by airplane. According to the Federal Aviation Administration, Alaska Region, by April 1988, there were close to 10,242 registered pilots — 1 out of every 53 Alaskans — and 9,225 registered aircraft — 1 for every 58 Alaskans. This figure is approximately 8 times as many pilots per capita and 15 times as many airplanes per capita as the rest of the United States.

According to FAA, Alaska has about 466 airports, 106 seaplane landing sites and 21 heliports. That puts Alaska seventh, behind Texas, Illinois, California, Pennsylvania, Ohio and Florida in the number of airports in the state. Of the seaplane bases, Lake Hood in Anchorage is the largest and the busiest in the world. On a yearly basis, an average of 233 takeoffs and landings occur daily, and more than 800 on a peak summer day. Merrill Field in Anchorage records more than 280,000 takeoffs and landings each year, making it one of the nation's busiest general aviation airports. Alaska's international airports saw 1,205,899 passengers pass through in 1987.

Flying in Alaska, as elsewhere, is not without its hazards. In 1988, there were 182 airplane accidents in which 44 persons lost their lives. In security, however, Anchorage International Airport ranked first in tests conducted by the FAA in late 1987. Pilots who wish to fly their own planes to Alaska may obtain a booklet titled *Flight Tips for Pilots in Alaska* from the Federal Aviation Administration, 222 W. 7th Ave., #14, Anchorage 99513-7587.

According to the Alaska Transportation Commission, certified air carriers with operating rights within Alaska as of January, 1988 included: 183 air taxi operators; 12 contract air carriers; 7 postal contract carriers; 12 subcontract carriers; and 41 scheduled air carriers. Scheduled passenger service is available to dozens of Alaskan communities (see Intrastate Service this section). Contact the airlines for current schedules and fares.

Air taxi operators are found in most Alaskan communities and aircraft can be chartered to fly you to a wilderness spot and pick you up later at a prearranged time and location. (Many charter services charge an hourly standby fee if the customer is not on time at the pickup point.) Most charter operators charge an hourly rate either per plane load or per passenger (sometimes with a minimum passenger requirement); others may charge on a per mile basis. Flightseeing trips to area attractions are often available at a fixed price per passenger. Charter fares range from $140 to $175 per person (four person minimum) for a short flightseeing trip to $350, an hour for an eight-passenger Cessna 404. Multi-engine planes are generally more expensive to charter than single-engine planes.

A wide range of aircraft is used for charter and scheduled passenger service in Alaska. The large interstate airlines — Alaska, Northwest, United and Delta — use jets (DC-8, DC-10, 727, 737, 757, 767); Reeve Aleutian flies Electra, YS-11, DC-4 and DC-6. MarkAir uses 737 and de Havilland Dash-7. Prop jets and single- or twin-engine prop planes on wheels, skis and floats are used for most intrastate travel. Here are just a few of the types of aircraft flown in Alaska: DC-3, 19-passenger Twin Otter, 10-passenger Britten-Norman Islander, 7-passenger Grumman Goose (amphibious), 5-passenger Cessna 185, 9-passenger twin engine Piper Navajo Chieftain, 5- to 8-passenger Beaver, 3- to 4-passenger Cessna 180, 5- to 6-passenger Cessna 206 and single-passenger Super Cub.

Interstate Service

U.S. carriers providing interstate passenger service: Alaska Airlines, Delta Air Lines, Hawaiian Air, Northwest Airlines, United Airlines and Reeve Aleutian Airways. These carriers and Flying Tigers also provide freight service between Anchorage and Seattle. Reeve Aleutian Airways provides freight and passenger service between Cold Bay and Seattle.

International carriers servicing Alaska through the Anchorage gateway: Air France, British Airways, China Airlines, KLM Royal Dutch Airlines, Korean Airlines, Japan Air Lines, Sabena-Belgian World Airlines, SAS Scandinavian Airlines and Swiss Air.

Intrastate Service
From Anchorage

Alaska Airlines, 4750 International Road, Anchorage 99502. Serves Cordova, Fairbanks, Gustavus/Glacier Bay, Juneau, Ketchikan, Kotzebue, Nome, Petersburg, Prudhoe Bay, Sitka, Wrangell, Yakutat. Additional routes served on a contract basis by local carriers.

Delta Air Lines. Serves Fairbanks.

Era Aviation, 6160 S. Airpark Drive, Anchorage 99502. Serves Homer, Kenai and Valdez.

MarkAir, P.O. Box 196769, Anchorage 99519. Serves Aniak, Barrow, Bethel, Dillingham, Dutch Harbor, Fairbanks, King Salmon, Kodiak, St. Marys and Unalakleet, with connections into 17 other cities.

Peninsula Airways, 6441 S. Airpark Drive, Anchorage 99502. Serves Cold Bay, Dillingham, King Salmon and Kodiak.

Reeve Aleutian Airways, 4700 W. International Airport Road, Anchorage 99502. Serves the Alaska Peninsula, Aleutian Islands and Pribilof Islands.

Ryan Air, 1205 E. International Airport Road, Suite 201, Anchorage 99518. Serves Anchorage, Bethel, Kotzebue, McGrath, Nome and many other communities in western Alaska.

Southcentral Air, 125 N. Willow St., Kenai 99611. Serves Homer, Kenai and Soldotna.

United Airlines. Serves Fairbanks.

From Barrow

Barrow Air, P.O. Box 184, Barrow 99723. Serves Atkasuk, Nuiqsut and Wainwright.

Cape Smythe Air, P.O. Box 549-VP, Barrow 99723. Serves Brevig Mission, Elim, Golovin, Shishmaref, Teller, Wales and White Mountain.

From Fairbanks

Frontier Flying Service, 3820 University Ave., Fairbanks 99701. Serves Allakaket, Anaktuvuk Pass and Bettles.

Larry's Flying Service, P.O. Box 2348, Fairbanks 99707. Serves Denali National Park and Preserve (McKinley Park airstrip).

From Galena

Galena Air Service, P.O. Box 188, Galena 99741. Serves Anchorage.

From Glennallen

Gulkana Air Service, P.O. Box 31, Glennallen 99588. Serves Anchorage.

From Gustavus

Glacier Bay Airways, P.O. Box 1, Gustavus 99826. Serves Excursion Inlet, Hoonah and Juneau.

From Haines
L.A.B. Flying Service, P.O. Box 272, Haines 99827. Serves Hoonah, Juneau and Skagway.

From Juneau
Wings of Alaska, 1873 Shell Simmons Drive, Suite 119, Juneau 99801. Serves Angoon, Elfin Cove, Gustavus/Glacier Bay, Haines, Hoonah, Kake, Pelican, Skagway and Tenakee.

From Kenai
Southcentral Air, 125 N. Willow St., Kenai 99611. Serves Anchorage, Homer, Seward and Soldotna.

From Ketchikan
Ketchikan Air Service, P.O. Box 6900, Ketchikan 99901. Serves Stewart, B.C., and Hyder.
Temsco Airlines, 1249 Tongass Ave., Ketchikan 99901. Serves Craig, Hydaburg, Klawock, Metlakatla and other Southeast points.

From McGrath
Hub Air Service, P.O. Box 2-TD, McGrath 99827. Serves Lime Village, Nikolai, Telida, Flat, Talalina Air Force Station and Takotna.

From Nome
Bering Air Inc., P.O. Box 1650, Nome 99762. Serves Kotzebue and points in western Alaska.

From Petersburg
Alaska Island Air, P.O. Box 508, Petersburg 99833. Serves Kake.

From Tanana
Tanana Air Service, P.O. Box 36, Tanana 99777. Serves Eagle, Fairbanks, Huslia, Manley Hot Springs, Nenana, New Minto and Rampart.

From Tok
40-Mile Air Ltd., P.O. Box 539, Tok 99780. Serves Boundary, Chicken, Delta Junction, Eagle, Fairbanks and Tetlin.

Related reading: *The Alaska Airlines Story.* History of one of Alaska's major commercial airlines. 224 pages, $12.95. See ALASKA NORTHWEST LIBRARY in the back of the book.

Alaska Highway

(*See also* Highways)

This highway runs 1,520 miles through Canada and Alaska from Milepost 0 at Dawson Creek, British Columbia, through Yukon Territory to Fairbanks, Alaska.

History
The highway was built to relieve Alaska from the wartime hazards of shipping and to supply a land route for wartime equipment.

By agreement between the governments of Canada and the United States, the highway was built in eight months by the U.S. Army Corps of Engineers and dedicated in November 1942. Crews worked south from Delta Junction, Alaska, north and south from Whitehorse, Yukon Territory and north from Dawson Creek, British Columbia.

Two major sections of the highway were connected on September 23, 1942, at Contact Creek, Milepost 588.1, where the Thirty-fifth Engineer Combat Regiment working west from Fort Nelson met the 340th Engineer General Service Regiment working east from Whitehorse. The last link in the highway was completed November 20, when the Ninety-seventh Engineer General Service Regiment, heading east from Tanacross, met the Eighteenth Engineer Combat Regiment, coming northwest from Kluane Lake, at Milepost 1200.9. A ceremony commemorating the event was held at Soldiers Summit on Kluane Lake, and the first truck to negotiate the entire highway left that day from Soldiers Summit and arrived in Fairbanks the next day.

After WWII, the Alaska Highway was turned over to civilian contractors for widening and graveling, replacing log bridges with steel and rerouting at many points. Construction continues on the Alaska Highway today.

Road Conditions
The Alaska Highway is a 2-lane road that winds and rolls across the wilderness. Some sections of road have no centerline, and some stretches of narrow road have little or no shoulder. The best driving advice on these sections is to take your time; drive with your headlights on at all times; keep to the right on hills and corners; and drive defensively.

There are relatively few steep grades on the Alaska Highway. The most mountainous section of highway is between Fort Nelson and Watson Lake, as the highway crosses the Rocky Mountains.

Almost the entire length of the Alaska Highway is asphalt-surfaced, ranging from poor to excellent condition. Some rugged stretches exist with many chuckholes, gravel breaks, hardtop with loose gravel, deteriorated shoulders and bumps.

On the Alaska portion of the highway, watch for frost heaves. This rippling effect in the pavement is caused by the alternate freezing and thawing of the ground. Drive slowly in sections of frost heaves to avoid breaking an axle or trailer hitch.

Travelers should keep in mind that road conditions are subject to change. Always be alert for bumps and holes in the road; some are signed or flagged, but many are not.

Always watch for construction crews along the Alaska Highway. Extensive road construction may require a detour, or travelers may be delayed while waiting for a pilot car to guide them through the construction. Motorists may also encounter some muddy roadways at construction areas if there are heavy rains while the roadbed is torn up.

Dust and mud are generally not a problem anymore, except in construction areas and on a few stretches of the highway.

On gravel, don't drive too fast. Gravel acts just like many little ball bearings and you could lose control of your vehicle. Driving too fast on gravel is also hard on your tires, raises dust and throws rocks at oncoming cars. Heavy rain on a gravel road generally means mud. Considerable clay in the road surface means very slippery when wet.

Gas, food and lodging are found along the Alaska Highway on an average of every 20 to 50 miles. The longest stretch without services is about 100 miles. Keep in mind that not all businesses are open year-round, nor are most services available 24 hours a day. Regular, unleaded and diesel gasoline, and propane fuel are available along the highway. Both government campgrounds and commercial campgrounds are located along the Alaska Highway.

Preparation for Driving the Alaska Highway

Make sure your vehicle and tires are in good condition before starting out. An inexpensive and widely available item to include is clear plastic headlight covers to protect your headlights from flying rocks and gravel.

You might also consider a wire-mesh screen across the front of your vehicle to protect paint, grill and radiator from flying rocks. These may be purchased ready-made, or you may manufacture your own.

For those hauling trailers, a piece of 1/4-inch plywood fitted over the front of your trailer offers protection from rocks and gravel.

You'll find well-stocked auto shops in the North, but may wish to carry the following for emergencies: flares; first-aid kit; trailer bearings; good bumper jack with lug wrench; a simple set of tools, such as crescent wrenches, socket and/or open-end wrenches, hammer, screwdrivers, pliers, wire, pry bar; electrician's tape; small assortment of nuts and bolts; fan belt; 1 or 2 spare tires (2 spares for traveling any remote road); and any parts for your vehicle that might not be available along the way. Include an extra few gallons of gas and also water, especially for remote roads. You may also wish to carry a can of fluid for brakes, power steering and automatic transmissions. You do not, however, want to overload your vehicle with too many spare parts.

Along the Alaska Highway dust is at its worst during dry spells, following heavy rain (which disturbs the road surface) and in construction areas. If you encounter much dust, check your air filter frequently. To help keep dust out of your vehicle, try to keep air pressure in the car by closing all windows and turning on the fan. Filtered heating and air-conditioning ducts in a vehicle bring in much less dust than open windows or vents. Mosquito netting placed over the heater/fresh air intake and flow-through ventilation will also help eliminate dust.

Related reading: *The MILEPOST®* All-the-North Travel Guide® All travel routes in western Canada and Alaska with photos and detailed maps, including the Alaska Highway. 546 pages, $14.95. See ALASKA NORTHWEST LIBRARY in the back of the book.

Alcoholic Beverages

At this writing, legal age for possession, purchase and consumption of alcoholic beverages is 21.

Any business which serves or distributes alcoholic beverages must be licensed by the state. The numbers of all types of licenses issued are limited to the population in a geographic area. Generally one license of each type may be issued for each 3,000 persons or fraction thereof. Licensed premises include bars, some restaurants, roadhouses and clubs. Packaged liquor, beer and wine are sold by licensed retailers. Recreational site licenses, caterer's permits and special events permits allow the holder of a beverage dispensary license to sell at special (usually sporting) events, and allow nonprofit fraternal, civic or patriotic organizations to serve beer and wine at certain activities.

State law allows liquor outlets to operate from 8 a.m. to 5 a.m., but provides that local governments can impose tighter restrictions. Juneau, Ketchikan and Anchorage have cut back on the number of hours liquor outlets may operate; a similar move to shorten bar hours in Fairbanks was killed by the assembly there in January 1982.

In fiscal year 1988, approximately $11.9 million was generated through taxes on alcoholic beverages.

Local governments may also ban the sale or otherwise restrict alcoholic beverages. Barrow and Bethel have banned the sale of alcoholic beverages. Communities that have banned possession, the sale and/or importation of alcoholic beverages (knowingly bringing, sending or transporting alcoholic beverages into the community) are:

Alakanuk
Ambler
Anaktuvuk Pass
Angoon
Atka
Atmautluak
Atqasuk
Barrow
Bethel
Birch Creek
Brevig Mission
Buckland
Chalkyitsik
Chefornak
Deering
Diomede
Eek
Ekwok
Elim
Emmonak
Gambell
Golovin
Goodnews Bay
Grayling
Holy Cross
Hooper Bay
Huslia
Iliamna
Kasigluk
Kiana
Kipnuk
Kivalina
Kokhanok
Kongiganak
Kotlik
Kotzebue
Koyuk
Kwethluk
Kwigillingok
Manokotak
Marshall
Mekoryuk
Minto
Mountain Village
Napakiak
Napaskiak
Newtok
Noatak
Nondalton
Noorvik
Nuiqsut
Nunipatchuk
Pilot Station
Platinum
Point Hope
Point Lay
Port Alexander
Quinhagak
Russian Mission
Saint Marys
Saint Michael
Savoonga
Scammon Bay
Selawik
Shageluk
Shaktoolik
Sheldon Point
Shishmaref
Shungnak
Stebbins
Stevens Village
Tanacross
Tatitlek
Teller
Tetlin
Togiak
Toksook Bay
Tuluksak
Tuntutuliak
Tununak
Wainwright
Wales

On July 20, 1983, Governor Sheffield signed into law a tougher driving while intoxicated law. Under the new law first offenders face a mandatory 72-hour jail sentence, a minimum fine of $250 and loss of driving privileges for 30 days. A second offense receives a minimum sentence of 20 days, a minimum fine of $500 and loss of license for 1 year. The third offense brings a 30-day sentence, a minimum $1,000 fine and loss of license for 10 years.

Alyeska

Pronounced Al*yes*-ka, this Aleut word means "the great land" and was one of the original names of Alaska. Also a 3,939-foot peak in the Chugach Mountains; Mount Alyeska is the site of the state's largest ski resort.

Amphibians

In Alaska, there are three species of salamanders, two species of frogs and one species of toad. In the salamander order there are the rough-skinned newt, long-toed salamander and northwestern salamander. In the frogs and toads order there are the boreal toad, wood frog and spotted frog. The northern limit of each species may be the latitude at which the larvae fail to complete their development in one summer. While some species of salamander can overwinter as larvae in temperate southeastern Alaska, the shallow ponds of cental Alaska freeze solid during the winter. All but the wood frog, *Rana sylvatica*, which with its shortened larval period is found widespread throughout the state and north of the Brooks Range, are found primarily in southeastern Alaska.

Arctic Circle

The Arctic Circle is the latitude at which the sun does not set for one day at summer solstice and does not rise for one day at winter solstice, when the sun is at its greatest distance from the celestial equator. The latitude, which varies slightly from year to year, is approximately 66°34′ from the equator.

On the day of summer solstice, on June 20 or 21, the sun does not set at the Arctic Circle; because of refraction of sunlight, it appears not to set for four days. Farther north, at Barrow (northernmost community in the United States), the sun does not set from May 10 to August 2.

At winter solstice, December 21 or 22, the sun does not rise for one day at the Arctic Circle. At Barrow, it does not rise for 67 days.

Arctic Winter Games

The Arctic Winter Games are a biennial event held in mid-March for northern athletes from Alaska, northern Alberta, Yukon Territory and Northwest Territories. The first games were held in 1970 in Yellowknife, NWT, and have since been held in Fairbanks and Whitehorse, YT.

Judo and table tennis were dropped from the 1984 games because the AWG board felt they didn't fit the northern spirit of the games and because Canadian teams were unable to field competitive teams.

Added in 1984 were speed skating and a speed skating-skiing-snowshoeing triathlon. Other arctic sports, such as ice hockey, indoor soccer and the snowshoe biathlon, were expanded by adding more athletes and splitting the competition into junior and open divisions. Other competition includes badminton, cross-country skiing, curling, figure skating, basketball, broomball, gymnastics, silhouette shooting, ski biathlon, snowshoeing and volleyball.

Aurora Borealis

The Phenomena

The aurora borealis is produced by charged electrons and protons striking gas particles in the earth's upper atmosphere. The electrons and protons are released through sunspot activity on the sun and emanate into space. A few drift the one- to two-day course to Earth where they are pulled to the most northern and southern latitudes by the planet's magnetic forces.

The color of the aurora borealis varies depending on how hard the gas particles are being struck. Auroras can range from simple arcs to draperylike forms in green, red, blue and purple. The lights occur in a pattern rather than as a solid glow because electric current sheets flowing through gases create V-shaped potential double layers. Electrons near the center of the current sheet move faster, hit the atmosphere harder and cause the different intensities of light observed in the aurora.

Displays take place as low as 40 miles above the Earth's surface, but usually begin about 68 miles above and extend hundreds of miles into space. They concentrate in two bands roughly centered above the Arctic Circle and Antarctic Circle (the latter known as aurora australis) that are about 2,500 miles in diameter. In northern latitudes the greatest occurrence of auroral displays is in the spring and fall months owing to the tilt of the planet in relationship to the sun's plane, but displays may occur on dark nights throughout the winter. If sunspot activity is particularly intense and the denser-than-usual solar wind heads to Earth, the resulting auroras can be so great they cover all but the tropical latitudes. However, the cycle of sunspot activity is such that it will be many years before the numerous, brilliant displays of the late 1950s are regularly seen again.

Some observers claim the northern lights make a noise similar to the rustle of taffeta, but scientists say the displays cannot be heard in the audible frequency range.

Photographing the Aurora Borealis

To capture the northern lights on film, you will need a sturdy tripod, a locking-type cable release (some 35mm cameras have both *time* and *bulb* settings, but most have *bulb only*, which calls for use of the locking-type cable release) and a camera with an f/3.5 lens (or faster).

It is best to photograph the lights on a night when they are not moving too rapidly. And, as a general rule, photos improve if you manage to include recognizable subjects in the foreground — trees and lighted cabins being favorites of many photographers. Set your camera up at least 75 feet back from the foreground objects to make sure that both the foreground and aurora are in sharp focus.

Normal and wide-angle lenses are best. Try to keep your exposures under a minute — 10 to 30 seconds are generally best. The following lens openings and exposure times are only a starting point, since the amount of light generated by the aurora is inconsistent. (For best results, bracket widely.)

	ASA 200	ASA 400
f1.5	3 sec.	2 sec.
f1.4	5	3
f1.8	7	4
f2	20	10
f2.8	40	20
f3.5	60	30

Ektachrome 200 and 400 color films can be push-processed in the home darkroom or by some custom-color labs, allowing use of higher ASA ratings (800, 1200 or even 1600 on the 400 ASA film, for example). Kodak will push-process film if you include an ESP-1 envelope with your standard film-processing mailer. (Consult your local camera store for details.)

A few notes of caution: Protect the camera from low temperatures until you are ready to make your exposures. Some newer cameras, in particular, have electrically controlled shutters that will not function properly at low temperatures. Wind the film slowly to reduce the possibility of static electricity, which can lead to streaks on the film. Grounding the camera when rewinding can help prevent the static-electricity problem. (To ground the camera, hold it against a water pipe, drain pipe, metal fence post or other grounded object.) Follow the basic rules and experiment with exposures.

The first photographs to show the aurora borealis in its entirety became public in early 1982. These historic photographs were taken from satellite-mounted cameras specially adapted to filter unwanted light from the sunlit portion of the earth, which is a million times brighter than the aurora. From space the aurora has the appearance of a nearly perfect circle.

Alaska Natives still use brownish black bowhead baleen to make baskets and model ships for the tourist trade.

Barabara

Pronounced *buh-rah-buh-ruh*, this traditional Aleut or Eskimo shelter is built of sod supported by driftwood or whalebone.

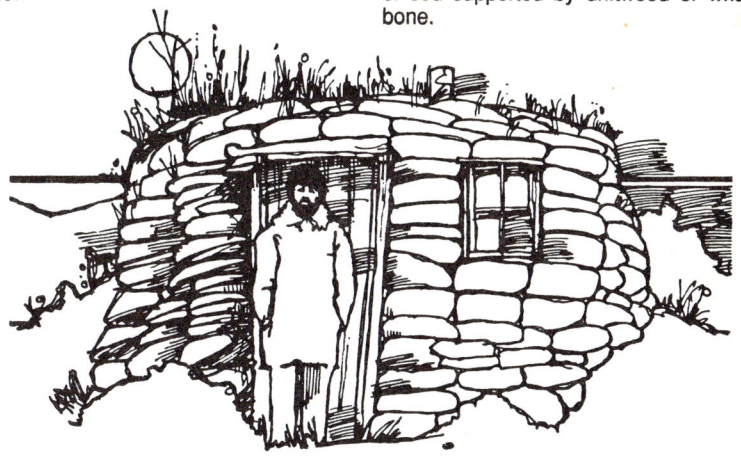

Baleen

(*See also* Baskets)

Long, fringed, bonelike strips that line the mouths of baleen whales. Baleen strains out plankton, the tiny, shrimplike creatures called krill, and small fish from the water. Humpback whales are the largest of the baleen whales, having a coarse baleen similar to human fingernails. The inside edges of the baleen plates end in coarse bristles that are similar in appearance to matted goat hair. The color of the plates varies from gray to almost black and the bristles from white to grayish white. The number of plates in an adult humpback mouth varies from 600 to 800 (300 to 400 per side), the roof of the mouth is empty of plates. The bowhead whale has 600 plates, longest of any whale species — some reach 12 feet or more in length. The sei whale has finely textured baleen and the minkes are the smallest of the baleen whales. Other baleen whales are the right, blue, fin and gray. Baleen was once used for corset stays and buggy whips. It is no longer of significant commercial use, although

Baseball

The Alaska Baseball League consists of eight All-Alaska amateur league teams: Anchorage Glacier Pilots (club started in 1969), Fairbanks Goldpanners (1966), Kenai Peninsula Oilers (1974), Mat-Su Miners (1980), North Pole Nicks (1980), Cook Inlet Bucs (1980), Hawaiian Rainbows (1986) and the Palouse Cougars (1986).

The baseball season opens in June and runs through the end of July. Each team plays a round-robin schedule with the other seven teams, as well as scheduling games with visiting Lower 48 teams, such as Athletes in Action. In 1988, for the first time, however, only the Oilers played due to insufficient funding for the other teams. The Oilers made it to the NBC tournament. The league has a championship series the first of August, followed by a state National Baseball Congress tournament leading up to the NBC nationals at Wichita.

The caliber of play in Alaska is some of the best nationwide at the amateur level. Since 1968, Alaska teams have won nine NBC championships. (The Glacier Pilots in 1969, 1971 and 1986; the Goldpanners in 1972-74, 1976 and 1980; and the Oilers in 1981.) Major league scouts rate Alaska baseball at A to AA.

The Alaska league teams are composed of walk-on and recruited players alike, but primarily of college players, many of whom go on to professional baseball. (Any college senior drafted by a major league team cannot play in the Alaska league.) Since its inception in 1969, the Alaska league has sent more than 150 players on to careers in major league baseball. The list is an impressive one, including such current stars as Tom Seaver, Chris Chambliss, Bruce Bochte and Dave Winfield.

Baskets

Native basketry varies greatly according to materials locally available. Athabascan Indians of the Interior, for example, weave baskets from willow root gathered in late spring. The roots are steamed and roasted over a fire to loosen the outer bark; weavers then separate the bark into fine strips by pulling the roots through their teeth.

Eskimo grass baskets are made in river delta areas of southwestern Alaska from Bristol Bay north to Norton Sound and from Nunivak Island east to interior Eskimo river villages. The weavers use very fine grass harvested in fall. A coil basketry technique is followed, using coils three-fourths to one-eighth inch wide. Seal gut, traditionally dyed with berries (today with commercial dyes), is often interwoven into the baskets.

Baleen, a glossy, hard material that hangs in slats from the upper jaw of a bowhead whale, is also used for baskets. Baleen basketry originated about 1905 when Charles D. Brower, trader for a whaling company at Point Barrow, suggested, after the decline of the whalebone (baleen) industry for women's corsets, that local Eskimos make the baskets as a source of income. The baskets were not produced in any number until 1916. The weave and shape of the baskets were copied from the split-willow Athabascan baskets acquired in trade. Men, rather than women, became the basket makers. Later, baleen baskets were also made in Point Hope and Wainwright.

Most birch bark baskets are made by Athabascan Indians, although a few Eskimos also produce them. Commonly, they are shaped as simple cylinders and are held together with root bindings. Sometimes the birch bark is cut into thin strips and woven into diamond or checkerboard patterns. Birch bark is usually collected in spring and early summer; large pieces free of knots are preferred. Birch bark baskets traditionally were used as cooking vessels; food was placed in them and hot stones added. Birch bark baby carriers also are made.

Among the finest of Alaskan baskets are the tiny, intricately woven Aleut

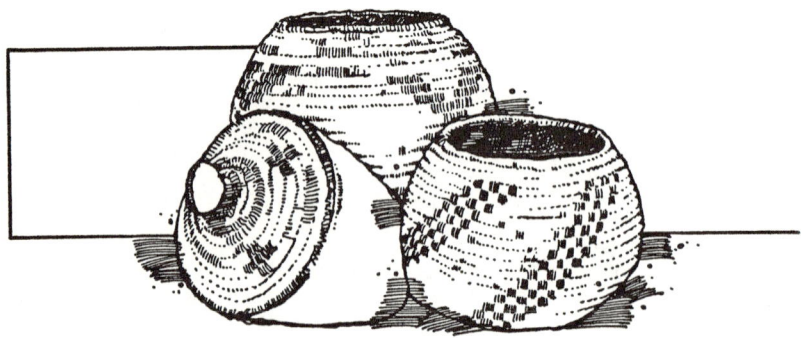

baskets made of rye grass, which in the Aleutians is abundant, pliable and very tough. The three main styles of Aleut baskets — Attu, Atka and Unalaska — are named after the islands where the styles originated. Although the small baskets are the best known, Aleuts also traditionally made large, coarsely woven baskets for utilitarian purposes.

Tlingit, Haida and Tsimshian Indians make baskets of spruce roots and cedar bark. South of Frederick Sound, basket material usually consists of strands split from the inner bark of red cedar. To the north of the sound, spruce roots are used. Maidenhair ferns are sometimes interwoven into spruce root baskets in a technique that looks like embroidery. A large spruce root basket may take months to complete.

Examples of Alaska Native basketry may be viewed in many museums within the state, including the University of Alaska Museum, Fairbanks; the Anchorage Museum of History and Art, Anchorage; the Sheldon Jackson Museum, Sitka; and the Alaska State Museum, Juneau.

Prices for Native baskets vary greatly. A fine-weave, coiled beach grass basket may cost from $30 to $450; birch bark baskets, which look like trays, may range from $10 to $100; willow root trays may cost $500; finely woven Aleut baskets may cost $200 to $600; cedar bark baskets may range from $30 to $80; and baleen baskets range in price from $450 to more than $1,100 for medium-sized baskets. These prices are approximate and are based on the weave, material used, size and decorations added, such as beadwork or ivory.

Beadwork

Eskimo and Indian women create a variety of handsomely beaded items. Before contact with Europeans, Indian women sometimes carved beads of willow wood, or made them from seeds of certain shrubs and trees. Glass seed beads became available to Alaskan Athabascan Indians in the mid-nineteenth century, although some types of larger trade beads were in use earlier. Beads quickly became a coveted trade item. The *Cornaline d'aleppo,* an opaque red bead with a white center, and the faceted Russian blue beads were among the most popular types.

The introduction of small glass beads sparked changes in beadwork style and design. More colors were now available, and the smaller, more easily maneuvered beads made it possible to work out delicate floral patterns impossible with larger trade beads.

Historically, beads were sewn directly onto leather garments or other items with the overlay stitch. Contemporary beadwork is often done on a separate piece of felt that is not visible once the beads are stitched in place.

Alaskan Athabascan beadworkers sometimes use paper patterns, often combining several motifs and tracing their outline on the surface to be worked. The most common designs include flowers, leaves and berries, some in very stylized form. Many patterns are drawn simply from the sewer's environment. Recently, magazines, advertisements and patriotic motifs have inspired Athabascan beadworkers, although stylized floral designs are still the most popular.

Designs vary regionally, as do the ways in which they are applied to garments or footgear. Women from some areas do beadwork so fine and distinctive it can be recognized at a glance.

Related reading: *Secrets pf Eskimo Skin Sewing,* by Edna Wilder. 125 pages, $9.95. See ALASKA NORTHWEST LIBRARY in the back of the book.

Berries

Wild berries abound in Alaska with the circumboreal lowbush cranberry (*Vaccinium vitis-idaea*) being the most widespread. Blueberries of one species or another grow in most of the state. Some 50 other species of wild fruit are

Lingonberry/ Lowbush Cranberry, *Vaccinium vitis-idaea* (Reprinted from *Alaska Wild Berry Guide and Cookbook*)

11

found in Alaska, and include strawberries, raspberries, cloudberries, salmonberries, crowberries, nagoonberries and crabapples.

Highbush cranberries (which are not really cranberries) can be found on bushes even in the dead of winter and the frozen berries provide a refreshing treat to the hiker.

The fruit of the wild rose, or rose hip, is not strictly a berry but is used in similar fashion and is an ideal source of vitamin C for bush dweller and city resident alike. A few hips will provide as much of the vitamin as a medium-sized orange. The farther north the hips are found, the richer they are in vitamin C.

Related reading: *Alaska Wild Berry Guide and Cookbook,* 216 pages, $14.95. *Discovering Wild Plants, Alaska, Western Canada, The Northwest,* by Janice Schofield. 350 pages of detailed facts about 130 plants. Illustrations and pictures. $34.95. *Plant Lore of an Alaskan Island,* by Frances Kelso Graham and the Ouzinkie Botanical Society. 194 pages, $9.95. See ALASKA NORTHWEST LIBRARY in the back of the book.

Billiken

This smiling ivory figure with a pointed head, though long a popular Northland souvenir, is not an Eskimo invention. The billiken was patented in 1908 by Florence Pretz of Kansas City. A small, seated, Buddhalike figure, the original billiken was manufactured by the Billiken Company of Chicago and sold as a good luck charm. During the 1909 Alaska-Yukon-Pacific Exposition in Seattle, thousands of these figurines were sold. Although billikens vanished soon afterward from most Lower 48 shops, someone had brought them to Nome, where King Island, Little Diomede and Wales Eskimos began carving replicas in ivory.

Billikens are still being made elsewhere in the world in such media as wood, concrete and glass. A popular notion contends that rubbing a billiken's tummy brings good fortune.

Birds

Authorities at the University of Alaska acknowledge 427 species of birds in Alaska. If unsubstantiated sightings are included, the species total increases. Thousands of ducks, geese and swans come north to breeding grounds each spring. Millions of seabirds congregate in nesting colonies on exposed cliffs along Alaska's coastline, particularly on the Aleutian Islands, and on islands in the Bering Sea.

Migratory birds reach Alaska from many corners of the world. Arctic terns travel up to 22,000 miles on their round trip each year from Antarctica. Others come from South America, the South Pacific islands and Asia.

Each May one of the world's largest concentrations of shorebirds funnels through the Copper River Delta near Cordova. Waterfowl such as trumpeter swans and the world's entire flock of dusky Canada geese breed there.

Other key waterfowl habitat includes the Yukon-Kuskokwim Delta, Yukon Flats, Innoko Flats and Minto Lakes. During migration, huge flocks gather at Egegik, Port Heiden, Port Moller, Izembek Bay, Chickaloon Flats, Susitna Flats and Stikine Flats.

Raptors, led by the bald eagle, range throughout the state. Alaska has three subspecies of peregrine falcon: Arctic, American and Peale's. Arctic and American peregrine falcons join the Eskimo

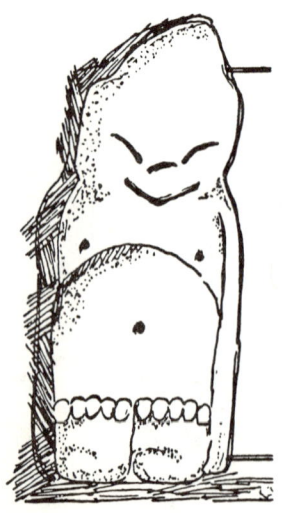

curlew, Aleutian Canada goose and short-tailed albatross on the endangered or threatened species list for the state.

Five chapters of the National Audubon Society are based in Alaska: the Anchorage Audubon Society, Inc. (P.O. Box 101161, Anchorage 99510), the Juneau Audubon Society (P.O. Box 021725, Juneau 99802), the Arctic Audubon Society (P.O. Box 82098, Fairbanks 99708), the Kenai Audubon Society (P.O. Box 3371, Soldotna 99669) and the Kodiak Audubon Society (Box 1756, Kodiak 99615). In addition to trying to help people increase their knowledge of birds, the groups (except for Fairbanks) coordinate over 20 annual Christmas bird counts around the state. The Fairbanks Bird Club (P.O. Box 81791, Fairbanks 99708) conducts the annual Christmas count for that area.

Related reading: *The Alaskan Bird Sketches of Olaus Murie.* With excerpts from his field notes, compiled and edited by Margaret E. Murie. 64 pages, $11.95. *A Guide to the Birds of Alaska,* including most species found in Alaska. 320 pages. $19.95. See ALASKA NORTHWEST LIBRARY in the back of the book.

Blanket Toss

As effective as a trampoline, the blanket toss (or *nalukataq*) features a walrus hide blanket grasped by a number of people in a circle. They toss a person on the blanket as high as possible for as long as that person can remain upright. Every true Eskimo festival and many non-Native occasions include the blanket toss, which was originally used to allow Eskimo hunters to spot game, such as walrus and seal, in the distance. Depending on the skill of the person being tossed and the number of

13

tossers, a medium-weight person might typically go 20 feet in the air.

Boating

Travel by boat is an important means of transportation in Alaska, where highways cover only about one-third of the state. Until the advent of the airplane, boats were often the only way to reach many parts of Alaska. Most of Alaska's supplies still arrive by water and in Southeast — where precipitous terrain and numerous islands make road building impossible — water travel is essential. (*See also* Ferries.)

The Alaska Department of Transportation and Public Facilities (P.O. Box Z, Juneau 99811), through its regional offices, has the major responsibility for providing public floats, grids, docks, launching ramps and associated small-boat harbor facilities throughout the coastal areas of the state. Often these facilities are leased to local governments at no cost. Moorage facilities constructed by the state are intended for boats up to a maximum of 100 feet, with a limited number of facilities for larger vessels where large boats are common. With the exception of Ketchikan, Sitka and Juneau, there are no private marine facilities.

According to the U.S. Coast Guard, there are 44,488 vessels registered in Alaska. Of these, approximately 3,258 are longer than 30 feet (many are commercial fishing vessels) and 16,219 are longer than 20 feet.

To accommodate the needs of this fleet, there are approximately 8,000 slips available at public small-boat harbors in Alaska. According to the state, actual service capacity is somewhat greater because of the transient nature of many boats and certain management practices allowing "double parking." There are also harbors at various remote locations; no services other than moorage are provided at these harbors.

Recreational boating opportunities in Alaska are too numerous and varied to list here; Alaska has thousands of miles of lakes, rivers and sheltered seaways. For information about boating on the rivers, lakes and seaways within national forests, parks, monuments, preserves and wildlife refuges, contact the appropriate federal agency (see related sections and Information Sources). For travel by boat in southeastern Alaska's sheltered seaways — or elsewhere in Alaska's coastal waters — NOAA nautical charts are available.

Canoe trails have been established on the Kenai Peninsula (contact Kenai National Wildlife Refuge, 2139 Ski Hill

Road, Soldotna 99669); in Nancy Lake State Recreation Area (contact Superintendent, Mat-Su District, HC32, Box 6706, Wasilla 99687); and on rivers in the Fairbanks and Anchorage areas (contact Bureau of Land Management, 1150 University Ave., Fairbanks 99709 and 222 W. 7th Ave., #13, Anchorage 99513).

Travel by water in Alaska requires extra caution, however. Weather changes fast and is often unpredictable; it's important to be prepared for the worst. Alaska waters, even in midsummer, are cold; a person falling overboard may become immobilized by the cold water in only a few minutes. And since many of Alaska's water routes are far from civilization, help may be a long way off.

Persons inexperienced in traveling Alaska's waterways might consider hiring a charter boat operator or outfitter. Guides offer local knowledge and provide all necessary equipment. The Division of Tourism (Pouch E-001, Juneau 99811) maintains current lists of such services. Recreation information on both state and federal lands is available at the three Alaska Public Lands Information Centers: 605 W. 4th Ave., Suite 105, Anchorage 99501; 250 Cushman St., Suite 1A, Fairbanks 99701; P.O. Box 359, Tok 99780.

Related reading: *A Guide to the Queen Charlotte Islands.* Valuable information, photos, separate large map. Revised 1989 edition, 95 pages, $9.95. *An Expedition to the Copper, Tanana and Koyukuk Rivers in 1885.* Adventures along waterways of Interior Alaska. 96 pages, $7.95. *Baidarka,* a history, development and redevelopment of the Aleut kayak. 218 pages. $24.95. See ALASKA NORTHWEST LIBRARY in the back of the book.

Bore Tide

(*See also* Tides)

A steep, foaming wall of water formed by a flood tide surging into a constricted inlet. In Cook Inlet, where maximum tidal range approaches 40 feet, incoming tides are further compressed in Knik and Turnagain arms and tidal bores may sometimes be seen. Though one- to two-foot-high bores are more common, spring tides in Turnagain Arm may produce bore tides up to six feet high, running at speeds of up to 10 knots, and even higher bores have been reported when unusually high tides come in against a strong southeast wind. Good spots to view bore tides in Turnagain Arm are along the Seward Highway, between 26 and 37 miles south of Anchorage; they can be expected to arrive there approximately 2 hours and 15 minutes later than the tide book prediction for low tide at Anchorage.

Breakup

(*See also* Nenana Ice Classic)

Breakup occurs when melting snows raise the level of streams and rivers sufficiently to cause the ice to break apart and float downstream. Breakup is one of two factors determining the open-water season for river navigation, the second being the depth of the river. Peak water conditions occur just after breakup.

The navigable season for the Kuskokwim and Yukon rivers is June 1 through September 30; Nushagak River, June 1 through August 31; and the Noatak River, late May through mid-June.

Breakup is a spectacular sight and sound show. Massive pieces of ice crunch and pound against each other as they push their way downriver racing for the sea, creating noises not unlike many huge engines straining and grating. The spine-tingling sound can be heard for miles. It marks the finale of winter and the arrival of spring in Alaska.

Sometimes great ice jams occur, causing the water to back up and flood inhabited areas, such as at Fort Yukon in spring 1982.

Bunny Boots

Large, insulated rubber boots to protect feet from frostbite; also called vapor barrier boots. Black bunny boots are generally rated to -20°F, while the more common white bunny boots are even warmer and used in the most extreme conditions, including the heights of Mount McKinley. (The cumbersome boots are adequate for easy climbing but unsuitable for technical mountain climbing.) Prices range from about $50 for used boots to about $175 for new ones.

Bus Lines

Scheduled bus service is available in summer to and within Alaska, although buses don't run as frequently as in the Lower 48. (Local transit service is also available in some major communities.) Consult current schedules as services often are not daily.

Alaska-Denali Transit, 608 W. 4th Ave., Anchorage 99501. Passenger van service between Anchorage, Tok, Haines, Denali National Park, Kenai, Homer and Fairbanks. Also provides service to Prudhoe Bay.

Alaska Sightseeing Tours, 543 W. 4th Ave., Anchorage 99501. Provides service between Anchorage, Denali National Park, Columbia Glacier, Fairbanks, Golden Circle, Haines and Valdez.

Alaska-Yukon Motorcoaches, 543 W. 4th Ave., Anchorage 99501. Provides service between Anchorage, Haines/Skagway, Valdez, Denali National Park and Preserve, and Fairbanks.

Atlas Tours Ltd., P.O. Box 4340, Whitehorse, Yukon Territory. Provides service between Whitehorse and Skagway.

Eagle Custom Tours, 614 W. 4th Ave., Anchorage 99501. Provides service between Anchorage, Portage Glacier and the Matanuska Valley.

Norline Coaches (Yukon), Ltd., 3211-A 3rd Ave., Whitehorse, Yukon Territory. Provides service between Whitehorse and Tok via Dawson City and Fairbanks.

Royal Hyway Tours, 2815 2nd Ave., Suite 410, Seattle, Washington 98121. Provides city tours and tour packages in many parts of Alaska.

Seward Bus Lines, P.O. Box 1338, Seward 99664. Provides service between Anchorage and Seward.

Valdez/Anchorage Bus Lines, P.O. Box 101388, Anchorage 99510. Provides service between Valdez and Anchorage via Glennallen.

Westours Motorcoaches, 547 W. 4th Ave., Anchorage 99501. Provides service throughout Alaska and the Yukon.

White Pass and Yukon Motorcoaches, 300 Elliott Ave. W., Seattle, Washington 98119. Provides service between Skagway, Haines, Valdez, Glennallen, Whitehorse and Anchorage.

Bush

Originally used to describe large expanses of wilderness beyond the fringes of civilization, inhabited only by trappers and miners, "Bush" has come to stand for any part of Alaska not accessible by road. A community accessible only by air, water, sled or snow machine is considered a bush village, and anyone living there is someone from the Bush.

The term bush has been adapted to the small planes and their pilots who service areas lacking roads. Bush planes are commonly equipped with floats and skis to match terrain and season.

Related reading: *The Alaska Airlines Story,* by Archie Satterfield. 224 pages, $12.95. *Canadian Bush Pilot,* Ernie Boffa, by Florence Whyard. 141 pages. $7.95. *The ALASKA WILDERNESS MILEPOST®,* 400 pages, $14.95. *The Long Dark,* by Slim Randles. 155 pages, $7.95. *Our Arctic Year,* by Vivian and Gil Staender. 160 pages, $12.95. *Frank Barr,* by Dermot Cole. 116 pages, $7.95. *Skystruck, Adventures of an Alaskan Pilot,* by Cliff Cernick. 175 pages, $9.95. See ALASKA NORTHWEST LIBRARY in the back of book.

Cabin Fever

A state of mind blamed on cold, dark winter weather when people are often housebound; characterized by depression, preoccupation, discontent and occasionally violence. Has beed described as "a 12-foot stare in a 10-foot room." Commonly thought to afflict miners and trappers spending a lonely winter in the wilderness, but, in truth, these people are active and outdoors enough to remain content. It is more likely to strike the snowbound or disabled. The arrival of spring or a change of scene usually relieves the symptoms.

Related reading: *Winter Watch,* by James Ramsey. For 266 days, the author tested himself against an Arctic winter in a remote cabin in the Brooks Range. 144 pages, $9.95. See ALASKA NORTHWEST LIBRARY in the back of the book.

Cabins

Rustic cabins in remote places can be rented from the Forest Service and the Bureau of Land Management. The modest price, $15 per night per cabin, makes this one of the best vacation bargains in Alaska. (Check with a local Forest Service office after January 1990, as the fee may increase.) It offers visitors a chance to try living "in the Bush."

Almost 200 of these cabins are scattered through Tongass and Chugach national forests in southeast and southcentral Alaska. Six BLM cabins are in the White Mountains National Recreation area east of Fairbanks. Some are located on saltwater; others on freshwater rivers, streams or lakes. Aluminum skiffs and oars are provided at most of the lake cabins.

Reservations may be made in person or by mail. Permits for use are issued on a first come, first serve basis, up to 179 days in advance. Length of stay is limited to 7 days from April 1 through October 31, and to 10 days from November 1 through March 31. The fee is due at the time the reservation is made.

The average cabin size is 12 by 14 feet, and usually equipped with a table, oil or wood stove and wooden bunks without mattresses. Most will accommodate a group of four to six. There is no electricity. Outhouses are down the trail a little way. Visitors will need to bring their own food, bedding and cooking utensils. In addition, it's nice to have a gas or propane stove for cooking, a lantern, air mattresses or sleeping pads and insect repellent.

Some of the cabins can be reached by boat or trail, but, because of the remote locations, visitors frequently come by chartered aircraft.

Further information on cabins and their locations may be obtained from the National Forest offices listed below. The Forest Service recommends that visitors contact the office nearest the area they

wish to visit, asking for a copy of the Recreation Facility booklet. In it are applications for cabin use plus tips on planning a stay.

Fairbanks Area
BLM Fairbanks Support Center, 1541 Gaffney Road, Fairbanks, Alaska 99703

Sitka Area
USDA Forest Service, Tongass National Forest, Sitka Ranger District, 204 Siginaka Way, Sitka, Alaska 99835

Ketchikan Area
USDA Forest Service, Tongass National Forest, Ketchikan and Misty Fiords Ranger District, Federal Building, Ketchikan, Alaska 99901

Petersburg Area
USDA Forest Service, Petersburg Ranger District, P.O. Box 309, Petersburg, Alaska 99833

Wrangell Area
USDA Forest Service, Wrangell Ranger District, P.O. Box 51, Wrangell, Alaska 99929

Juneau Area and Admiralty Island
USDA Forest Service, Juneau Ranger District, 8465 Old Dairy Road, Juneau, Alaska 99801

Anchorage, Cordova, Seward Areas
Cabin reservations may be made *in person* at the following locations:

Glacier Ranger District, Chugach National Forest, Monarch Mine Road, Girdwood, Alaska 99587

Cordova Ranger District, P.O. Box 280, Cordova, Alaska 99574

Seward Ranger District, P.O. Box 390, Seward, Alaska 99664

Cabin reservations may be made *by mail or in person* at:

Chugach National Forest, 201 East 9th Avenue, Suite 206, Anchorage, Alaska 99501

Cache

Pronounced *cash*, this small storage unit is built to be inaccessible to marauding animals. A cache resembles a miniature log cabin mounted on stilts. It is reached by a ladder that bears, dogs, foxes and other hungry or curious animals can't climb. Extra precautions include wrapping tin around the poles to prevent climbing by clawed animals and extending the floor a few feet in all directions from the top of the poles to discourage those clever enough to get that high.

Squirrels are the most notorious of Alaska's cache-marauding critters. To be truly animal-proof, a cache should be built in a clearing well beyond the 30-foot leaping distance a squirrel can manage from treetop.

Bush residents use the cache as a primitive food freezer in winter. A cache may also contain extra fuel and bedding. Size is determined by need. Sometimes a cache will be built between three or four straight trees growing close together.

Calendar of Events

JANUARY
Anchorage — Nastar Ski Races, Alyeska Ski Resort; Sled Dog Races; Hatcher Cup Series, Hatcher Pass Lodge. **Bethel** — Sled Dog Races. **Fairbanks** — Sled Dog Races. **Haines** — Snowmachine Rally. **Homer** — Snowmachine Races. **Juneau** — Rainier Downhill Challenge Cup; Alascom Ski Challenge; State Legislature Convenes. **Ketchikan** — Winter Festival. **Kodiak** — Russian Orthodox Starring Ceremony; Russian Orthodox Masquerade Ball. **Seward** — Polar Bear Jump. **Sitka** — Russian Christmas and Starring; Alaska Airlines Basketball Tournament.

Soldotna — Winter Games; Sled Dog Races. **Tok** — Sled dog races. **Unalakleet** — January Jamboree.

FEBRUARY
Anchorage — Fur Rendezvous; Iron Dog Iditarod; Sled Dog Races; Northern Lights Women's Invitational. **Big Lake** — Winter Carnival. **Cordova** — Ice Worm Festival. **Fairbanks** — Sled Dog Races; Festival of Native Arts; Yukon Quest Sled Dog Race. **Homer** — Winter Carnival. **Juneau** — Taku Rendezvous; Alascom Divisional Championships. **Ketchikan** — Festival of the North. **Knik** — Iditaski Nordic Ski Race. **Nenana** — Ice Classic Tripod Raising Festival. **Nome** — Dexter Creek Sled Dog Race; Heart Throb Bi-Athalon. **Palmer** — Sled Dog Races. **Sitka** — Basketball Tournament. **Soldotna** — Alaska State Championship Dog Sled Races. **Valdez** — Ice Climbing Festival. **Wasilla** — Iditarod Days. **White-** Folk Fest. **Kodiak** — Survival Suit Races; Mountain Golf Classic; Comfish Alaska. **Nome** — Ice Golf Classic on the Bering Sea; Month of Iditarod; Sled Dog Races; Snowmachine Race; Dog Weight Pull; Basketball Tournament. **North Pole** — Winter Carnival. **Sitka** — Bazaar and Totem Trot; Herring Festival. **Skagway** — Windfest '89; Buckwheat Ski Classic. **Talkeetna** — St. Patrick's Day Bash. **Tok** — Race of Champions Sled Dog Race. **Trapper Creek** — Cabin Fever Reliever Days. **Valdez** — Winter Carnival. **Wasilla** — Iditarod Days. **Whitehorse** — Curling Bonspiel.

APRIL
Anchorage — Spring Carnival, Alyeska Ski Resort; Native Youth Olympics. **Barrow** — Spring Festival. **Cordova** — Copper Day Celebrations. **Haines** — ARTFEST Drama Festival. **Homer** — Spring Arts Fesival. **Juneau** — Folk Festi-

horse — Sourdough Rendezvous; Yukon Quest Sled Dog Race. **Wrangell** — Tent City Days.

MARCH
Anchorage — Iditarod Sled Dog Race begins. **Chatanika** — Chatanika Days. **Dillingham** — Beaver Roundup. **Fairbanks** — Arctic Winter Games; Curling Bonspiel; Ice Festival; Sled Dog Races; Athabascan Old-Time Fiddling Festival. **Homer** — Snowmachine Poker Run. **Juneau** — Sourdough Pro/Am Ski Race; Southeast Championships; Rainier Downhill Challenge Cup. **Ketchikan** — val; Ski to Sea Race. **Kotzebue** — Arctic Circle Sunshine Festival. **Nome** — Sled Dog Race. **Whittier** — Crab Festival.

MAY
Anchor Point — King Salmon Derby. **Delta Junction** — Buffalo Wallow Square Dance Jamboree. **Haines** — King Salmon Derby. **Homer** — Halibut Derby. **Juneau** — Jazz and Classics Festival; May Day Mud Race. **Ketchikan** — Ocean Race; Rainbreak; Salmon Derby. **Kodiak** — Crab Festival; Chad Ogden Ultramarathon. **Nenana** — River Daze. **Nome** — Annual Polar Bear Swim in the

19

Bering Sea; Firemen's Ball; Stroak and Cloak Tri-Athalon. **Petersburg** — Little Norway Festival; Salmon Derby. **Savoonga** — Walrus Festival, St. Lawrence Island. **Seward** — Exit Glacier Run. **Sitka** — Salmon Derby. **Skagway** — Gold Rush Stampede. **Talkeetna** — Miners Day Festival. **Valdez** — Salmon Derby. **Wrangell** — Halibut Derby; King Salmon Derby.

JUNE
Anchorage — Renaissance Faire; Kite Day; Mayor's Midnight Sun Marathon; Basically Bach Festival; Midnight Sun Hot Air Balloon Classic; Semi-Pro Baseball. **Delta Junction** — Softball Tournament. **Fairbanks** — Tanana River Raft Classic; Yukon 800 Marathon River Boat Race; Midnight Sun Run; Sunfest '90; Midnight Sun Baseball Game; Air Show. **Kenai** — Kenai Kapers. **Ketchikan** — Salmon Derby. **Knik** — Museum Pot Luck. **Kodiak** — Freedom Days. **Nenana** — River Daze. **Nome** — Midnight Sun Softball Tournament, Festival and Raft Race; ARCO-Jesse Owens Games. **Palmer** — Colony Days; Mat-Su Miners baseball season opens; Bluegrass Festival. **Sitka** — All Alaska Logging Championships; Writer's Symposium; Summer Music Festival. **Tanana** — Nuchalawoya Festival. **Valdez** — Halibut Derby. **Wasilla** — Museum Garden Party. **Whitehorse** — Dog Show.

JULY
Fourth of July celebrations take place in most towns and villages.
Anchorage — Freedom Days Festival; Bluegrass and Folk Festival. **Big Lake** — Regatta Water Festival. **Dawson City** — Yukon Gold Panning Championship. **Delta Junction** — Softball Tournament. **Fairbanks** — World Eskimo-Indian Olympics; Renaissance Faire; Golden Days; Summer Arts Festival. **Girdwood** — Girdwood Forest Faire. **Hatcher Pass** — Rock Climbing Festival. **Homer** — Halibut Derby. **Ketchikan** — Salmon Derbies. **Kodiak** — Freedom Days. **Kotzebue** — Northwest Native Trade Fair. **Palmer** — KSKA Bluegrass Festival. **Seward** — Mount Marathon Race; Softball Tournaments; Silver Salmon Derby. **Sitka** — Fourth of July Celebration (four days). **Skagway** — Soapy Smith's Wake. **Soldotna** — Progress Days. **Sterling** — Moose River Log Raft Race. **Talkeetna** — Moose Dropping Festival; Mountain Bike Rush. **Valdez** — Pink Salmon Derby; Gold Rush Days.

AUGUST
Anchorage — Air Show. **Cordova** — Silver Salmon Derby. **Craig** — Prince of Wales Island Fair and Logging Show. **Dawson City** — Discovery Days. **Delta**

Junction — Deltana Fair. **Eagle River** — Alaskan Scottish Highland Games. **Fairbanks** — Tanana Valley Fair; Idita-foot Race; Summer Arts Festival. **Haines** — Southeast Alaska State Fair; Horse Show. **Juneau** — Golden North Salmon Derby. **Ketchikan** — Alaska Seafest; Silver Salmon Derby; Blueberry Festival. **Kodiak** — *Cry of the Wild Ram,* (outdoor historical pageant); Rodeo and State Fair; Pilgrimage to St. Herman's Monks Lagoon. **Ninilchik** — Kenai Peninsula State Fair. **Palmer** — Alaska State Fair. **Seward** — Silver Salmon Derby; Tok

Run; Softball Tournament. **Sitka** — Labor Day Classic Softball Tournament. **Skagway** — Hugs and Kisses Run. **Talkeetna** — Bluegrass Festival. **Valdez** — Gold Rush Days; Silver Salmon Derby. **Wasilla** — Museum Antique Show. **Wrangell** — Coho Derby. **Yukon** — Fireweed Festival.

SEPTEMBER
Anchorage — Oktoberfest; UAA Crafts Fair. **Dawson City** — Klondike International Outhouse Race. **Dillingham** — Fall Fair. **Fairbanks** — Tanana-Rampart Labor Day Race; Equinox Marathon. **Kenai** — Silver Salmon Derby. **Ketchikan** — Salmon Derby. **Knik** — Museum Open House. **Kodiak** — Silver Salmon Derby. **Nome** — Worm-Burning Golf Tournament; Great Bathtub Race. **Sitka** — Softball Tournament. **Skagway** — Klondike Trail of '98 Road Relay; Antique Auto Show. **Valdez** — Silver Salmon Derby. **Whittier** — Silver Salmon Derby. **Wrangell** — Silver Salmon Derby.

OCTOBER
Anchorage — Quiana Alaska. **Fairbanks** — Oktoberfest. **Petersburg** — October Arts Festival. **Sitka** — Alaska Day Festival. **Wrangell** — Winter Fishing Derby.

NOVEMBER
Anchorage — Great Alaska Shootout; Symphony of Trees. **Delta Junction** — EMT Winter Carnival. **Fairbanks** — Northern Invitational Curling Spiel; Athabascan Old-Time Fiddling Festival. **Juneau** — Veterans 10K Run. **Kenai** — Christmas Comes to Kenai Celebration. **Ketchikan** — Singing in the Rain Festival. **Wrangell** — Winter Derby.

DECEMBER
Anchorage — Christmas Tree Lighting Ceremony. **Barrow** — Christmas Festival. **Cordova** — North Country Faire. **Delta Junction** — Winter Carnival. **Homer** — Renaissance Fair. **Ketchikan** — Festival of Lights. **Nome** — Firemen's Carnival. **North Pole** — Candle Lighting Ceremony. **Palmer** — Colony Christmas. **Seward** — Christmas Parade. **Sitka** — Christmas Boat Parade. **Talkeetna** — Christmas Lighting; Bachelor Society Ball. **Wrangell** — Midnight Madness and Christmas Tree Lighting.

Camping

(*See also* State Park System; National Wildlife Refuges; Hiking; Cabins; National Parks, Preserves and Monuments; and National Forests)

Numerous public and privately operated campgrounds are found along Alaska's highways, although electrical hookups and dump stations are scarce. The dump station at Russian River campground is available for Chugach National Forest visitors at this campground. Alaska's back country offers virtually limitless possibilities for wilderness camping. Get permission before camping on private land. If the land is publicly owned, it's worthwhile to contact the agency that manages the land regarding regulations and hiking/camping conditions.

Additional details about camping are found in *The MILEPOST®* (see ALASKA NORTHWEST LIBRARY at the back of the book).

The USDA Forest Service maintains 25 campgrounds in Tongass and Chugach national forests, most with tent and trailer sites and minimum facilities. Camp stamps for use at any USDA Forest Service campground in Alaska, and 43 other states, may be

21

purchased in advance with a 15 percent discount off the one-time camp fee. All campgrounds are available first-come, first-served, and stays are limited to 14 days. Campground fees vary, from four to eight dollars per night depending upon facilities, which in the Chugach can include firegates, pit toilets, garbage pickup, picnic tables and water. Chugach campgrounds are open from Memorial Day through Labor Day, or until snow conditions cause closing. For further information write National Forests of Alaska, Regional Office, USDA Forest Service, P.O. Box 1628-RN, Juneau, Alaska 99802.

The National Park Service (Alaska Regional Office, 2525 Gambell St., Anchorage 99503) at Denali National Park offers one walk-in campground and six campgrounds accessible by road; all are available on a first-come, first-served basis. Four of them require an $10 fee. Situated near the park entrance and open year-round are Riley Creek, for tents and trailers, and Morino, for walk-in tent campers. The others are open between May and September, depending on weather. Brochures may be obtained from Denali National Park, P.O. Box 9, Denali Park 99755.

Glacier Bay and Katmai national parks each offer one campground for walk-in campers, and Katmai now requires reservations. Backcountry camping is permitted in Denali, Glacier Bay, Katmai and Klondike Gold Rush parks, as well as other national parks and monuments.

Alaska Division of Parks (Pouch 7-001, Anchorage 99510) maintains the most extensive system of roadside campgrounds and waysides in Alaska. Fees are charged, and a yearly pass is offered.

U.S. Fish and Wildlife Service (State Office, 1011 E. Tudor, Anchorage 99503) has several wildlife refuges open to campers, although most are not accessible by highway. The Kenai National Wildlife Refuge, P.O. Box 2139, Soldotna 99669, however, has several campgrounds accessible from the Sterling Highway linking Homer and Anchorage.

The Bureau of Land Management (District Office, 1150 University Ave., Fairbanks 99709) maintains about 25 campgrounds in interior Alaska. BLM campgrounds are free. BLM has six public-use cabins in the White Mountains National Recreation Area. A user fee of $15 per party per night (maximum of three nights) is required for permits, which may be obtained at the BLM Fairbanks District Office. Brochures describing BLM campgrounds are also available.

Canada-Alaska Boundary

In 1825, Russia, the owner of Alaska, and Great Britain, the owner of Canada, established the original boundary between Alaska and Canada. The demarcation was to begin at 54°40´ north latitude, just north of the mouth of Portland Canal, follow the canal to 56° north latitude, then traverse the mountain summits parallel to the coast as far as 141° west longitude. From there it would conform with that meridian north to the Arctic Ocean. The boundary line along the mountain summits in southeastern Alaska was never to be farther inland than 10 leagues — about 30 miles.

After purchasing Alaska, the United States found that the wording about the boundary line was interpreted differently by the Canadians. They felt the measurements should be made inland from the mouths of bays, while Americans argued the measurements should be made from the heads of the bays. In 1903, however, an international tribunal upheld the American interpretation of the treaty, providing Alaska the 1,538-mile-long border it enjoys with Canada today. If the Canadians had won their argument they would have had access to the sea, and Haines, Dyea and Skagway now would be in Canada.

The 20-foot-wide vista — a swath of land cleared 10 feet on each side of the boundary between southeastern Alaska, British Columbia and Yukon Territory — was surveyed and cleared between 1904 and 1914. Portions of the 710-mile-long boundary were again cleared in 1925, 1948, 1978 and 1982 by the International Boundary Commission. Monument and vista maintenance of 1978 and 1982 was conducted by the Canadian section of the commission and by the U.S. section in 1983, 1984 and 1985.

The Alaska-Canada border along the 141st meridian was surveyed and cleared between 1904 and 1920. Astronomical observations were made to find the meridian's intersection with the Yukon River, then, under direction of the International Boundary Commission, engineers and surveyors of the U.S. Coast and Geodetic Survey and the Canadian Department of the Interior worked together north and south from the Yukon. The vista extends from Demarcation Point on the Arctic Ocean south to Mount Saint Elias in the Wrangell Mountains (from there the border cuts east to encompass southeastern Alaska). This 647-mile stretch is one of the longest straight lines on record, varying less than 50 feet along its entire length.

Monuments are the actual markers of the boundary and are located so they tie in with survey networks of both the United States and Canada. Along the Alaska boundary most monuments are two-and-a-half-foot-high cones of aluminum-bronze set in concrete bases or occasionally cemented into rock. A large pair of concrete monuments with pebbled finish mark major boundary road crossings, and, because the boundary is not just a line but in fact a vertical plane dividing land and sky between the two nations, bronze plates mark tunnel and bridge crossings. One hundred ninety-one monuments stretch along the meridian, beginning 200 feet from the Arctic Ocean and ending at the south side of Logan Glacier.

Chambers of Commerce

(*See also* Convention and Visitors Bureaus)
Area code through Alaska: 907.

Alaska State Chamber, 217 2nd St., Suite 201, Juneau 99801, 586-2323; 801 B St., Suite 406, Anchorage 99501, 278-3741
Anchorage Chamber, 437 E St., Anchorage 99501, 272-2401
Chugiak-Eagle River Chamber, P.O. Box 353, Eagle River 99599, 694-4702
Greater Copper Valley Chamber, P.O. Box 469, Glennallen 99588
Cordova Chamber, P.O. Box 99, Cordova 99574, 424-7260
Delta Chamber, P.O. Box 987, Delta Junction 99737, 895-5068
Dillingham Chamber, P.O. Box 348, Dillingham 99576, 842-2588
Greater Fairbanks Chamber, P.O. Box 74446, Fairbanks 99707, 452-1105
Haines Chamber, P.O. Box 518, Haines 99827, 766-2202
Homer Chamber, P.O. Box 541, Homer 99603, 235-7740
Greater Juneau Chamber, P.O. Box 1227, Juneau 99802, 586-6420
Kenai Chamber, P.O. Box 497, Kenai 99611, 283-7989
Greater Ketchikan Chamber, P.O. Box 5957, Ketchikan 99901, 225-3184
Kodiak Area Chamber, P.O. Box 1485, Kodiak 99615, 486-5557
Mid Valley Chamber, P.O. Box 86, Houston 99694, 376-7533
City of Nenana, P.O. Box 00070, Nenana 99760, 832-5441
Nome Chamber, P.O. Box 251, Nome 99762, 443-5535
North Pole Community Center, P.O. Box 55071, North Pole 99705, 488-2242
Greater Palmer Chamber, P.O. Box 45, Palmer 99645, 745-2880
Petersburg Chamber, P.O. Box 649, Petersburg 99833, 772-3646
Seldovia Chamber, Drawer F, Seldovia 99663, 234-7816
Seward Chamber, P.O. Box 749, Seward 99664, 224-8051
Greater Sitka Chamber, P.O. Box 638, Sitka 99835, 747-8604
Skagway Chamber, P.O. Box 194, Skagway 99840, 983-2472
Soldotna Chamber, P.O. Box 236, Soldotna 99669, 262-9814
Talkeetna Chamber, P.O. Box 334, Talkeetna 99676, 733-2330
Tok Chamber, P.O. Box 389, Tok 99780, 883-2318
Valdez Chamber, P.O. Box 512, Valdez 99686, 835-2330
Greater Wasilla Chamber, P.O. Box 871826, Wasilla 99687, 376-1299
Wrangell Chamber, P.O. Box 49, Wrangell 99929, 874-3901

Cheechako

Pronounced *chee-chak-ko,* or *chee-hak-er* by some old-time Alaskans, the word means tenderfoot or greenhorn. According to *The Chinook Jargon,* a 1909 dictionary of the old trading language used by traders from the Hudson's Bay Company in the early 1800s, the word cheechako comes from combining the Chinook Indian word *chee,* meaning new, fresh, or just now, with the Nootka Indian word *chako,* which means to come, to approach, or to become.

Chilkat Blankets

Dramatic, bilaterally symmetrical patterns, usually in black, white, yellow and blue, adorn these heavily fringed ceremonial blankets.

The origin of the dancing blanket pinpoints legend to the Tsimshian. Knowledge of the weaving techniques apparently diffused north to the Tlingit, where blanket-making reached its highest form among the Chilkat group. Visiting traders coined the blanket's name during the late nineteenth century.

Time, technical skill and inherited privileges were required to weave Chilkat blankets and other ceremonial garments. Both men and women wore the blankets and heavily decorated aprons and tunics.

Yarn for Chilkat dancing blankets was spun primarily from the wool of the mountain goat. The designs woven into Chilkat blankets consist of geometric totemic shapes that can be reproduced by the method known as twining. (Early blankets are unadorned or display geometric patterns lacking curvilinear elements.) Often, the placement of totemic crests on painted house posts and the designs woven into garments were quite similar. Weavers re-used pattern boards of wood painted with a design.

A few weavers are producing the blankets today.

Chilkoot Trail

The Chilkoot Trail, from Skagway over Chilkoot Pass to Lake Bennett, British Columbia, was one of the established routes to Yukon Territory gold fields during the Klondike gold rush of 1897-98. Thousands of gold stampeders climbed the tortuous trail over Chilkoot Pass that winter. Those who reached Lake Bennett built boats to float down the Yukon River to Dawson City.

Today, the 33-mile Chilkoot Trail is part of Klondike Gold Rush National Historical Park and is climbed each year by hundreds of backpackers. The Chilkoot Trail begins about 8 miles from Skagway on Dyea Road. There are a dozen campgrounds along the trail and ranger stations on both the Alaska and British Columbia portions of the trail (the trail crosses the international border at 3,739-foot Chilkoot Pass, 16.5 miles from the trail head). The trail ends at Bennett, site of a White Pass and Yukon Route railway station, but since the railway suspended service, hikers must walk another 7 miles along the tracks to the Skagway-Carcross Highway, where they can catch a bus to either Skagway or Carcross. For more information, contact Klondike Gold Rush National Historical Park, Box 517, Skagway 99840.

Related reading: *Chilkoot Pass: The Most Famous Trail in the North.* Revised and expanded second edition by Archie Satterfield. History and a hiking guide. 214 pages, $9.95. See ALASKA NORTHWEST LIBRARY in the back of the book.

Chill Factor

Wind chill can lower the effective temperature many degrees. While Alaska's regions of lowest temperatures also generally have little wind, activities such as riding a snowmobile or even walking can produce the same effect on exposed skin.

Temperature (Fahrenheit)	Wind Chill Temperature at			
	10 mph	20 mph	30 mph	45 mph
40	28	18	13	10
30	16	4	-2	-6
20	4	-10	-18	-22
10	-9	-25	-33	-38
0	-21	-39	-48	-54
-10	-33	-53	-63	-70
-20	-46	-67	-79	-85
-30	-58	-82	-94	-102
-40	-70	-96	-109	-117

The wind's chill factor, when severe, can lead to frostnip (the body's early-warning signal of potential damage from cold — a "nipping" feeling in the extremities), frostbite (formation of small ice crystals in the body tissues) or hypothermia (dangerous lowering of the body's general temperature). Other factors that combine with wind chill and bring on these potentially damaging or fatal effects are exposure to wet exhaustion and lack of adequate clothing.

Chitons

World famous as edible delicacies are two of Alaska's marine invertebrates, king and tanner crabs. However, other shallow-water invertebrates, the gumboot and the Chinese slipper chiton, are also favorites of many Alaskans. Chitons are oval creatures with shells made up of eight overlapping plates. They fasten themselves tightly to rocks and must be pried loose. The gumboot, largest chiton in the world, is named for the tough, leathery, reddish brown covering that hides its plates. It has long been traditional food for southeastern Alaska Indians.

Related reading: *Cooking Alaskan*, over 1,500 recipes explain everything about the art of cooking the Alaska way. 500 pages, $16.95. *Under Alaskan Seas, The Shallow Water Marine Invertebrates*, by Lou and Nancy Barr. The complete guidebook and reference work to more than 240 varied and fascinating species of Alaska marine invertebrates. Color photographs. 208 pages, $14.95. See ALASKA NORTHWEST LIBRARY in the back of the book.

Climate

According to the Alaska state climatologist, Alaska's climate zones are maritime, transition, continental and arctic. With the exception of the transition zone along western Alaska, the zones are divided by mountain ranges that form barriers to shallow air masses and modify those deep enough to cross the ranges. The Brooks Range inhibits the southward movement of air from the Arctic Ocean, thus separating the Arctic climate zone from the Interior. The Chugach, Wrangell, Aleutian and Alaska mountain ranges often limit northward air movement; they at least dry the air before it reaches the Interior's continental zone.

Other meteorologic/oceanographic factors affecting Alaska's climate zones are air temperature, water temperature, cloud coverage, and wind and air pressure. The amount of moisture that air can hold in a gaseous state is highly dependent on its temperature. Warm air can contain more water vapor than cold air. Therefore, precipitation, as rain or snow or other forms, is likely to be heavier from warm than from cold air. Water temperatures change more slowly and much less than land temperatures. For this reason, coastal area temperatures vary less than those farther inland.

Clouds act as insulation for the earth's surface, reflecting solar radiation, yet preventing heat which is already present from escaping into space.

Wind results from air pressure differences and the tendency of the atmosphere to equalize these differences. If the only influence on the wind were atmospheric pressures, air would flow directly from high to low pressure. However, since the earth is rotating, wind tends to blow around a low pressure center in a counterclockwise direction and around a high pressure center in a clockwise direction. The greater the pressure difference between two points, the stronger the wind.

Climate Zones

The maritime climate zone includes Southeast, the northern gulf coast and the Aleutian Chain. Temperatures are mild — relatively warm in the winter and cool in summer. Precipitation is heavy, 50
(Continued on page 28)

Average Temperatures (Fahrenheit) and Precipitation (Inches)

	ANCHORAGE	BARROW	BETHEL	COLD BAY	FAIRBANKS	HOMER	JUNEAU
January							
Temperature	14.8	-13.7	6.6	28.4	-10.3	22.7	23.1
Precipitation	0.80	0.20	0.81	2.71	0.55	2.23	3.98
February							
Temperature	18.5	-19.2	7.3	27.5	-4.1	25.3	28.2
Precipitation	0.86	0.18	0.71	2.30	0.41	1.78	3.66
March							
Temperature	24.7	-15.4	12.3	29.5	10.0	28.3	32.0
Precipitation	0.65	0.15	0.80	2.19	0.37	1.57	3.24
April							
Temperature	35.2	-2.2	24.7	33.0	30.0	35.3	39.2
Precipitation	0.63	0.20	0.65	1.90	0.28	1.27	2.83
May							
Temperature	46.5	18.9	40.2	39.5	48.3	42.6	46.7
Precipitation	0.63	0.16	0.83	2.40	0.57	1.07	3.46
June							
Temperature	54.4	33.7	51.5	45.5	59.5	49.1	53.0
Precipitation	1.02	0.36	1.29	2.13	1.29	1.00	3.02
July							
Temperature	58.1	39.0	54.7	50.3	61.7	53.0	55.9
Precipitation	1.96	0.87	2.18	2.50	1.84	1.63	4.09
August							
Temperature	56.1	37.9	52.7	51.4	56.3	52.8	54.8
Precipitation	2.31	0.97	3.65	3.71	1.82	2.56	5.10
September							
Temperature	48.0	30.6	45.1	47.5	45.0	47.2	49.3
Precipitation	2.51	0.64	2.58	4.06	1.02	2.96	6.25
October							
Temperature	34.7	14.5	30.5	39.7	25.2	37.8	41.9
Precipitation	1.86	0.51	1.48	4.45	0.81	3.41	7.64
November							
Temperature	21.8	-0.7	17.4	34.4	3.8	28.8	32.8
Precipitation	1.08	0.27	0.98	4.33	0.67	2.74	5.13
December							
Temperature	15.2	-11.8	6.9	30.1	-8.1	23.3	27.2
Precipitation	1.06	0.17	0.95	3.16	0.73	2.71	4.48
Snowfall (mean)	14.0	7.1	9.0	9.7	12.5	11.7	23.2
Annual							
Temperature	35.7	9.3	29.1	38.1	26.5	37.2	40.3
Precipitation	15.37	4.67	16.90	35.84	10.37	24.93	53.15

KETCHIKAN	KING SALMON	KODIAK	McGRATH	NOME	PETERSBURG	VALDEZ	
							January
34.2	15.0	32.3	-8.3	6.5	27.6	22.6	Temperature
14.01	1.11	9.52	0.81	0.88	9.31	5.63	Precipitation
							February
36.4	15.1	30.5	-1.7	3.5	31.1	24.3	Temperature
12.36	0.82	5.67	0.74	0.56	7.85	5.08	Precipitation
							March
38.6	21.7	34.4	9.1	8.3	34.7	30.3	Temperature
12.22	1.06	5.16	0.75	0.63	7.19	4.06	Precipitation
							April
43.0	30.8	37.6	26.0	17.3	40.4	37.0	Temperature
11.93	1.07	4.47	0.73	0.67	6.94	2.89	Precipitation
							May
49.2	42.3	43.6	44.3	35.5	47.2	45.3	Temperature
9.06	1.25	6.65	0.84	0.58	5.92	2.74	Precipitation
							June
54.7	50.0	49.6	55.4	45.7	53.0	52.0	Temperature
7.36	1.54	5.72	1.56	1.14	5.00	2.64	Precipitation
							July
58.0	54.5	54.5	58.4	50.8	55.8	55.0	Temperature
7.80	2.10	3.80	2.16	2.18	5.36	3.77	Precipitation
							August
58.7	53.8	55.2	53.9	49.8	55.0	53.6	Temperature
10.60	2.96	4.03	2.87	3.20	7.57	5.73	Precipitation
							September
54.0	47.0	50.2	43.9	42.3	50.3	47.3	Temperature
13.61	2.75	7.18	2.19	2.59	11.15	7.99	Precipitation
							October
47.0	32.6	41.2	25.4	28.3	43.5	38.1	Temperature
22.55	1.98	7.85	1.24	1.38	16.83	8.23	Precipitation
							November
40.4	22.9	35.0	5.0	16.6	35.6	27.8	Temperature
17.90	1.45	6.89	1.18	1.02	11.99	6.09	Precipitation
							December
36.0	14.7	32.1	-7.6	6.2	30.5	22.5	Temperature
15.82	1.19	7.39	1.12	0.82	10.66	6.65	Precipitation
							Snowfall
9.2	7.8	9.9	17.1	8.7	23.9	62.9	(mean)
							Annual
45.9	33.4	41.3	25.3	25.6	42.1	38.0	Temperature
155.22	19.28	74.33	16.18	15.64	105.77	61.50	Precipitation

(Continued from page 25)
to 200 inches annually along the coast and up to 400 inches on mountain slopes. Storms are frequently from the west and southwest, resulting in strong winds along the Aleutian Islands and the Alaska Peninsula. Amchitka Island's weather station has recorded the windiest weather in the state, followed by Cold Bay. Frequent storms with accompanying high winds account for rough seas with occasional waves up to 50 feet in the Gulf of Alaska, particularly in fall and winter.

The transition zone is, in effect, two separate zones. One is the area between the coastal mountains and the Alaska Range, which includes Anchorage and the Matanuska Valley. Summer temperatures are higher than those of the maritime climate zone, with colder winter temperatures and less precipitation. Temperatures, however, are not as extreme as in the continental zone. Another transition zone includes the west coast from Bristol Bay to Point Hope. This area has cool summer temperatures that are somewhat colder than those of the maritime zone and cold winter temperatures similar to the continental zone. Cold winter temperatures are partly due to the sea ice in the Chukchi and Bering seas.

The continental climate zone covers the majority of Alaska except the coastal fringes and the arctic slope. It has extreme high and low temperatures and low precipitation. There are fewer clouds in the continental zone than elsewhere so there is more warming by the sun during the long days of summer and more cooling during the long nights of winter. Precipitation is light because air masses affecting the area lose most of their moisture crossing the mountains to the south.

The Arctic, north of the Brooks Range, has cold winters, cool summers and desertlike precipitation. Prevailing winds are from the northeast off the arctic ice pack, which never moves far offshore. Summers are generally cloudy and winters are clear and cold. The cold air allows little precipitation and inhibits evaporation. Because continuous permafrost prevents the percolation of water into the soil, the area is generally marshy with numerous lakes. (*See also* Permafrost.)

The chart on pages 26-27 shows normal monthly temperatures and precipitation for 14 communities in Alaska. Included are maximum monthly snowfall for December and annual precipitation. The chart is based on data from NOAA and the Alaska state climatologist.

CLIMATE RECORDS
Highest temperature: 100°F, at Fort Yukon, June 27, 1915.
Lowest temperature: -80°F, at Prospect Creek Camp, January 23, 1971.
Most precipitation in one year: 332.29 inches, at MacLeod Harbor (Montague Island), 1976.
Most precipitation in 24 hours: 15.2 inches, in Angoon, October 12, 1982.
Most monthly precipitation: 70.99 inches, at MacLeod Harbor, November, 1976.
Least precipitation in a year: 1.61 inches, at Barrow, 1935.
Most snowfall in a season: 974.5 inches, at Thompson Pass, 1952-53.
Most snowfall in 24 hours: 62 inches, at Thompson Pass, December, 1955.
Most monthly snowfall: 297.9 inches, at Thompson Pass, February, 1953.
Least snowfall in a season: 3 inches, at Barrow, 1935-36.
Highest recorded snow pack (also highest ever recorded in North America): 356 inches on Wolverine Glacier, Kenai Peninsula, after winter of 1976-77.
Highest recorded wind speed: 139 mph, at Shemya Island, December, 1959.

Coal

(*See also* Minerals and Mining)
About half of the coal resource of the United States is believed to be in Alaska. The demonstrated coal reserve base of the state is over 6 billion short tons, identified coal resources are about 160 billion short tons, and hypothetical and speculative resource estimates range upward to 6 trillion short tons. The three provinces containing the most coal are northwestern Alaska, Cook Inlet-Susitna Lowland and the Nenana Trend. Geologists estimate that perhaps 80 percent of Alaska's

coal underlies the 23-million-acre National Petroleum Reserve on the North Slope. Although the majority of the coals are of bituminous and sub-bituminous ranks, anthracite coal does occur in the Bering River and Matanuska fields. In addition to the vast resource base and wide distribution, the extremely low sulfur contents and near proximity to coastal access in certain areas, and to the Far East in general, are important selling points for Alaska coal.

Exploration, technology and economics will ultimately determine the marketability of Alaska's coal resources. Large-scale exploration programs have been conducted in most of Alaska's coal fields by private industry and state and federal governments. Maxus Energy, Inc. and Placer U.S. are developing the Beluga coal field west of Anchorage on Cook Inlet. Exploration is under way on Wish Bone Hill, and in Nenana and Cape Beaufort in northwest Alaska.

Alaska's production of coal in 1988 was estimated to be 1.55 million tons and came exclusively from the Usibelli Coal Mine near Healy. Of that estimate, 727,000 tons were burned in interior Alaska power plants; 810,800 short tons were shipped to Korea; and 13,500 tons were shipped to Japan for testing.

Coal production in Alaska was over $44 million in 1988, up from $42 million in 1987.

Conk

Alaskans apply this term to a type of bracket fungus. The platelike conks grow on dead trees. When dry and hard, conks are snapped off and used to paint on.

Constitution of Alaska

One of the most remarkable achievements in the long battle for Alaskan statehood was the creation of the constitution of the state of Alaska in the mid-1950s. Statehood supporters believed that creation of a constitution would demonstrate Alaska's maturity and readiness for statehood, so in 1955 the territorial legislature appropriated $300,000 for the costs of holding a Constitutional Convention in Fairbanks.

For 73 days in 1955-1956, a total of 55 elected delegates from all across the territory of Alaska met in the new Student Union Building (now called Constitution Hall) on the University of Alaska campus. William A. Egan, a territorial legislator and former mayor of Valdez, who later became the first governor of the state of Alaska, was president of the convention. Under his leadership, the disparate group of Alaskans hammered out a document that is considered a model for a state constitution.

The National Municipal League said that the brief 14,000-word document drafted by the convention delegates was "one of the best, if not the best, state constitutions ever written." By an overwhelming margin the people of Alaska approved the new constitution at the polls in 1956, paving the way for the creation of the 49th state in 1959.

Preamble

We the people of Alaska, grateful to God and to those who founded our nation and pioneered this great land, in order to secure and transmit to succeeding generations our heritage of political, civil and religious liberty within the Union of States, do ordain and establish this constitution for the State of Alaska.

Article I
Declaration of Rights

SECTION 1. This constitution is dedicated to the principles that all persons have a natural right to life, liberty, the pursuit of happiness, and the enjoyment of the rewards of their own industry; and all persons are equal and entitled to equal rights, opportunities, and protection under the law; and that all persons have corresponding obligations to the people and to the State.

SECTION 2. All political power is inherent in the people. All government originates with the people, is founded upon their will only, and is instituted solely for the good of the people as a whole.

SECTION 3. No person is to be denied the enjoyment of any civil or political right because of race, color, creed, sex, or national origin. The legislature shall implement this section. *(The above Constitutional Amendment was approved by the voters of the State on August 22, 1972. The amendment added the word "sex" to this section.)*

SECTION 4. No law shall be made respecting an establishment of religion, or prohibiting the free exercise thereof.

SECTION 5. Every person may freely speak, write, and publish on all subjects, being responsible for the abuse of that right.

SECTION 6. The right of the people peaceably to assemble, and to petition the government shall never be abridged.

SECTION 7. No person shall be deprived of life, liberty, or property, without due process of law. The right of all persons to fair and just treatment in the course of the legislative and executive investigations shall not be infringed.

SECTION 8. No person shall be held to answer for a capital, or otherwise infamous crime, unless on a presentment or indictment of a grand jury, except in cases arising in the armed forces in time of war or public danger. Indictment may be waived by the accused. In that case the prosecution shall be by information. The Grand Jury shall consist of at least twelve citizens, a majority of whom concurring may return an indictment. The power of grand juries to investigate and make recommendations concerning the public welfare or safety shall never be suspended.

SECTION 9. No person shall be put in jeopardy twice for the same offense. No person shall be compelled in any criminal proceeding to be a witness against himself.

SECTION 10. Treason against the state consists only in levying war against it, or in adhering to its enemies, giving them aid and comfort. No person shall be convicted of treason, unless on the testimony of two witnesses to the same overt act, or on confession in open court.

SECTION 11. In all criminal prosecutions, the accused shall have the right to a speedy and public trial, by an impartial jury of twelve; except that the legislature may provide for a jury of not more than twelve nor less than six in courts not of record. The accused is entitled to be informed of the nature and cause of the accusation; to be released on bail, except for capital offenses when the proof is evident or the presumption great; to be confronted with the witnesses against him; to have compulsory process for obtaining witnesses in his favor, and to have the assistance of counsel for his defense.

SECTION 12. Excessive bail shall not be required, nor excessive fines imposed nor cruel and unusual punishments inflicted. Penal administration shall be based on the principle of reformation and upon the need for protecting the public.

SECTION 13. The privilege of the writ of habeas corpus shall not be suspended, unless when in cases of rebellion or actual or imminent invasion, the public safety requires it.

SECTION 14. The right of the people to be secure in their persons, houses and other property, papers and effects, against unreasonable searches and seizures, shall not be violated. No warrants shall issue, but upon probable cause supported by oath or affirmation, and particularly describing the place to be searched, and the persons or things to be seized.

SECTION 15. No bill of attainder or ex post facto law shall be passed. No law impairing the obligation of contracts, and no law making any irrevocable grant of special privileges or immunities shall be passed. No conviction shall work corruption of blood or forfeiture of estate.

SECTION 16. In civil cases where the amount in controversy exceeds two hundred fifty dollars, the right of trial by a jury of twelve is preserved to the same extent as it existed at common law. The legislature may make provision for a verdict by not less than three-fourths of the jury and, in courts not of record, may provide for a jury of not less than six or more than twelve.

SECTION 17. There shall be no imprisonment for debt. This section does not prohibit civil arrest of absconding debtors.

SECTION 18. Private property shall not be taken or damaged for public use without just compensation.

SECTION 19. A well-regulated militia being necessary to the security of a free state, the right of the people to keep and bear arms shall not be infringed.

SECTION 20. No member of the armed forces shall in time of peace be quartered in any house without the consent of the owner or occupant, or in time of war except as prescribed by law. The military shall be in strict subordination to the civil power.

SECTION 21. The enumeration or rights in this constitution shall not impair or deny others retained by the people.

SECTION 22. The right of the people to privacy is recognized and shall not be infringed. The legislature shall implement this section. *(This section was added as a new amendment approved by the voters of the State on August 22, 1972.)*

Article II
The Legislature

SECTION 1. The legislature power of the State is vested in the legislature consisting of a senate with a membership of twenty and a house of representatives with a membership of forty.

SECTION 2. A member of the legislature shall be a qualified voter who has been a resident of Alaska for at least three years and of the district from which elected for at least one year, immediately preceding his filing for office. A senator shall be at least twenty-five years of age and a representative at least twenty-one years of age.

SECTION 3. Legislators shall be elected at general elections. Their terms begin on the fourth Monday of the January following election unless otherwise provided by law. The term of representatives shall be two years, and the term of senators, four years. One-half of the senators shall be elected every two years. *(Exercising its authority under this section the legislature has provided that legislative terms begin on the second Monday in January; see AS 24.05.080.)*

SECTION 4. A vacancy in the legislature shall be filled for the unexpired term as provided by law. If no provision is made, the governor shall fill the vacancy by appointment.

SECTION 5. No legislator may hold any other office or position of profit under the United States or the State. During the term for which elected and for one year thereafter, no legislator may be nominated, elected, or appointed to any other office or position of profit which has been created, or the salary or emoluments of which have been increased, while he was a member. This section shall not prevent any person from seeking or holding the office of governor, lieutenant governor, or member of Congress. This section shall not apply to employment by or election to a constitutional convention. *(The above Constitutional Amendment was approved by the voters of the State August 25, 1970. The words secretary of state were changed to lieutenant governor.)*

SECTION 6. Legislators may not be held to answer before any other tribunal for any statement made in the exercise of their legislative duties while the legislature is in session. Members attending, going to, or returning from legislative sessions are not subject to civil process and are privileged from arrest except for felony or breach of the peace.

SECTION 7. Legislators shall receive annual salaries. They may receive a per diem allowance for expenses while in session and are entitled to travel expenses going to and from sessions. Presiding officers may receive additional compensation.

SECTION 8. The legislature shall convene each year on the fourth Monday in January, but the month and day may be changed by law. *(Exercising its authority under this section, the legislature has provided that it shall convene on the second Monday in January except in the year immediately following a gubernatorial election, when it shall convene on the third Monday in January; see AS 24.05.090. The above Constitutional Amendment was approved by the voters of the State on August 22, 1972. A further amendment approved by the* voters of the State on November 6, 1984, adds a limit on the length of regular sessions of the state legislature. The legislature must adjourn no later than 120 consecutive calendar days after the date it convenes in regular session each year. If at least two-thirds of each house of the legislature votes to extend the regular session, the session may be extended once for up to 10 calendar days. The legislature will adopt deadlines for scheduling session work in keeping with these provisions.)

SECTION 9. Special sessions may be called by the governor or by vote of two-thirds of the legislators. The vote may be conducted by the legislative council or as prescribed by law. At special sessions called by the governor, legislation shall be limited to subjects designated in his proclamation calling the session, or to subjects presented by him, and the reconsideration of bills vetoed by him after adjournment of the last regular session. Special sessions are limited to thirty days. *(The above Constitutional Amendment was approved by the voters of the State on November 2, 1976. The amendment added the reconsideration of vetoed bills.)*

SECTION 10. Neither house may adjourn or recess for longer than three days unless the other concurs. If the two houses cannot agree on the time of adjournment and either house certifies the disagreement to the governor, he may adjourn the legislature.

SECTION 11. There shall be a legislative council, and the legislature may establish other interim committees. The council and other interim committees may meet between legislative sessions. They may perform duties and employ personnel as provided by the legislature. Their members may receive an allowance for expenses while performing their duties.

SECTION 12. The houses of each legislature shall adopt uniform rules of procedure. Each house may choose its officers and employees. Each is the judge of the election and qualifications of its members and may expel a member with the concurrence of two-thirds of its members. Each shall keep a journal of its proceedings. A majority of the membership of each house constitutes a quorum to do business, but a smaller number may adjourn from day to day and may compel attendance of absent members. The legislature shall regulate lobbying.

SECTION 13. Every bill shall be confined to one subject unless it is an appropriation bill or one codifying, revising,or rearranging existing laws. Bills for appropriations shall be confined to appropriations. The subject of each bill shall be expressed in the title. The enacting clause shall be: "Be it enacted by the Legislature of the State of Alaska."

SECTION 14. The legislature shall establish the procedure for enactment of bills into law. No bill may become law unless it has passed three readings in each house on three separate days, except that any bill may be advanced from second to third reading on the same day by concurrence of three-fourths of the house considering it. No bill may become law without an affirmative vote of a majority of the membership of each house. The yeas and nays on final passage shall be entered in the journal.

SECTION 15. The governor may veto bills passed by the legislature. He may, by veto, strike or reduce items in appropriations bills. He shall return any vetoed bill, with a statement of his objections, to the house of origin.

SECTION 16. Upon receipt of a veto message during a regular session of the legislature, the legislature shall meet immediately in joint session and reconsider passage of the vetoed bill or item. Bills to raise revenue and appropriation bills or items, although vetoed, become law by affirmative vote of three-fourths of the membership of the legislature. Other vetoed bills become law by affirmative vote of two-thirds of the membership of the legislature. Bills vetoed after adjournment of the first regular session of the legislature shall be reconsidered by the legislature sitting as one body no later than the fifth day of the next regular or special session of that legislature. Bills vetoed after adjournment of the second regular session shall be reconsidered by the legislature sitting as one body no later than the fifty day of a special session of that legislature, if one is called. The vote on reconsideration of a vetoed bill shall be entered on the journals of both houses. *(The above Constitutional Amendment was approved by the voters of the State on November 2, 1976. The amendment added bills vetoed after adjournment.)*

SECTION 17. A bill becomes law if, while the legislature is in session, the governor neither signs nor vetoes it within fifteen days, Sundays excepted, after its delivery to him. If the legislature is not in session and the governor neither signs nor vetoes a bill within twenty days, Sundays excepted, after its delivery to him, the bill becomes law.

SECTION 18. Laws passed by the legislature become effective ninety days after enactment. The legislature may, by concurrence of two-thirds of the membership of each house, provide for another effective date.

SECTION 19. The legislature shall pass no local or special act if a general act can be made applicable. Whether a general act can be made applicable shall be subject to judical determination. Local acts necessitating appropriations by a political subdivision may not become effective unless approved by a major of the qualified voters voting thereon in the subdivision affected.

SECTION 20. All civil officers of the State are subject to impeachment by the legislature. Impeachment shall originate in the senate and must be approved by a two-thirds vote of its members. The motion for impeachment shall list fully the basis for the proceeding. Trial on impeachment shall be conducted by the house or representatives. A supreme court justice designated by the court shall preside at the trial. Concurrence of two-thirds of the members of the house is required for a judgment of impeachment. The judgment may not extend beyond removal from office, but shall not prevent proceedings in the courts on the same or related charges.

SECTION 21. The legislature shall establish procedures for suits against the State.

Article III
The Executive

SECTION 1. The executive power of the State is vested in the governor.

SECTION 2. The governor shall be at least thirty years of age and a qualified voter of the State. He shall have been a resident of Alaska at least seven years immediately preceding his filing for office, and he shall have been a citizen of the United States for at least seven years.

SECTION 3. The governor shall be chosen by the qualified voters of the State at a general election. The candidate receiving the greatest number of votes shall be governor.

SECTION 4. The term of office of the governor is four years, beginning at noon on the first Monday in December following his election and ending at noon on the first Monday in December four years later.

SECTION 5. No person who has been elected governor for two full successive terms shall be again eligible to hold that office until one full term has intervened.

SECTION 6. The governor shall not hold any other office or position of profit under the United States, the State, or its political subdivisions.

SECTION 7. There shall be a lieutenant governor.

He shall have the same qualifications as the governor and serve for the same term. He shall perform such duties as may be prescribed by law and as may be delegated to him by the governor. *(The above Constitutional Amendment was approved by the voters of the State August 25, 1970. The words secretary of state were changed to lieutenant governor.)*

SECTION 8. The lieutenant governor shall be nominated in the manner provided by law for nominating candidates for other elective office. In the general election the votes cast for a candidate for governor shall be considered as cast also for the candidate for lieutenant governor running jointly with him. The candidate whose name appears on the ballot jointly with that of the successful candidate for governor shall be elected lieutenant governor. *(The above Constitutional Amendment was approved by the voters of the State August 25, 1970. The words secretary of state were changed to lieutenant governor.)*

SECTION 9. In case of the temporary absence of the governor from office, the lieutenant governor shall serve as acting governor. *(The above Constitutional Amendment was approved by the voters of the State August 25, 1970. The words secretary of state were changed to lieutenant governor.)*

SECTION 10. If the governor-elect dies, resigns, or is disqualified, the lieutenant governor elected with him shall succeed to the office of governor for the full term. If the governor-elect fails to assume office for any other reason, the lieutenant governor elected with him shall serve as acting governor, and shall succeed to the office if the governor-elect does not assume his office within six months of the beginning of the term. *(The above Constitutional Amendment was approved by the voters of the State August 25, 1970. The words secretary of state were changed to lieutenant governor.)*

SECTION 11. In case of a vacancy in the office of governor for any reason, the lieutenant governor shall succeed to the office for the remainder of the term. *(The above Constitutional Amendment was approved by the voters of the State August 25, 1970. The words secretary of state were changed to lieutenant governor.)*

SECTION 12. Whenever for a period of six months, a governor has been continuously absent from office or has been unable to discharge the duties of his office by reason of mental or physical disability, the office shall be deemed vacant. The procedure for determining absence and disability shall be prescribed by law.

SECTION 13. Provisions shall be made by law for succession to the office of governor and for an acting governor in the event that the lieutenant governor is unable to succeed to the office or act as governor. No election of a lieutenant governor shall be held except at the time of electing a governor. *(The above Constitutional Amendment was approved by the voters of the State August 25, 1970. The words secretary of state were changed to lieutenant governor.)*

SECTION 14. When the lieutenant governor succeeds to the office of governor, he shall have the title, power, duties and emoluments of that office. *(The above Constitutional Amendment was approved by the voters of the State August 25, 1970. The words secretary of state were changed to lieutenant governor.)*

SECTION 15. The compensation of the governor and the lieutenant governor shall be prescribed by law and shall not be diminished during their term of office, unless by general law applying to all salaried officers of the State. *(The above Constitutional Amendment was approved by the voters of the State August 25, 1970. The words secretary of state were changed to lieutenant governor.)*

SECTION 16. The governor shall be responsible for the faithful execution of the laws. He may, by appropriate court action or proceeding brought in the name of the State, enforce compliance with any constitutional or legislative mandate, or restrain violation of any constitutional or legislative power, duty, or right by any officer, department, or agency of the State or any of its political subdivisions. This authority shall not be construed to authorize any action or proceeding against the legislature.

SECTION 17. Whenever the governor considers it in the public interest, he may convene the legislature, either house, or the two houses in joint session.

SECTION 18. The governor shall, at the beginning of each session, and may at other times, give the legislature information concerning the affairs of the State and recommend the measures he considers necessary.

SECTION 19. The governor is commander-in-chief of the armed forces of the State. He may call out these forces to execute the laws, suppress or prevent insurrection or lawless violence, or repel invasion. The governor, as provided by law, shall appoint all general and flag officers of the armed forces of the State, subject to confirmation by a majority of the members of the legislature in joint session. He shall appoint and commission all other officers.

SECTION 20. The governor may proclaim martial law when the public safety requires it in case of rebellion or actual or imminent invasion. Martial law shall not continue for longer than twenty days without the approval of a majority of the members of the legislature in joint session.

SECTION 21. Subject to procedures prescribed by law, the governor may grant pardons, commutations, and reprieves, and may suspend and remit fines and forfeitures. This power shall not extend to impeachment. A parole system shall be provided by law.

SECTION 22. All executive and administrative offices, departments, and agencies of the state government and their respective functions, powers, and duties shall be allocated by the law among and within not more than twenty principal departments, so as to group them as far as practicable according to major purposes. Regulatory quasijudicial, and temporary agencies may be established by law and need not be allocated within a principal department.

SECTION 23. The governor may make changes in the organization of the executive branch or in the assignment of functions among its units which he considers necessary for efficient administration. Where these changes require the force of law, they shall be set forth in executive orders. The legislature shall have sixty days of a regular session, or a full session if of shorter duration, to disapprove these executive orders. Unless disapproved by resolution concurred in by a majority of the members in joint session, these orders become effective at a date thereafter to be designated by the governor.

SECTION 24. Each principal department shall be under the supervision of the governor.

SECTION 25. The head of each principal department shall be a single executive unless otherwise provided by law. He shall be appointed by the governor, subject to confirmation by a majority of the members of the legislature in joint session, and shall serve at the pleasure of the governor, except as otherwise provided in this article with respect to the lieutenant governor. The heads of all principal departments shall be citizens of the United States. *(The above Constitutional Amendment was approved by the voters of the State August 25, 1970. The words secretary of state were changed to lieutenant governor.)*

SECTION 26. When a board or commission is at the head of a principal department or a regulatory or quasi-judicial agency, its members shall be appointed by the governor, subject to confirmation by a majority of the members of the legislature in joint session, and may be removed as provided by law. They shall be citizens of the United States. The board or commission may appoint a principal executive officer when authorized by law, but the appointment shall be subject to the approval of the governor.

SECTION 27. The governor may make appointments to fill vacancies occurring during a recess of the legislature, in offices requiring confirmation by the legislature. The duration of such appointments shall be prescribed by law.

Article IV
The Judiciary

SECTION 1. The judicial power of the State is vested in a supreme court, a superior court and the courts established by the legislature. The jurisdiction of courts shall be prescribed by law. The courts shall constitute a unified judicial system for operation and administration. Judicial districts shall be established by law.

SECTION 2. (a) The supreme court shall be the highest court of the State, with final appellate jurisdiction. It shall consist of three justices, one of whom is chief justice. The number of justices may be increased by law upon the request of the supreme court.

(b) The chief justice shall be selected from among the justices of the supreme court by a majority vote of the justices. His term of office is three years. A justice may serve more than one term as chief justice but he may not serve consecutive terms in that office. *(The above Constitutional Amendment was approved by the voters of the State August 25, 1970. Subsection (b) was added.)*

SECTION 3. The superior court shall be the trial court of general jurisdiction and shall consist of five judges. The number of judges may be changed by law.

SECTION 4. Supreme court justices and superior court judges shall be citizens of the United States and of the State, licensed to practice law in the State, and possessing any additional qualifications prescribed by law. Judges of other courts shall be selected in a manner, for terms, and with qualifications prescribed by law.

SECTION 5. The governor shall fill any vacancy in an office of supreme court justice or superior court judge by appointing one of two or more persons nominated by the judicial council.

SECTION 6. Each supreme court justice and superior court judge shall, in the manner provided by law, be subject to approval or rejection on a nonpartisan ballot at the first general election held more than three years after his appointment. Thereafter, each supreme court justice shall be subject to approval or rejection in a like manner every tenth year, and each superior court judge, every sixth year.

SECTION 7. The office of any supreme court justice or superior court judge becomes vacant ninety days after the election at which he is rejected by a majority of those voting on the question, or for which he fails to file his declaration of candidacy to succeed himself.

SECTION 8. The judicial council shall consist of seven members. Three attorney members shall be appointed for six-year terms by the governing body of the organized state bar. Three non-attorney members shall be appointed for six-year terms by the governor subject to confirmation by a majority of the members of the legislature in joint session. Vacancies shall be filled for the unexpired term in like manner. Appointments shall be made with due consideration to area representation and without regard to political affiliation. The chief justice of the supreme court shall be ex officio the seventh member and chairman of the judicial council.

No member of the judicial council, except the chief justice, may hold any other office or position of profit under the United States or the State. The judicial council shall act by concurrence of four or more members and according to rules which it adopts.

SECTION 9. The judicial council shall conduct studies for improvement of the administration of justice, and make reports and recommendations to the supreme court and to the legislature at intervals of not more than two years. The judicial council shall perform other duties assigned by law.

SECTION 10. The commission on judicial qualifications shall consist of nine members, as follows: three persons who are justices or judges of state courts, elected by the justices and judges of state courts; three members who have practiced law in this state for ten years, appointed by the governor from nominations made by the governing body of the organized bar and subject to confirmation by a majority of the members of the legislature in joint session; and three persons who are not judges, retired judges, or members of the state bar, appointed by the governor and subject to confirmation by a majority of the members of the legislature in joint session. In addition to being subject to impeachment under Section 12 of this article, a justice or judge may be disqualified from acting as such and may be suspended, removed from office, retired, or censured by the supreme court upon the recommendation of the commission. The powers and duties of the commission and the bases for judicial disqualification shall be established by law. *(The above Constitutional Amendment was approved by the voters of the State August 27, 1968. Section 10, Article IV, pertaining to Incapacity of Judges was repealed. A second Constitutional Amendment approved by the voters of the State November 2, 1982 changed the selection process for the nine members.)*

SECTION 11. Justices and judges shall be retired at the age of seventy except as provided in this article. The basis and amount of retirement pay shall be prescribed by law. Retired judges shall render no further service on the bench except for special assignments as provided by court rule.

SECTION 12. Impeachment of any justice or judge for malfeasance or misfeasance in the performance of his official duties shall be according to procedure prescribed for civil officers.

SECTION 13. Justices, judges, and members of the judicial council and the commission on judicial qualifications shall receive compensation as prescribed by law. Compensation of justices and judges shall not be diminished during their terms of office, unless by general law applying to all salaried officers of the State. *(The above Constitutional Amendment was approved by the voters of the State August 27, 1968. The words "and the commission on judicial qualifications" were incorporated in this Section.)*

SECTION 14. Supreme court justices and superior court judges while holding office may not practice law, hold office in a political party, or hold any other office or position of profit under the United States, the State, or its political subdivisions. Any supreme court justice or superior court judge filing for another elective public office forfeits his judicial position.

SECTION 15. The supreme court shall make and promulgate rules governing the administration of all courts. It shall make and promulgate rules governing practice and procedure in civil and criminal cases in all courts. These rules may be changed by the legislature by two-thirds vote of the members elected to each house.

SECTION 16. The chief justice of the supreme court shall be the administrative head of all courts. He may assign judges from one court or division thereof to another for temporary service. The chief justice shall, with the approval of the supreme court, appoint an administrative director to serve at the pleasure of the supreme court and to supervise the administrative operations of the judicial system. *(The above Constitutional Amendment was approved by the voters of the State August 25, 1970. The amendment substituted "the pleasure of the supreme court" for "his pleasure" in the last sentence.)*

Article V
Suffrage and Elections

SECTION 1. Every citizen of the United States who is at least eighteen years of age, who meets registration requirements which may be prescribed by law, and who is qualified to vote under this article, may vote in any state or local election. A voter shall have been, immediately preceding the election, a thirty day resident of the election district in which he seeks to vote, except that for purposes of voting for President and Vice President of the United States other residency requirements may be prescribed by law. Additional voting qualifications may be prescribed by law for bond issue elections of political subdivisions. *(The above Constitutional Amendment was approved by the voters of the State August 25, 1970. It changed the voting age from nineteen years to eighteen years and deleted the sentence: "A voter shall be able to read or speak the English language as prescribed by law, unless prevented by physical disability." A further amendment approved by the voters on August 22, 1972 gave the legislature authority to prescribe registration residency requirements and changed the residency requirements from one year in the state and thirty days in the election district to thirty days in the election district.)*

SECTION 2. No person may vote who has been convicted of a felony involving moral turpitude unless his civil rights have been restored. No person may vote who has been judicially determined to be of unsound mind unless the disability has been removed.

SECTION 3. Methods of voting, including absentee voting, shall be prescribed by law. Secrecy of voting shall be preserved. The procedure for determining election contests, with right of appeal to the courts, shall be prescribed by law.

SECTION 4. The legislature may provide a system of permanent registration of voters, and may establish voting procincts within election districts.

SECTION 5. General elections shall be held on the second Tuesday in October of every even-numbered year, but the month and day may be changed by law. *(Exercising its authority under this section, the legislature has provided that the date of general election is the Tuesday after the first Monday in November in every even-numbered year; See AS 15.15.020.)*

Article VI
Legislative Apportionment

SECTION 1. Members of the house of representatives shall be elected by the qualified voters of the respective election districts. Until reapportionment, election districts and the number of representatives to be elected from each district shall be as set forth in Section 1 of Article XIV.

SECTION 2. Members of the senate shall be elected by the qualified voters of the respective senate districts. Senate districts shall be as set forth in Section 2 of Article XIV, subject to changes authorized in this article.

SECTION 3. The governor shall reapportion the house of representatives immediately following the official reporting of each decennial census of the United States. Reapportionment shall be based upon civilian population within each election district as reported by the census.

SECTION 4. Reapportionment shall be by the methods of equal proportions, except that each election district having the major fraction of the quotient obtained by dividing total civilian population by forty shall have one representative.

SECTION 5. Should the total civilian population within any election district fall below one-half of the quotient, the district shall be attached to an election district within its senate district, and the reapportionment for the new district shall be determined as provided in Section 4 of this article.

SECTION 6. The governor may further redistrict by changing the size and area of election districts, subject to the limitations of this article. Each new district so created shall be formed of contiguous and compact territory containing as nearly as practicable a relatively integrated socio-economic area. Each shall contain a population at least equal to the quotient obtained by dividing the total civilian population by forty. Consideration may be given to local government boundaries. Drainage and other geographic features shall be used in describing boundaries whenever possible.

SECTION 7. The senate districts, described in Section 2 of Article XIV, may be modified to reflect changes in election districts. A district, although modified, shall retain its total number of senators and its approximate perimeter.

SECTION 8. The governor shall appoint a reapportionment board to act in an advisory capacity to him. It shall consist of five members, none of whom may be public employees or officials. At least one member each shall be appointed from the Southeastern, Southcentral, Central and Northwestern Senate Districts. Appointments shall be made without regards to political affiliation. Board members shall be compensated.

SECTION 9. The board shall elect one of its members chairman and may employ temporary assistants. Concurrence of three members is required for a ruling or determination, but a lesser number may conduct hearings or otherwise act for the board.

SECTION 10. Within ninety days following the official reporting of each decennial census, the board shall submit to the governor a plan for reapportionment and redistricting as provided in this article. Within ninety days after receipt of the plan, the governor shall issue a proclamation of reapportionment and redistricting. An accompanying statement shall explain any change from the plan of the board. The reapportionment and redistricting shall be effective for the election of members of the legislature until after the official reporting of the next decennial census.

SECTION 11. Any qualified voter may apply to the superior court to compel the governor, by mandamus or otherwise to perform his reapportionment duties or to correct any error in redistricting or reapportionment. Application to compel the governor to perform his reapportionment duties must be filed within thirty days of the expiration of either of the two ninety-day periods specified in this article. Application to compel correction of any error in redistricting or reapportionment must be filed within thirty days following the proclamation. Original jurisdiction in these matters is hereby vested in the superior court. On appeal, the cause shall be reviewed by the supreme court upon the law and the facts.

Article VII
Health, Education, and Welfare

SECTION 1. The legislature shall by general law establish and maintain a system of public schools open to all children of the State, and may provide for other public educational institutions. Schools and institutions so established shall be free from sectarian control. No money shall be paid from public funds for the direct benefit of any religious or other private educational institution.

SECTION 2. The University of Alaska is hereby established as the state university and constituted a body corporate. It shall have title to all real and personal property now or hereafter set aside for or conveyed to it. Its property shall be administered and disposed of according to law.

SECTION 3. The University of Alaska shall be governed by a board of regents. The regents shall be appointed by the governor, subject to confirmation by a majority of the members of the legislature in joint session. The board shall, in accordance with law, formulate policy and appoint the president of the university. He shall be the executive officer of the board.

SECTION 4. The legislature shall provide for the promotion and protection of public health.

SECTION 5. The legislature shall provide for public welfare.

Article VIII
Natural Resources

SECTION 1. It is the policy of the State to encourage the settlement of its land and the development of its resources by making them available for maximum use consistent with the public interest.

SECTION 2. The legislature shall provide for the utilization, development, and conservation of all natural resources belonging to the State, including land and waters, for the maximum benefit of its people.

SECTION 3. Wherever occurring in the natural state, fish, wildlife, and waters are reserved to the people for common use.

SECTION 4. Fish, forests, wildlife, grasslands, and all other replenishable resources belonging to the State shall be utilized, developed, and maintained on the sustained yield principle, subject to preferences among beneficial uses.

SECTION 5. The legislature may provide for facilities, improvements, and services to assure greater utilization, development, reclamation, and settlement of lands, and to assure fuller utilization and development of the fisheries, wildlife, and waters.

SECTION 6. Lands and interests therein, including submerged and tidal lands, possessed or acquired by the State, and not used or intended exclusively for governmental purposes, constitute the state public domain. The legislature shall provide for the selection of lands granted to the State by the United States, and for the administration of the state public domain.

SECTION 7. The legislature may provide for the acquisition of sites, objects, and areas of natural beauty or of historic, cultural, recreational, or scientific value. It may reserve them from the public domain and provide for their administration and preservation for the use, enjoyment, and welfare of the people.

SECTION 8. The legislature may provide for the leasing of, and the issuance of permits for exploration of, any part of the public domain or interest therein, subject to reasonable concurrents uses. Leases and permits shall provide, among other conditions, for payment by the party at fault for damage or injury arising from noncompliance with terms governing concurrent use, and for forfeiture in the event of breach of conditions.

SECTION 9. Subject to the provisions of this section, the legislature may provide for the sale or grant of state lands, or interests therein, and establish sales procedures. All sales or grants shall contain such reservations to the State of all resources as may be required by Congress or the State and shall provide for access to these resources. Reservation of access shall not unnecessarily impair the owners' use, prevent the control of trespass, or preclude compensation for damages.

SECTION 10. No disposals or leases of state lands, or interests therein, shall be made without prior public notice and other safeguards of the public interest as may be prescribed by law.

SECTION 11. Discovery and appropriation shall be the basis for establishing a right in those minerals reserved to the State which, upon the date of ratification of this constitution by the people of Alaska, were subject to location under the federal mining laws. Prior discovery, location, and filing, as prescribed by law, shall establish a prior right to these minerals and also a prior right to permits, leases, and transferable licenses for their extraction. Continuation of these rights shall depend upon the performance of annual labor, or the payment of fees, rents, or royalties, or upon other requirements as may be prescribed by law. Surface uses of land by a mineral claimant shall be limited to those necessary for the extraction or basic processing of the mineral deposits, or for both. Discovery and appropriation shall initiate a right, subject to further requirements of law, to patent of mineral lands if authorized by the State and not prohibited by Congress. The provisions of this section shall apply to all other minerals reserved to the State which by law are declared subject to appropriation.

SECTION 12. The legislature shall provide for the issuance, types and terms of leases for coal, oil, gas, oil shale, sodium, phosphate, potash, sulfur, pumice, and other minerals as may be prescribed by law. Leases and permits giving the exclusive right of exploration for these minerals for specific periods and areas, subject to reasonable concurrent exploration as to different classes of minerals, may be authorized by law. Like leases and permits giving the exclusive right of prospecting by geophysical, geochemical, and similar methods for all minerals may also be authorized by law.

SECTION 13. All surface and subsurface waters reserved to the people for common use, except mineral and medicinal waters, are subject to appropriation. Priority of appropriation shall give prior right. Except for public water supply, an appropriation of water shall be limited to stated purposes and subject to preferences among beneficial uses, concurrent or otherwise, as prescribed by law, and to the general reservation of fish and wildlife.

SECTION 14. Free access to the navigable or public waters of the State, as defined by the legislature, shall not be denied any citizen of the United States or resident of the State, except that the legislature may by general law regulate and limit such access for other beneficial uses or public purposes.

SECTION 15. No exclusive right or special privilege of fishery shall be created or authorized in the natural waters of the State. This section does not restrict the power of the State to limit entry into any fishery for purposes of resource conservation, to prevent economic distress among fishermen and those dependent on them for a livelihood and to promote the efficient development of the aquaculture in the State. *(The above Constitutional Amendment was approved by the voters of the State August 22, 1972. The sentence about not restricting the power of the State was added.)*

SECTION 16. No person shall be involuntarily divested of his right to the use of waters, his interests in lands, or improvements affecting either, except for a superior beneficial use or public purpose and then only with just compensation and by operation of law.

SECTION 17. Laws and regulations governing the use or disposal of natural resources shall apply equally to all persons similarly situated with reference to the subject matter and purpose to be served by the law or regulation.

SECTION 18. Proceeding in eminent domain may be undertaken for private ways of necessity to permit essential access for extraction or utilization of resources. Just compensation shall be made for property taken or for resultant damages to other property rights.

Article IX
Finance and Taxation

SECTION 1. The power of taxation shall never be surrendered. This power shall not be suspended or contracted away, except as provided in this article.

SECTION 2. The lands and other property belonging to the citizens of the United States residing without the State shall never be taxed at a higher rate than the lands and other property belonging to the residents of the State.

SECTION 3. Standards for appraisal of all property assessed by the State or its political subdivisions shall be prescribed by law.

SECTION 4. The real and personal property of the State or its political subdivisions shall be exempt from taxation under conditions and exceptions which may be provided by law. All, or any portion of, property used exclusively for nonprofit religious, charitable, cemetery, or educational purposes, as defined by law, shall be exempt from taxation. Other exemptions of like or different kind may be granted by general law. All valid existing exemption shall be retained until otherwise provided by law.

SECTION 5. Private leaseholds, contracts, or interests in land or property owned or held by the United States, the State, or its political subdivisions, shall be taxable to the extent of the interests.

SECTION 6. No tax shall be levied, or appropriation of public money made, or public property transferred, nor shall the public credit be used, except for a public purpose.

SECTION 7. The proceeds of any state tax or license shall not be dedicated to any special purpose, except as provided in section 15 of this article or when required by the federal government for state participation in federal programs. This provision shall not prohibit the continuance of any dedication for special purposes existing upon the date of ratification of this section by the people of Alaska. *(The above Constitutional Amendment was approved by the voters of the State November 2, 1976. It extended special purposes to those provided in section 15 of this article.)*

SECTION 8. No state debt shall be contracted unless authorized by law for capital improvements or unless authorized by law for housing loans for veterans, and ratified by a majority of the qualified voters of the State who vote on the question. The State may, as provided by law and without ratification, contract debt for the purpose of repelling invasion, suppressing insurrection, defending the State in war, meeting natural disasters, or redeeming indebtedness outstanding at the time this constitution becomes effective. *(The above Constitutional Amendment was approved by the voters of the State November 2, 1982. Housing loans for veterans were added.)*

SECTION 9. No debt shall be contracted by any political subdivision of the State, unless authorized for capital improvements by its governing body and ratified by a majority vote of those qualified to vote and voting on the question.

SECTION 10. The State and its political subdivisions may borrow money to meet appropriations for any fiscal year in anticipation of the collection of the revenues for that year, but all debt so contracted shall be paid before the end of the next fiscal year.

SECTION 11. The restrictions on contracting debt do not apply to debt incurred through the issuance of revenue bonds by a public enterprise or public corporation of the State or a political subdivision, when the only security is the revenues of the enterprise or corporation. The restrictions do not apply to indebtedness to be paid from special assessments on the benefited property, nor do they apply to refunding indebtedness of the State or its political subdivisions.

SECTION 12. The governor shall submit to the legislature, at a time fixed by law, a budget for the next fiscal year setting forth all proposed expenditures and anticipated income of all departments, offices, and agencies of the state. The governor, at the same time, shall submit a general appropriation bill to authorize the proposed expenditures, and a bill or bills covering recommendations in the budget for new or additional revenues.

SECTION 13. No money shall be withdrawn from the treasury except in accordance with appropriations made by law. No obligation for the payment of money shall be incurred except as authorized by law. Unobligated appropriations outstanding at the end of the period of time specified by law shall be void.

SECTION 14. The legislature shall appoint an auditor to serve at its pleasure. The auditor shall conduct post-audits as prescribed by law and shall report to the legislature and to the governor.

SECTION 15. At least twenty-five percent of all mineral lease rentals, royalties, royalty sale proceeds, federal mineral revenue sharing payments and bonuses received by the State shall be placed in a permanent fund, the principal of which shall be used only for those income-producing investments specifically designated by law as eligible for permanent fund investments. All income from the permanent fund shall be deposited in the general fund unless otherwise provided by law. *(This section was added as a new amendment approved by the voters of the State November 2, 1976.)*

SECTION 16. Except for appropriations for Alaska permanent fund dividends, appropriations of revenue bond proceeds, appropriations required to pay the principal and interest on general obligation bonds, and appropriations of money received from a non-State source in trust for a specific purpose, including revenues of a public enterprise or public corporation of the State that issues revenue bonds, appropriations from the treasury made for a fiscal year shall not exceed $2,500,000,000 by more than a cumulative change, derived from federal indices as prescribed by law, in population and inflation since July 1, 1961. Within this limit, at least one-third shall be received for capital projects and loan appropriations. The legislature may exceed this limit in bills for appropriations to the Alaska permanent fund and in bills for appropriations for capital projects, whether of bond proceeds or otherwise, if each bill is approved by the governor, or passed by affirmative vote of three-fourths of the membership of the legislature over a veto or item veto, or becomes law without signature, and is also approved by the voters as prescribed by law. Each bill for appropriations for capital projects in excess of the limit shall be confined to capital projects of the same type, and the voters shall, as provided by law, be informed of the cost of operations and maintenance of the capital projects. No other appropriation in excess of this limit may be made except to meet a state of disaster declared by the governor as prescribed by law. The governor shall cause any unexpended and unappropriated balance to be invested so as to yield competitive market rates to the treasury. *(This section was added as a new amendment approved by the voters of the State November 2, 1982.)*

Article X
Local Government

SECTION 1. The purpose of this article is to provide for maximum local self-government with a minimum of local government units, and to prevent duplication of tax-levying jurisdictions. A liberal construction shall be given to the powers of local government units.

SECTION 2. All local government powers shall be vested in boroughs and cities. The State may delegate taxing powers to organized boroughs and cities only.

SECTION 3. The entire State shall be divided into boroughs, organized or unorganized. They shall be established in a manner and according to standards provided by law. The standards shall include population, geography, economy, transportation, and other factors. Each borough shall embrace an area and population with common interests to the maximum degree possible. The legislature shall classify boroughs and prescribe their powers and functions. Methods by which boroughs may be organized, incorporated, merged, consolidated, reclassified, or dissolved shall be prescribed by law.

SECTION 4. The governing body of the organized borough shall be the assembly, and its composition shall be established by law or charter. *(The above Constitutional Amendment was approved by the voters of the State August 22, 1972. It established that assembly representation is to be based on law or chatter.)*

SECTION 5. Service areas to provide special services within an organized borough may be established, altered, or abolished by the assembly, subject to the provisions of law or charter. A new service area shall not be established if, consistent with the purposes of this article, the new service can be provided by an existing service area, by incorporation as a city, or by annexation to a city. The assembly may authorize the levying of taxes, charges, or assessments within a service area to finance the special services.

SECTION 6. The legislature shall provide for the performance of services it deems necessary or advisable in unorganized boroughs, allowing for maximum local participation and responsibility. It may exercise any power or function in an unorganized borough which the assembly may exercise in an organized borough.

SECTION 7. Cities shall be incorporated in a manner prescribed by law, and shall be part of the borough in which they are located. Cities shall have the powers and functions conferred by law or charter. They may be merged, consolidated, classified, reclassified, or dissolved in the manner provided by law.

SECTION 8. The governing body of a city shall be the council.

SECTION 9. The qualified voters of any borough of the first class or city of the first class may adopt, amend, or repeal a home rule charter in a manner provided by law. In the absence of such legislation, the governing body of a borough or city of the first class shall provide the procedure for the preparation and adoption or rejection of the charter. All charters, or parts or amendments of charters, shall be submitted to the qualified voters of the borough or city, and shall become effective if approved by a majority of those who vote on the specific question.

SECTION 10. The legislature may extend home rule to other boroughs and cities.

SECTION 11. A home rule borough or city may exercise all legislative powers not prohibited by law or by charter.

SECTION 12. A local boundary commission or board shall be established by law in the executive branch of the state government. The commission or board may consider any proposed local government boundary change. It may present proposed changes to the legislature during the first ten days of any regular session. The change shall become effective forty-five days after presentation or at the end of the session, whichever is earlier, unless disapproved by a resolution concurred in by a majority of the members of each house. The commission or board, subject to law, may establish procedures whereby boundaries may be adjusted by local action.

SECTION 13. Agreements, including those for cooperative or joint administration of any functions or powers, may be made by any local government with any other local government, with the State, or with the United States, unless otherwise provided by law or charter. A city may transfer to the borough in which it islocated any of its powers or functions unless prohibited by law or charter, and may in like manner revoke the transfer.

SECTION 14. An agency shall be established by law in the executive branch of the state government to advise and assist local governments. It shall review their activities, collect and publish local government information, and perform other duties prescribed by law.

SECTION 15. Special service districts existing at the time a borough is organized shall be integrated with the government of the borough as provided by law.

Article XI
Initiative, Referendum, and Recall

SECTION 1. The people may propose and enact laws by the initiative, and approve or reject acts of the legislature by the referendum.

SECTION 2. An initiative or referendum is proposed by an application containing the bill to be initiated or the act to be referred. The application shall be signed by not less than one hundred qualified voters as sponsors, and shall be filed with the lieutenant governor. If he finds it in proper form he shall so certify. Denial of certification shall be subject to judicial review. *(The above Constitutional Amendment was approved by the voters of the State August 25, 1970. The words secretary of state were changed to lieutenant governor.)*

SECTION 3. After certification of the application, a petition containing a summary of the subject matter shall be prepared by the lieutenant governor for circulation by the sponsors. If signed by qualified voters, equal in number to ten per cent of those who voted in the preceding general election and resident in at least two-thirds of the election districts of the State, it may be filed with the lieutenant governor. *(The above Constitutional Amendment was approved by the voters of the State August 25, 1970. The words secretary of state were changed to lieutenant governor.)*

SECTION 4. An initiative petition may be filed at any time. The lieutenant governor shall prepare a ballot title and proposition summarizing the proposed law, and shall place them on the ballot for the first statewide election held more than one hundred twenty days after adjournment of the legislative session following the filing. If, before the election, substantially the same measure has been enacted, the petition is void. *(The above Constitutional Amendment was approved by the voters of the State August 25, 1970. The words secretary of state were changed to lieutenant governor.)*

SECTION 5. A referendum petition may be filed only within ninety days after adjournment of the legislative session at which the act was passed. The lieutenant governor shall prepare a ballot title and proposition summarizing the act and shall place them on the ballot for the first statewide election held more than one hundred eighty days after adjournment of that session. *(The above Constitutional Amendment was approved by the voters of the State August 25, 1970. The words secretary of state were changed to lieutenant governor.)*

SECTION 6. If a majority of the votes cast on the

proposition favor its adoption, the initiated measure is enacted. If a majority of the votes cast on the proposition favor the rejection of an act referred, it is rejected. The lieutenant governor shall certify the election returns. An initiated law becomes effective ninety days after certification, is not subject to veto, and may not be repealed by the legislature within two years of its effective date. It may be amended at any time. An act rejected by referendum is void thirty days after certification. Additional procedures for the initiative and referendum may be prescribed by law. *(The above Constitutional Amendment was approved by the voters of the State August 25, 1970. The words secretary of state were changed to lieutenant governor.)*

SECTION 7. The initiative shall not be used to dedicate revenues, make or repeal appropriations, create courts, define the jurisdiction of courts or prescribe their rules, or enact local or special legislation. The referendum shall not be applied to dedications of revenue, to appropriations, to local or special legislation, or to laws necessary for the immediate preservation of the public peace, health, or safety.

SECTION 8. All elected public officials in the State, except judicial officers, are subject to recall by the voters of the State or political subdivision from which elected. Procedures and grounds for recall shall be prescribed by the legislature.

Article XII
General Provisions

SECTION 1. The State of Alaska shall consist of all the territory, together with the territorial waters appurtenant thereto, included in the Territory of Alaska upon the date of ratification of this consitituton by the people of Alaska.

SECTION 2. The State and its political subdivisions may cooperate with the United States and its territories, and with other states and their political subdivisions on matters of common interest. The respective legislative bodies may make appropriations for this purpose.

SECTION 3. Service in the armed forces of the United States or of the State is not an office or position of profit as the term is used in this constitution.

SECTION 4. No person who advocated, or who aids or belongs to any party or organization or association which advocates, the overthrow by force or violence of the government of the United States or of the State shall be qualified to hold any public office of trust or profit under this constitution.

SECTION 5. All public officers, before entering upon the duties of their offices, shall take and subscribe to the following oath or affirmation: "I do solemnly swear (or affirm) that I will support and defend the Constitution of the United States and the Constitution of the State of Alaska, and that I will faithfully discharge my duties as _____ to the best of my ability." The legislature may prescribe further oaths or affirmations.

SECTION 6. The legislature shall establish a system under which the merit principle will govern the employment of persons by the State.

SECTION 7. Membership in employee retirement systems of the State or its political subdivisions shall constitute a contractual relationship. Accrued benefits of these systems shall not be diminished or impaired.

SECTION 8. The enumeration of specified powers in this constitution shall not be construed as limiting the powers of the State.

SECTION 9. The provisions of this constitution shall be construed to be self-executing whenever possible.

SECTION 10. Titles and subtitles shall not be used in construing this constitution. Personal pronouns used in this constitution shall be construed as including either sex.

SECTION 11. As used in this constitution the terms "by law" and "by the legislature," or variations of these terms, are used interchangeably when related to law-making powers. Unless clearly inapplicable, the law-making powers assigned to the legislature may be exercised by the people through the initiative, subject to the limitations of Article XI.

SECTION 12. The State of Alaska and its people forever disclaim all right and title in or to any property belonging to the United States or subject to its disposition, and not granted or confirmed to the State or its political subdivisions, by or under the act admitting Alaska to the Union. The State and its people further disclaim all right or title in or to any property, including fishing rights, the right or title to which may be held by or for any Indian, Eskimo, or Aleut, or community thereof, as that right or title is defined in the act of admission. The State and its people agree that, unless otherwise provided by Congress, the property, as described in this section, shall remain subject to the absolute disposition of the United States. They further agree that no taxes will be imposed upon any such property, until otherwise provided by the Congress. This tax exemption shall not apply to property held by individuals in fee without restrictions on alienation.

SECTION 13. All provisions of the act admitting Alaska to the Union which reserve rights or powers to the United States, as well as those prescribing the terms or conditions of the grants of lands or other property, are consented to fully by the State and its people.

Article XIII
Amendment and Revision

SECTION 1. Amendments to this constitution may be proposed by a two-thirds vote of each house of the legislature. The lieutenant governor shall prepare a ballot title and proposition summarizing each proposed amendment, and shall place them on the ballot for the next statewide election. If a majority of the votes cast on the proposition favor the amendment, it shall be adopted. Unless otherwise provided in the amendment, it becomes effective thirty days after the certification of the election returns by the lieutenant governor. *(The above Constitutional Amendment was approved by the voters of the State August 25, 1970. The words secretary of state were changed to lieutenant governor.)*

SECTION 2. The legislature may call constitutional conventions at any time.

SECTION 3. If during any ten-year period a constitutional convention has not been held, the lieutenant governor shall place on the ballot for the next general election the question: "Shall there be a Constitutional Convention?" If a majority of the votes cast on the question are in the negative, the question need not be placed on the ballot until the end of the next ten-year period. If a majority of the votes cast on the question are in affirmative delegates to the convention shall be chosen at the next regular statewide election, unless the legislature provides for the election of the delegates at a special election. The lieutenant governor shall issue the call for the convention. Unless other provisions have been made by law, the call shall conform as nearly as possible to the act of calling the Alaska Constitutional Convention of 1955, including, but not limited to, number of members, districts, election and certification of delegates, and submission and ratification of revisions and ordinances. The appropriation provisions of the call shall be self-executing and shall constitute a first claim on the state treasury. *(The above Constitutional Amendment was approved by the voters of the State August 25, 1970. The words secretary of state were changed to lieutenant governor.)*

SECTION 4. Constitutional Conventions shall have plenary power to amend or revise the constitution, subject only to ratification by the people. No call for a constitutional convention shall limit these powers of the convention.

Article XIV
Apportionment Schedule
Amended November 2, 1982, by voters of Alaska. *(For previous apportionment schedules refer to past issues of THE ALASKA ALMANAC®.)*

SECTION 1. Members of the House of Representatives shall, according to the reapportionment schedule of the governor, dated July 24, 1981, be elected from the election districts and in the numbers shown below:

1 Ketchikan-Wrangell-Petersburg — 2(A-B)
2 Inside Passage-Cordova — 1
3 Baranof-Chichagof — 1
4 Juneau — 2(A-B)
5 Kenai-Cook Inlet — 2(A-B)
6 North Kenai-South Coast — 1
7 South Anchorage — 1
8 Hillside — 2(A-B)
9 Sand Lake — 1
10 Mid-Town — 2(A-B)
11 West Side — 2(A-B)
12 Downtown — 2(A-B)
13 Mountain View-University — 2(A-B)
14 Muldoon — 2(A-B)
15 Chugiak-Eagle River Bases — 2(A-B)
16 Matanuska-Susitna — 2(A-B)
17 Interior Highways — 1
18 Southeast North Star Borough — 1
19 Outer Fairbanks — 1
20 Fairbanks City — 2(A-B)
21 West Fairbanks — 1
22 North Slope-Kotzebue — 1
23 Norton Sound — 1
24 Interior Rivers — 1
25 Lower Kuskokwim — 1
26 Bristol Bay-Aleutian Islands — 1
27 Kodiak-East Alaska Peninsula — 1

In all two member house districts candidates will run for designated seats indicated by Seat A and Seat B. Candidates will file for one of the available seats. Each qualified voter in the district may cast one vote for their choice among the candidates for each seat. The candidate receiving the greatest number of votes cast for each seat is elected.

SECTION 2. Members of the senate shall be elected in 1982 from the following senate districts except those seats where an asterisk (*) indicates the existing senator's term will continue until January 1985:

Senate District	Composed of Election Districts	Length of Term
A.	Ketchikan-Wrangell-Petersburg	4 years
B.	Inside Passage-Cordova-Baranof-Chichagof	2 years*
C.	Juneau	4 years
D.	Kenai-Cook Inlet-North Kenai-South Coast	Seat A—2 years
	South Anchorage	Seat B—4 years
E.	Hillside-Sand Lake	Seat A—2 years
		Seat B—4 years
F.	Mid-Town-West Side	Seat A—2 years
		Seat B—4 years
G.	Downtown-Mountain View-University	Seat A—2 years
		Seat B—4 years
H.	Muldoon-Chugiak-Eagle River-Bases	Seat A—2 years
		Seat B—4 years
I.	Matanuska-Susitna	2 years*
J.	Interior Highways-Southeast North Star Borough	2 years*
K.	Outer Fairbanks-Fairbanks City-West Fairbanks	Seat A—2 years
		Seat B—4 years
L.	North Slope-Kotzebue-Norton Sound	4 years
M.	Interior Rivers-Lower Kuskokwim	4 years
N.	Bristol Bay-Aleutian Islands-Kodiak-East Alaska Peninsula	2 years

In all two member senate districts candidates will run for designated seats indicated by Seat A and Seat B. Candidates will file for one of the available seats. Each qualified voter may cast one vote for their choice among the candidates for each seat. The candidate receiving the greatest number of votes cast for each seat is elected.

SECTION 3. The election districts set forth in Section 1 shall include the following territory:
1. *Ketchikan-Wrangell-Petersburg* — District 1 is an area within a line proceeding from Dixon Entrance in a northerly direction up Clarence Strait, passing west of Zarembo Island, northerly up Duncan Canal, across Frederick Sound to a point just north and west of Cape Fanshaw, then northeasterly to the Canadian border to the point of beginning at Dixon Entrance. The district includes the Ketchikan Gateway Borough, Wrangell, Petersburg, Metlakatla, Hyder, Saxman, Meyers Chuck and Kupreanof.
2. *Inside Passage-Cordova* — District 2 is composed of that portion of Southeast Alaska between Dixon Entrance and Port Gravina on Prince William Sound that is not contained in Districts 1, 3 and 4. Included within its boundaries are the communities of Cordova, Yakutat, Haines, Skagway, Klukwan, Gustavus, Angoon, Kake, Thorne Bay, Klawock, Craig and Hydaburg.
3. *Baranof-Chichagof* — District 3 consists of Baranof Island and Chichagof Island. The communities on the islands include Sitka, Pelican, Hoonah, Tenakee Springs and Port Alexander.
4. *Juneau* — District 4 boundaries coincide with those of the City and Borough of Juneau.
5. *Kenai-Cook Inlet* — District 5 includes all of the coastal areas of the east and west sides of Cook Inlet that lie south and west of Nikishka. Sterling is also within the district.
6. *North Kenai-South Coast* — District 6 includes the northern quarter of the Kenai Peninsula, Nikishka, Hope, Cooper Landing, Moose Pass, Seward, Whittier and Valdez.
7. *South Anchorage* — District 7 contains the suburban southern and southeastern reaches of the Municipality of Anchorage, including the community council areas of Eldon, Old Seward/Oceanview, Rabbit Creek, Turnagain Arm and Girdwood Valley. Its northern boundary proceeds east from the inlet on Klatt Road to the New Seward Highway, southerly on the New Seward Highway to DeArmoun Road, east on DeArmoun Road to Morgaard Road, easterly on Morgaard Road to DeArmoun Road, easterly and southerly on Rabbit Creek.
8. *Hillside* — District 8 is bounded on the south by Rabbit Creek, Morgaard Road and DeArmoun Road and on the west by the Seward Highway. At Tudor Road

39

the boundary proceeds east to Bragaw Road where it turns south. This district includes the neighborhood council areas of Campbell Park, Abbott Loop, Huffman-O'Malley, Mid-Hillside, Hillside East and Glen Alps.

9. *Sand Lake* — District 9 is bounded by a line beginning at the inlet and proceeding east on Klatt Road. The line proceeds north on the New Seward Highway to Dimond Boulevard where it turns west. At Minnesota Drive the line turns north and proceeds to International Airport Road where it turns west and extends to the inlet. The district includes the community council areas of Sand Lake and Klatt Road.

10. *Mid-Town* — District 10 is bounded by a line beginning at the Intersection of the Seward Highway and Dimond Boulevard. The line proceeds west to Minnesota Drive, north to International Airport Road, east to the Alaska Railroad, north by northwest along the railroad right of way to Tudor Road, east to Arctic Boulevard, north to 36th Avenue, east on 36th Avenue to C Street, north to Northern Lights Boulevard, west to Spenard Road, north to W. 25th Street, west to Minnesota Drive, north to Chester Creek, easterly to Lake Otis Road, south to Tudor Road, west to the New Seward Highway and south to the point of beginning. The district includes the community council areas of North Star, Rogers Park, Tudor, and parts of Spenard and Taku-Campbell.

11. *West Side* — District 11 is bounded by the boundary of District 10 on the east, International Airport Road on the south, and the inlet and Chester Creek on the north. It includes the community council area of Turnagain and the major part of the Spenard area.

12. *Downtown* — District 12 is bounded by Chester Creek on the south, Bragaw Road on the east, Commercial Drive and Elmendorf reservation boundary on the north and the inlet on the west. Included are the community council areas of Government Hill, Downtown, Penland Park and South Addition, and parts of areas of Fairview, North Mountain View and Airport Heights.

13. *Mountain View-University* — District 13 is bounded by a line beginning at the intersection of Tudor Road and Lake Otis Road proceeding east to Baxter Road, north to Northern Lights Boulevard, west to Boniface Road, north to the Glenn Highway, west on the Glenn Highway, northerly and westerly around North Mountain View along the Elmendorf military reservation boundary, south to the Glenn Highway, east to Bragaw Road, south to Chester Creek, westerly to Lake Otis Road and south to the point of beginning. The district includes the community council areas of Russian Jack Park and University, and parts of the North Mountain View and Airport Heights areas.

14. *Muldoon* — District 14 includes Stuckagain Heights and the community council areas of Northeast and Scenic Park. That part of the Northeast area bounded by Boniface Road, DeBarr Road, Turpin Street and the Glenn Highway is included in District 15.

15. *Chugiak-Eagle River-Bases* — District 15 includes the community council areas of Eklutna Valley, Chugiak, Birchwood, and Eagle River Valley. Also included are Fort Richardson, Elmendorf Air Force Base and that area of the Northeast community council area bounded by Boniface Road, DeBarr Road, Turpin Street and the Glenn Highway.

16. *Matanuska-Susitna* — District 16 is comprised of the Matanuska-Susitna Borough, including the communities of Talkeetna, Willow, Houston, Big Lake, Wasilla, Bodenburg Butte, Palmer, Sutton, Peter's Creek, Montana and Chickaloon.

17. *Interior Highways* — District 17 is made up of those areas outside of the Matanuska- Susitna Borough and the Fairbanks North Star Borough which are along the Glenn, Parks, Richardson and Alaska Highways.

Included are Paxson, Gulkana, Glennallen, Copper Center, Tonsina, Tazlina, McCarthy, Eagle, Delta, Fort Greely, Tanacross, Tok, Tetlin, Northway, Nenana, Anderson, Healy and Cantwell.

18. *Southeast North Star Borough* — District 18 encompasses the southeast section of the Fairbanks North Star Borough. It includes North Pole, Eielson Air Force Base, Salcha and Harding Lake.

19. *Fort Wainwright-Outer Fairbanks* — District 19 includes Livengood, Ester, Goldstream Road, the Steese Highway, the eastern half of the Farmers Loop Road, Fort Wainwright, Chena Hot Springs Road, Circle, Central and Circle Hot Springs.

20. *Fairbanks City* — District 20 is bounded by the Noyes Slough and University Avenue on the west, the Fairbanks International Airport on the Southwest, the Tanana River on the south and Fort Wainwright on the east. The Creamers Field area is included as the northern edge of the district.

21. *West Fairbanks* — District 21 includes the western half of Farmers Loop Road and the area west of the Noyes Slough and University Avenue to, but not including, the Ester area.

22. *North Slope-Kotzebue* — District 22 includes the areas of the North Slope Borough/Arctic Slope Regional Corporation and the Northwest Alaska Native Association.

23. *Norton Sound* — District 23 includes the area of the Bering Straits Regional Corporation; Shishmaref, Diomede, Teller, Nome, Koyuk and Saint Michael, and the coastal communities as far south as Hooper Bay and Paimiut. Chevak is also included along the Yukon River villages down river from Mountain Village.

24. *Interior Rivers* — District 24 includes the community on or near the great interior rivers, the Yukon, the Koyukuk and the Kuskokwim, as far down river as Mountain Village on the Yukon and Tuluksak on the Kuskokwim. Minto and Manley Hot Springs are included; Eagle and Circle are not included.

25. *Lower Kuskokwim* — District 25 includes the Kuskokwim River communities down river from Aklak and the coastal communities from Newtok to Platinum.

26. *Bristol Bay-Aleutian Islands* — District 26 includes all of the Bristol Bay Native Corporation area except Ivanof Bay, Perryville, Chignik Lake, Chignik Lagoon and the Lake Clark-Lake Iliamna communities. Included are the remainder of the Alaska Peninsula communities, the Aleutian communities, the Bristol Bay communities as far west as Twin Hills, communities as far up river as Aleknagik and Koliganek and the Lake Clark and Lake Iliamna communities. The Bristol Bay Borough is also included.

27. *Kodiak-East Alaska Peninsula* — District 27 covers the Kodiak Island Borough and the Alaska Peninsula communities of Ivanof Bay, Perryville, Chignik Lake, Chignik and Chignik Lagoon.

Continental Divide

(*See also* Mountains)

The Continental Divide extends into Alaska, but unlike its portions in the Lower 48, which divide the country into east-west watersheds, the Continental Divide in Alaska trends through the Brooks Range, separating water sheds that drain north into the Arctic Ocean and west and south into the Bering Sea.

According to *Alaska Science Nuggets*, until recently geologists thought of the Brooks Range as a structural extension of the Rocky Mountains, but recent thinking now assumes the range to be 35 million to 200 million years older than the Rockies. The Alaska Range, on the other hand, is comparatively young, only about 5 million years.

Convention and Visitors Bureaus

Anchorage Convention and Visitors Bureau, 201 E. 3rd Ave., Anchorage 99501. Phone (907) 276-4118.
Barrow Convention and Visitors Bureau, P.O. Box 1060, Barrow 99723. Phone (907) 852-5211.
Fairbanks Visitors and Convention Bureau, 550 1st Ave., Fairbanks 99701. Phone (907) 456-5774.
Homer Convention and Visitors Bureau, P.O. Box 541, Homer 99603. Phone (907) 235-5300.
Juneau Convention and Visitors Bureau, 134 3rd St., Juneau 99801. Phone (907) 586-2201.
Kenai Peninsula Convention and Visitors Bureau, P.O. Box 497, Kenai 99611. Phone (907) 283-7989.
Ketchikan Visitors Bureau, 131 Front St., Ketchikan 99901. Phone (907) 225-6166.
Kodiak Island Convention and Visitors Bureau, 100 Marine Way, Kodiak 99615. Phone (907) 486-4782.
Mat-Su Convention and Visitors Bureau, 191 E. Swanson Ave., #201, Wasilla 99687. Phone (907) 376-8000
Nome Convention and Visitors Bureau, P.O. Box 251, Nome 99762. Phone (907) 443-5535.
Sitka Visitors Bureau, P.O. Box 1226, Sitka 99835. Phone (907) 747-5940.
Skagway Convention and Visitors Bureau, P.O. Box 415, Skagway 99840. Phone (907) 983-2854.
Valdez Convention and Visitors Bureau, 333 Fairbanks St., Suite 18, Valdez 99686. Phone (907) 835-2984.
Wrangell Visitors Bureau, P.O. Box 1078, Wrangell 99929. Phone (907) 874-3800.

Coppers

(*See also* Potlatch)

Coppers (*tinnehs*) were beaten copper plaques, shaped something like a keyhole, usually two or three feet long and weighing approximately 40 pounds. Coppers varied in value from tribe to tribe and were especially prized among the Tlingit.

Early coppers were made of ore from the Copper River area, although western traders quickly made sheet copper available. Some scholars believe that Tlingit craftsmen shaped placer copper into the desired form themselves, while others maintain that coppers were formed by Athabascans or may even have been artifacts of some kind. The impressive plaques were engraved or carved in relief with totemic crests.

The value of coppers increased as they were traded or sold, and their transfer implied that a potlatch would be given by the new owner. Coppers were anthropomorphized — given names such as "Cloud," "Point of Island" or "Killer Whale" — and were spoken of in sentimental and respectful terms. They were thought of as powerful, and their histories were as well-known as those of the noblest families.

Coppers were often broken and destroyed during public displays of wealth. Some parts of the coppers were valued nearly as much as the whole.

To this day, certain coppers that have been part of museum collections for years are still valued highly by some tribes, and are used as symbols of wealth and prestige during marriage ceremonies and potlatches.

Cost of Living

The cost of living in Alaska is high, as is income. For example, the main methods of travel in the state are by sea and by air. The size of the state and its remoteness from the Lower 48 make personal and business travel expensive. Similarly, providing goods and services, such as medical care, to remote areas of the state is also costly.

Since agriculture and manufacturing in the state are limited, most consumption items are shipped in from Outside, adding to their cost. Lack of competition, particularly in the rural areas and in locations with small population bases, also keeps prices of goods and services high. Nevertheless, in recent years the increase in Anchorage consumer prices has been lower than the national average. Medical care is an exception to this trend of moderating prices: it rose at a higher rate than other prices and kept pace with the nationwide trend.

A housing market analysis done at the beginning of 1987 in more than 200 cities across the nation found that the price of a standard-quality Anchorage house, in what was judged to be an above-average to prime neighborhood, was 55 percent above the median price. The $131,655 Anchorage price compared to $92,341 in Seattle, Washington; $156,000 in San Jose, California; and $135,000 in New York City suburbs.

Food — average cost for one week at home for a family of four with elementary schoolchildren (compiled September 1988; U.S. average $88.20):
Juneau .... $ 92.95
Anchorage .... $ 90.99
Fairbanks .... $ 94.74
Nome $147.69
Dillingham $144.78

Housing — average cost of single-family residence with three bedrooms, including land (compiled April 1987):
Juneau $124,750
Anchorage $131,333
Fairbanks $112,988
Nome $135,000
Kotzebue $140,000

Gasoline — average cost for 55-gallon drum (compiled September 1988):
Juneau $71.63
Anchorage $51.65
Fairbanks $56.24
Nome $95.10
Dillingham $89.65

Heating Oil — average cost for 55-gallon drum (compiled September 1988):
Juneau $67.19
Anchorage $49.98
Fairbanks $49.20
Nome $76.18
Dillingham $84.54

Taxes — city and borough (Alaska has no state income tax), as of September 1988:
Juneau .... 4 percent sales
Anchorage .... none
Fairbanks .... none
Nome .... 4 percent sales
Dillingham .... 3 percent sales

Annual per capita personal income: At $18,230, Alaska was 118 percent higher than the national average in 1987, and fifth highest in the nation in income standings.

Courts

The Alaska court system operates at four levels: the supreme court, the court of appeals, superior court and district court. The Alaska judiciary is funded by the state and administered by the supreme court.

The five-member supreme court, established by the Alaska Constitution in 1959, has final appellate jurisdiction of all actions and proceedings in lower courts. It sits monthly in Anchorage and Fairbanks, quarterly in Juneau and occasionally in other court locations.

The three-member court of appeals was established in 1980 to relieve the supreme court of some of its ever-increasing caseload. The supreme court retained its ultimate authority in all cases, but concentrated its attention on civil appellate matters, giving authority in criminal and quasi-criminal matters to the court of appeals. The court of appeals has appellate jurisdiction in certain superior court proceedings and jurisdiction to review district court decisions. It meets regularly in Anchorage and travels occasionally to other locations.

The superior court is the trial court with original jurisdiction in all civil and criminal matters, and appellate jurisdiction over all matters appealed by the district court. The superior court has exclusive jurisdiction in probate and in cases concerning minors. There are 29 superior court judges.

The district court has jurisdiction over misdemeanor violations and violations of ordinances of political subdivisions. In civil matters, the district court may hear cases for recovery of money, damages or specific personal property if the amount does not exceed $35,000. The district court may also establish death and issue marriage licenses, summons, writs of habeas corpus and search and arrest warrants. District court criminal decisions may be appealed directly to the court of appeals, bypassing the superior court. There are 17 district court judges.

Administration of the superior and district courts is divided by region into four judicial districts: First Judicial District, Southeast; Second Judicial District, Nome-Kotzebue; Third Judicial District, Anchorage-Kodiak-Kenai; and Fourth Judicial District, Fairbanks.

District magistrates serve rural areas and help ease the work load of district courts in metropolitan areas. In criminal matters, magistrates may give judgment of conviction upon a plea of guilty to any state misdemeanor and may try state misdemeanor cases if the defendant waives his right to a district court judge. Magistrates may also hear municipal ordinance violations and state traffic infractions without the consent of the accused. In civil matters, magistrates may hear cases for recovery of money, damages, or specific personal property if the amount does not exceed $5,000.

Selection of justices, judges and magistrates

Supreme court justices and judges of the court of appeals, superior court and district court are appointed by the governor from candidates submitted by the Alaska Judicial Council. All justices and judges must be citizens of the United States and have been residents of Alaska for at least five years. A justice must be licensed to practice law in Alaska at the time of appointment and have engaged in active law practice for eight years. A court of appeals judge must be a state resident for five years immediately preceding appointment, have been engaged in the active practice of law not less than eight years immediately preceding appointment and be licensed to practice law in Alaska. Qualifications of a superior court judge are the same as for supreme court justices, except that only five years of active practice are necessary. A district court judge must be 21 years of age, a resident for at least five years, and (1) be licensed to practice law in Alaska and have engaged in active practice of law for not less than three years immediately preceding appointment, *or* (2) have served for at least seven years as a magistrate in the state and have graduated from an accredited law school.

The chief justice of the supreme court is selected by majority vote of the justices, serves a three year term and cannot succeed him or herself.

Each supreme court justice and each judge of the court of appeals is subject to approval or rejection by a majority of the voters of the state on a nonpartisan ballot at the first general election held more than three years after appointment. Thereafter, each justice must participate in a retention election every 10 years. A court of appeals judge must participate every eight years.

Superior court judges are subject to approval or rejection by voters of their judicial district at the first general election held more than three years after appointment. Thereafter, it is every sixth year. District court judges must run for retention in their judicial districts in the first general election held more than one year after appointment and every fourth year thereafter.

District magistrates are appointed for an indefinite period by the presiding superior court judge of the judicial district in which they will serve.

The Alaska State Supreme Court, 1959-1989

Justice	Tenure
John H. Dimond	1959-1971
Walter H. Hodge	1959-1960
Buell A. Nesbett	1959-1970
Chief Justice:	1959-1970
Harry O. Arend	1960-1965
Jay A. Rabinowitz	1965-
Chief Justice:	1972-1975
	1978-1981
	1984-1987
George F. Boney	1968-1972
Chief Justice:	1970-1972
Roger G. Connor	1968-1983
Robert C. Erwin	1970-1978
Robert Boochever	1972-1980
Chief Justice	1975-1978
James M. Fitzgerald	1972-1975

Edmond W. Burke 1975-
  Chief Justice 1981-1984
Warren W. Mathews 1978-
  Chief Justice: 1987-
Allen T. Compton 1980-
Daniel A. Moore, Jr. 1983-

**The Alaska State
Court of Appeals, 1980-1989**
Judge   Tenure
Alexander O. Bryner 1980-
  Chief Judge 1980-
James K. Singleton, Jr. 1980-
Robert G. Coats 1980-

Cruises

There are many opportunities for cruising Alaska waters, aboard either charter boats, scheduled boat excursions or luxury cruise ships. (*See also* Ferries.)

Charter boats are readily available in southeastern and southcentral Alaska. Charter boat trips range from day-long fishing and sightseeing trips to overnight and longer customized trips or package tours. There is a wide range of charter boats, from simple fishing boats to sailboats, yachts and mini-class cruise ships.

In summer, scheduled boat excursions — from all-day trips to overnight cruises — are available at the following locations: Ketchikan (Misty Fiords); Sitka (harbor and area tours); Bartlett Cove and Gustavus (Glacier Bay); Valdez and Whittier (Columbia Glacier, Prince William Sound); Seward (Resurrection Bay, Kenai Fjords); Homer (Kachemak Bay); and Fairbanks (Chena and Tanana rivers).

For details and additional information on charter boat operators and scheduled boat excursions, contact the Alaska Division of Tourism, P.O. Box E-101, Juneau 99811.

From May through September, luxury cruise ships carry visitors to Alaska via the Inside Passage. There are 25 ships to choose from and almost as many itineraries. There's also a bewildering array of travel options. Both round-trip and one-way cruises are available, or a cruise may be sold as part of a packaged tour which includes air, rail and/or motorcoach transportation. Various shore excursions may be included in the cruise price or offered to passengers for added cost.

Because of the wide variety of cruise trips available, it is wise to work with your travel agent.

Following is a list of cruise ships serving Alaska in the 1989-90 season:

Admiral Cruises, 1220 Biscayne Blvd., Miami, FL 33101. The MV *Stardancer,* carrying 1,200 passengers, 350 vehicles, offers 3-, 4- and 7-night round-trip cruises between Vancouver, BC, and Skagway, AK.

Costa Cruises, Inc., 80 SW 8th St., Miami, FL 33130. MTS *Daphne,* 400 passengers, 7-night round-trip from Vancouver, BC.

Cunard/NAC Lines, 555 5th Ave., New York, NY 10017. *Sagafjord,* 589 passengers, 11-day cruise between Vancouver, BC, and Anchorage.

Holland America Lines/Westours, 300 Elliott Ave. W., Seattle, WA 98119. MS *Noordam,* 1,214 passengers; MS *Nieuw Amsterdam,* 1,214 passengers; *Westerdam* and the SS *Rotterdam,* 1,114 passengers, offer 3-, 4- and 7-night round-trip cruises from Vancouver, BC. The *Rotterdam* also offers 7- and 14-night cruises between Vancouver, BC, and Seward, AK.

Princess Cruises, 2029 Century Park E., Los Angeles, CA 90025. *Sea Princess* and *Island Princess,* 730 and 626 passengers, offer 7-day cruises between Vancouver, BC, and Whittier, AK. *Fair Princess,* 890 passengers, 7-day round-trip from Vancouver. *Star Princess,* 1,470 passengers, 12-day round-trip from San Francisco.

Regency Cruises, 260 Madison Ave., New York, NY 10016. MV *Regent Sea,* 717 passengers, and MV *Regent Sun,* 832 passengers, 7 nights between Vancouver, BC, and Whittier, AK.

Royal Viking Line, 750 Battery St., San Francisco, CA 94111. *Royal Viking Sea,* 725 passengers, 11-day cruises from Vancouver, BC.

Sea Venture Cruises, 5217 NW 79th Ave., Miami, FL 33166. *Sea Venture,* 352 passengers, 10- and 11-day cruises between Vancouver, BC, and Anchorage.

Travalaska, 4th and Battery Bldg., Suite 808, Seattle, WA 98111. The 35-passenger *Sheltered Seas* offers

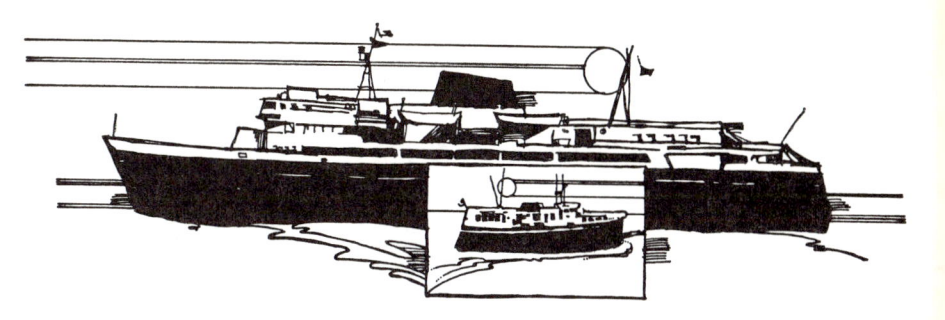

4-night cruises between Ketchikan and Juneau.
World Explorer Cruises, 555 Montgomery St., San Francisco, CA 94111. SS *Universe,* 554 passengers, 11- and 14-day round-trip from Vancouver, BC.

Dalton Highway

This all-weather gravel road bridges the Yukon River, climbs the Brooks Range and crosses the tundra plains before reaching the Prudhoe Bay oil fields on the coast of the Arctic Ocean.

Named for James Dalton, a post-World War II explorer who played a large role in the development of North Slope oil and gas industries, the 416-mile road was built to provide access to the northern half of the 800-mile trans-Alaska oil pipeline during construction.

The Dalton Highway has been partially opened by the state for public use. The public may drive the road's first 215.4 miles to Disaster Creek at Dietrich. North of Dietrich, the highway is closed to the public. Permits to travel north of Disaster Creek are issued for commercial or industrial purposes, mass transit, official government travel, access to property by the owners or university-affiliated Arctic Research. Permits may be obtained from the Alaska Department of Transportation and Public Facilities, 2301 Peger Road, Fairbanks 99709.

Fuel, limited food services and tire repairs, as well as wrecker service at $5 per mile, are available (for cash) at the Yukon Bridge and at Coldfoot. Travelers are advised that dust clouds, soft shoulders, large trucks traveling fast and sometimes narrow, rough road surfaces may make stopping along the roadway dangerous. Also, since safe drinking water is not available along the road, travelers should carry their own.

The Dalton Highway begins at Milepost 73.1 on the Elliott Highway.

Daylight Hours

(*See also* Arctic Circle)

Maximum (At Summer Solstice, June 20 or 21)

	Sunrise	Sunset	Hours of daylight
Barrow	May 10	August 2	84 days continuous
Fairbanks	1:59 a.m.	11:48 p.m.	21:49 hours
Anchorage	3:21 a.m.	10:42 p.m.	19:21 hours
Juneau	3:51 a.m.	10:09 p.m.	18:18 hours
Ketchikan	4:04 a.m.	9:33 p.m.	17:29 hours
Adak	6:27 a.m.	11:10 p.m.	16:43 hours

Minimum (At Winter Solstice, December 21 or 22)

	Sunrise	Sunset	Hours of daylight
Barrow	*	*	0:00 hours
Fairbanks	10:59 a.m.	2:41 p.m.	3:42 hours
Anchorage	10:14 a.m.	3:42 p.m.	5:28 hours
Juneau	9:46 a.m.	4:07 p.m.	6:21 hours
Ketchikan	9:12 a.m.	4:18 p.m.	7:06 hours
Adak	10:52 a.m.	6:38 p.m.	7:46 hours

*For the period November 18 through January 24 — 67 days — there is no daylight in Barrow.

Diamond Willow

Fungi, particularly *Valsa sordida Nitschke,* are generally thought to be the cause of diamond-shaped patterns in the wood of some willow trees. There are 33 varieties of willow in Alaska, of which at least 5 can develop diamonds. They are found throughout the state, but are most plentiful in river valleys. Diamond willow, stripped of bark, is used to make lamps, walking sticks and novelty items.

Dog Mushing

(*See also* Iditarod Trail Sled Dog Race)

In many areas of the state where snow machines had just about replaced the working dog team, the sled dog has made a comeback, due in part to a rekindled appreciation of the reliability of nonmechanical transportation. In addition to working and racing dog teams, many people keep 2 to 10 sled dogs for recreational mushing.

Sled dog racing is Alaska's official state sport. Races ranging from local club meets to world championship class are held throughout the winter.

The sprint or championship races are usually run over two or three days with the cumulative time for the heats deciding the winner. Distances for the heats vary from about 12 miles to 30 miles. The size of dog teams also varies, with mushers using anywhere from 7 to 16 dogs in their teams. Since racers are not allowed to replace dogs in the team, most finish with fewer than they started with (attrition may be caused by anything from tender feet to sore muscles).

Purses range from trophies for the club races to $50,000, including heat money, for the championships. The purse is split between the finishers.

Statistics for two of the biggest races follow.

World Championship Sled Dog Race, Anchorage

Held in February. Best elapsed time in three heats over three days, 24 miles each day. The 1989 race saw two firsts: it was the first time in the history of the race that a woman won, and the purse reached an all-time high of $50,000.

	Day 1	Day 2	Day 3	Total	Purse
1974 Roland Lombard	105:32	108:34	101:36	310:10	$10,000
1975 George Attla	98:09	107:01	104:18	309:28	12,000
1976 George Attla	98:39	102:64	102:32	303:35	12,000
1977 Carl Huntington	97:42	105:29	*	201:11	12,000
1978 George Attla	102:59	108:38	107:11	318:48	15,000
1979 George Attla	99:51	97:23	99:07	296:21	15,000
1980 Dick Brunk	83:25	82:35	*	166:00	15,000
1981 George Attla	90:04	85:43	91:34	267:21	20,000
1982 George Attla	73:19	75:36	76:56	225:51	20,000
1983 Harris Dunlap	82:29	88:58	89:05	260:32	25,000
1984 Charlie Champaine	82:55	84:06	85:03	254:04	26,000
1985 Eddie Streeper	83:08	85:32	88:36	251:16	30,000
1986 — Race cancelled for the first time due to lack of snow					
1987 Eddy Streeper	87:07	88:36	86:05	261:48	30,000
1988 Charlie Champaine	103:53	92:00	89:33	285:26	30,000
1989 Roxy Wright-Champaine	87:30	90:32	89:22	266.84	50,000

*Trail conditions shortened race

Open North American Sled Dog Championship, Fairbanks

Held in March. Best elapsed time in three heats over three days; 20 miles on Days 1 and 2, 30 miles on Day 3.

	Day 1	Day 2	Day 3	Total	Purse
1974 Alfred Attla	72:00	74:25	108:29	254:54	$9,000
1975 George Attla	69:56	70:16	104:05	244:17	9,000
1976 Harvey Drake	72:00	73:43	116:00	261:43	10,000
1977 Carl Huntington	71:20	71:40	109:00	252:00	12,000
1978 George Attla	71:07	68:05	106:53	246:53	15,000
1979 George Attla	68:41	70:07	104:44	243:32	15,000
1980 Harvey Drake	63:48	66:49	94:30	225:07	15,000
1981 Peter Norberg	73:01	70:55	109:07	253:03	15,000
1982 Harris Dunlap	69:17	72:14	105:43	247:14	15,000
1983 Gareth Wright*	65:43	68:31	99:36	233:50	15,000
1984 Doug McRae	—	—	—	235:04	17,500
1985 Eddy Streeper	61:88	64:16	98:52	224:56	25,000
1986 George Attla	63:95	65:99	103:07	233:01	25,000
1987 George Attla	63:50	68:10	97:21	229:03	25,000
1988 Marvin Kokrine	63:52	66:16	95:42	225:49	30,000
1989 Roxy Wright-Champaine	62:10	62:42	92:07	216:59	44,000

*This was Gareth's second win of this race. He took his first championship in 1950.

Other major races round the state are:

Alaska State Championship Race, Kenai-Soldotna. Two heats in two days, 15.4 miles each day. Held in February.

All-Alaska Sweepstakes. The Nome Kennel Club sponsors this 408-mile Nome to Candle and back race. Held in March, not always an annual event.

Clark Memorial Sled Dog Race, Soldotna to Hope, 100 miles. Held in January.

Iditarod Trail Sled Dog Race (*See* Iditarod Trail Sled Dog Race).

Kusko 300, Bethel to Aniak. Held in January.

Tok Race of Champions, Tok. Two heats in two days, 20.5 miles a day. Held in March.

Willow Winter Carnival Race, Willow. Two heats in two days, 18 miles each day. Held in January.

Women's World Championship Race, Anchorage. Three heats in three days, 12 miles each day. Held in February.

Yukon Quest International Sled Dog Race, Fairbanks to Whitehorse in even numbered years, with trail reversing on odd numbered years, 1,000 miles. Held in February.

Earthquakes

Between 1899 and mid-1989, ten Alaska earthquakes occurred that equaled or exceeded a magnitude of 8 on the Richter scale. During the same period, more than 70 earthquakes took place that were of magnitude 7 or greater, the most recent occurring in the Gulf of Alaska on March 6, 1988, and registering 7.6 on the Richter scale.

According to the Alaska Tsunami Warning Center, earthquake activity in Alaska typically follows the same pattern from month to month, interspersed with sporadic swarms, or groups of small earthquakes, and punctuated every decade or so by a great earthquake and its aftershocks. Alaska is the most seismic of all the 50 states and the most seismically active part of the state is the Aleutian Islands arc system. Seismicity related to this system extends into the Gulf of Alaska and northward into interior Alaska to a point near Mount McKinley. These earthquakes are largely the result of underthrusting of the North Pacific plate with most seismic activity taking place along the Aleutian Island chain. Many earthquakes resulting from this underthrusting occur in Cook Inlet — particularly near Mount Illiamna and Mount Redoubt — and near Mount McKinley. North of the Alaska Range, in the central interior, most earthquakes are of shallow origin.

An earthquake created the highest seiche, or splash wave, ever recorded when, on the evening of July 9, 1958, a quake with a magnitude of 7.9 on the Richter scale rocked the Yakutat area. A landslide containing approximately 40 million cubic yards of rock plunged into Gilbert Inlet at the head of Lituya Bay. The gigantic splash resulting from the slide sent a wave 1,740 feet up the opposite mountain side, denuding it of trees and soil down to bedrock. It then fell back and swept through the length of the bay and out to sea. One fishing boat anchored in Lituya Bay at the time was lost with its crew of two; another was carried over a spit of land by the wave and soon after foundered, but its crew was saved. A third boat anchored in the bay miraculously survived intact. A total of four square miles of coniferous forest was destroyed.

The most destructive earthquake to strike Alaska occurred at 5:36 p.m. on Good Friday, March 27, 1964, — a day now referred to as Black Friday. Registering between 8.4 and 8.6 on the Richter scale in use at the time, its equivalent moment magnitude has since been revised upward to 9.2, making it the strongest earthquake ever recorded in North America. With its primary epicenter deep beneath Miners Lake in northern Prince William Sound, the earthquake spread shock waves that were felt 700 miles away. The earthquake and seismic waves that followed killed 118 persons, 103 of them Alaskans. The death tally was: Chenega, 23; Kodiak 12; Point Nowell, 1; Point Whitshed, 1; Port Ashton, 1; Port Nellie Juan, 3; Seward, 11; Valdez, 31; Whittier, 12; Kalsin Bay, 6; Cape St. Elias, 1; Spruce Cape, 1.

The 1964 earthquake released 80 times the energy of the San Francisco earthquake of 1906 and moved more earth farther, both horizontally and vertically, than any other earthquake ever recorded, save the 1960 Chilean earthquake. In the 69-day period after the main quake, there were 12,000 jolts of 3.5 magnitude or greater.

The highest sea wave caused by the 1964 earthquake occurred when an undersea slide near Shoup Glacier in Port Valdez triggered a wave that toppled trees 100 feet above tidewater and deposited silt and sand 220 feet above salt water.

Education

(*See also* School Districts *and* Universities and Colleges)

Alaskans are well educated. The 1980 Population Census reported 83 percent of persons older than twenty-four as having had twelve or more years of education. This compares to 67 percent for the rest of the country.

Elementary and secondary education in Alaska is provided largely by the state, with a small percentage of private and denominational schools. According to the 1989 *Alaska Education Directory,* Alaska has approximately 463 public schools and over 100 private and denominational schools. The Bureau of Indian Affairs operated schools in Alaska until 1985.

The state Board of Education has seven members appointed by the governor. (In addition, two non-voting members are appointed by the board to represent the military and public school students.) The board is responsible for setting policy for education in Alaska schools and appoints a commissioner of education to carry out its decisions. The 463 public schools are controlled by 55 school districts and each school district elects its own school board. There are 22 Regional Education Attendance Areas which oversee education in rural areas outside the 33 city and borough school districts.

Any student in grades K-12 may choose to study at home through the unique state-operated Centralized Correspondence Study program, which also serves traveling students, GED students, migrant students and students living in remote areas. Summer school classes are also available through correspondence. Each year, up to 2,000 students are enrolled in this program. Home study has been an option for Alaskan students since 1939.

The state Department of Education also operates the Alaska Vocational Technical Center at Seward and a number of other education programs ranging from adult basic education to literacy skills.

Alaskans aged 7 through 16 are required to attend school. According to state regulations a student must earn a minimum of 21 high school credits to receive a high school diploma. The state Board of Education has stipulated that four credits must be earned in language arts; three in social studies; two each in math and science; and one in physical education. Local school boards set the remainder of the required credits.

Since 1976, the state has provided

secondary school programs to any community in which an elementary school is operated and one or more children of high school age wish to attend high school. This mandate was the result of a suit initiated on behalf of Molly Hootch, a high school age student from Emmonak. Prior to the so-called Molly Hootch Decree, high school age students in villages without a secondary school attended high school outside their village. Of the 127 villages originally eligible for high school programs under the Molly Hootch Decree, only a few remain without any.

There were approximately 7,735 teachers and administrators in the public schools and approximately 101,365 students enrolled in public schools in 1988-1989. The Anchorage School District accounted for more than 38 percent of the state's student enrollment. Private schools had about 5,400 students. The size of schools in Alaska varies greatly, from 1,993-student high schools in Anchorage to one or two-teacher, one-room schools in remote rural areas.

Of the school district's operating fund, 73.6 percent is provided by the state, 20.6 percent by local governments and 5.8 percent by the federal government. Alaska's teachers receive the highest average salaries in the nation.

Employment

The average number of people employed in the state in 1988 was about 212,300. The annual average unemployment rate for 1988 was 9.5 percent, down significantly from the 10.9 percent unemployment rates posted in 1986 and 1987.

After a two-year recession caused by an overbuilt construction market and collapsing world oil prices, Alaska's economy returned to growth. As of March 1989, the statewide growth in employment was between 1 and 2 percent on an annual basis. This follows two years of employment losses of more than 4 percent each.

During the recession not many of Alaska's industries were spared. Many job losses occurred in Anchorage, Alaska's largest city, and the construction and financial industries statewide were particularly hard hit. The oil and gas industry and Alaska's large government sectors were also adversely affected.

The recovery in 1988 was spurred on by a resurgence in Alaska's traditional resource based industries of fishing and timber. This growth recovery was augmented by a growing tourist trade and an increasing military presence in the state. Higher oil prices in late 1987 and most of 1988 returned stability to the oil and gas industry as well as to government sectors dependant on revenue generated by oil. In the immediate future hard rock mining will be a growing employer. One major mine opened in 1989, another is scheduled for early 1990 and several other major projects are in the works.

Although Alaska's 9.5 percent unemployment rate is well above the national average, it is best characterized by a very seasonal labor market. Increased activity of all types in the summer makes unemployment fairly low, while a lack of activity pushes up the unemployment rate in the winter months.

Unemployment figures vary dramatically from winter to summer and from one region to another. High unemployment rates in Alaska's rural areas are common. In Interior Alaska for example, the unemployment rate approaches 20 percent in the winter months. On the other hand bustling seaports such as Kodiak experience unemployment rates below 3 percent during the summer. Unemployment figures for March 1989 by selected areas are as follows: Statewide 9.5 percent; Anchorage 6.7 percent; Fairbanks 12.1 percent; Juneau 6.5 percent; Kodiak 3.9 percent; Nome 10.4 percent; Yukon-Koyukuk 19.0 percent.

The presence of a high level of transient population is another characteristic of the Alaskan labor market that presumably aggravates the unemployment rate.

In the last decade, employment in Alaska grew at an average of 5 percent annually. During this period Alaska's economy experienced two surges: the construction of the trans-Alaska pipeline system in the mid-seventies and the increase in petroleum-based government revenues in the early eighties. In early 1986, concurrent with the world-wide drop in the price of oil, the Alaskan economy began its first major contraction since World War II. More than 4 percent of total employment was lost in 1987, with a tapering off to under 1 percent for 1988.

While the government sector (state, local and federal) is generally a significant force in the economies of most states, historically this is particularly true in Alaska. In 1988, government employment in Alaska, excluding federal military personnel, was highest in employment numbers and total wage and salary payroll. In contrast, the average government-sector employment in the U.S. was about 18.7 percent of total payroll by industry. In 1988, Alaska ranked first among all states in government employment, both on a percent of total and per capita basis.

In 1987, employment percentages in the mining, construction, transportation-communications-utilities and government industry groups were typically higher than their U.S. averages, while percent employment in the retail trade, finance-insurance-real estate and service industry groups were comparable to or slightly lower than, their U.S. averages. The smallest industry groups in Alaska, relative to the U.S., were manufacturing and wholesale trade.

Alaska law requires that for state-funded projects, 95 percent of the employees be state residents.

If you're seriously considering a move to Alaska to seek a job, first make a visit and see it for yourself. Jobs are scarce in Alaska and housing is expensive — there are now, and will be in the foreseeable future, plenty of Alaska residents out of work and anxious to find jobs. For additional information, write: Alaska Department of Labor, Alaska State Employment Service, P.O. Box 3-7000, Juneau 99811. Employment offices are located in most major communities.

End of the Trail®
1989-90

The trademark name "End of the Trail" belongs to *ALASKA*® magazine, which reports the passing of old-timers and prominent Alaskans in its monthly "End of the Trail" column. *ALASKA*® magazine has graciously given THE ALASKA ALMANAC® permission to use the title and pick up listings from its column. To be eligible for listing, the deceased must have achieved pioneer status by living at least thirty years in the North, or have made a significant impact upon the northern scene.

ADAMS, Fred, 76, retired construction worker, died January 12, 1988, in Anchorage. He was born in Kotzebue and served in the U.S. Army during World War II. Following his discharge, he worked in construction and as a commercial fisherman. Survivors include his wife, Elsie of Kotzebue, and two sons, James of Nome and David of Porterville, CA.

ALBERT, Thomas Noah, 72, grandson of Alaska Native Land Claims proponent Chief Thomas, died November 6, 1988, in Fairbanks. He spent most of his life in the Wood River and Nenana districts, where he worked as a commercial fisherman and trapper. He was a member of Doyon Ltd., Nenana Native Corp. and the Episcopal church. Survivors include three daughters, Virginia Albert of Fairbanks, Judith Butler of Anchorage and Dinah Burke of Palmer.

ALEX, Edward William, 73, a retired contractor and service station owner, died June 14, 1988, at his home in Slana. A World War II veteran, he was a 40-year resident of Alaska. Survivors include two sons and four daughters.

ANDERSON, Andrew Nels Jensen, 84, a 50-year Alaska resident, died September 20, 1988, in Spanaway, WA. He retired from Pelican Storage in Juneau after working there for 34 years. He was a member of the Pioneers of Alaska Igloo No. 6. Survivors include his wife, Lilian of Spanaway, three sons and a daughter.

ASPEN, Sigurd Magnar Sr., 74, an Alaska resident since 1940, died July 26, 1988, in Juneau. Born in Norway, he moved to Aberdeen, WA, in 1929, and later made Alaska his permanent home. He worked as a fisherman, longshoreman and bartender before his retirement in 1985. Survivors include three daughters and a son.

AVAKOFF, Emily Curley Mullen Meyers, 92, died May 13, 1988, in Northbrook, IL. She arrived in Alaska in 1946 from Illinois and eventually helped run Avakoff's Jewelry Store in Fairbanks. She was a member of the Pioneers of Alaska Auxiliary No. 8, the Emblem Club and a charter member of the Quota Club. She is survived by two granddaughters and a grandson.

BAILEY, Warren "Moose," 61, died February 15, 1989, in Sylmar, CA. Born and lived in Anchorage until his retirement. Survived by his sister, Lucile of Seattle; and four brothers, Albert and Stan of Anchorage, Bill of Simi Valley, CA, and Bob of Seattle.

BAKER, William Irey "Wild Bill", 80, died May 21, 1988, at his home near Sheep Creek. He had lived in Alaska since the 1940s, working as a carpenter throughout the state. Survivors include his brother, Charles of Loon Lake, WA, and sisters, Wave Warren of Volney, VA, and Mary Boyd of New Providence, PA.

BARNETT, Virginia Wassam, 73, former Anchorage homesteader and retired Anchorage School District employee, died August 20, 1988, in Portland, OR. She and her husband came to Alaska in 1945 and began homesteading in 1949. In 1960, she began working as an elementary school secretary until she retired in 1977. She is survived by her daughters, Robie Webb of Spokane, WA, Glenna Rodriguez of Chicago, IL; and her son, Jack Richmond, CA.

BARRY, Elizabeth Lee, 67, died late 1988, in Spokane, WA. A 31-year resident of Wasilla, she began working for the Mat-Su Borough in 1969 before becoming a tax assessor in 1973. She retired from the borough in 1983. Survivors include a son, James Barry of Spokane, WA, and four daughters, Suzan Barry, Anne Ellis and Helen Barry, all of Wasilla, and Mary McCarver of Fairbanks.

BEACH, Markel, 51, died February 19, 1989, in Fair-

51

banks. Born in Seldovia and worked as a seine fisherman until moving to Fairbanks. Survived by his daughter, Samantha Lynn Williams of Fairbanks; and three sons, Mark of Anchorage, Nathanial of Fairbanks, John of Lynnwood, WA, and Wade of Seattle.

BECKHORN, Ruby, 71, retired secretary for the State of Alaska, died June 16, 1988, in Anchorage. She came to Alaska 45 years ago, and she and her husband ran a trapline in interior Alaska until the mid-1950s, when the couple homesteaded on the Kenai Peninsula. She retired from her job with the state in 1975. Survivors include a daughter, Judy Beckhorn of Anchorage.

BENSHOOF, William W., 80, died July 10, 1988, in Kingston, WA. He came to Alaska in 1943 and worked on the Alaska Highway. He later moved to Fairbanks where he was superintendent of the Sunday school at Fairbanks Lutheran Church. Survivors include his wife, Emma of Kingston, and three sons.

BERG, Geraldine H., 81, a longtime Seward resident, died September 20, 1988, in Bigfork, MT. She arrived in 1938 in Seward, where she was a music teacher and a member of the Methodist church. Survivors include her husband, Claude of Bigfork, and a son, Charles of Ketchikan.

BERRY, Clifford William, 70, of Sitka, died June 23, 1988, in Anchorage. He served in the U.S. Army from 1944 to 1946 and later worked as a union carpenter and a millwright. Survivors include three children, Georgia Lynn of Seattle, Francis Clifford of North Pole, and Susan Catherine of Cazadero, CA.

BESSER, Irma C., 69, a former Anchorage Parks and Recreation board member, died November 10, 1988, in Anchorage. She lived in Alaska for 42 years and was known for her hand-stitched doll clothes and knitted items. She was a member of the Anchorage Lionesses, Ladies of the Oriental Shrine, Pioneers of Alaska, Order of the Eastern Star and Anchorage Women's Club. Survivors include her husband, W.A. "Bill" Besser, and a daughter, Roxie Ottley, both of Anchorage.

BIGELOW, Lowell Curtis "Bolly", 81, a retired dock builder, died July 30, 1988, in Wrangell. He came to Wrangell in 1934 as a commercial fisherman and later made his living building docks. His work took him to Cold Bay, Kodiak, Seward and Soldotna. In 1977, he and his wife started the Our Collections Museum in Wrangell. Survivors include his wife, Elva of Wrangell.

BINGHAM, Carl Eugene, 77, a former Knik homesteader, died January 29, 1989, in Anchorage. He came in 1951 to Alaska, where he and his wife homesteaded near the Knik River. He later moved to Anchorage where he worked for Glass, Sash and Door Supply for 26 years. He was a member of the Church of Jesus Christ of Latter-day Saints, Anchorage 12th Ward. Survivors include his wfie, Raone "Sammi" Bingham of Anchorage.

BITTNER, William E., 71, a lifelong Alaskan and father-in-law of senior U.S. Senator Ted Stevens, died January 22, 1989, in Phoenix, AZ. Born in Anchorage, he graduated from Anchorage High School in 1934. He continued his education at the University of Southern California and was a Navy Flight instructor during World War II. He brought his family to Alaska in 1950 where he worked as a tax collector for the territory and later started two construction companies. He was the first president of the Mount McKinley Lions Club. Survivors include his wife, Elladean of Phoenix, two daughters and a son.

BIXLER, Vivian Talbot, 84, died July 6, 1988. Born and raised in Skagway, she became known in the community for her piano and accordion playing. During the 1930s, she lived in Wasilla, Hope and Seldovia, where her husband taught school, before moving to Anchorage in 1940. She belonged to a number of organizations including the Anchorage Musicians Association and Pioneers of Alaska. Survivors include her daughters, Janet B. Porter of Anchorage and Jo Ann Kirk of Seattle.

BOGAN, Jean H., 66, a third-generation Alaskan, died August 6, 1988, in Anchorage. She was raised in Seward and made her living as a courier for the U.S. Army Corps of Engineers. She later hosted a popular weekly radio show for the visually impaired. She was a member of the Seward Pioneer Lodge and Anchorage Greatland Toastmasters Club. Survivors include a daughter, Patti Lash of Anchorage.

BRANNAM, Neta Alene, 69, died January 5, 1989, in Anchorage. She arrived in Ketchikan in 1954 and was a dispatcher and taxi driver for Yellow Cab until she moved to Anchorage in 1975. She was a member of the Ketchikan Eagles Lodge and was active in Tri-Chem Painting. Survivors include four sons.

BRECKENRIDGE, Jess J., 79, a retired builder, died May 14, 1988, in Cathlamet, WA. He worked as a miner in southcentral Alaska and as a commercial fisherman in Cook Inlet and Kodiak. He served in the U.S. Navy during World War II and later made his living in construction. Survivors include his wife, Esther of Astoria, OR.

BRODERICK, Gwenn K., 66, died August 19, 1988, in Ketchikan. A schoolteacher, she taught in Fairbanks, Kenai and Ketchikan. Survived by her husband, Francis of Ketchikan; a daughter, Ruth Gundersen of Juneau; and three sons, Mark of Ketchikan, Kent of Willow and Kirk of South Carolina.

BROOKMAN, Albert John, 82, a longtime commercial fisherman, died December 31, 1988, in Sitka. He came to Alaska in 1926 to fish for king salmon. He spent his life as a commercial fisherman and wrote a book, *Sitka Man*, which recounted his 60 years of fishing, hunting and trapping in southeastern Alaska. He wa a member of the Elks Lodge and Pioneers of Alaska. Survivors include four daughters and two sons.

BRYMER, Alvin H., 62, died July 2, 1988, in Anchorage. He served with the U.S. Navy during World War II and was a sergeant in the U.S. Air Force from 1948 to 1949. He came to Alaska with his family in 1955 and homesteaded in Anchor Point. He later founded Brymer's Backhoe and Dozer Works of Soldotna until he retired in 1972. A member of the Kenai Elks Lodge and the Palmer American Legion Post 15, he leaves his wife, Frances of Anchor Point.

BUCHANAN, Rev. John R., 73, known as the "Pack-Rat" priest, died November 26, 1988, in Spokane, WA. He arrived in Alaska in the early 1940s when he was assigned by the Catholic Church to Holy Cross. He later moved to Tok Junction, where he once said there were more huskies in his parish than people. His ability to persuade people to donate materials for building schools and churches earned him his nickname. Survivors include a sister, Mary McGuire of southern California.

BUTLER, William L., 74, died late 1988, in Valdez. He spent 34 years working for Standard Oil and running his own refrigeration business in Valdez. Survivors include his wife, Ruby of Valdez.

CAMP, Thelma P., 76, died July 4, 1988, at her home in Juneau. She moved with her husband to Alaska in 1947 and worked as a hardware clerk in Juneau for many years. She was a member of the Women of the Moose, Pioneers of Alaska Igloo No. 6 and Benevolent Protective Order of Elks.

CHANDLER, Barbara Rose, 71, died March 20, 1989, in Scottsdale, AZ. One of the original four charter members of the Alaska Mechanical Contractors Auxiliary and a member of the Pioneers of Alaska. Survived by her daughter, Patricia Gail of Chandler, AZ; and a step-daughter, Donna Dannell of Oxnard, CA.

CHANDLER, Don C., 77, died February 19, 1989, in Scottsdale, AZ. Longtime Fairbanks resident, he was a partner in Acme Electric, served on the Alaska National Bank board of directors and as chairman of the board for seven years. Survived by his daughters, Donna Danell of Oxnard, CA, and Patricia Gail of Chandler, AZ.

CHEEK, Joseph A., 69, died August 18, 1988, in Fairbanks. Fairbanks resident since 1956, he opened his home to children when the need arose. Survived by his wife, Georgette; a daughter Darlene; and three sons, Allen, Allbert and Curtis, all of Fairbanks.

CHURCH, Lawrence F., 78, a retired employee of the Anchorage Parks and Recreation Department, died February 12, 1989, in Lewiston, ID. He came to Alaska in 1939 and served with the U.S. Army at Fort Richardson from 1942 to 1945. He later worked as an equipment operator for the City of Anchorage until his retirement in 1972. Survivors include his wife, Marguerite of Lewiston.

CLOSE, Carroll C., 82, died June 25, 1988, in Palmer. He had lived in Alaska since 1928 and operated the Talkeetna Roadhouse, now a registered historical building. He also was a member of the Anchorage Elks Lodge. Survivors include three brothers and three sisters.

CONGER, Jack Aaron, 77, a 37-year Alaska resident, died December 27, 1988, in Fairbanks. He came to Alaska in 1951 and worked as a painter and business agent for the Painter's Union Local 1555 until his retirement in 1976. He was a member of the Eagles Lodge and Pioneers of Alaska. Survivors include his wife, Marjorie, and a son, Floyd, both of Fairbanks.

COOGAN, Anne L., 67, died July 11, 1988, in Juneau. In 1957, she arrived in Juneau, where she operated a professional photography service and later worked for RCA Alascom. She was active in the Catholic church and was a volunteer for Senior Citizens and a women's crisis center in Juneau. Survivors include her husband, Jack of Juneau, three sons and a daughter.

CORLISS, Jessie, 79, a native of Girdwood, died September 23, 1988, in Phoenix, AZ. She spent part of her life in Seward, where she operated a beauty salon, and later moved to Cordova, where she worked for the New England Fish Co. and Cordova Drug Co. Survivors include two daughters, Janet Corliss Shaw of Cordova, and Nancy Corliss Peifer of Phoenix.

COTTER, Cora Belle, 79, a former Anchorage chef, died January 31, 1989, in Anchorage. She came to Alaska in 1946 and worked in Healy as a cook at an Alaska Railroad bridge and building camp. She moved to Anchorage in 1947 and worked as a cook for the Anchorage firemen at old city hall. She later worked as a master chef in several Anchorage restaurants before her retirement in 1951. Survivors include two daughters and a son.

COYLE, Ruby, 73, a 40-year Alaskan resident, died October 4, 1988, in Kenai. She and her husband came to Alaska in 1948 and homesteaded on the Kenai Peninsula. She was a cannery worker, commercial fisherman and an avid gardener. Survivors include her husband, Waldo of Kenai.

CROCK, J. Paul, 73, died September 5, 1988, in Juneau. He came to Alaska in 1937 as an engineer and trapper for Kanaga Ranching Co., and he trapped throughout the Aleutians. He later operated a herring seiner out of Kodiak and served as general field superintendent during World War II for A.J. McMillan Construction Co.

DALY, Virginia Y., 82, died August 13, 1988, in Ketchikan. She arrived in Ketchikan on New Year's Eve in 1927 and taught high school for many years. She was a member of St. John's Episcopal Church, Pioneer's Auxiliary and Hospital Advisory Board. She is survived by two sons, James of Ketchikan and John of Anchorage, and a daughter, Margaret Lynne of Ketchikan.

DEGNAN, Caroline H., 72, former co-owner of the McGrath Roadhouse, died October 27, 1988, in Coos Bay, Oregon. She came to Alaska in 1937 and spent 50 years operating a placer mine with her husband in the Ophir area. In conjunction with the mine, the couple also owned the McGrath Roadhouse, which they ran when they were not mining.

DOUGLAS, Elsie U., 67, lifelong Alaskan, died September 2, 1988, in Anchorage. Born in Kobuk Village, she and her husband were among the original founding families of Ambler. She traveled throughout the Kotzebue Sound region for the past 10 years as a pastor. Survivors include her husband, Douglas of Ambler, two sons, Peter of Anchorage and James of Ambler, and a daughter, Harriet Blair of Kiana.

DOYLE, Margaret Kiloh, 80, a 75-year resident of Juneau, died April 28, 1988, in Juneau. She retired from Alaska Coastal Airlines and had previously worked with the Alaska Game Commission. She is survived by a sister, Lillian Lane of Florence, OR.

DUNLAP, Jack, 44, died July 24, 1988, in California. Raised in Fairbanks and resident of Cordova at the time of his death, he worked as an electrician and piloted his own plane. Survived by his son, Robert of Fairbanks.

DUVAL, Clara G., 85, died May 10, 1988, in Petersburg. She was active in the Lutheran Church and was a volunteer swimming instructor for preschool children. Survivors include a son, Robert of Olympia, WA, and a daughter, Ruth Dawson of Petersburg.

EBY, Florence O., 84, died May 3, 1988, in Saint Augustine, FL. She worked in bush communities for the Alaska Department of Health in the late 1940s and early 1950s. Survivors include a sister, Marion Randolph of Saint Augustine.

EDMOND, Myrtle, 89, a longtime Cordova resident, died September 18, 1988, in Grass Valley, CA. She arrived in 1927 in Cordova, where she was a homemaker and accomplished seamstress. She was a former Worthy Matron of the Cordova Order of Eastern Star. Survivors include her son, Joe of Weimer, CA.

EGAN, Clinton J. "Truck", 91, an Alaska resident for 86 years, died October 4, 1988, in Valdez. He came to Alaska with his family in 1902 and later received commendations from Presidents Franklin Delano Roosevelt and Harry S. Truman for his service on the draft board. Survivors include his sister, Alice Horton of Palmer.

FALK, Jessie James, 85, known for her traditional Indian basketry skills, died September 10, 1988, in Pinconning, MI. She spent much of her life as a cook and baker for the Alaska Native Service Hospital, Copper Center Lodge, Tolsona Lodge and the Chistochina Trading Post. Survivors include two sons and two daughters.

53

FARO, Robert J. "Bobby", 19, two-time Alaska State Poster Child for the Muscular Dystrophy Association, died November 29, 1988, in Bellevue, WA. As a poster child, he traveled throughout the state as a goodwill ambassador. Despite his illness, he earned his high school diploma from Bartlett-Begich High School in Anchorage. Survivors include his mother, Gail, of Bellevue, father Robert of West Milford, NJ, four brothers and four sisters.

FLEMING, Frances B., 79, a longtime Cordova resident, died August 6, 1988, in Valdez. In 1939, she settled in Cordova, where she worked in the commercial fishing industry. Survivors include a son, Tom of Cordova, and five daughters, Jesse Jewell of Kimberly, OR, Pearl Langenfeld of Burns, OR, Anna Briedford of Palmer, Donna Barclay of Tidewater, OR, and Jerri Hunnicutt of Cordova.

FOUNTAIN, G.F., Sr., 77, died October 10, 1988, in Fairbanks. Fairbanks resident since 1951, he owned Fountain's Texaco for many years. Survived by his wife, Thelma of Anchorage; a daughter, Patsy Gossett of Minnesota; a step-daughter, Mable Schouten of Anchorage; four sons, G.F., Jr. and Perry of Fairbanks, Otis of Alabama and Charles of North Pole; and two step-sons, Herman Schouten of Minnesota and Hugh Schouten of Anchorage.

FRAZIER, Francis "Bill", 73, retired highway foreman for the state of Alaska, died July 10, 1988. In 1950, he brought his family to Alaska, where he was employed in the construction of the Alaska Highway. He later moved to Seward, where he helped build the Seward Highway. He eventually became highway foreman for the state until his retirement in 1980. He is survived by his wife, Patricia of Seward, and three daughters.

FREY, Homer Leroy Jr., 59, an Alaska resident for more than 30 years, died August 11, 1988, in Anchorage. He served in the U.S. Navy during the Korean conflict and later became a cook on the North Slope. He is survived by his son, Jim Dailey of Wichita, KS.

FULLER, Harold Bill, 72, died August 22, 1988, in Cooper Landing. He had lived in Cooper Landing for the past 36 years and was the owner of Bill's Gun Shop. He was a member of the National Rifle Association and the Cooper Landing Gun Club. Survivors include his wife, Betty of Cooper Landing.

GALLAGHER, Don F., 83, a retired merchant vessel captain, died October 25, 1988, in Juneau. Between 1927 and 1948, he served as engineer or master on 22 different boats. In 1949, he founded Island Transportation in Juneau, where he operated the MV Forester for 19 years, delivering mail and freight throughout southeastern Alaska. He retired in 1968 and moved to Hoonah. Survivors include two sons, Dennis of Anchorage and Terry of Yakutat, and two daughters, Fay Gallagher and Lydonna Dybdahl, both of Hoonah.

GELLATLY, Amanda Cook, 87, a retired Juneau schoolteacher, died December 22, 1988, in Woodburn, OR. She came to Alaska in 1926 and lived in Ketchikan for two years before moving to Juneau, where she taught high school business classes until her retirement in 1965. She was a member of the Order Eastern Star, Delta Kappa Gamma, Pioneers of Alaska and the Northern Light Presbyterian Church. Survivors include two daughters.

GEORGE, Thelma, 80, died in early 1989, in Seattle. Longtime Juneau resident, she and her husband owned George's Gift Shop, and she was a member of the Pioneers of Alaska. Survived by her aunt and uncle, Elizabeth and Adrian Carr of Port Orchard, WA.

GILBERT, Donald Philo, 65, died September 4, 1988, in Fairbanks. Longtime Fairbanks businessman, he owned the Ranch Dinner House on the Richardson Highway and the A & W Drive-In. Survived by his wife, Lucille of Fairbanks; three daughters, Barbara Taylor and Donna Gilbert of Fairbanks, and Vicki Shoffstall of Mesa, AZ; and two sons, William of Fairbanks and Mark of Washington, D.C.

GLAVINOVICH, Mary Alma, 84, died July 9, 1988, in Seattle. Longtime resident of Alaska living in Nome and Fairbanks, she was a member of the Pioneers of Alaska and the Sacred Heart Cathedral auxiliary. Survived by her husband, Walter of Seattle; and two daughters, Helen Enyeart of Florida and Alice Ehli of Seattle.

GOOCH, Mary "Eleanor", 81, a former Anchorage florist, died January 14, 1989, in Anchorage. She came to Alaska in 1941 and later owned and operated the Anchorage Floral Shop. Survivors include two sisters, Alice Floyd and Betty Sweatte, both of Spokane, WA.

GOULD, Peter Gordon, 88, founder of Alaska Methodist University, died November 23, 1988, in Medina, NY. The first Alaska Native to become an ordained United Methodist minister, he was superintendent of Methodist work in Alaska from 1948 to 1965. He served as vice president of AMU (now Alaska Pacific University) during the late 1960s and was an honorary member of the Anchorage Chamber of Commerce. Survivors include his wife and three sons.

GRAVES, Hazel Paramore, 85, former Alaskan missionary, died August 4, 1988, in Yuba City, CA. She arrived in Unga in 1939 as a missionary of the Methodist Church. She and her husband later traveled throughout the state, building church facilities. Survivors include two sons, Eric and Gary of Fairbanks, and two daughters, Kathleen Moore of Homer and Sheila Pennell of Eagle River.

GREER, Mike, 56, a retired schoolteacher, died August 4, 1988, in Anchorage. He spent many years as a teacher in McGrath, Holy Cross and Anchorage. He was a master cook, and while living in the bush, he enjoyed providing meals for Bureau of Land Management firefighting crews. Survivors include a son, Michael of Kotzebue.

GRONROOS, Harold B., 69, died September 3, 1988, in Anchorage. He arrived in Alaska in 1933 and later graduated from the University of Alaska Fairbanks. Following a tour of duty with the U.S. Army during World War II, he returned to Alaska and worked for the Labor Department in Juneau, the Bureau of Indian Affairs and the National Park Service. He was a member of the Ketchikan Elks Lodge, Mount Juneau Lodge, American Legion and many other social organizations. Survivors include his wife, Earline of Anchorage.

HAGE, Agner, 78, former co-owner of Curtis and Hage Construction Co., died January 21, 1988, in Anchorage. A 47-year resident of Alaska, he built homes, schools and business buildings throughout the state. He was a life member of the Fraternal Order of Eagle No. 13 in Washington state. Survivors include his wife Elaine of Anchorage; daughter Joyce Vance of Anchorage; and son, Charles Peters of Saudi Arabia.

HALL, Tekla Alexandra Nordstrom, 91, died August 8, 1988, in Petersburg. She came to Alaska in 1916 from Sweden and homesteaded at Point Agassiz from 1924 to 1931. She was a member of the Eastern Star and the local hospital guild. Survivors include her husband, Ralph of Petersburg.

HALLBACK, Kenneth H., 65, a 30-year resident of Alaska, died January 26, 1989, in Anchorage. He spent his career working for the state Division of Lands and retired as Chief of Land Section. Survivors include three daughters, Debra Anderson of Anchorage, Gail Dexter of Bloomington, MN, and Jill Hallback of Orinda, CA.

HANCOCK, Leland "Lee", 84, a longtime Alaskan guide, died November 17, 1988, in Anchorage. He came to Alaska in 1929 and worked as a wrangler for a guide out of Rainy Pass. He later worked for the Alaska Railroad, as a commercial fisherman and as a hunting guide based in Kodiak. He was a member of the Pioneers of Alaska Igloo No. 17. Survivors include his wife, Laura of Nabesna, and three sons.

HANSEN, Chris, 82, a native of Norway who had lived in Alaska for 60 years, died August 5, 1988, at his son's home in San Diego. He worked as a chief engineer for Alaska Steamship Co., before being employed by the Municipality of Anchorage for 32 years. He is survived by his son, Arthur of Lemon Grove, CA.

HARBISON, Seward B., 73, died September 15, 1988, in Tok. Longtime resident of Tok, he worked for the Alaska Road Commission and the Haines-Fairbanks Pipeline. Survived by two daughters, Diane Batchelder and Mary Wallis of Fairbanks; and a son, James of Tok.

HARRELSON, Orval Wayne, 72, longtime Alaska resident, died August 14, 1988, in Fairbanks. He brought his family to Alaska in the 1950s. He worked as an equipment operator, mechanic and helped build the Parks Highway with the Alaska Department of Highways. He is survived by his wife, Maxiene of Fairbanks, two daughters and four sons.

HASSEL, Harold, 89, retired gold miner, died September 28, 1988, in Fairbanks. He arrived in Alaska in 1924 and took a job with a mining company in Fairbanks. He later developed Ready Bullion Mining Co. in Ester, becoming one of Alaska's most successful gold mining pioneers. He was a member of the Lutheran Church, Alaska Miners Association, Pioneers of Alaska Igloo No. 4 and many other social organizations. Survivors include a son, Jerald of Ester, and a daughter, Marian Schafer of Juneau.

HEDGES, Marian, 77, died January 25, 1989, in Maui, Hawaii. Longtime resident of Juneau and employee of B.M. Behrends Bank in Juneau, she was also active in scouting. Survived by her husband, Art of Maui, HI; a son, Gary of Juneau; and four grandchildren.

HEDSTROM, Elmer, 75, a lifetime Alaska resident, died January 15, 1989, in Anchorage. A native of Cordova, he worked as a trapper, commercial fisherman and operated a crab cannery. He later worked for the Federal Aviation Administration maintaining equipment in remote sites of Prince William Sound. He was a life member of Pioneers of Alaska Igloo No. 19. Survivors include his wife, Irene of Anchorage.

HELLENTHAL, John, 73, died February 5, 1989, in Anchorage. Lifelong Alaskan born in Juneau, he was an attorney, a delegate to the territory's constitutional convention and a member of the first two state legislatures. Survived by his wife, LaRue of Anchorage, a daughter, Cathy Braund of Anchorage; and two sons, Mark of Anchorage and Steve of Texas.

HERBERT, Roberta, 78, died February 24, 1989, in Anchorage. Active in dog shows, she was president of the Anchorage Kennel Club, and worked as a traveling field editor for The MILEPOST® when living in Anchorage and Juneau. Survived by her husband, Charles of Anchorage; and two stepsons, Stephen of Honolulu and Paul of Friday Harbor, WA.

HERNING, Carl Roland, 73, a 50-year Alaska resident, died October 5, 1988, in Fairbanks. He arrived in Cordova in 1938 and traveled to Fairbanks, where he built gold dredges for the Fairbanks Exploration Co. He served with the U.S. Air Force in Alaska during World War II and homesteaded near Chena Hot Springs after the war. He is best known for pioneering and maintaining bus transportation for schoolchildren in the Chena Hot Springs area. Survivors include his wife, Mattie Lee of Fairbanks.

HICKOX, Helen, 62, died March 30, 1989, in Wasilla. She lived and worked throughout the state as an educator, and a women's and children's advocate. Survived by her husband, Dean of Wasilla; two daughters, June Kinney and Alicen Phipps, both of Anchorage; two step-daughters, Pamela Clark of Vancouver, WA and Deanna Sterret of Tigard, OR; two sons, Barry Weaver of Juneau and John Williams of Sitka; and a step-son, John Hickox of Portland.

HILL, Laverne C., 82, died February 4, 1989, in Anchorage. A nurse, she had been in public health, and on the staff of the old railroad hospital and Providence Hospital. She was active in many organizations. Survived by two daughters, Elizabeth Robinson of Port Republic, Virginia and Marie Brown of Anchorage; and two sons, Fred and Oliver, both of Anchorage.

HODGE, Leon, 73, died March 9, 1989, in Fairbanks. Alaska resident since 1940, he worked as a bartender and was in the U.S. Army during World War II. Survived by his wife, Lorna of Fairbanks; and a daughter, Beverly Jean Marquez of Sacramento, CA.

HODGSON, Lawrence W. "Larry," 76, longtime Alaska resident, died December 15, 1988, in Soldotna. He came to Alaska in 1927 and worked as a commercial fisherman, bush pilot and road construction laborer. Survivors include his wife, Margaret of Soldotna.

HOLLOWELL, McLoyd M., 64, a 30-year resident of North Pole, died January 19, 1988, in Lake Havasu, AZ. He was employed with the Civil Service at Eielson Air Force Base until his retirement in 1979. He was a member of the original Planning and Zoning board for the North Star Borough and was former president of the Fairbanks Golf and Country Club. Survivors include a son, Morry of Eagle River, and three daughters, Sandy Casey and Betty Burkett of North Pole, and Sue Goodman of San Antonio, TX.

HOLLYWOOD, William James, 74, a lifelong Alaskan, died August 30, 1988, in Sitka. He graduated from Sitka High School and worked for Columbia Lumber until 1953. He later moved to Ketchikan, where he worked for Ketchikan Pulp Co. until his retirement in 1979. He was a member of the Loyal Order of Moose, Shee Atika Corp. and Sealaska. Survivors include his wife, Carol of Ketchikan.

HOYT, Norma Jordet, 87, died February 10, 1989, in Anchorage. Longtime resident of Alaska, she taught school in Fairbanks and worked summers at McKinley Park. She was a world traveler and active in many clubs. Survived by her son, Harold of Yuba City, CA; and two grandchildren.

HOYT, Sylvester A. "Bunk", 80, a Kenai Peninsula homesteader, died December 29, 1988, in Kenai. He came to Alaska in 1954 and began homesteading in 1958. He also worked as a commercial fisherman and operated a sawmill. He was a lifetime member of the Eagles, a member of Kenai

55

Elks Lodge No. 2425, the Moose Lodge and was active at the Kenai Senior Citizens Center. Survivors include two daughters.

HUBBARD, Lee Dale, 83, a retired state roads engineer, died January 27, 1989, in Anchorage. He traveled to Alaska by steamship in 1938. During World War II he worked as an engineer for the Civil Aeronautics Administration, building roads, airfields and related work in Juneau, Gustavus, Galena, Bethel, Cordova and Petersburg. He retired in 1971 from the Alaska Highway Department in Juneau as secondary roads engineer. He was a member of the Mount Juneau Masonic Lodge No. 147 and Pioneers of Alaska Igloo No. 6. Survivors include two daughters, Diana Weaver of Anchorage and Sylvia Ann Heath of Seattle.

HUTCHISON, Lavena A., 68, died October 26, 1988, in Juneau. She came to Juneau in 1959, where she worked as a schoolteacher. She was active in the Chapel-by-the-Lake church, where she taught Sunday school, served on the board of deacons and was editor of the church newsletter. Survivors include her husband, Keith of Juneau.

HUTTULA, William, 75, died March 10, 1989, in Juan de Fuca Strait, WA. Born near Fairbanks, he was active with the Junior Chamber of Commerce and Pioneers of Alaska. Survived by his wife, Rachel of Sequim, WA; three daughters, Maija Rippee of Lynwood, WA, Ann Henley of Richland and Carol Sande of Shelton, WA; and two sons, Bill of Bainbridge Island and Tom of Bothell, WA.

ISAAK, G.R. "Mex", 79, a resident of Alaska for 60 years, died at his home in Douglas on June 8, 1988. He arrived in Juneau in 1928 and worked for the Alaska-Juneau gold mine for 11 years and later entered the carpentry trade. Survivors include his wife, Helen of Douglas.

JACK, Edward B., 58, a 23-year Kodiak resident, died November 11, 1988, in Seattle. He drove a cab, fished commercially and worked as an investigator in Kodiak. He later owned and operated Ocean Air Emergency Safety Service Co. in Kodiak. Survivors include his wife, Natalie of Kodiak, four daughters and four sons.

JAMES, Philip "Peewee", 67, a longtime Sitka resident, died July 26, 1988, in Anchorage. Born in Hoonah, he later attended Sheldon Jackson School in Sitka, then joined the Army in 1942. After serving on Attu in the Aleutian Islands, he left the Army and worked as a commercial fisherman and as an electrician. He was a lifetime member of the Sitka Sportsman's Association, American Legion Post No. 13 and the National Rifle Association. Survivors include his wife, Elsie of Sitka, seven daughters and two sons.

JENSEN, Louis W., 82, a longtime Sitka resident, died November 13, 1988, in Sitka. He came to Sitka in 1951, where he owned and operated Sitka Marine Shop. His expertise and ingenuity as a machinist were well-known throughout the community. He was a member of the Elks Lodge, the Masonic Lodge and the National Rifle Association. Survivors include a son, John of Anchorage.

JERSILD, Elva N., 80, died November 11, 1988, in Foley, AL. She arrived in Juneau in 1946, where she worked as a registered nurse. In 1956, she transferred to Kotzebue, and she worked there until her retirement in 1969. Survivors include her husband, Gordon K. Chappel of Fairbanks, a son, Simeon of Fairbanks, and a daughter, E.J. Morena of Kiana.

JIM, Charlie, Sr., 76, chief of the End of the Trail House of the Raven Clan in Angoon, died October 29, 1988, in Sitka. Born in Killisnoo, he was president of the Indian Heritage Foundation, and treasurer and lifetime member of the Alaska Native Brotherhood of Angoon. Survivors include his wife, Jennie of Angoon, seven sons and eight daughters.

JOHN, Albert, 67, died late February, 1989, in Nenana. Lifelong Alaskan born in Shageluk and known as "Elbow" John. Survived by two brothers, Eluska and Simon, both of Shageluk.

JOHNSON, Myrtle B., 76, died January 17, 1989, in Juneau. Longtime Juneau resident, she owned the Owl Grocery and was active in several organizations. Survived by her son, Ken Thompson and his family, of Juneau.

JOHNSON, Terry E., died October 9, 1988, in Fairbanks. An avid outdoorsman, he owned Johnson Fish Co., was a pilot, fisherman, guide and trapper. Survived by his wife, Alice; and six daughters, Kim Taylor, Linda Colang, Marsha Woods, Camille, Laura and Holly Johnson, all of Fairbanks.

KARELLA, Ambrose J., 61, died March 4, 1989, in Fairbanks. Owner of several businesses in Fairbanks, he also served on the assembly for three years. Survived by his wife, Rosemary of Fairbanks; six daughters, Ivy Lichtenberger of New Jersey, Deena Stout, Carlene Cipra and Lewanne Karella of Fairbanks, and Cathy Ward and Gwen Tyson of Anchorage; and four sons, Fred and Howard of Fairbanks, Justin of Anchorage, and Kevin of Alabama.

KETURI, Hildur Kathryn, 76, died March 5, 1989, in Carlsbad, CA. A 43-year resident of Alaska, she was a teacher and shared a gold mining operation with her husband. Survived by her husband, Elmer of Carlsbad; a daughter, Lynn Erickson of Seattle; a son, Raymond of Fairbanks; and four granchildren.

KINDRED, Herbert Matthew, 83, a veteran seaman, died August 1, 1988, in Ketchikan. He arrived in Alaska in 1928 and worked on the oil Tanker, *Alaska Standard*. He later became assistant agent for the Alaska Steamship Co. He was a member of the Pioneers of Alaska. He is survived by his wife, Eunice of Ketchikan, two sons and a daughter.

KLOUDA, Joseph C., 65, died October 21, 1988, in Anchorage. Lifelong Alaskan, he grew up on a homestead at 8th and F streets. He was the great-grandson of Adam Bloch who was dispatched to Sitka in 1867 for the transfer of the Alaska territory from Russia to America. Survived by his wife, Patricia; and two sons, Bernard and Terry, all of Anchorage.

KRIGER, Kenneth J., 78, died July 9, 1988, in Aurora, CO. He was an adult education instructor with the Bureau of Indian Affairs in several rural Alaskan school districts prior to his retirement in 1972. He is survived by his wife, Eva of Aurora.

KRIZE, Rudolph B. "Rudy", 87, a 50-year resident of Fairbanks, died January 27, 1989, in Phoenix, AZ. He came to Alaska in 1939 and mined for gold in the Wiseman and Manley regions. He later moved to Fairbanks and became a businessman. Survivors include his brothers, Louis and Ed, both of Fairbanks.

LAKE, James M., 70, died March 11, 1989, in Fairbanks. Longtime Fairbanks resident, he owned Lake and Boswell Consulting Electrical Engineers, Inc. Active in many organizations, he was also honored professionally as Engineer of the Year in 1982. Survived by his wife, Katherine of Fairbanks.

LARRABEE, Bonnie June, 59, a 30-year resident of Alaska, died August 3, 1988, in Fairbanks. Since her arrival in Alaska in 1958, she worked as an office assistant and as a cook. She was a member of the American Legion Auxiliary, Delta Senior Citizens and the Delta Ladies Community Club. Survivors include three daughters and four sons.

LATTIN, Bill, 69, a well-known Ketchikan photographer, died October 6, 1988, in Seattle. He arrived with his family in Ketchikan at the age of 12 and graduated from Ketchikan High School. He served in the U.S. Air Force during World War II and later owned Southeast Electric Co. in Ketchikan. Survivors include his wife, Agnes, and sons Tom and Michael, all of Ketchikan.

LAUESEN, Elstun W. "Bud", 82, of Sourdough, died October 21, 1988, in Anchorage. He came to Alaska in 1950 with the Army Corps of Engineers. He later worked as chief engineer at Eielson Air Force Base until his retirement in the early 1970s. Survivors include his wife, Charlene of Sourdough, sons Raymond and Elstun II, and daughters Linda Brechan, and Fairbanks North Star Borough Mayor Juanita Helms, all of Fairbanks.

LEASK, Bertram James, 71, a native of Metlakatla, died November 4, 1988, in Sitka. He attended Sheldon Jackson School in Sitka followed by four years at the University of Dubuque in Iowa. He later flew B-25 bombers during World War II and received the Purple Heart and the Distinguished Flying Cross. Following his discharge from the Air Force, he worked as an accountant. Survivors include his wife, Ethel of Metlakatla.

LESH, Keith M., 80, died March 13, 1989, in Anchorage. Longtime Anchorage businessman, he established a number of businesses and was heavily involved in banking. He served on the Anchorage School Board for 17 years and was a member of many organizations. Survived by his wife, Mae; and a daughter, Nancy, both of Anchorage.

LINDBERG, Carroll L. "Lindy", 82, a Fairbanks grocery store operator for more than 50 years, died December 11, 1988, in Fairbanks. He arrived in Fairbanks in 1935 and worked for Lavery's Grocery. He served in the U.S. Army from 1943 to 1945 at Ladd Field. He later opened his own grocery store in Fairbanks and, in 1957, opened another in College. He was a charter member and former president of the Fairbanks Kiwanis Club, served on the Fairbanks City Council and spent 26 years serving on the First National Bank board of directors. Survivors include his wife, Barbara of Fairbanks.

LINN, Alfred, 70, died August 14, 1988, at his home in Kaktovik. He was born in Barrow and grew up in the Sagavanirktok River area, where he hunted and trapped. From 1947 to 1953, he and his family lived at Herschel Island, Canada, where he worked for the Royal Canadian Mounted Police. In 1953, he moved to Kaktovik, where he was a successful whaling captain. Survivors include four sons and three daughters.

LITTLEFIELD, Henry, 74, a Metlakatla fisherman, died September 28, 1988, in Ketchikan. He was a second lieutenant in the Alaska Territorial Guard, mayor of Metlakatla for 12 consecutive years, member of the city council for 57 years and a Presbyterian elder. He also owned and operated three seine boats out of Metlakatla. Survivors include his wife, Esther of Metlakatla, three sons and a daughter.

LLORENTE, S.J., The Rev. Segundo, 82, died January 26, 1989, in Spokane, WA. Born in Spain, he came to Alaska in 1935 and ministered to people from Kotzebue to Cordova. He was elected to the House of Representatives, and wrote and published several books on Alaska and her people.

LOBBAN, Leonard LeRoy, retired restaurant and club owner, died December 23, 1988, in Fairbanks. He served in the U.S. Army during World War II before arriving in Alaska 38 years ago. He made his home in Fairbanks and worked as a volunteer for the civil defense during the 1967 flood. He was co-owner of the Club 11 restaurant in Fairbanks until his death. He was a member of the American Legion Post No. 11, the Elks Lodge, Veterans of Foreign Wars and the Baptist Church. Survivors include three daughters.

LOKKE, Jacob Chris, 66, a lifelong Alaska resident, died August 9, 1988, in Juneau. Born in Sitka, he served in the U.S. Army in the Pacific during World War II. He moved to Juneau in 1950, where he worked as a commercial fisherman, longshoreman and for Alaska Coastal Airlines. He leaves his wife, Ruth, and three daughters, Kathy Polk, Marge Vonda and Julie Williams, all of Juneau.

LONGACRE, Connie, 65, died February 6, 1989, in Sun City West. Longtime Alaska resident, she was a stewardess for Alaska Airlines and active in many clubs. Survived by her daughter, Kathy Ybarra of Palmer.

LORD, Meda, 74, died March 26, 1989, in Fairbanks. Lifelong Alaskan, she was born in Coldfoot and lived in the Fort Yukon-Porcupine River area, Fairbanks and Nenana. She owned a restaurant, trapped, fished and had a mink ranch at various times. Survived by her four daughters, Mary Alice Wedde of Tacoma, WA, Alfrieda Edgington of Point Barrow, Rhoda Mancuso of Fairbanks and Susan Peter of Fort Yukon; and seven sons, Edmond of Nenana, Walter of Fairbanks, Gilbert, William, Delano, and George Ahmaogak of Point Barrow, and Olaf of Anchorage.

LUCAS, Harry I., 68, a native of Juneau, died December 21, 1988, in Juneau. He graduated from Juneau High School in 1938 and later attended the University of Alaska Fairbanks. He served in the U.S. Army from 1945 until 1953 and later became the commissioner of Veterans Affairs for the Territory of Alaska. Survivors include his wife, Eleanor of Juneau, and three daughters.

LUTHER, Howard C., 83, well-known realtor, died November 2, 1988, in Anchorage. He arrived in Alaska in 1943 and worked for the Alaska Railroad until 1948. He owned and operated Pioneer Realty. In 1963, he served as president of the Board of Realtors. Survivors include his wife, Betty, and a son, Howard, both of Anchorage.

LYNCH, Paul Patrick, 68, died April 4, 1989, in Anchorage. Longtime Anchorage resident, he owned the Irish Setter Lounge, and was active in the Pioneers of Alaska and the Anchorage Elks Lodge. Survived by his wife, June; and two daughters, Susan Trotter and Abby Rutherford, all of Anchorage.

MARTIN, Shirley Ann, 53, a lifelong resident of Juneau, died July 13, 1988. She was a member of the Juneau Seventh-Day Adventist Church, the Pioneers of Alaska and Perseverance Rebekah Lodge. She is survived by a sister, Patti Sidor of Great Falls, MT.

MCLAUGHLIN, Helen, 78, died March 16, 1989, in Anchorage. Alaska resident for 50 years, she was a retired school teacher. Survived by her daughter, Molly Windred of Juneau; and three sons, Terry of Juneau, Tim of Anchorage and Tom of Seattle.

MCNULTY, Thomas H., 65, a native of Sitka, died August 14, 1988, in Seattle. He served in the U.S. Army in Europe during World War II. He returned to Sitka following his discharge and worked there as a logger. Survivors include three sisters and a brother.

McRAE, Ella Margaret Johnston, 75, a lifelong Alaskan, died November 1, 1988, in Anchorage. She was born on Latouche Island and graduated from Seward High School. She moved to Anchorage in 1934 and homesteaded in the Sand Lake area. She was a member of the Pioneers of Alaska. Survivors include three sons and six daughters.

METCALFE, Vern, 65, a two-term territorial legislator and journalist, died January 18, 1989, in Juneau. He came to Alaska in 1941 and, after a four-year stint in the U.S. Army, worked with his father in a Juneau sheet-metal business. He later worked at the *Juneau Empire* newspaper, was editor of the weekly *Juneau Independent* in the 1950s, and worked for two radio stations. He served in the territorial legislature in 1951 to 1953 and 1955 to 1957, as a Democrat in the House.

MILLER, Evan L., 74, died January 24, 1989, in Seattle. Longtime Alaska resident, he worked as a welder throughout Alaska. He was a member of Pioneers of Alaska and the Masonic Lodge.

MILLER, Harry T., 75, died October 29, 1988, in Fairbanks. Alaskan since 1938, he was a member of the Carpenters Local. Survived by two sons, Barron of Fairbanks and Tony of Italy.

MILLER, William Ross, 79, a longtime Alaska resident, died November 13, 1988, in Kurtistown, HI. He arrived in Seward in 1942 and found work in a sawmill. He later homesteaded in Hope and worked as a construction foreman on the Sterling Highway. In 1957, he moved to Homer and established and operated the Homer Lumber Co., until the late 1960s. Survivors include his wife, Alma of Kurtistown.

MILNE, Harold, 77, died October 17, 1988, in Palmer. He arrived in Anchorage in 1952 and was a construction worker for the federal government. He later worked as an engineer in the civil service until his retirement in 1973. Survivors include two daughters.

MONSMA, Albert F., 62, an Alaskan for 35 years, died August 11, 1988, in Fairbanks. He came to Alaska in 1953, where he worked for the city of Anchorage as a lineman. He later moved to Fairbanks, and worked as a lineman and supervisor for the city. Survivors include two daughters and three sons.

MONTGOMERY, Ethel M., 92, died early 1989, in Juneau. Longtime Alaskan, she was advisor to the Alaska Native Arts and Crafts Cooperative, and had been adopted into the Kaagwaan Taan Wolf Clan of the Eagle Tribe. Survived by two daughters, Jean C. Berg of Seattle and Chloe M. Porter of Chula Vista, CA; and a son, Neil of Lebanon, PA.

MULLER, Meta E. "Auka", 77, a Native Alaskan, died January 5, 1989, in Anchorage. She was born in Teller in 1911 and eventually moved to Nome where she worked as a clerk at the Nome Drug and Jewelry Store. She later moved to Anchorage where she worked for the Alaska Native Medical Center until her retirement in 1977. She was known to her family and friends as "Auka," meaning "Mother" in Eskimo.

NELSON, Hilda O., 97, a longtime Ketchikan resident, died August 2, 1988, in Puyallup, WA. She came to Alaska with her husband in 1925. She was employed by several canneries and worked for *The Alaska Sportsman*. Survivors include a son, Ralph of Nancy Lake and a daughter, Lillian Landoe of Puyallup.

NEWELL, Hollis Maxwell, 86, a longtime Alaskan, died January 8, 1989, in Palmer. He came to Alaska in 1947, pulling one of the first trailer houses over the Alcan Highway. He homesteaded in Spenard and worked at Elmendorf Air Force Base as an accountant-auditor. In 1950, he opened Mountain View Service Station and later built an apartment complex and a mobile home park in the Mountain View area. Survivors include his wife, Delia of Big Lake, two sons and two daughters.

NICHOLOFF, Perry Peter, 60, died June 20, 1988, in Naknek. Lifelong Alaskan, he worked at sea as a deckhand and fisherman. Survived by his daughters, Perri of Fairbanks and Sherry of Cordova; and a son, Peter of Seattle.

NOSICH, John, 73, a 37-year resident of Kodiak, died August 16, 1988. A bartender since 1953, he was a member of Local 878 Bartenders, Hotel and Motel Workers Union. Survivors include his wife, Sally of Kodiak.

NUNLEY, Leo Marvin, 71, first mayor of Wasilla, died January 23, 1989, in Palmer. He arrived in Alaska in 1947 and homesteaded in the Fairview Loop area. He worked as a correctional officer in Palmer until his retirement in 1982. He was an active member of the Wasilla Veterans of Foreign Wars Post 9365, and the National Community Activities Committee. Survivors include his wife, June of Wasilla, four sons and three daughters.

NYGARD, Flora, 82, a longtime Alaskan, died December 9, 1988, in Ketchikan. She came to Alaska in 1914 and made Ketchikan her home. She spent her life as a homemaker and was a member of Moose Lodge No. 162, Eagles Lodge and Pioneers of Alaska. Survivors include her husband, Haakon, son Norman and daughter Joanne Shepard, all of Ketchikan.

O'NEILL, Iloe Slade, 86, a territorial schoolteacher in Alaska during the 1920s, died June 28, 1988, in Seattle. She was raised in Juneau and earned a teaching degree in Bellingham, WA. She returned to Alaska in 1923 and taught throughout the state. Survivors include a daughter, Patricia of Anchorage, and a son, Tom of Seattle.

OFFIELD, Audrey S, 69, a retired civil service worker, died November 12, 1988, in Anchorage. She lived in Alaska for 25 years and resided in Delta Junction for most of that time. Survivors include a son, Ronald of Anchorage, and a daughter, Janice Soderling of Southfield, MI.

OLSEN, Toiva, 68, died October 22, 1988, in Anchorage. Born in Douglas, he was a fisherman and worked in airport maintenance. Survived by his sister, Vleno Evans; and a brother, Donald, both of Anchorage.

OLSON, Edward, 90, a retired miner, died December 23, 1988, in Seattle. He came to Alaska in 1931 and worked in a gold mine near Flat. He helped open a platinum mine on Goodnews Bay in 1934 and served as president and general manager of Goodnews Bay mining Co. until he retired. In 1980, he was awarded the University of Alaska's School of Mineral Industry's Distinguished Award for his mining achievements. Survivors include a daughter, Karen Enberg of Anchorage, and a son, Eugene Olson of Bakersfield, CA.

PARKER, Martha Louise, 82, died March 8, 1989, in Anchorage. Longtime Alaska resident, she worked at Ladd Air Force Base and was active in several organizations. Survived by her two sons, Marvon of Manteca, CA, and James of Anchorage.

PEGUES, Geoffrey P., 54, a native of Juneau, died August 11, 1988, in Anchorage. A Juneau High School graduate, he attended Washington State College and the University of Alaska Fairbanks. He later worked as a right-of-way agent for the state Department of Highways and for the Department of Natural Resources until his retirement two years ago. Survivors include four sons and a daughter.

PERATROVICH, Roy, 88, died in early 1989, in Juneau. Lifelong Alaska resident, he was a grand president emeritus and a lifelong member of the Alaska Native Brotherhood Executive Committee. Survived by his daughter, Loretta Montgomery of Moses Lake, WA; two sons, Frank of Juneau and Roy Jr. of Anchorage; and numerous grandchildren and great-grandchildren.

PERKINS, Margaret C. 84, a 62-year resident of Alaska, died December 24, 1988, in Fairbanks. She arrived in Alaska in 1927 and worked as a nurse for the copper mine in Kennecott. She later moved to Fairbanks, where she and her husband owned Sig Wold Storage and Transfer. She retired in 1965 and made her home at Harding Lake. She was a member of the Eagles Lodge, Eastern Star and Pioneers of Alaska.

PERME, Louis Frank, 70, a retired construction worker and World War II Veteran, died July 21, 1988. He served in the U.S. Army from 1941 to 1945. In 1947, he moved to Fairbanks, where he entered the construction trade. He was a member of the American Legion Dorman H. Baker Post No. 11 and Carpenters Local No. 1243. He is survived by five sisters and one brother.

PERRY, Joseph Andrew "Sonny", 60, died June 16, 1988, in Anchorage. He came to Alaska in 1958 and worked as an operator and welder in various oil fields in Alaska. He leaves behind two sons and three daughters.

PERRY, Mary, 83, longtime Fairbanks resident, died late 1988, in Payson, AZ. She came to Fairbanks in the early 1940s and was a nurse at St. Joseph Hospital for many years. Survivors include her husband, Bob of Payson.

PHILLIPS, Phil D., 53, of Valdez, died August 13, 1988, in Anchorage. He came to Alaska in 1966, and worked as a heavy equipment operating engineer and as a commercial fisherman. He was a 15-year member of the Eagles Aerie No. 1971 in Valdez. Survivors include his wife, Jean of Valdez, four daughters and three sons.

POLIS, John Sr., 81, a longtime Alaskan, died October 29, 1988, in Anchorage. He came to Alaska in 1930 and worked in the Kennecott Copper Mine and for the Alaska Railroad. In the early 1950s, he purchased the Wasilla Bar and Polis' Lakeside Hotel on the Parks Highway, where he cooked and tended bar before retiring in 1973. Survivors include two sons and three daughters.

POWERS, Warren D., 83, a 40-year resident of Wrangell, died October 21, 1988, in Ketchikan. He came to Alaska in 1929 as a merchant marine and jumped ship in Kake. He later moved to Ketchikan and then to Wrangell, where he made his living as a commercial fisherman. Survivors include three sons, Warren, Jr. and Darrell, both of Wrangell, and Jerry of Tacoma, WA., and a daughter, Donna Roach of Wrangell.

PRESCOTT, Edith "Peggy", 88, died August 9, 1988, in Wrangell. She arrived in 1935 in Wrangell, where she worked for the U.S. Weather Bureau for more than 20 years. Survivors include a daughter, Mercedes Angerman, and a son, Mitchell Prescott, both of Wrangell.

PRINGLE, Archie, 86, died March 19, 1989, in Tagert, OR. Alaska resident since 1927, he mined and lived at Manley Hot Springs until 1985.

RADFORD, Seba "Jean", 70, died June 27, 1988, in Anchorage. She had lived in Alaska for 35 years and was the owner/operator of LaHonda Trailer Court in Anchorage. She enjoyed politics and was an avid gardener. Survivors include her son, Milton of Anchorage.

RAPUZZI, Edna Dorothy Nelson, 87, of Skagway, died July 31, 1988, in San Diego. She came to Skagway in the late 1920s as a schoolteacher. She and her husband were later known for their extensive collection of gold rush artifacts. Survivors include a sister, Florence Olsen Batty of San Diego.

RASMUSSEN, Mae Lorraine "Larry", 70, a former Anchorage wine consultant, died November 1, 1988, in Modesto, CA. She came to Anchorage in 1952, where she worked for 22 years as a wine consultant and manager of the Library of Fine Spirits. She also founded a wine appreciation club called Les Amis du Vin. Survivors include four sons and two daughters.

RAUSCH, Frances G., 65, of Juneau, died October 11, 1988, in Honolulu. She drove to Alaska in 1956 with a friend, expecting to stay a week, but stayed for 33 years. A retired U.S. Fish & Wildlife employee, she spent the remainder of her life traveling. Survivors include her daughter, Ann of Juneau.

REECE, William S. "Bish" Sr., a Metlakatla native, died August 22, 1988, in Metlakatla. He spent most of his life in southeastern Alaska. He worked as a power and light operator, a police officer and a commercial fisherman. He later worked for the Federal Aviation Administration in Ketchikan and Anchorage. Survivors include his wife, Doris of Metlakatla, three sons and two daughters.

REED, Lela, 73, of Moose Pass, died October 10, 1988, in Charlo, MT. In 1956, she and her husband came to Moose Pass, where they owned and operated Reed's Jewelry. Survivors include a daughter, Jackie Firestone of Charlo.

REED, Morgan William Sr., 84, a resident of Skagway for more than 40 years, died July 21, 1988. He came to Alaska 46 years ago to work on the Alaska Highway and soon thereafter made Skagway his home. He is survived by his wife, Blodwen of Skagway, and five sons.

REINDL, Joseph A., 65, founder and president of Geophysical Corporation of Alaska, died August 14, 1988, in Anchorage. A 42-year resident of Alaska, he was a graduate of the University of Alaska School of Mines in Fairbanks. He served with the U.S. Navy during World War II aboard a destroyer in the Pacific theater. He spent his career in the geophysical industry and, in addition to establishing his own company, was an early pioneer in oil exploration in Alaska. Survivors include his wife, Natalie of Anchorage.

REYNOLDS, William A., 75, an Anchorage resident for more than 40 years, died August 17, 1988, in Anchorage. A U.S. Marine Corps veteran, he moved to Alaska 41 years ago to work for the Alaska Railroad. He was later employed by Chugach Electric Association until he co-founded Alchem Inc., a local construction company. He was a member of the Alaska Building Industry Association, National Association of Home Builders and the Pioneers of Alaska Igloo No. 4. Survivors include his wife, Louise, and twin sons, Philip and Kent, all of Anchorage.

ROBERTSON, Wayne E., 56, an Alaska resident for more than 40 years, died August 11, 1988, in Anchorage. He was a veteran of the U.S. Army and worked in construction throughout Anchorage in the early 1950s. He owned and operated a heating and oil company from 1961 to 1974, and then tended an Anchorage bar until 1982. He was a member of the American Legion Post No. 15 in Palmer. Survivors include his wife, Rosel of Anchorage, and three sons, Charles and Christopher of Seattle, WA, and Wayne of Anchorage.

RONHOLDT, Roy, 72, died April 5, 1989, in Anchorage.

Longtime Alaska resident, he worked in logging, lumber mills and fishing, and was part-owner of Columbia Lumber Company. Survived by his wife, Emma; three daughters, Roylene McElroy, Shirley Otte and Cindy McCullough; and four sons, Roy Jr., John and Robert Ronholdt, and Sid McCullough, all of Anchorage.

ROOT, Mary Elizabeth, 71, died October 27, 1988, in Kodiak. A resident of Kodiak since 1941, she worked for Pacific Northern Airlines and Western Airlines for 25 years. Survivors include her husband, Vincent W. Root of Kodiak.

RUST, Elizabeth F., 62, died October 24, 1988, in Ukiah, CA. Born to pioneers, Clara and Jesse Rust of Fairbanks, she operated a marina, and was a member of the Pioneers and the Emblem Club. She was also the author of This Old House, the story of her mother and family. Survived by her daughter, Barbara Buchignani of Sebastopol, CA; and two sons, Joseph Aggi of Chico, CA and Christopher Aggi of Ukiah; and five granchildren.

RUST, George, F., 66, a lifelong Alaskan, died October 8, 1988, in Kenai. He lived in Fairbanks until World War II, when he joined the U.S. Navy and served overseas. After the war, he settled on the Kenai Peninsula, where he made his living as an iron-worker and as a commercial fisherman. He was a member of the Pioneers of Alaska, the Fraternal Order of Eagles, the American Legion and other social organizations. Survivors include his wife, Helene, and sons Ronald and Donald, all of Kenai.

SCHMIDT, Charles A., 82, a longtime Juneau resident, died November, 1988, in Juneau. He was a stunt pilot in the 1920s before moving to Ketchikan to work for Ellis Airlines. He moved to Juneau in 1949 and worked for the Government Services Administration until his retirement. Survivors include his wife, Juliet of Juneau, and two sons.

SCHWANDT, Albert E., 82, a longtime Alaska resident, died June 23 at his home in Copper Center. A retired Teamsters Union member, he had worked on the construction of the Alaska Highway during World War II. He was an avid outdoorsman and big game hunter. He had lived in Alaska for 46 years, and in Copper Center for the last 30 years. Survivors include his son, Dale, and his daughter, Shirley Dedrick, both of Milwaukee, WI.

SCOBY, Mabel K., 77, a 40-year Alaska resident, died December 6, 1988, in Smyrna, GA. She and her husband built Forty-Mile Roadhouse at Tetlin Junction in 1948. The roadhouse became a popular truckstop which she operated until 1976. She was an ardent supporter of the Tok Dog Musher's Association. Survivors include a daughter, Joann Henry of Smyrna, and a son, Jack of Seward.

SCROGGS, Don Roy, 52, died September 16, 1988, in Topeka, KS. He grew up in Kodiak and later homesteaded on the Kenai Peninsula. In his youth, he fished commercially for king crab, and later worked in construction. Survivors include three sons and three daughters.

SELMER, Elizabeth "Betty", 87, a longtime resident of Skagway, died January 30, 1989, in Sitka. She arrived in Skagway in 1925 as a tourist aboard the Princess Nora and adopted Alaska as her home. She taught at the Pius X Mission and Skagway Public School until retiring in 1966. She was a founder of the Trail of '98 Museum and served as a library volunteer for 50 years. Survivors include a daughter and a son.

SENUNGETUK, Stanley "Skip", 50, a lifelong Alaskan, died May 27, 1988, in Anchorage. Born in the village of Wales, he attended the University of Alaska Fairbanks and later spent 15 years as a schoolteacher. Survivors include his wife, Edna of Shishmaref, and his mother, Helen of Nome.

SHAFFER, Ellen Nelson, 83, died September 9, 1988, in Seattle. She came to Alaska in 1921, and lived in Juneau and Ketchikan. She enjoyed music and was known for her piano performances. She also was a member of the Pioneers of Alaska. Survivors include a son, Edward Shaffer of Seattle, and a daughter, Patricia Soroko of Wallingford, CT.

SHIPMAN, John L., 73, a retired U.S. Air Force officer, died May 17, 1988, at Elmendorf Air Force Base. He arrived in Alaska in 1951, leaving temporarily for tours of duty in Vietnam. He was a Boy Scout leader and a member of the Masonic Lodge in Iowa and Chi Epsilon. Survivors include his wife, Enafae of Anchorage, a son and three daughters.

SIDARS, James R., 65, a 39-year Alaska resident, died November 20, 1988, in Fairbanks. He served with the U.S. Army Corps of Engineers during World War II and was later assigned to Ladd Field. Following his discharge, he joined the Civil Service and worked with the Post Engineers until his retirement. He was a member of the Shriners, Masons, Pioneers of Alaska Igloo No. 4 and the Horseless Carriage Club. Survivors include his wife, June Rust Sidars of Fairbanks, one son and three daughters.

SIMPSON, James "Big Jim", 85, a lifelong cook, died January 1, 1989, in Fairbanks. He came to Alaska in 1930 after a career in the Merchant Marine. He worked as a cook with the Bristol Bay salmon fishing fleet during the 1930s. In 1946 he cooked for crews in the Aleutians that were dismantling military equipment. He also worked for the hospital in Tanana, the U.S. Dredge and Mining Co. at Chatanika, and at Chicken when the gold dredges were operating.

SING, Sam A. "Spike", 66, a Sitka native, died August 10, 1988, in San Antonio, TX. He served with the U.S. Army during World War II and later joined Alaska's first National Guard company. He was employed by the Bureau of Indian Affairs before moving to Seattle in the early 1960s to work as a painter at a U.S. Navy shipyard. Survivors include four daughters.

SMITH, Walter Willis, 60, a retired construction worker, died in Anchorage February 1, 1988. He arrived in Ketchikan in 1954 and later made Anchorage his permanent home. His work took him throughout the state where the construction of schools, hospitals and power plants were among his many projects. A member of the Asbestos Workers Local No. 97 for 33 years, he also belonged to a number of social organizations and was an avid outdoorsman. He is survived by his wife, Mary.

SNYDER, Marvin C. "Tige", 79, a retired cannery foreman, died January 13, 1989, in Cathlamet, WA. A resident of Yakutat in the early 1950s, he recently retired from Bumble Bee Inc. in Naknek after working 41 years in Alaska canneries. Survivors include his wife, Ora of Cathlamet, and two sons.

SOCKPICK, Teddy O., 81, died June 14, 1988, in Anchorage. He was a custodian for the state of Alaska. Survivors include his wife, Holly of Nome.

SOLOMON, Madeline "Halohooltunn", 83, a Native Alaskan, died September 18, 1988, in Galena. Born on the Kateel River, she attended the Holy Cross Catholic Mission for four years. She later became a faculty member at the University of Alaska Fairbanks, where she taught Native culture. She also wrote the book Koyukon Athabscan Dance Songs.

SPALDING, Robert F., 77, died February 1, 1989, in Fairbanks. He came to Alaska in 1941 and worked throughout the state as a plumber. He joined the United Association of Plumbers and Pipefitters in

1934 and was a member of Local 375 in Fairbanks for 26 years. He also was a member of Pioneers of Alaska Igloo No. 4, Fraternal Order of the Eagles, National Rifle Association and many other social organizations. Survivors include a sister, Virginia Murray of Huntington Beach, CA.

STADEM, Peder K., 87, a longtime Alaska resident, died December 9, 1988, in Palmer. He came to Alaska in 1928 and worked for Diamond X cannery in Bristol Bay. He later made his living as a trapper, shipwright and as a commercial fisherman in the Bristol Bay region. He was a member of the Bering Sea Fisherman's Association and the Alaska Fisherman's Union. Survivors include two sons and a daughter.

STEVENS, Mike, 86, died June 15, 1988, in a nursing home in Grants Pass, OR. He moved to Alaska with his family in 1948, where he spent 15 years as a logger in Seward and Haines before moving to Skagway. Survivors include his wife, Helen of Anchorage.

STOLL, Lawrence A., 74, died August 27, 1988, in Seattle. He arrived in Alaska in 1953 and worked for the Alaska Department of Fish & Game and, later, the University of Alaska. He was a member of the Pioneers of Alaska Igloo No. 34. Survivors include his wife, Harriet of Haines.

STOLTZ, Roy James Sr., 71, bar owner and bush pilot, died October 10, 1988, in Fairbanks. He came to Alaska in 1947 and became a bartender in Fairbanks. He began taking flying lessons in 1978 and eventually became a bush pilot, transporting outdoorsmen to and from remote points of the state. Survivors include his wife, Vera of Fairbanks.

STOWELL, Charles W. "Charlie," 60, died December 28, 1988, in Fairbanks. He came to Alaska in 1947 and worked as a gold miner and heavy equipment mechanic. He was a member of Operating Engineers Local 302 since 1949. Survivors include his wife, Rosalyn of Fairbanks, two sons and three daughters.

SUCKLING, Elizabeth, 72, died September 4, 1988, in Sequim, WA. Longtime Alaska resident, she taught school in Fairbanks and Bethel, and was principal and superintendent of schools at Ladd Field. Survived by her sister, Dr. Minnie Wells of Sequim.

SWIFT-CARTER, Sarah, 92, died August 15, 1988, in Juneau. She arrived in Juneau in 1963. She taught music for 15 years and was active in the Church of the Holy Trinity. Survivors include two sons, Robert C. Townsend of Higganum, CT, and Christopher R. Townsend of Scottsdale, AZ.

THOMPSON, Charles O. "Tommy", 85, early Fairbanks pioneer, died October 1, 1988, in Daytona Beach, FL. He came in 1922 to Alaska, where he worked as a miner in Livengood. He attended the University of Alaska and graduated in 1930. Survivors include his wife, Florence and two sons.

THOMPSON, Wilma F. "Granny", 92, mother of former Kenai Peninsula Borough Mayor Stan Thompson, died September 22, 1988, in Anchorage. She arrived in Alaska with her husband in 1944 and taught school in Nenana. She later taught in Nome, Seldovia, Fairbanks and Kenai. She was a charter member of the Church of the New Covenant in Kenai and was known for her instrumental role in building the church. Survivors include a son, Jerry Thompson of Kenai, and daughters Martha Anderson of Kenai and Mary Eidem of Anchorage.

TRENT, Walter M., 67, a longtime Sitka resident, died December 29, 1988, in Sitka. He came to Sitka in 1932 and worked as a commercial fisherman. He was inducted into the U.S. Army during World War II and was in command of an Army supply boat in the Aleutian Islands. He returned to Sitka after the war and worked as an engineer for Sitka Cold Storage Co. He later worked for Alaska Lumber and Pulp Co. He was a member of the Benevolent and Protective Order of the Elks, Sitka Lodge 1662; the Coast Guard Auxiliary Search and Rescue Unit; Pioneers of Alaska; Sitka Sportsman's Association and many other social organizations. Survivors include his wife, Nellie, two daughters, a son and a stepson.

TURNER, Caroline "Charlie", 84, a longtime Juneau resident died August 10, 1988, in Sitka. She arrived in Juneau in 1943, where she was manager of MacKinnon Apartments for 26 years. She was a member of Rebecca Lodge, Pioneers of Alaska and United Methodist Women. She is survived by a daughter, Phyllis T. Cashen of San Diego, CA.

URIE, Sidney M "Sid", 61, of Seward, died September 8, 1988, in Kailua-Kona, HI. Born near Seward, he joined the U.S. Navy when he was 17 and returned to Seward in 1944 to graduate from the local high school. He attended the University of Alaska Fairbanks for two years and later became a business owner in Kodiak. He was a member of the Seward Elks Club, Masonic Lodge and VFW.

WARDLE, Harold C., 64, a retired Anchorage bartender, died August 12, 1988, in Anchorage. He had lived in Alaska for 45 years. He served with the Alaska Scouts in World War II and later tended bar in Anchorage until 1977. Survivors include his wife, Helen "Pat" Wardle of Anchorage, three sons and two daughters.

WARNER, Nova Eldon, 70, a longtime Skagway resident, died September 3, 1988, in Skagway. He came to Alaska in 1948 and worked as a longshoreman in Skagway until his retirement in 1983. He also owned and operated a propane business called the White House. He was active in the Presbyterian church where he served as an elder. Survivors include his wife, Wanda of Skagway, three sons and a daughter.

WEBER, Rika V., 59, died October 15, 1988, in Kodiak. Legally blind since birth, she spent her early childhood battling tuberculosis in a Seattle hospital. She later returned to her home in Kodiak, where she married and raised a family. Survivors include her husband, William, and three daughters, Helen M. Wandersee, Cindy Weber, and Frances Weber, all of Kodiak.

WENNERSTROM, Bertel A., 85, one of the last members of the Golden Spike Veterans Club, died November 12, 1988, in Anchorage. He came to Alaska in 1920 and went to work with the Alaska Railroad. When he retired in 1964, he was one of two employees who had been with the Alaska Railroad since President Harding drive the golden spike on July 15, 1923, that signified the completion of the railroad. He was a member of the Elks Lodge and Pioneers of Alaska Igloo No. 15. Survivors include his wife, Mae of Anchorage.

WENTZ, Henry Ernest, 66, a lifelong Alaskan, died November 13, 1988, in Juneau. He served with the U.S. Army in World War II and the Korean War. He later settled in Juneau. He made his living as a commercial fisherman, boat builder, cannery worker and Native artist. Survivors include his wife, Mary Ann of Juneau, a daughter and four sons.

WERNER, Harold J. "Buz", 74, died April 4, 1989, in Anchorage. Longtime Alaska resident, he worked as a trucker, and was a member of the Pioneers of Alaska, the Teamsters and the Elks Club. Survived by his wife, Mollie of Palmer; a daughter, Deborah Tolen of Portland, OR; and two stepdaughters,

Nancy Brauch and Candice Dielema, both of Anchorage.

WESCOTT, Libby, 74, champion dog musher and pioneer, died October 1, 1988, in Fairbanks. She came to Alaska with her husband in 1942 and worked for the U.S. Army in Whittier and Seward. After World War II, she moved to Fairbanks, where she worked as secretary of the Tanana Valley Fair Association. Dog mushing was her passion and she won the American Sled Dog Championship in 1960.

WICKERSHAM, Martha E., 75, former Homer restaurant owner, died October 7, 1988, in Homer. She came to Alaska in 1950, where she and her husband owned and operated several restaurants in Anchorage and Homer. She was known for her hospitality and excellent culinary skills. Survivors include a son and five daughters.

WIDMARK, Dr. Alfred E. Sr., 84, a lifelong Alaskan, died January 10, 1989, in Seattle. Born in Haines, he attended Sheldon Jackson School and received a degree from Oregon State University in 1935, where he majored in pharmacy. He moved to Klawock in 1937 where he owned and operated the Sand Point Co. general store until 1967. He was one of the first Tlingits to serve as a member of the Alaska State Legislature in 1961 and 1962. In 1967 he was appointed deputy director of the Local Affairs Office to handle government relations with the state. He was a past grand president of the Alaska Native Brotherhood, former executive committee member of the Tlingit-Haida Central Council and an ANB representative and vice president to the National Congress of American Indians. Survivors include five daughters and two sons.

WILCOX, Helen Elizabeth Upper, 94, died February 10, 1989, in Anchorage. Longtime Alaska resident, she taught school in Fairbanks and Anchorage, and was librarian at the University of Alaska. She was active in many clubs and as a volunteer. Survived by a daughter, Elizabeth of Seattle; two sons, Donald of Anchorage and James of Seattle; 17 grandchildren; 32 great-grandchildren; and five great-great-grandchildren.

WILSON, Stanley G., 62, a native of Kenai, died December 18, 1988, in Kenai. He worked as a laborer and bartender prior to his retirement. He was a member of the Kenai Moose Lodge and American Legion Post 20. Survivors include a brother, Howard Wilson of Kenai.

WINSOR, Charlotte S., 75, died December 21, 1988, in Portland, OR. She came to Alaska in 1950 and was a teacher for the Bureau of Indian Affairs in Hooper Bay. She later taught in Bethel, Fairbanks, Anchorage and Juneau. Survivors include her husband, Paul L. Winsor.

WOLFE, Vera, 82, died July 17, 1988, in Seward. She arrived in 1947 in Seward, where she taught school. In 1949, she moved to Moose Pass, where she continued to teach and became active in the local United Methodist Church. She is survived by her husband, Delbert of Moose Pass and her son, Matthew of Seward.

WOOD, Vincent Vernon, 66, died June 24 in Anchorage. He moved to Alaska in 1953, where he worked as an aircraft mechanic at Elmendorf Air Force Base and Anchorage International Airport. He was a member of the Elks Club and the Veterans of Foreign Wars in Valley City, ND. Survivors include his wife, Mary of Anchorage.

WOODRUFF, James R., 73, died January 22, 1989, in Seattle. He worked several years as circulation manager of the *Juneau Empire* and started his own newspaper, the *Juneau Independent* in the mid-1950s. He later worked for the Bureau of Indian Affairs from which he retired in 1979. Survivors include his wife, Gertrude of Gresham, OR.

WRIGHT, Cherie Louise, 74, died November 26, 1988, in Sitka. She came to Alaska in 1953, and operated the Federal Cafe and the Totem Cafe in Ketchikan for a short time before moving to Fairbanks. In 1958, she moved to Sitka and operated an auto dealership with her husband. Survivors include her husband, Virgil of Sitka, two sons and three daughters.

WRIGHT, Neal, 83, died April 13, 1989, in Snohomish, WA. Alaska resident since 1933, and Palmer pharmacist and businessman since 1935. His store, long a Palmer landmark, was the central gathering point for many years. Survived by his wife, Marie of Snohomish; and a daughter, Bridgie Peruse of Auburn, WA.

ZAHN, Milstead "Mil", 57, retired executive director of the Alaska Department of Fish & Game board of game and fish, died September, 1988. He worked for the U.S. Fish & Wildlife Service and enforced fish and game regulations prior to statehood. He moved in 1964 to the National Marine Fisheries Service, where he investigated treaty violations in the fisheries of the Aleutian Islands and the Bering Sea. Survivors include his wife, Mary, and daughters Tanya and Natasha, all of Juneau.

ZIEGMAN, Irving John "Ziggy", 79, former manager of K&L Distributors in Anchorage, died July 25, 1988, in Seattle, WA. Born in Russia in 1909, he later came to Alaska and served as a U.S. Navy Sea Bee in the Aleutians during World War II. He moved to Anchorage in 1946 and was general manager of K&L Distributors until 1969. He is survived by his wife, Anne of Seattle, his two daughters, Vivian of Israel, and Lori of Los Angeles, CA, and a son, Steve of Healy.

Energy and Power

For the purposes of classifying power usage, the state of Alaska can be divided into three major regions, each having similar energy patterns, problems and resources: the Extended Railbelt region; the Southeast region; and the Bush region.

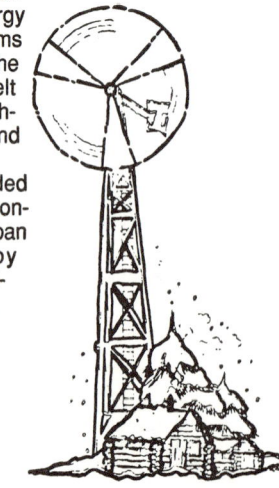

The Extended Railbelt region consists of major urban areas linked by the Alaska Railroad (Seward, Anchorage and Fairbanks). The south-central area of this region uses relatively inexpensive natural gas in Cook Inlet and small hydroelectrical power plants for electrical production and heating. The Fairbanks-Tanana Valley area uses primarily coal, and also oil, to meet its electrical needs. Future electrical demand for the Railbelt region will be met by a combination of hydropower and coal- and gas-fired generators. Currently in the planning stages are several major hydropower projects for this region.

The Southeast region relies on hydropower for a large portion of its electrical generation. (Most of the existing hydroelectric power projects in Alaska are located in the Southeast region and more are planned.) In the smaller communities, diesel generators are used.

The Bush region includes all communities that are remote from the major urban areas of the Extended Railbelt and Southeast regions. Electricity in bush communities is typically provided by small diesel generators. Thirty-four wind turbines are currently operating in the windy coastal areas of the Bush region and more are planned. Where wind projects are feasible, such as those at Nelson Lagoon and Unalakleet, wind power can be a viable, fuel-saving alternative to diesel-powered generators. Thermal needs in the Bush are currently being met almost entirely by heating oil. Wood and kerosene heaters are used to a limited extent. Natural gas is available in Barrow.

Eskimo Ice Cream

Also called *akutak* (Yup'ik Eskimo word for Eskimo ice cream), this classic Native delicacy, popular throughout Alaska, is traditionally made of whipped berries, seal oil and snow. Sometimes shortening, raisins and sugar are added. In different regions, different variations are found. One favored variation uses the soopalallie berry, *Shepherdia canadensis,* a bitter species that forms a frothy mass like soapsuds when beaten. Another name for the soopalallie berry is soapberry.

Related reading: *Alaska Wild Berry Guide and Cookbook,* by the Alaska Northwest Publishing editors. How to find, identify and prepare Alaska's wild berries.

216 pages, $14.95. From the same people, *Cooking Alaskan.* More than 1,500 recipes for cooking Alaska style. 500 pages, $16.95. See ALASKA NORTHWEST LIBRARY in the back of the book.

Ferries

The state Department of Transportation and Public Facilities, Marine Highway System, provides year-round scheduled ferry service for passengers and vehicles to communities in southeastern and southwestern Alaska. (The southeastern and southwestern Alaska state ferry systems do not connect with each other.)

A fleet of seven ferries on the southeastern system connects Bellingham, Washington and Prince Rupert, British Columbia, with the Southeastern Alaska ports of Hyder/Stewart, Ketchikan, Metlakatla, Hollis, Wrangell, Petersburg, Kake, Sitka, Angoon, Pelican, Hoonah, Tenakee Springs, Juneau, Haines and Skagway. These southeastern communities — with the exception of Hyder, Haines and Skagway — are accessible only by ferry or by airplane. The seven vessels of the southeastern system are the *Aurora, Columbia, Chilkat, LeConte, Malaspina, Matanuska* and *Taku.*

Southwestern Alaska is served by two ferries. The *Tustumena* serves Seward, Port Lions, Kodiak, Homer, Seldovia, Cordova and Valdez, with limited summer service to Chignik, Sand Point, King Cove, Cold Bay and Dutch Harbor. In summer, the *Bartlett* provides service between Valdez, Cordova and Whittier.

Scheduled state ferry service to southeastern Alaska began in 1963; ferry service to Kodiak Island began in 1964. The first three ferries of the Alaska ferry fleet were the *Malaspina, Matanuska* and *Taku,* built at an approximate cost of $4.5 million each. The names were selected by then-governor William A. Egan.

Reservations should be made for all sailings. Senior Citizen passes and Handicapped Persons passes are available. The address of the main office of the Alaska Marine Highway System is Box R, Juneau 99811; phone (907) 465-3941; or toll free, 1-800-642-0066.

Embarking Passenger and Vehicle Totals (in thousands) on Alaskan Mainline Ferries**

Southeastern System

	Passengers	Vehicles
1988	234.6	62.2
1987	215.2	55.8
1986	214.8	56.5
1985	213.0	56.4
1984	57.8	214.9
1983	52.6	206.1
1982	51.0	220.0
1981	44.1*	181.5*
1980	44.3	189.5
1979	42.9	169.4
1978	38.6	161.9
1977	40.0	148.5
1976	46.3	181.7
1975	45.9	184.5
1974	41.4	174.7
1973	38.4	162.7
1972	39.4	162.7
1970	28.5	137.2
1965	25.8	123.7

Southwestern System

	Passengers	Vehicles
1988	50.4	16.6
1987	52.0	16.5
1986	51.8	16.0
1985	56.1	16.4
1984	55.8	15.5
1983	55.5	15.9
1982	57.0	15.5
1981	55.8	15.1
1980	49.4	14.0
1979	48.9	13.8
1978	46.6	13.2
1977	38.8	12.5
1976	44.4	11.7
1975	45.0	12.8
1974	44.6	12.4
1973	40.7	11.3
1972	35.9	9.9
1971	25.8	7.7
1970	6.9	3.2

*Does not include totals of passengers (9.5) and vehicles (2.9) on the MV *Aurora*.
**Mainline ports for Southeast are: Seattle, Vancouver (1970 to 1973 only), Prince Rupert, Ketchikan, Wrangell, Petersburg, Sitka, Juneau, Haines and Skagway. Mainline ports for southwestern Alaska are: Anchorage (1970 to 1973 only), Cordova, Valdez, Whittier, Homer, Seldovia, Kodiak, Seward and Port Lions.

Alaska State Ferry Data

Aurora: (235 feet, 14 knots), 250 passengers, 47 vehicles, no cabins, began service in 1977.
Bartlett: (193 feet, 14 knots), 170 passengers, 38 vehicles, no cabins, began service in 1969.
Chilkat: (99 feet, 10 knots), 75 passengers, 15 vehicles, no cabins, began service in 1959.
Columbia: (418 feet, 19 knots), 1,000 passengers, 170 vehicles, 96 cabins, began service in 1973.
LeConte (235 feet, 14 knots), 258 passengers, 47 vehicles, no cabins, began service in 1974.
Malaspina: (408 feet, 16.5 knots), 750 passengers, 120 vehicles, 86 cabins, began service in 1963 and was lengthened and renovated in 1972.
Matanuska: (408 feet, 16.5 knots), 750 passengers, 120 vehicles, 112 cabins, began service in 1963.
Taku: (352 feet, 16 knots), 500 passengers, 105 vehicles, 30 cabins, began service in 1963.
Tustumena: (296 feet, 14 knots), 220 passengers, 50 vehicles, 27 cabins, began service in 1964.

Nautical Miles between Ports
Southeastern System

Seattle-Ketchikan	650
Seattle-Prince Rupert	573
Prince Rupert-Ketchikan	91
Ketchikan-Metlakatla	16
Ketchikan-Hollis	40
Hollis-Petersburg	122
Hollis-Wrangell	95
Ketchikan-Wrangell	89
Wrangell-Petersburg	41
Petersburg-Juneau	108
Petersburg-Kake	59
Kake-Sitka	110
Sitka-Angoon	66
Angoon-Tenakee	33
Tenakee-Hoonah	47
Angoon-Hoonah	60
Hoonah-Juneau (AB)*	45
Sitka-Hoonah	115
Hoonah-Pelican via South Pass	58
Hoonah-Juneau	68
Juneau-Haines	91
Haines-Skagway	13
Juneau (AB)-Haines	68
Petersburg-Juneau (AB)	120
Petersburg-Sitka	156
Juneau (AB)-Sitka	136

*AB-Auke Bay

Southwestern System
Seward-Cordova 146
Seward-Valdez 143
Cordova-Valdez 73
Valdez-Whittier 84
Seward-Kodiak 175
Kodiak-Port Lions 27
Kodiak-Homer 126
Homer-Seldovia 16
Kodiak-Sand Point via
  Sitkinak Strait 353

Fires on Wild Land

The 1988 fire season saw continued inter-agency cooperation in fighting fires on state and federal lands throughout Alaska, in the worst fire season in more than a decade.

The state of Alaska and the Bureau of Land Management share responsibility for fighting wild land fires in Alaska. The BLM Alaska Fire Service fights all fires in the northern part of the state, and the state of Alaska Division of Forestry is responsible for fires in the southern part of the state.

Since 1982, the Department of the Interior has operated the Alaska Fire Service, which is responsible for initial fire control on all lands in the northern section of the state. The development of the AFS allowed the Bureau of Land Management, the National Park Service, Fish and Wildlife Service, Bureau of Indian Affairs, Native corporations and the state, to develop fire protection goals and guidelines for public lands in Alaska.

The AFS and the state share training and use of fire-fighting personnel. They also send fire fighters to the Lower 48 when necessary and receive assistance from fire fighters in other states. In 1988, Alaska sent about 1,400 fire fighters to other states, particularly to Montana to help with the Yellowstone National Park wildfires. The AFS has approximately 1,100 emergency fire fighters and 400 fire management personnel in Alaska (95 are smoke jumpers). Most emergency fire fighters are village residents who are trained by AFS personnel and hired on a temporary basis for fire emergencies.

Lightning is the leading cause of wild land fires in Alaska, accounting for 80.7 percent of reported fires in 1986 — a typical year. Man-caused fires followed at 9.6 percent. False alarms also accounted for 9.6 percent of the reports.

The largest single fire ever recorded in Alaska burned 1,161,200 acres 74 miles northwest of Galena in 1957, according to BLM. In 1977, the Bear Creek fire, largest in the United States that year, consumed 361,000 acres near the Farewell airstrip. The same fire season, the BLM logged 24,000 flying hours and smoke jumpers made a record 1,795 jumps.

The chart below shows the number of fires and acres burned from 1956 through mid-September 1988. The 1983, 1984, 1987 and 1988 figures show combined totals: fires dealt with by the Alaska Fire Service plus those put out by the state of Alaska. Separately, in 1987, the AFS fought 165 fires over 146,551 acres, and the state controlled 541 fires over 12,300 acres.

Calendar Year	No. of Fires	Acres Burned
1956	226	476,593
1957	391	5,049,661
1958	278	317,215
1959	320	596,574
1960	238	87,180
1961	117	5,100
1962	102	38,975
1963	194	16,290
1964	164	3,430
1965	148	7,093
1966	256	672,765
1967	207	109,005
1968	442	1,013,301
1969	511	4,231,820
1970	487	113,486
1971	472	1,069,108
1972	641	963,686
1973	336	59,816
1974	782	662,960
1975	344	127,845
1976	622	69,119
1977	681	2,209,408
1978	356	7,757
1979	620	432,425
1980	417	188,778
1981	556	758,335
1982	283	70,798
1983	800	109,187*
1984	845	122,901*
1985	261	372,230
1986	396	395,169
1987	706	158,851*
1988	639	2,167,795*

*Combined AFS (federal) and state coverage.

Fish Wheel

Widely used for subsistence salmon, the fish wheel, fastened to a river shore, is a current-propelled machine that scoops up fish heading upstream to spawn, providing an easy and inexpensive way of catching salmon without injuring them. Contrary to popular belief, Alaska Natives did not invent the fish wheel. Non-natives apparently first introduced the fish wheel on the Tanana River in 1904. Soon after, it appeared on the Yukon River, where it was used by both settlers and Natives. It first appeared on the Kuskokwim in 1914, when prospectors introduced it for catching salmon near Georgetown.

Today, subsistence fishing with the use of a fish wheel is allowed on the Copper River as well as the Yukon River and its tributaries. Currently, there are 166 limited-entry permits for the use of fish wheels by commercial salmon fishermen on the Yukon River system — the only district where subsistence fishermen use the same gear. Commercial and subsistence fishing times with the wheels are regulated.

Prior to its appearance in Alaska, the fish wheel was used on the East Coast, on the Sacramento River in California and on the Columbia River.

Fishing

COMMERCIAL

Alaska's commercial fish production is greater in value than that of any other state in the country ($1.3 billion in 1988), and first in volume (2.6 billion pounds in 1988) according to the National Marine Fisheries Service.

Value and Volume of Alaska Fish and Shellfish Landings

Year	Value	Volume (in pounds)
1976	$219,071,000	600,203,000
1977	333,844,000	658,754,000
1978	482,207,000	767,167,000
1979	622,284,000	854,247,000
1980	561,751,000	983,664,000
1981	639,797,000	975,245,000
1982	575,569,000	878,935,000
1983	543,941,000	963,765,000
1984	509,300,000	1,002,909,000
1985	590,751,000	1,184,807,000
1986	752,417,000	1,236,062,000
1987	941,690,000	1,697,547,000
1988	1,339,394,000	2,639,250,000

Source: National Marine Fisheries Service, U.S. Department of Commerce

Value of U.S. commercial fish landings caught off Alaska in 1988 of $1.3 billion was followed by: Louisiana, second in value at $317 million; Massachusetts, $274 million; and California, $199 million.

Volume of Alaska's commercial fish landings in 1988 (another record year) of 2.6 billion pounds exceeded Louisiana, which recorded a volume of 1.4 billion pounds. In 1987, in world commercial fishery landings, Japan was first with 26.1 billion pounds, the USSR was second with 24.6 billion pounds, China was third with 20.6 billions pounds, and the U.S. fourth with 12.7 billion pounds.

In 1988, out of the top 10 U.S. ports in terms of value, Alaska held six positions. Kodiak was first with $166.3 million in commercial fish landings; Dutch Harbor-Unalaska was third with $100.9 million; Kenai was fourth with $99.3 million; Petersburg was sixth with $58.5 million; Cordova was eighth with $46.4 million; and Ketchikan was tenth with $43.5 million.

Joint venture fisheries peaked in 1987, and though there was a decline in volume in 1988, value continued to increase. Joint ventures are catches by U.S. vessels unloaded onto foreign vessels within the U.S. Exclusive Economic Zone (EEZ). Partnerships have been formed between 18 U.S. companies and 38 foreign companies: 18 Japanese, 15 Korean, 3 Polish, 1 Chinese and 1 Russian.

Foreign Fishing

In 1987, U.S. fishermen participated in joint ventures delivering 3.5 billion pounds of fish valued at $213.8 million to foreign processors. These figures represent significant increases over 1986 landings (2.9 billion pounds worth $154.9 million).

Foreign fishing in Alaska waters, as in other U.S. waters, is governed by the Magnuson Fishery Conservation and Management Act of 1976. This act provides for the conservation and exclusive management by the U.S. of all fishery resources within the U.S. Exclusive Economic Zone (except for highly migratory species of tuna). The U.S. EEZ established by the act extends from 3 nautical miles from shore to 200 nautical miles from shore. In addition, the act provides for exclusive management authority over continental shelf fishery resources and anadromous species (those that mature in the ocean, then ascend streams to spawn in fresh water) beyond the 200-mile limit, except when they are within any recognized foreign nation's territorial sea. Foreign countries fishing within the U.S. zone do so under agreement with the U.S. and are subject to various fees.

Foreign catch within the United States EEZ was 328.4 million pounds in 1987, with Alaska supplying the largest share (46 percent) of the foreign catch, according to the National Marine Fisheries Service. This was a 75 percent decrease compared to 1986. Leading all other countries in the U.S. EEZ was Japan with 45 percent of the total catch. Poland was second with 33 percent of the 1987 catch. The total foreign catch of trawl fish in Alaska waters was 69,051 tons, a decrese of more than 400 thousand tons over 1986. The total catch came from the Bering Sea and Aleutian Islands. In 1988, there was no foreign-directed fishery for groundfish off Alaska.

Types of Fish Caught

A dramatic strengthening of salmon runs in the mid-seventies brought new vitality to the Alaska fishing industry. Since 1977, the salmon catch more than doubled, reaching new highs in 1986. In 1988, Alaska landings of salmon were 526 million pounds valued at $745 million, a record value. The shellfish industry is suffering setbacks from the decline of all shellfish stocks except tanner crab.

The priority of the U.S. industry to harvest within the 200-mile Exclusive Economic Zone, which became effective in 1977, has increased the future prospects, especially in the domestic U.S. market, of the Alaska groundfish industry. While the price per pound of groundfish is much lower than that of salmon, the richness of the resource and the potential for value-added products such as surimi, is beginning to capture the attention of the U.S. food industry. With surimi growing in popularity, Alaska pollock landings were valued at $95 million in 1988, an increase over 1987. Surimi is a fish paste made from minced pollock and used as a base for manufactured products like imitation crab legs.

Alaska landings of salmon in 1988 were 526.4 million pounds, valued at $744.9 million — a 63 percent increase in value over 1987. Halibut landings off Alaska in 1988 totaled 76.5 million pounds, valued at $66.1 million.

Alaska's 1988 king crab harvest decreased with a reported total catch of 21 million pounds. This was down from 29.1 million pounds in 1987. The statewide totals for other shellfish landed in 1988, included Dungeness crab, 10.3 million pounds; tanner crab, 132 million pounds; and shrimp, 2.5 million pounds. All shellfish but tanner crab showed a decrease over 1987 totals.

Halibut landings and value continued to increase. The 1988 volume of 76.5 million pounds was the second-largest landing in recorded history, and was valued at $66.1 million. The herring harvest also increased in 1988, with a harvest of 115 million pounds valued at $56 million.

Following are Alaska Department of Fish & Game ex-vessel value figures:

Value of Alaska's Commercial Fisheries to Fisherman (in millions of dollars)

Species	1981	1982	1983	1984*	1985	1986	1987	1988
Salmon	484.9	310.3	320.6	335.0	389.0	414.0	457.9	744.9
Shellfish	245.5	213.5	147.0	102.1	106.3	186.4	213.5	235.6
Halibut	19.3	21.4	37.9	24.9	40.3	63.2	60.9	66.1
Herring	18.6	20.2	28.3	19.8	38.0	38.5	41.8	56.0
Groundfish	24.0	40.9	78.8**	108.4**	137.5**	197.9**	324.3	441.1

*Preliminary estimates.
**Includes international, joint-venture landings not previously shown in table.

1988 Preliminary Commercial Salmon Harvest (in thousands of fish)

Region	King	Red	Silver	Pink	Chum	Total
Southeast	265	1,460	1,043	11,202	3,535	17,505
Central (Prince William Sound, Cook Inlet, Kodiak, Chignik and Bristol Bay)	108	21,902	1,232	14,050	4,344	41,635
Arctic-Yukon-Kuskokwim	178	151	728	113	3,117	4,288
Western (Alaska Peninsula, and Aleutian Islands)	58	6,409	1,374	24,162	3,941	35,944
Total	609	29,922	4,377	49,526	14,937	99,371

Note: Preliminary statistics are from ADF&G, 1988.

Related reading: *Alaska Blues: A Fisherman's Journal,* by Joe Upton, Award-winning saga of salmon fishing in southeastern Alaska. Cloth, 236 pages, 198 black-and-white photos, $14.95. *Fisheries of the North Pacific,* by Robert J. Browning; 1980 revision of the earlier classic. Paper, 424 pages, $24.95. *Pacific Troller: Life on the Northwest Fishing Grounds,* by Francis E. Caldwell. Paper, 144 pages, $5.95. *The Pacific Halibut: The Resource and the Fishery,* by F. Heward Bell. Paper, $19.95 and cloth, $24.95. Includes nearly 300 pages of history on the fishery; with more than 300 photos, maps, and illustrations. See ALASKA NORTHWEST LIBRARY in the back of the book.

SPORT

There are 12 sport fishing management areas in Alaska, each with its own bag and possession limits and possible special provisions. Current copies of *Alaska Sport Fishing Regulations Summary* are available from the Department of

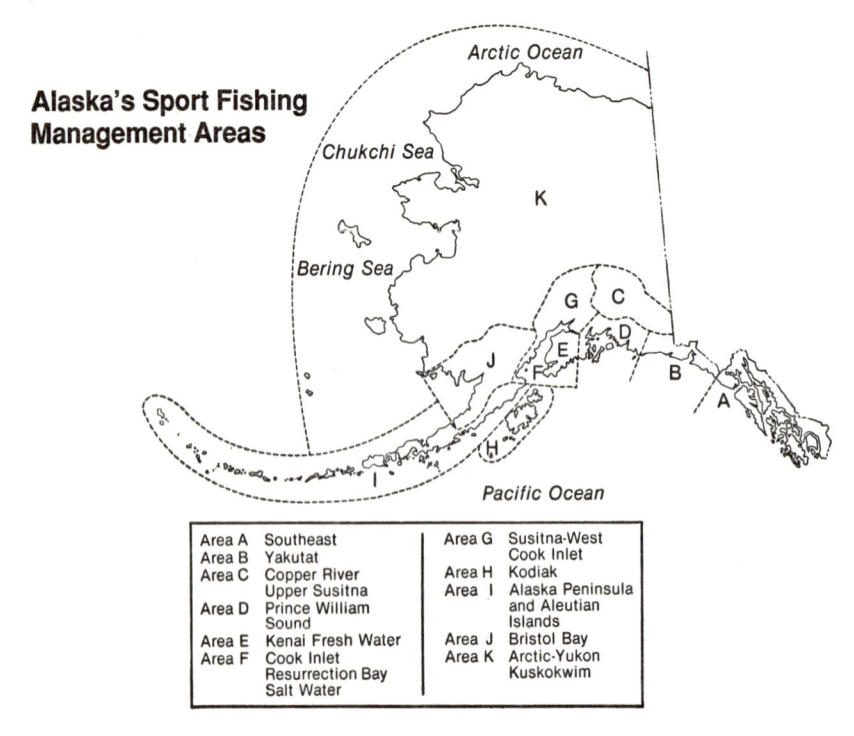

Alaska's Sport Fishing Management Areas

Area A	Southeast
Area B	Yakutat
Area C	Copper River Upper Susitna
Area D	Prince William Sound
Area E	Kenai Fresh Water
Area F	Cook Inlet Resurrection Bay Salt Water
Area G	Susitna-West Cook Inlet
Area H	Kodiak
Area I	Alaska Peninsula and Aleutian Islands
Area J	Bristol Bay
Area K	Arctic-Yukon Kuskokwim

Alaska Sport Fishing Regulations Summary are available from the Department of Fish and Game, Box 3-2000, Juneau 99802. Also available from the department are the free booklets *Sport Fishing Predictions* and the *Alaska Sport Fishing Guide.*

Regulations

A sport fishing license is required for residents and nonresidents 16 years of age or older. (Alaskan residents 60 years of age or more who have been residents one year or more do not need a sport fishing license as long as they remain residents; a special identification card is issued for this exemption.)

Resident sport fishing licenses cost $10, valid for the calendar year issued (nonresident, $36; 3-day nonresident, $10; 14-day nonresident, $20). A resident is a person who has maintained a permanent place of abode within the state for 12 consecutive months and has continuously maintained a voting residence in the state. Military personnel on active duty permanently stationed in the state and their dependents can purchase a nonresident military sport fishing license ($10).

Nearly all sporting goods stores in Alaska sell fishing licenses. They are also available by mail from the Alaska Department of Revenue, Fish and Game License Section, 1111 W. 8th St., Room 108, Juneau 99801.

Sport fish species information below includes the best bait or lure followed by the state record fish weight in pounds and ounces.

Arctic char — spoon, eggs	17.8
Arctic grayling — flies	4.13
Burbot — bait	24.12
Chum salmon — spoon	32.0
Cutthroat trout — bait, spin, flies	8.6
Dolly Varden — bait, spin, flies	17.8
Halibut — octopus, herring	450.0
King salmon — herring	97.4
Kokanee — spin, eggs	2.0
Lake trout — spoon, plug	47.0
Northern pike — spoon, spin	38.0
Pink salmon — small spoon	12.9
Rainbow trout — flies, lures, bait	42.3
Red salmon — flies	16.0
Sheefish — spoon	53.0
Silver salmon — herring, spoon	26.0
Steelhead trout — spoon, eggs	42.3
Whitefish — flies, eggs	7.2

Related reading: *The ALASKA WILDERNESS MILEPOST®* 1990 edition. Includes information on sport fishing throughout the entire state on all major river systems. 416 pages, $14.95. *Alaska's Saltwater Fishes.* A field guide designed for quick identification of 365 species of saltwater fishes. 384 pages, $19.95. See ALASKA NORTHWEST LIBRARY in the back of the book.

Furs and Trapping

According to the state fur bearer biologist, the major sources of harvested Alaska furs are the Yukon and Kuskokwim valleys. The Arctic provides limited numbers of Arctic fox, wolverine and wolf, but the gulf coast areas and Southeast are more productive. Southeast Alaska is a good source of mink and otter.

Trapping is seasonal work, and most trappers work summers at fishing or other employment. (Licenses are required for trapping. See Hunting Section for cost of licenses.)

State regulated furbearers are: beaver; coyote; red (includes cross, black or silver color phases) and Arctic (white or blue) fox; lynx; marmot; marten; mink; muskrat; raccoon; river (land) otter; squirrel (parka or ground, flying and red); weasel; wolf; and wolverine. Very little harvest or use is made of parka squirrels and marmots. Flying squirrels are not caught deliberately, and raccoons, introduced in a couple of coastal locations years ago, appear to have been exterminated.

Prices for raw skins are extremely variable and depend on the buyer, quality, condition and size of the fur. Pelts accepted for purchase are: beaver, coyote, lynx, marten, mink, muskrat, otter, red and white fox, red squirrel, weasel (ermine), wolf and wolverine. Check with a buyer for current prices.

Related reading: *Land of Fur and Gold,* by Raymond Thompson. The story of a loved and respected man. 208 pages, $5.95. *Trapline Twins.* Identical twin girls trap, canoe, dogsled and live off the land. 215 pages, $12.95. See ALASKA NORTHWEST LIBRARY in the back of the book.

Glaciers and Ice Fields

The greatest concentrations of glaciers are in the Alaska Range, Wrangell Mountains and the coastal ranges of the Chugach, Coast, Kenai and Saint Elias mountains, where annual precipitation is high. All of Alaska's well-known glaciers fall within these areas. According to the U.S. Geological Survey, distribution of glacier ice is as follows (the map key and region is followed by the approximate square miles):

glaciers in Alaska, ranging from tiny cirque glaciers to huge valley glaciers.

Glaciers are formed where, over a number of years, more snow falls than melts. Alaska's glaciers fall roughly into five general categories: alpine, valley, piedmont, ice fields and icecaps. Alpine (mountain and cirque) glaciers head high on the slopes of mountains and plateaus. Valley glaciers are an overflowing accumulation of ice from mountain or plateau basins. Piedmont glaciers form when one or more glaciers join to form a fan-shaped ice mass at the foot of a mountain range. Ice fields develop when large valley glaciers interconnect, leaving only the highest peaks and ridges to rise above the ice surface. Icecaps are smaller snow- and ice-filled basins or plateaus.

Major Ice Fields

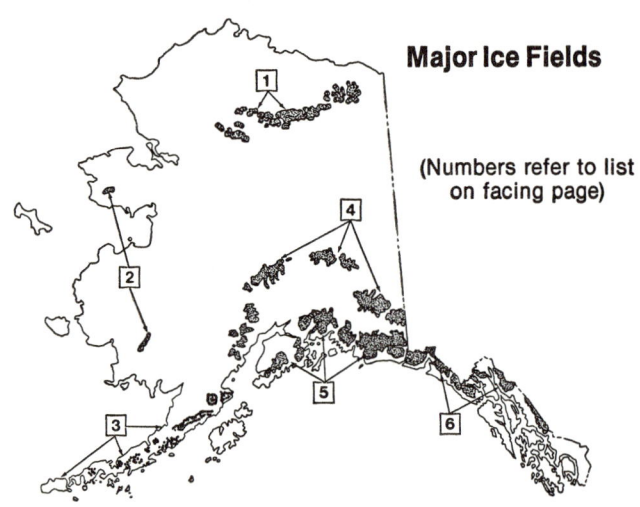

(Numbers refer to list on facing page)

1 North: Brooks Range 279
2 West: Seward Peninsula 2
    Kilbuk-Wood River mountains 89
3 Southwest: Aleutian Islands 371
    Alaska Peninsula 483
4 Interior: Alaska Range 5,367
    Talkeetna Mountains 309
    Wrangell Mountains 3,205
5 Southcentral: Kenai Mountains .. 1,776
    Chugach Mountains 8,340
6 Southeast: Saint Elias Mtns 4,556
    Coast Mountains 4,055
Total: 28,842

Glaciers cover approximately 30,000 square miles — or 3 percent — of Alaska, which is 128 times more area covered by glaciers than in the rest of the United States. There are an estimated 100,000

Most of Alaska's major rivers originate at glaciers. The runoff from glaciers is naturally regulated: because clean (new) snow reflects most of the sun's energy, the more snowfall, the less melt and runoff there is. The converse is also true: a year at low snowfall allows the older snow to be exposed longer, so melting and runoff are greater. This is opposite to the regime of a nonglacial-fed stream.

Alaska's better-known glacier accessible by road are: Worthington and Black Rapids (Richardson Highway); Matanuska (Glenn Highway); Portage (Seward Highway) and Mendenhall (Glacier Highway). In addition, Childs and Sheridan glaciers may be reached by car from Cordova, and Valdez Glacier is only a few miles from the town of Valdez. The sediment-covered terminus of Muldrow Glacier in Denali National Park and Preserve is visible at a distance along several miles of the park road.

Many spectacular glaciers in Glacier Bay National Park and Preserve and in Prince William Sound are accessible by tour boat.

Glacier ice often appears blue because its great thickness absorbs all the colors of the spectrum except blue, which is reflected back.

— About three-fourths of all the fresh water in Alaska is stored as glacial ice. This is many times greater than the volume of water stored in all the state's lakes, ponds, rivers and reservoirs.

— Longest tidewater glacier in North America is Hubbard, 76 miles in length (heads in Canada). In 1986, Hubbard rapidly advanced and blocked Russell Fiord near Yakutat. Later in the year, the ice dam gave way.

— Longest glacier is Bering (including Bagley Icefield), over 100 miles in length.

— Southernmost active tidewater glacier in North America is LeConte.

— Greatest concentration of tidewater-calving glaciers is in Prince William Sound, with 20 active tidewater glaciers.

— Largest glacier is Malaspina, 850 square miles; the Malaspina glacier complex (including tributary glaciers) is approximately 2,000 square miles in area. The Bering glacier complex, which includes Bagley Icefield, is approximately 2,250 square miles.

— La Perouse glacier is the only calving glacier in North America that discharges icebergs directly into the open Pacific Ocean.

— Iceberg production in Prince William Sound is expected to increase fourfold in the next 20 years as Columbia glacier retreats.

— There are more than 750 glacier-dammed lakes in Alaska, the largest at the present time is 28-square-mile Chakachamna Lake west of Anchorage.

Gold

The largest gold nugget ever found in Alaska was discovered near Nome. The nugget, weighing 155 troy ounces, was found September 29, 1903, on Discovery Claim on Anvil Creek, Nome District. The nugget was 7 inches long, 4 inches wide and 2 inches thick.

Four other large nuggets have been found in Alaska, another of which also came from Discovery Claim on Anvil Creek, Nome District in 1899. It was the largest Alaska nugget found up to that time, weighing 82.2 troy ounces, and was 6-1/4 inches long, 3-1/4 inches wide, 1-3/8 inches thick at one end and 1/2 inch thick at the other. In 1914, the second-largest nugget mined, weighing 138.8 troy ounces, was found near Discovery Claim on Hammond River, Wiseman District. Two of the two five nuggets have been discovered this decade, with one coming from Lower Glacier Creek, Kantishna District in 1984, weighing 91.8 troy ounces, and the other from Ganes Creek, Innoko District in 1986, weighing 122 troy ounces.

According to *Alaska's Mineral Industry 1988*, a publication of the Alaska Division of Geological and Geophysical Surveys, major operators produced 265,500 troy ounces of gold in 1988. This was a 16 percent increase from 1987. In 1987, the price of gold averaged $447 an ounce, and in 1988, the average was $425.

Following are volume and value figures for recent years of Alaska gold production.

Gold Production in Alaska, 1980-87

Year	Volume (in troy ounces)	Value
1980	75,000	$32,000,000
1981	134,000	55,200,000
1982	174,900	69,960,000
1983	169,000	67,600,000
1984	175,000	63,000,000
1985	190,000	61,175,000
1986	160,000	60,800,000
1987	229,700	104,500,000
1988	265,500	112,837,000

The chart following shows the fluctuation in the price of gold after the gold standard was lifted in 1967. Note that these are average annual prices and do not reflect the highest or lowest prices during the year.

Average Annual Price of Gold, per Troy Ounce

Prior to 1934	$20.67
1934 to 1967	35.00
1968	39.26
1969	41.51
1970	36.41
1971	41.25
1972	58.60
1973	97.81
1974	159.74
1975	161.49
1976	125.32
1977	148.31
1978	193.55
1979	307.50
1980	569.73
1981	548.90
1982	461.00
1983	400.00
1984	360.00
1985	325.00
1986	380.00
1987	447.00
1988	425.00

If you are interested in gold panning, sluicing or suction dredging in Alaska — whether for fun or profit — you'll have to know whose land you are on and familiarize yourself with current regulations.

Panning, sluicing and suction dredging on private property, established mining claims and Native lands is considered trespassing unless you have the consent of the owner. On state and federal lands, contact the agency for the area you are interested in for current restrictions on mining.

You can pan for gold for a small fee by visiting one of the commercial gold panning resorts in Alaska. These resorts rent gold pans and let you try your luck on gold-bearing creeks and streams on their property.

If you want to stake a permanent claim, the state Department of Natural Resources has a free booklet, *Regulations and Statutes Pertaining to Mining Rights of Alaska Lands,* which can be obtained by contacting the department office in Juneau (907) 465-3400; Ketchikan (907) 225-4181; Fairbanks (907) 474-7062; and Anchorage (907) 276-2653.

Gold Strikes and Rushes

1848 — First Alaska gold discovery (Russian on Kenai Peninsula)
1861 — Stikine River near Telegraph Creek, British Columbia
1872 — Cassiar district in Canada (Stikine headwaters country)
1872 — Near Sitka
1874 — Windham Bay near Juneau
1880 — Gold Creek at Juneau
1886 — Fortymile discovery
1887 — Yakutat beach areas and Lituya Bay
1893 — Mastodon Creek, starting Circle City
1895 — Sunrise district on Kenai Peninsula
1896 — Klondike strike, Bonanza Creek, Canada
1898 — Anvil Creek, Nome; Atlin district,
1898 — British Columbia
1900 — Porcupine rush out of Haines
1902 — Fairbanks (Felix Pedro, Pedro Dome)
1906 — Innoko
1907 — Ruby
1908 — Iditarod
1913 — Marshall
1913 — Chisana
1914 — Livengood

Related reading: *In Search of Gold, The Alaska Journals of Horace S. Conger, 1889-1899,* by Carolyn Jean Holeski and Marlene Conger Holeski, 314 pages, $9.95; *The Gold Hustlers,* by Lewis Green, 339 pages, $7.95; *Nome Nuggets,* by L.H. French, 64 pages, $5.95. See ALASKA NORTHWEST LIBRARY in the back of the book.

Government

(*See also* Courts *and* Officials)

The capital of Alaska is Juneau. In November of 1976, Alaskan voters chose Willow as their new capital site. In a second election six years later, voters chose to keep Juneau as the capital city.

Alaska is represented in the U.S. Congress by two senators and one representative.

A governor and lieutenant governor are elected by popular vote for four-year terms on the same ticket. The governor is termed strong because of extensive powers given under the constitution. He administers 15 major departments: Administration, Commerce and Economic Development, Community and Regional Affairs, Corrections, Education, Environmental Conservation, Fish and Game, Health and Social Services, Labor, Law, Military Affairs, Natural Resources, Public Safety, Revenue, and Transportation and Public Facilities.

The legislature is bicameral, with 20 senators elected from 14 senate districts for four-year terms, and 40 representatives from 27 election districts for two-year terms. Under the state constitution, redistricting is accomplished every 10 years, after the reporting of the decennial federal census. The latest redistricting occurred in 1981 and was accomplished by the governor's office with assistance of an advisory apportionment board. The judiciary consists of a state supreme court, court of appeals, superior court, district courts and magistrates.

Local government is by a system of organized boroughs, much like counties in other states. Several areas of the state are not included in any borough because of sparse population. Boroughs generally provide a more limited number of services than cities. There are three classes. First- and second-class boroughs have three mandatory powers: education, land use planning and tax assessment and collection. The major difference between the two classes is how they may acquire other powers. Both classes have separately elected borough assemblies and school boards. A third-class borough has two mandatory powers: operation of public schools and taxation. All boroughs may assess, levy and collect real and personal property taxes.

Incorporated cities are small units of local government, serving one community. There are two classes. First-class cities, generally urban areas, have six-member councils and a separately elected mayor. Taxing authority is somewhat broader than second-class cities and responsibilities are broader. A first-class city that has adopted a home rule charter is called a home rule city; adoption allows the city to revise its ordinances, to the extent that the powers it assumes are those not prohibited by law or charter. Second-class cities, generally places with fewer than 400 people (but not less than 25), are governed by a seven-member council, one of whom serves as mayor. Taxing authority is limited. A borough and all cities located within it may unite in a single unit of government called a unified municipality.

There is also one community organized under federal law. Originally an Indian reservation, Metlakatla was organized so municipal services could effectively be provided to its residents.

In 1989, there were 14 organized boroughs and unified home rule municipalities: 3 unified home rule municipalities, 2 home rule boroughs, 1 first-class borough, 8 second-class boroughs and 1 third-class borough. Alaska's 148 incorporated cities include: 12 home rule cities, 22 first-class cities and 114 second-class cities. One city, Metlakatla, is organized under federal law.

Borough Addresses and Contacts
(Area code throughout Alaska is 907)

Aleutians East Borough
P.O. Box 249
Sand Point 99661
Telephone: 383-2696

Bristol Bay Borough
Contact: Borough Clerk
P.O. Box 189
Naknek 99633
Telephone: 246-4224

City and Borough of Juneau
Contact: City-Borough Manager
155 S. Seward St.
Juneau 99801
Telephone: 586-5241

City and Borough of Sitka
Contact: Administrator
304 Lake St., Room 104
Sitka 99835
Telephone: 747-3294
Fairbanks North Star Borough
Contact: Clerk
P.O. Box 1267
Fairbanks 99707
Telephone: 452-4761
Haines Borough
Contact: Borough Secretary
Box H
Haines 99827
Telephone: 766-2711
Kenai Peninsula Borough
Contact: Borough Clerk
P.O. Box 850
Soldotna 99669
Telephone: 262-4441
Ketchikan Gateway Borough
Contact: Borough Manager
344 Front St.
Ketchikan 99901
Telephone: 225-6151
Kodiak Island Borough
Contact: Borough Mayor or Borough Clerk
710 Mill Bay Road
Kodiak 99615
Telephone: 486-5736
Lake and Peninsula Borough
c/o Lake and Peninsula School District
P.O. Box 498
King Salmon 99613
Telephone: 276-4280
Matanuska-Susitna Borough
Contact: Borough Manager
P.O. Box B
Palmer 99645
Telephone: 745-4801
Municipality of Anchorage
Contact: Mayor's Office or Manager's Office
Pouch 6-650
Anchorage 99502
Telephone: 264-4431
North Slope Borough
Contact: Borough Mayor
P.O. Box 69
Barrow 99723
Telephone: 852-2611
Northwest Arctic Borough
P.O. Box 1110
Kotzebue 99752
Telephone: 442-2500

Highways

(*See also* Alaska Highway *and* Dalton Highway)

Major Highways in Alaska

	Route#	Year Completed	Total length (miles) paved	gravel	Open
Alaska	2	1942	298.2*	—	All yr.
Copper River	10	see note	12.4	35.7	Apr.-Oct.
Dalton	12	1974	—	416	All yr.
Denali	8	1957	21	115	Apr.-Oct.
Edgerton	10	1923	19	14	All yr.
Elliott	2	1959	28	124	All yr.
George Parks	3	1971	322.7	—	All yr.
Glenn	1	1942	328*	—	All yr.
Haines	7	1947	40.5	—	All yr.
Klondike	11	1978	14.6	—	All yr.
Richardson	4	1923	368*	—	All yr.
Seward	1&9	1951	127	—	All yr.
Steese	6	1928	43.8	118.2	All yr.
Sterling	1	1950	135.8	—	All yr.
Taylor	5	1953	—	161	Apr.-Oct.

*The Richardson shares a common alignment with the Alaska Highway (98 miles) and with the Glenn (14 miles).
NOTE: Construction on the Copper River Highway — which was to link up with Chitina on the Edgerton — was halted by the 1964 Good Friday earthquake which damaged the Million Dollar Bridge and by local Cordova citizens who desired semi-isolation.

As of December 31, 1984, the state Department of Transportation and Public Facilities showed 15,779 miles of highways, including those in national parks and forests (2,223), and 1,435 miles of ferry routes. Of the total, 4,778 miles were unpaved, 4,821 miles were paved, 979 were local city streets, 2,321 were borough roads and 2,880 were listed as "other." Alaska's relative sparseness of roadway is accentuated by a comparison to Austria, a country only one-eighteenth the size of Alaska but with nearly twice as many public roads.

The chart above lists each major highway in Alaska, its route number, the year the highway opened to vehicle traffic and its total length within Alaska (most of the Alaska Highway, Haines Highway and Klondike Highway 2 lie within Canada). Also indicated is whether the highway is open all year or closed in winter.

Related reading: *The MILEPOST®* All-the-North Travel Guide®. A 546-page comprehensive travel guide with mile-by-mile logs of all access highways and travel by air, rail, water. Includes accommodations, cities, villages, parks, wildlife; hints for fishermen, bicyclists, hikers. Numerous photos and maps. $14.95. See ALASKA NORTHWEST LIBRARY in the back of the book.

Hiking

A variety of hiking trails for all levels of ability may be found in the state. The experienced hiker with proper topographic maps will find some of the best Alaska hiking is cross-country above tree line. Using both maps and tide tables, it is also feasible to hike along ocean shorelines at low tide.

Hikers in Alaska must plan for rapidly changing, inclement weather. Take rain gear. If staying overnight in the back country, it's wise to carry a tent if a cabin is unavailable. Above tree line, snow can be encountered at any time of year.

Sporting goods stores in Alaska feature an excellent selection of hiking equipment. Back country guides often furnish equipment on escorted expeditions.

Information on hiking in Alaska's national parks and monuments is available from the Alaska Public Lands Information Centers, 605 W. 4th Ave., Suite .105, Anchorage 99501; 250 Cushman Street, Suite 1A, Fairbanks 99701; and P.O. Box 359, Tok 99780, or from park headquarters for the area you're interested in. (*See* National Parks, Preserves and Monuments.)

The Alaska Division of Parks (*see* State Park System) has information on hiking on lands managed by that agency.

History

6,000-11,000 years ago — Human culture in southeastern, Aleutians interior, and northwestern Arctic Alaska.

6,000 years ago — Most recent migration from Siberia across the land bridge. Earliest migration believed to have gone back 25,000 years ago.

3,000-5,000 years ago — Human culture on the Bering Sea coast.

200-300 years ago — Tlingits and Haidas arrive.

1725 — Vitus Bering sent by Peter the Great to explore the North Pacific.

1741 — On a later expedition, Bering in one ship and Alexei Chirikof in another discover Alaska. Chirikof, according to ship logs, probably sees land on July 15, a day ahead of his leader, who was perhaps 300 miles or more to the north. Georg Steller goes ashore on Kayak Island, becoming the first white man known to have set foot on Alaska soil.

1743 — Russians begin concentrated hunting of sea otter, continuing until the species is almost decimated; fur seal hunting begins later.

1774-94 — Explorations of Alaska waters by Juan Perez, James Cook and George Vancouver.

1784 — First Russian settlement in Alaska, at Three Saints Bay, Kodiak Island.

1794 — Vancouver sights Mount McKinley.

1799 — Alexander Baranof establishes the Russian post known today as Old Sitka; a trade charter is granted to the Russian-American Company.

1821 — Russians prohibit trading in Alaska waters by other nations, making the Russian-American Company the sole trading firm.

1824-42 — Russian exploration of the mainland leads to discovery of the Kuskokwim, Nushagak, Yukon and Koyukuk rivers.

1847 — Fort Yukon established by Hudson's Bay Company.

1848 — First mining in Alaska, on the Kenai Peninsula.

1853 — Russian explorers-trappers find the first oil seeps in Cook Inlet.

1857 — Coal mining begins at Coal Harbor, Kenai Peninsula, to supply steamers.

1859 — Baron Edoard de Stoecki, minister and charge d'affaires of the Russian delegation to the United States, is given authority to negotiate the sale of Alaska.

1867 — United States under President Andrew Johnson buys Alaska from Russia for $7.2 million; treaty signed March 30, formal transfer takes place on October 18 at Sitka. Fur seal population begins to stabilize. U.S. Army is given jurisdiction over the Department of Alaska the following year.

1872 — Gold discovered near Sitka. Later discoveries include Windham, 1874, and Juneau, 1880; Fortymile, 1886; Circle City, 1893; Sunrise District (Kenai Peninsula), 1895; Nome, 1898; Fairbanks, 1902; Innoko, 1906; Ruby, 1907; Iditarod, 1908; Marshall, 1913; Chisana, 1913; and Livengood, 1914.

1878 — First salmon canneries at Klawock and Old Sitka.

1887 — Tsimshians, under Father William Duncan, arrive at Metlakatla from British Columbia.

1891 — First oil claims staked in Cook Inlet area.

1897-1900 — Klondike gold rush in Yukon Territory; heavy traffic through Alaska.

1902 — First oil production, at Katalla; telegraph from Eagle to Valdez completed.

1906 — Peak gold production year; Alaska granted a nonvoting delegate to Congress.

1911 — Copper production begins at Kennicott.

1912 — Territorial status for Alaska; first territorial legislature is convened the following year.
1913 — First airplane flight in Alaska, at Fairbanks; first auto trip from Fairbanks to Valdez.
1914 — President Wilson authorizes construction of the Alaska Railroad.
1916 — First bill proposing Alaska statehood introduced in Congress; peak copper production year.
1922 — First pulp mill starts production at Speel River, near Juneau.
1923 — President Warren Harding drives spike completing the Alaska Railroad.
1930 — The first "talkie" motion picture is shown in Fairbanks, featuring the Marx Brothers in *The Coconuts.*
1935 — Matanuska Valley Project, which establishes farming families in Alaska, begins. First Juneau to Fairbanks flight.
1936 — All-time record salmon catch in Alaska — 126.4 million fish.
1940 — Military build-up in Alaska; Fort Richardson, Elmendorf Air Force Base established. At this point there are only about 40,000 non-Native Alaskans and 32,458 Natives. Pan American Airways inaugurates twice-weekly service between Seattle, Ketchikan and Juneau, using Sikorsky flying boats.
1942 — Dutch Harbor bombed and Attu and Kiska islands occupied by Japanese forces. Alaska Highway built; first overland connection to Lower 48.
1943 — Japanese forces driven from Alaska.
1944 — Alaska-Juneau Mine shuts down.
1953 — Oil well drilled near Eureka, on the Glenn Highway, marking the start of modern oil history; first plywood mill at Juneau; first big pulp mill at Ketchikan.
1957 — Kenai oil strike.
1958 — Statehood measure passed by Congress; statehood proclaimed officially January 3, 1959. Sitka pulp mill opens.
1964 — Good Friday earthquake, March 27, causes heavy damage throughout the gulf coast region; 131 people lose their lives.
1967 — Alaska Centennial celebration; Fairbanks flood.
1968 — Oil and gas discoveries at Prudhoe Bay on the North Slope; $900 million North Slope oil lease sale the following year; pipeline proposal follows.
1971 — Congress approves Alaska Native Land Claims Settlement Act, granting title to 40 million acres of land and providing more than $900 million in payment to Alaska Natives.
1974 — Trans-Alaska pipeline receives final approval; construction build-up begins.
1975 — Population and labor force soar with construction of pipeline; Alaska Gross Products hits $5.8 billion — double the 1973 figure.
1976 — Voters select Willow area for new capital site.
1977 — Completion of the trans-Alaska pipeline from Prudhoe Bay to Valdez; shipment of first oil by tanker from Valdez to Puget Sound.
1978 — 200-mile fishing limit goes into effect. President Jimmy Carter withdraws 56 million acres to create 17 new national monuments as of December 1, 1978.
1979 — State of Alaska files suit to halt the withdrawal of 56 million acres of Alaska land by President Carter under the Antiquities Act.
1980 — Special session of the Alaska legislature votes to repeal the state income tax and provides for refunds of 1979 taxes. Legislature establishes a Permanent Fund as a repository for one-fourth of all royalty oil revenues for future generations. Census figures show Alaska's population grew by 32.4 percent during the 1970s. The Alaska Lands Act of 1980 puts 53.7 million Alaska acres into the national wildlife refuge system, parts of 25 rivers to the national wild and scenic rivers system, 3.3 million acres to national forest lands and 43.6 million acres to national park land.
1981 — Legislature puts on the ballot a constitutional amendment proposal to limit state spending. Secretary of the Interior James Watt initiates plans to sell oil and gas leases on 130 million acres of Alaska's nonrestricted federal land and announces a tentative schedule to open 16 offshore areas of Alaska as part of an intense national search for oil and gas on the outer continental shelf.

1982 — Oil revenues for state decrease. Vote for funding of capital move from Juneau to Willow defeated. First permanent fund dividend checks of $1,000 each are mailed to every six-month resident of Alaska.

1983 — Salmon harvest in Bristol Bay broke records. Building permits set a record at just under $1 billion.

1984 — State of Alaska celebrates its 25th birthday.

1985 — Anchorage receives the U.S. bid for the 1994 Olympics. The Iditarod race won by a woman for the first time.

1986 — World Championship Sled Dog Race held during Fur Rendezvous is cancelled due to lack of snow. Iditarod race once again won by a woman.

1987 — Alaska is retained as America's choice for the 1994 Olympics. The Iditarod race is won by a woman for the third straight year.

1988 — First successful solo winter ascent of Mount McKinley is accomplished by Vern Tejas of Anchorage. The Iditarod race is won by Susan Butcher of Manley for the third year in a row. Two sets of orphaned polar bear cub twins are on view in Anchorage before going to zoos in the Lower 48. Anchorage loses its bid to Norway for the 1994 Olympics.

1989 — Record-breaking cold hits entire state lasting for weeks. Worst oil spill in history happens in Prince William Sound. Soviets visit Alaska, and the Bering Bridge Expedition crosses the Bering Strait by dogsled and skis.

Related reading: Many of the books listed in the ALASKA NORTHWEST LIBRARY in the back of the book are totally or in part about Alaska history.

Holidays 1990

New Year's Day .... January 1
Martin Luther King Day .... January 15
Lincoln's Birthday .... February 12
Washington's Birthday
— holiday .... February 19
— traditional .... February 22
Seward's Day* .... March 26
Memorial Day
— holiday .... May 28
— traditional .... May 30
Independence Day .... July 4
Labor Day .... September 3
Alaska Day* .... October 18
Veterans Day .... November 11
Thanksgiving Day .... November 22
Christmas Day .... December 25

*Seward's Day commemorates the signing of the treaty by which the United States bought Alaska from Russia, signed on March 30, 1867. Alaska Day is the anniversary of the formal transfer of the territory and the raising of the U.S. flag at Sitka on October 18, 1867.

Hooligan

Smelt, also known as eulachon or candlefish (because the oily little fish can be burned like a candle). These small fish, known as "ooligan" in southeastern Alaska, are caught by dip-netting as they travel upriver to spawn.

Hospitals and Health Facilities

Alaska has numerous hospitals, nursing homes and other health facilities. (*See also* Pioneers' Homes.) The only hospital in the state currently offering specialized care units is Providence Hospital in Anchorage, with its thermal unit (burn and frostbite), cancer treatment center and neonatal intensive care nursery.

A list of emergency medical services on Alaska's highways and marine highways are detailed in a brochure available from the Office of Emergency Medical Services, Division of Public Health, Dept. of Health & Social Services, P.O. Box H-06C, Juneau 99811.

Municipal, Private and State Hospitals
Anchorage, Alaska Psychiatric Institute (176 beds), 2900 Providence Drive, 99508.
Anchorage, Alaska Treatment Center (out-patient rehabilitation facility), 3710 E. 20th Ave., 99504.
Anchorage, Charter North Hospital (80 beds), 2530 DeBarr Road, 99514.
Anchorage, Humana Hospital (238 beds), 2801 DeBarr Road, P.O. Box 143889, 99514.
Anchorage, North Star Hospital (34 beds), 1650 S. Bragaw, 99508.

Anchorage, Providence Hospital (303 beds), 3200 Providence Drive, P.O. Box 196604, 99519.
Cordova, Cordova Community Hospital (23 beds), Box 160, 99574.
Fairbanks, Fairbanks Memorial Hospital (177 beds), 1650 Cowles St., 99701.
Glennallen, Cross Road Medical Center (6 beds), Box 5, 99588.
Homer, South Peninsula Hospital (39 beds), 4300 Bartlett St., 99603.
Juneau, Bartlett Memorial Hospital (51 beds), 3260 Hospital Drive, 99801.
Juneau, Juneau Recovery Unit (15 alcoholism treatment beds), 3250 Hospital Drive, 99801.
Ketchikan, Ketchikan General Hospital (46 beds), 3100 Tongass Ave., 99901.
Kodiak, Kodiak Island Hospital (44 beds), 1915 E. Rezanof Drive, 99615.
Palmer, Valley Hospital (36 beds), P.O. Box 1687, 99645.
Petersburg, Petersburg General Hospital (25 beds), Box 589, 99833.
Seward, Seward General Hospital (32 beds), Box 365, 99664.
Sitka, Sitka Community Hospital (24 beds), 209 Moller Drive, 99835.
Soldotna, Central Peninsula General Hospital (62 beds), 250 Hospital Place, 99669.
Valdez, Harborview Developmental Center (state operated residential center for the mentally handicapped; 80 beds), Box 487, 99686.
Valdez, Valdez Community Hospital (15 beds), Box 550, 99686.
Wrangell, Wrangell General Hospital (9 beds), Box 80, 99929.

U.S. Public Health Service Hospitals
Anchorage, Alaska Native Medical Center (170 beds), Box 7-741, 99510.
Barrow, PHS Alaska Native Hospital (14 beds), 99723.
Bethel, Yukon-Kuskokwim Delta Service Unit (51 beds), 99559.
Dillingham, Bristol Bay Area Kanakanak Hospital (15 beds), P.O. Box 10320, 99576.
Kotzebue, Kotzebue Service Unit (31 beds), 99752.
Nome, Norton Sound Regional Hospital (22 beds), P.O. Box 966, 99672.
Sitka, SEARHC Medical Center (78 beds), 222 Tongass Drive, 99835.

Military Hospitals
Adak, Branch Hospital, Box NAS ADAK, FPO Seattle 98791.
Adak, Naval Regional Medical Center, NAVSTA Adak, FPO Seattle 98791.
Eielson AFB, Eielson Air Force Base Clinic, 99702.
Elmendorf AFB, Elmendorf Air Force Base Hospital, 99506.
Fort Greely, Fort Greely Dispensary, Box 488, APO Seattle 98733.
Fort Richardson, U.S. Army Health Clinic, 99505.
Fort Wainwright, Bassett Army Community Hospital, 99703.
Ketchikan, Ketchikan Coast Guard Dispensary, 99901.
Kodiak, Kodiak Coast Guard Dispensary, Box 2, 99619.
Mount Edgecumbe, Sitka Coast Guard Air Station, Box 6-5000, 99835.

Nursing Homes
Anchorage, Our Lady of Compassion (224 beds), 4900 Eagle, 99503.
Cordova, Cordova Community Hospital Nursing Home (10 beds), P.O. Box 160, 99574.
Fairbanks, Denali Center (101 beds), 1949 Gillam Way, 99701.
Homer, South Peninsula Hospital (16 beds), 4300 Bartlett 99603.
Juneau, Saint Ann's Nursing Home (45 beds), 415 Sixth St., 99801.
Ketchikan, Island View Manor (44 beds), 3100 Tongass Ave., 99901.
Petersburg, Petersburg General Hospital (14 beds), P.O. Box 589, 99833.
Seward, Wesleyan Nursing Home (66 beds), Box 430, 99664.
Soldotna, Heritage Place (45 beds), 232 Rockwell Ave., 99669.
Wrangell, Wrangell General Hospital (14 beds), P.O. Box 80, 99929.

Hostels

Alaska has 13 youth hostels, located as follows:
Anchorage International Hostel, 700 H St., Anchorage 99501. Located downtown on the corner of 7th and H streets.
Alyeska International Youth Hostel, P.O. Box 10-4099, Anchorage 99510. Located 40 miles south of Anchorage on Alpina in Girdwood.

Bear Creek Camp and Hostel, P.O. Box 334, Haines 99827. Located along Small Tract Road, two miles from town.
Delta Youth Hostel, P.O. Box 971, Delta Junction 99737. Located three miles in from Milepost 272 of Richardson Highway.
Fairbanks Youth Hostel, P.O. Box 2196, Fairbanks 99701. Located at Tanana Valley Fairgrounds.
Juneau International Hostel, 614 Harris St., Juneau 99801. Located four blocks northeast of the capitol building.
Ketchikan Youth Hostel, P.O. Box 8515, Ketchikan 99901. Located in United Methodist Church, Grant and Main streets.
Mentasta Mountain Wilderness Lodge, P.O. Box 950, Slana 99586. Write for details.
Sheep Mountain Lodge, SRC Box 8490, Palmer 99645. Located at Mile 113.5 of the Glenn Highway.
Sitka Youth Hostel, P.O. Box 2645, Sitka 99835. Located in United Methodist Church, Edgecumbe and Kimsham streets.
Snow River International Hostel, HRC 64, Box 425, Seward 99664. Located at Mile 16 of the Seward Highway.
Soldotna International Youth Hostel, P.O. Box 327, Soldotna 99669. Located at 444 Riverview Drive.
Tok International Youth Hostel, P.O. Box 532, Tok 99780. Located one mile south of Mile 1322.5 of the Alaska Highway.

The hostels in Alyeska, Anchorage, Juneau, Slana, Soldotna and Seward are open year-round. All others are open only in the summer, and all of the hostels accept reservations by mail. Opening and closing dates, maximum length of stay and hours vary depending on the hostel.

Hostels are available to anyone with a valid membership card issued by one of the associations affiliated with the International Youth Hostel Federation. Membership is open to all ages. By international agreement, each youth hostel member joins the association of his own country. A valid membership card, which ranges from $10 (one night temporary membership) to $200 (life), entitles a member to use hostels.

Hostel memberships and a guide to American youth hostels can be purchased from the state office (Alaska Council, AYH, P.O. Box 91461, Anchorage 99509), national office (American Youth Hostels, 1332 I St. N.W., Suite 800, Washington, D.C. 20005) or from local hostels. For more information regarding Alaska youth hostels write the Alaska Council, AYH, 700 H St., Anchorage 99501 or the Department of Natural Resources, Division of Parks, Pouch 7-001, Anchorage 99510.

Hot Springs

The U.S. Geological Survey identifies 79 thermal springs in Alaska. Almost half of these hot springs occur along the volcanic Alaska Peninsula and Aleutian Chain. The second greatest regional concentration of such springs is in southeastern Alaska. Hot springs are scattered throughout the Interior and western Alaska, as far north as the Brooks Range and as far west as the Seward Peninsula.

Early miners and trappers were quick to use the naturally occurring warm waters for baths. Today approximately 25 percent of the recorded thermal springs are used for bathing, irrigation or domestic use. However, only a handful can be considered developed resorts.

Resorts (with swimming pools, changing rooms and lodging) are found at Chena Hot Springs, a 62-mile drive east of Fairbanks and Circle Hot Springs, 136 miles by road from Fairbanks. The less-developed Manley Hot Springs, at the small community of the same name at the end of the Elliott Highway, is privately owned and the primitive bathhouse is used mainly by local residents. Developed, but not easily accessible, is Melozi Hot Springs at Melozi Hot Springs Lodge, some 200 miles northwest of Fairbanks by air. The community of Tenakee Springs on Chichagof Island in southeastern Alaska maintains an old bathhouse near the waterfront. Goddard Hot Springs near Sitka was at one time owned by the Territory and operated as a Pioneer Home for Alaskan women. Temperature of the hot springs here is about 106°F/ 41°C. The state Marine Highway System provides ferry service to Tenakee. On Baranof Island in Southeast there are two hot springs: Baranof Hot Springs on the east shore of the island, and Goddard Hot Springs behind Sitka. Both are accessible by private boat or by air; both have bathhouses.

Hunting

There are 26 game management units in Alaska with a wide variety of both seasons and bag limits. Current copies of the *Alaska Game Regulations* and a map delineating game unit boundaries are available from the Alaska Department of Fish and Game (P.O. Box 3-2000, Juneau 99802) or from Fish and Game offices and sporting goods stores throughout the state.

Regulations

A hunting or trapping license is required for all residents and non-residents with the exception of Alaska residents under 16 years of age and Alaska residents over 60 years of age. A special identification card is issued for the senior citizen exemption.

A resident hunting license (valid for calendar year) costs $12; trapping license (valid until September 30 of the year following the year of issue), $10; hunting and trapping license, $22; hunting and sport fishing license, $22; hunting, trapping and sport fishing license, $32.

A nonresident hunting license (valid for calendar year) costs $60; hunting and sport fishing license, $96; hunting and trapping license, $200.

Military personnel stationed in Alaska may purchase a small game hunting license for $12, and a small game hunting and sport fishing license for $22. Military personnel must purchase a nonresident hunting license at full cost ($60) and pay nonresident military fees for big game tags (one-half the nonresident rate), unless they are hunting big game on military property.

Licenses may be obtained from any designated issuing agent or by mail from the Alaska Department of Fish and Game, Licensing Section, P.O. Box 3-2000, Juneau 99802. Licenses are also available at Fish and Game regional offices in Anchorage, Fairbanks, Juneau and Kodiak.

Big game tags and fees are required for residents hunting musk oxen and brown/grizzly bear and for nonresidents hunting any big game animal. These non-refundable, nontransferable, metal locking tags (valid for calendar year) must be purchased prior to the taking of the animal. A tag may, however, be used for any species for which the tag fee is of equal or less value. Fees quoted below are for *each* animal.

All residents (regardless of age) and nonresidents intending to hunt brown/grizzly bear must purchase tags (resident, $25; nonresident, $350). Both residents and nonresidents are also required to purchase musk oxen tags (resident, $500 each bull taken on Nunivak Island, $25 each bull from Nelson Island or in Arctic National Wildlife Refuge $25 cow; nonresident, $1,100).

Nonresident tag fees for other big game animals are as follows: deer, $135; wolf or wolverine, $150; black bear, $200; elk or goat, $250; caribou or moose, $300; bison, $350; and sheep, $400.

Nonresidents hunting brown/grizzly bear, Dall sheep or mountain goat are required to have a guide or be accompanied by an Alaska resident relative over 19 years of age within the second degree of kindred (includes parents, children, sisters or brothers). Nonresident aliens hunting big game must have a guide. A current list of registered Alaska guides is available from the Department of Commerce, Guide Licensing and Control Board, P.O. Box D-LIC, Juneau 99811 for $5, or *The ALASKA WILDERNESS MILEPOST®*.

Residents and nonresidents 16 years of age or older hunting waterfowl must have a signed federal migratory bird hunting stamp (duck stamp) and a state waterfowl conservation stamp. The Alaska duck stamp is available from agents who sell hunting licenses or by mail from the Alaska Department of Fish and Game, Licensing Section.

Trophy Game

Record big game in Alaska as recorded by the Boone and Crockett Club in the latest (1981) edition of *Record Big Game of North America* are as follows:

Black bear: Skull 13-7/16 inches wide (1966).
Brown bear (coastal region): Skull 17-5/8 inches long, 12-13/16 inches wide (1952).
Grizzly bear (inland): Skull 16-5/8 inches long, 9-7/8 inches wide (1970).
Polar bear: Skull 18-1/2 inches long, 11-7/16 inches wide (1963). It is currently illegal for anyone but an Alaskan Eskimo, Aleut or Indian to hunt polar bear in Alaska.
Bison: Right horn 18-1/8 inches long, base circumference 15 inches; left horn 21 inches long, base circumference 15-1/4 inches; greatest spread 31-7/8 inches (1977).
Barren Ground caribou: Right beam 51-1/4 inches, 22 points; left beam 51-5/8 inches, 23 points (1967).
Moose: Right palm length 49-5/8 inches, width 20-3/4 inches; left palm length 49-5/8 inches, width 15-5/8 inches; right beam 18 points, left 16 points; greatest spread 77 inches (1978).
Mountain goat: Right horn 11-5/8 inches long, base circumference 5-3/4 inches; left horn 11-5/8 inches long, base circumference 5-5/8 inches (1933).
Musk ox: Right horn 26-3/4 inches, left horn 26-1/2 inches, tip-to-tip spread 27-7/8 inches (1976).
Dall sheep: Right horn 48-5/8 inches long, base circumference 14-5/8 inches; leftthorn 47-7/8 inches long, base circumference 14-3/4 inches (1961).

Related reading: *Alaska Game Trails With a Master Guide,* compiled by Charles J. Keim; foreword by Lowell Thomas Sr. True stories about a legendary Alaska guide, Hal Waugh. 310 pages, $8.95. *Trails Of An Alaska Game Warden,* by Ray Tremblay. Lively tales that entertain and inform. 176 pages, $9.95. *Northwest Sportsman Almanac,* informative guide to outdoor recreation. 291 pages, $34.95. See ALASKA NORTHWEST LIBRARY in the back of the book.

Hypothermia

(*See also* Chill Factor)

The body's reaction when it is exposed to cold and cannot maintain normal temperatures. In an automatic survival reaction, blood flow to the extremities is shut down in favor of preserving warmth in the vital organs. As internal temperature drops, judgment and coordination become impaired. Allowed to continue, hypothermia leads to stupor, collapse and death. Immersion hypothermia occurs in cold water.

Ice

(*See* Glaciers and Ice Fields)

Icebergs

Icebergs are formed in Alaska wherever glaciers reach salt water or a freshwater lake. Some accessible places to view icebergs include Glacier Bay, Icy Bay, Yakutat Bay, Taku Inlet, Endicott Arm, portions of northern Prince William Sound (College Fiord, Barry Arm, Columbia Bay), Mendenhall Lake and Portage Lake.

If icebergs contain little or no sediment, approximately 75 percent to 80 percent of their bulk may be underwater. The more sediment an iceberg contains, the greater its density, and an iceberg containing large amounts of sediment will float slightly beneath the surface. Glaciologists of the U.S. Geological Survey believe that some of these "black icebergs" may actually sink to the bottom of a body of water. Since salt water near the faces of glaciers may be liquid to temperatures as low as 28°F, and icebergs melt at 32°F, some of these underwater icebergs may remain unmelted indefinitely.

Alaska's icebergs are comparatively small compared to the icebergs found near Antarctica and Greenland. One of the largest icebergs ever recorded in Alaska was formed in May, 1977, in Icy Bay. Glaciologists measured it at 346 feet long, 297 feet wide, and 99 feet above the surface of the water.

Sea Ice

Sea water typically freezes at -1.8°C or 28.8°F. The first indication that sea water is freezing is the appearance of frazil — tiny needlelike crystals of pure ice — in shallow coastal areas of low current or areas of low salinity, such as near the mouths of rivers. Continued freezing turns the frazil into a soupy mass called grease ice and eventually into an ice crust approximately four inches thick. More freezing, wind and wave action thicken the ice and break it into ice floes ranging from a few feet to several miles across. In the Arctic Ocean, ice floes can be 10 feet thick. Most are crisscrossed with 6- to 8-foot-high walls of ice caused by the force of winds.

Sea salt that is trapped in the ice during freezing is leached out over time, making the oldest ice the least saline. Meltwater forming in ponds on multi-year-old ice during summer months is a fresh water source for native marine life.

Refreezing of meltwater ponds and the formation of new ice in the permanent ice pack (generally north of 72° north latitude) begins in mid-September. While the ice pack expands southward, new ice freezes to the coast (shorefast ice) and spreads seaward. Where the drifting ice pack grinds against the relatively stable shorefast ice, tremendous walls or ridges of ice are formed, some observed to be 100 feet thick and grounded in 60 feet of water. They are impenetrable by all but the most powerful icebreakers. By late March the ice cover has reached its maximum extent, approximately from Port Heiden on the Alaska Peninsula in the south to the northern Pribilof Islands and northwestward to Siberia. In Cook Inlet, sea ice, usually no more than two feet thick, can extend as far south as Anchor Point and Kamishak Bay on the east and west sides of the inlet respectively. The ice season usually lasts from mid-November to mid-March.

In 1954, the Navy began observing and forecasting sea ice conditions in support of the construction of defense sites along the Arctic coast. In 1969 the National Weather Service began a low-profile sea ice reconnaissance program, which expanded greatly during the summer of 1975, when during a year of severe ice, millions of dollars of material had to be shipped to Prudhoe Bay. Expanded commercial fisheries in the Bering Sea also heightened the problem of sea ice for crabbing and bottom fish trawling operations. In 1976, headquarters for a seven-day-a-week ice watch was established at Fairbanks; it was moved to Anchorage in 1981.

The National Weather Service operates a radio facsimile broadcast service, making current ice analysis charts, special oceanographic charts and standard weather charts available to the public via standard radios equipped with "black box" receivers. Commercial fishing operators, particularly in the Bering Sea, use the radio-transmitted charts to steer clear of problem weather and troublesome ice formations. More information is available from the National Weather Service in Kodiak or Anchorage.

Related reading: *Icebound in the Siberian Arctic,* by Robert J. Gleason. Rescue of a ship by early aviators. 164 pages, $4.95. See ALASKA NORTHWEST LIBRARY in the back of the book.

Ice Fog

A fog of tiny, spherical ice crystals formed when air just above the ground becomes so cold it can no longer retain water vapor. Most common in Arctic and subarctic regions in winter when clear skies create an air inversion. Surface heat radiates into space, forming a warm-air cap that contains cold air at low elevations. Most noticeable when man-made pollutants are also trapped at low levels by the air inversion.

Iceworm

Although generally regarded as a hoax, iceworms actually exist. These small, thin, segmented black worms, usually less than one inch long, thrive at temperatures just above freezing. Observers as far back as the 1880s report that at dawn, dusk or on overcast days, the tiny worms, all belonging to the genus *Mesenchytraeus*, may literally carpet the surface of glaciers. When sunlight strikes them, they burrow back down into the ice.

The town of Cordova commemorates its own version of the iceworm each February in the Iceworm Festival, when a 150-foot-long, multilegged "iceworm" marches in a parade down Main Street.

Iditarod Trail Sled Dog Race

The first race, conceived and organized by Joe Redington, Sr., of Knik, and historian Dorothy Page, of Wasilla, was run in 1967 and covered only 56 miles. The race was lengthened in 1973, and the first ever 1,100-mile sled dog race began in Anchorage on March 3, and ended April 3, 1973, in Nome. Of the 34 who started the race, 22 finished. The Iditarod has been run every year since its inception. In 1976, Congress designated the Iditarod as a National Historic Trail.

Following the old dog team mail route blazed in 1910 from Knik to Nome, the trail crosses two mountain ranges, follows the Yukon River for about 150 miles, runs through several bush villages and crosses the pack ice of Norton Sound.

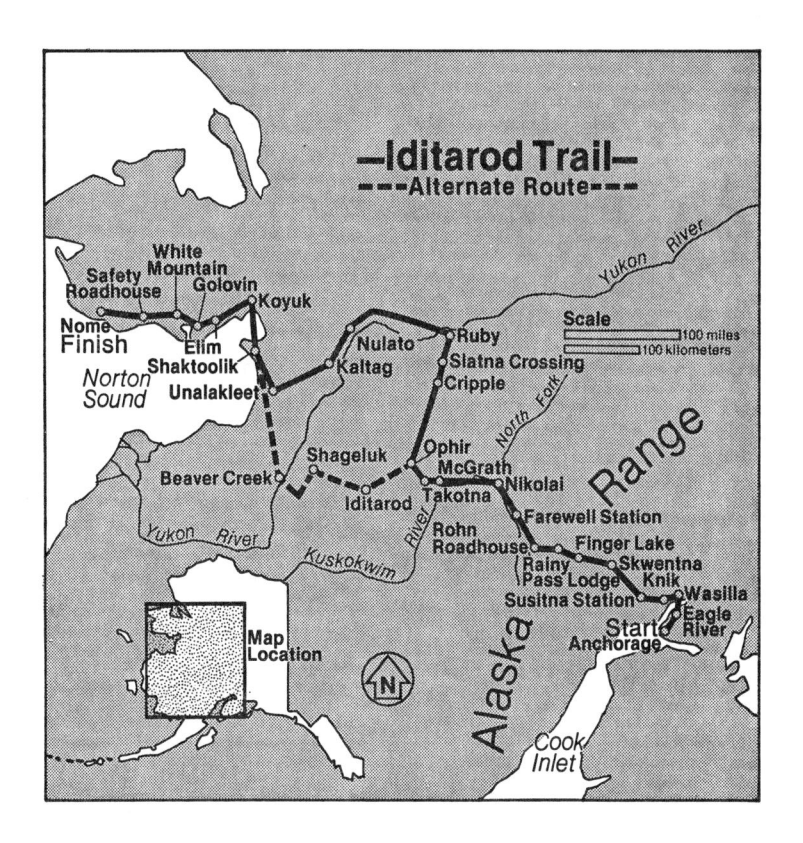

Strictly a winter trail because the ground is mostly spongy muskeg swamps, the route attracted national attention in 1925 when sled dog mushers, including the famous Leonhard Seppala, relayed 300,000 units of life-saving diphtheria serum to epidemic-threatened Nome. However, as the airplane and snowmobile replaced the sled dog team, the trail fell into disuse. Thanks to Redington, the trail has been assured a place in Alaska history.

Each year the Iditarod takes a slightly different course, following an alternate southern route in odd years (see map). While the route is traditionally described as 1,049 miles long (a figure that was selected because Alaska is the 49th state), actual distance is close to 1,100 miles. Part of it is run on frozen river ice.

The Iditarod purse is divided among the first 20 finishers. In 1989, Susan Butcher received $3,000 in silver ingots for being the first to hit the halfway checkpoint at Cripple.

In 1989, 49 mushers started the world's longest and richest sled dog race. Of those, 38 finished the Anchorage to Nome ordeal. Joe Runyan of Nenana, the 1989 winner, received the first-place check of $50,000 from a $249,500 purse. During the 1989 race, several mushers put the race aside, and any hopes of finishing in the top 20, to come to the aid of musher Mike Madden. Between Ophir and Iditarod, Madden fell victim to severe hypothermia aggravated by an internal infection. The help provided by Jerry Austin, Mitch Brazen, Kathy Halverson, Jamie Nelson, Linwood Fielder and Bernie Willis saved Madden's life.

Winners and Times

Year	Musher	Days	Hrs.	Min.	Sec.	Prize
1989	Joe Runyan, Nenana	11	05	24	34	$50,000
1988	Susan Butcher, Manley	11	11	41	40	30,000
1987	Susan Butcher, Manley	11	02	05	13	50,000
1986	Susan Butcher, Manley	11	15	06	00	50,000
1985	Libby Riddles, Teller	18	00	20	17	50,000
1984	Dean Osmar, Clam Gulch	12	15	07	33	24,000*
1983	Dick Mackey, Wasilla	12	14	10	44	24,000
1982	Rick Swenson, Eureka	16	04	40	10	24,000
1981	Rick Swenson, Eureka	12	08	45	02	24,000
1980	Joe May, Trapper Creek	14	07	11	51	12,000
1979	Rick Swenson, Eureka	15	10	37	47	12,000
1978	Dick Mackey, Wasilla	14	18	52	24	12,000
1977	Rick Swenson, Eureka	16	16	27	13	9,600
1976	Jerry Riley, Nenana	18	22	58	17	7,000
1975	Emmitt Peters, Ruby	14	14	43	45	15,000
1974	Carl Huntington, Galena	20	15	02	07	12,000
1973	Dick Willmarth, Red Devil	20	00	49	41	12,000

*Does not include $2,000 in silver ingots for reaching the halfway checkpoint first.

1989 Results

Place	Musher	Days	Hrs.	Min.	Sec.	Prize
1	Joe Runyan, Nenana	11	05	24	34	$50,000
2	Susan Butcher, Manley	11	06	28	50	35,000
3	Rick Swenson, Two Rivers	11	08	50	50	27,000
4	Dee Dee Jonrowe, Willow	11	13	47	16	20,000
5	Lavon Barve, Wasilla	11	16	46	53	15,000
6	Martin Buser, Big Lake	12	02	06	05	12,000
7	Guy Blankenship, Fairbanks	12	02	22	24	11,000
8	Rick Mackey, Trapper Creek	12	02	25	00	10,000
9	Joe Redington, Sr., Knik	12	02	57	16	9,000
10	Tim Osmar, Clam Gulch	12	03	33	03	8,000
11	Jacques Philip, By Thomery, France	12	04	40	46	7,500
12	Matt Desalernos, Nome	12	05	33	38	7,000
13	Bob Chlupach, Willow	12	06	17	41	6,500
14	John Barron, Big Lake	12	08	10	08	6,000
15	Joe Garnie, Teller	12	08	33	28	5,500
16	Libby Riddles, Nome	12	08	34	44	5,000
17	Jerry Riley, Nenana	12	13	35	21	4,500
18	Bill Cotter, Nenana	12	15	22	59	4,000
19	Frank Teasley, Jackson, WY	12	16	54	19	3,500
20	Terry Adkins, Sand Coulee, MT	13	07	13	57	3,000

Igloo

Also known as snowhouses, these snow block structures provided temporary shelter for Arctic Alaska Eskimos. Igloos are built in a spiral with each tier leaning inward at a greater angle. The entrance is a tunnel with a cold trap in front of the sleeping platform. A vent at the top allows for ventilation, and an ice window lets in light.

Imports and Exports

Alaska's most important trading partner is Japan, to which it sent 71 percent of its exports in 1988. Two other Asian nations were significant markets: Korea (8.7 percent) and Taiwan (4.5 percent). The state received 55.6 percent of its 1988 imports from Canada, 22.9 percent from Japan, 1.4 percent from Korea and 0.16 percent from Taiwan.

Alaska's exports for 1988 were valued at over two billion dollars by the International Trade Administration, U.S. Department of Commerce. Of this total, the state's most valuable exports were fish (41.6 percent), lumber (24 percent), petrol products (18.7 percent), minerals (6.3 percent) and coal (1.4 percent).

Income

In many sectors of the economy, Alaskans earn higher incomes than their counterparts in the Lower 48. On the average, Alaskans' net earnings was 76.7 percent of their total personal income in 1987 (most current information available), versus 68.9 percent in the Lower 48. A great deal of this difference, however, is due to Alaska's younger population. In general, Alaskans are younger, and the total population has less dividends, interest and rent income.

A wide variation is apparent when comparing the average earnings by industry between the U.S. and Alaska. The ratio of Alaska to U.S. wage and salary earnings are highest in mining and government, and lowest in the manufacturing industry.

In 1987, total personal income earned by Alaskans was $9.57 billion. On a per capita basis, that ranked Alaska fifth in the nation at $18,230 per person. This was 118 percent above the national average per capita income. Alaska's per capita income position among the states has eroded in the past several years. In 1985, Alaska had the highest per capita income in the nation, but the two-year recession dropped per capita income nearly 3 percent from 1985 to 1987.

Alaska is characterized by a wide disparity in incomes. According to the September 1987 issue of *Alaska Economic Trends,* income statistics show that Alaska had one of the highest concentrations of millionaires in the nation, as well as more than one in five people living below the poverty level.

Personal income in Alaska has followed the same pattern as employment, rising during construction of the trans-Alaska pipeline and during the construction boom of the early 1980s. Following those, personal income has either dropped or increased at a very gradual rate. The 1986-88 recession spared few industries, adversely affecting all income averages. A slow recovery was being seen in 1988.

Industry

In 1988, third quarter statistics, the highest income earning sectors of the economy were: government ($482.8 million), services ($233.2 million), trade (wholesale and retail, $200.3 million), transportation ($155.2 million), mining ($152.4 million), manufacturing ($141.3 million) and construction ($120.6 million).

Fiscal budgets provide another perspective on the importance of oil and gas to the state's economy. Approximately 85 percent of the state's 1989 fiscal year budget (July 1988 to June 1989) will come from the oil and gas industry.

With the major exception of oil and gas, industries yielding the highest gross state product are also among the top employers. According to statistics provided by the Alaska Department of Labor, state, federal and local governments were among the largest employers in the state in 1988. The three levels of government employed an average of 66,600 people in 1988. Following government, in rank by the average number of people employed annually, came services (42,900); wholesale and retail trade (42,000); transportation, communications and utilities, (17,200); manufacturing (14,800); finance, insurance and real estate (10,700); mining (9,500); and construction (8,700).

Information Sources

Agriculture: State Division of Agriculture, P.O. Box 949, Palmer 99645; Cooperative Extension Service, University of Alaska, Fairbanks 99701.
Alaska Natives: Alaska Federation of Natives, 411 W. 4th Ave., Anchorage 99501.
Boating, Canoeing and Kayaking: Alaska Dept. of Transportation and Public Facilities, Pouch Z, Juneau 99811; State of Alaska, Division of Parks and Outdoor Recreation, 3601 C St., Suite 1200, Anchorage 99503.
Business: Alaska Department of

- **Commerce and Economic Development**, Pouch D, Juneau 99811; State Chamber of Commerce, 217 2nd St., Suite 201, Juneau 99801.
- **Camping and Hiking:** U.S. Forest Service, P.O. Box 1628-RN, Juneau 99802; Bureau of Land Management, 222 W, 7th Ave., #13, Anchorage 99513; Supervisor, Chugach National Forest, 201 E. 9th Ave., Suite 206, Anchorage 99501; National Park Service, 2525 Gambell St., Anchorage 99503; Supervisor, Tongass National Forest, P.O. Box 1628, Juneau 99802; U.S. Fish and Wildlife Service, 1011 E. Tudor Road, Anchorage 99503.
- **Census Data:** Alaska Department of Labor, Research and Analysis, P.O. Box 107018, Anchorage 99510.
- **Climate:** State Climatologist, University of Alaska, Arctic Environmental and Data Center, 707 A St., Anchorage 99501.
- **Education:** Alaska Department of Education, P.O. Box GA, Juneau 99811.
- **Gold Panning:** State Division of Geological and Geophysical Surveys, Mines Information Office, 3601 C St., Anchorage 99503; Alaska Miners Association, 501 W. Northern Lights, Suite 203, Anchorage 99503.
- **Health:** State Department of Health and Social Services, Division of Public Health, Pouch H-06C, Juneau 99811.
- **Housing:** State Housing Authority, Box 100080, Anchorage 99510.
- **Hunting and Fishing Regulations:** State Department of Fish and Game, P.O. Box 3-2000, Juneau 99802.
- **Job Opportunities:** State Employment Service, Box 3-7000, Juneau 99802.
- **Labor:** State Department of Labor, P.O. Box 25501-5501, Juneau 99802.
- **Land:** State Division of Lands, Pouch 7-005, Anchorage 99510; Bureau of Land Management, 222 W. 7th Ave., #13, Anchorage 99513; Alaska Public Lands Information Centers; 605 W. 4th Ave., Suite 105, Anchorage 99501; 250 Cushman St., Suite 1A, Fairbanks 99701; P.O. Box 359, Tok 99780.
- **Legislature:** Legislative Information Office, 3111 C St., Anchorage 99503.
- **Made in Alaska Products:** Alaska Association of Manufacturers, P.O. Box 142831, Anchorage 99514.
- **Maps (topographic):** U.S. Geological Survey, 222 W. 7th Ave., Room F-146, Anchorage 99513
- **Military:** Department of the Air Force, Headquarters, Alaskan Air Command, Elmendorf Air Force Base 99506; Department of the Army, Headquarters, 6th Infantry Brigade (Alaska), Fort Richardson 99505; State Department of Military Affairs, Office of the Adjutant General, 3601 C St., Anchorage 99503; Department of Transportation, U.S. Coast Guard, 17th Coast Guard District, P.O. Box 3-5000, Juneau 99802.
- **Mines and Petroleum:** State Division of Geological and Geophysical Surveys, 3601 C Street, Anchorage 99503; Petroleum Information Corp., P.O. Box 102278, Anchorage 99510; Alaska Miners Association, 501 W. Northern Lights, Suite 203, Anchorage 99503.
- **River Running:** National Park Service, 2525 Gambell St., Anchorage 99503; U.S. Dept. of the Interior, Fish and Wildlife Service, 1011 E. Tudor Road, Anchorage 99503; BLM, 222 W. 7th Ave., #13, Anchorage 99513.
- **Travel and Visitor Information:** State Division of Tourism, Pouch E-001, Juneau 99811; Alaska Visitors Association, P.O. Box 102220, Anchorage 99510.

Islands

Southeastern Alaska contains about 1,000 of the state's 1,800 named islands, rocks and reefs; several thousand remain unnamed. The Aleutian Island chain, stretching southwest from the mainland, contains more than 200 islands.

Of the state's 10 largest islands, 6 are in southeastern Alaska. Of the remainder, Unimak is in the Aleutians, Nunivak and Saint Lawrence are in the Bering Sea off the west coast of Alaska, and Kodiak is in the Gulf of Alaska. The state's 10 largest islands, according to U.S. Geological Survey and Bureau of Land Management figures, are:

	Square Miles
Kodiak	3,588
Prince of Wales	2,731*
Chichagof	2,062
Saint Lawrence	1,780
Admiralty	1,709
Baranof	1,636
Nunivak	1,600**
Unimak	1,600
Revillagigedo	1,134
Kupreanof	1,084

*The figure 2,770 square miles reported in earlier editions of The ALASKA ALMANAC® included associated islands.
**Estimate

Related reading: *A Guide to The Queen Charlotte Islands.* 90 pages, $9.95. See ALASKA NORTHWEST LIBRARY in the back of the book.

Ivory

Eskimos traditionally carved ivory to make such implements as harpoon heads, dolls and *ulu* (fan-shaped knife) handles. For the past 80 years, however, most carvings have been made to be sold. Etching on ivory originally was done with hand tools and the scratches were filled in with soot. Today power tools supplement the hand tools and carvers may color the etching with India ink, graphite, hematite or commercial coloring.

The large islands of the Bering Sea — Saint Lawrence, Little Diomede and Nunivak — are home to the majority of Alaska's ivory carvers. Eskimos from King Island, renowned for their carving skill, now live in Nome along with talented artists from many other villages.

The bulk of the ivory used today comes from walrus tusks and teeth, seasoned for a few months. Old walrus ivory, often mistakenly called fossil ivory, is also used. This ivory has been buried in the ground or has been on beaches for years, and contact with various minerals has changed it from white to tan or any of a multitude of colors. Some highly prized old ivory exhibits rays of deep blue or areas of brown and gold that shine. Most old ivory comes from ancient sites or beaches on Saint Lawrence Island and is sold by the pound to non-Native buyers, generally for use in some kind of artwork.

Mastodon tusks are often unearthed in the summer by miners or found eroding from river cutbanks where they have been buried for thousands of years. Although these tusks are enormous and their colorations often beautiful, the material cannot be used as efficiently as walrus ivory. Mastodon ivory dries and separates into narrow ridges.

Various federal prohibitions govern the collection of old walrus, mammoth and mastodon ivory. Such materials may be gathered from private or reservation lands, but may not be traded or sold if found on public lands. The taking of fresh walrus ivory is prohibited to non-Natives in accordance with the Marine Mammal Protection Act of 1972.

In the 19th century, Native artists who came in contact with whalers etched realistic scenes on sperm whale teeth. Today, with the ban on the taking of sperm whales, this type of ivory is not available to Native scrimshanders.

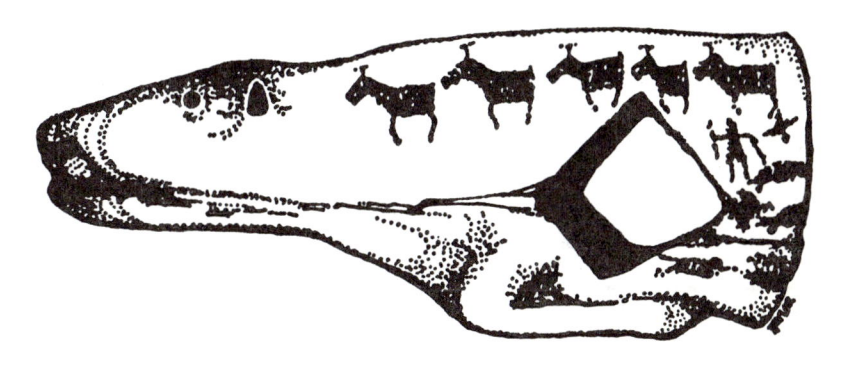

Walrus may be taken only by Alaska Natives (Aleuts, Eskimos and Indians) who dwell on the coast of the North Pacific Ocean or the Arctic Ocean, for subsistence purposes or for the creation and sale of authentic Native articles of handicrafts or clothing.

Raw walrus ivory and other parts can be sold only by an Alaska Native to an Alaska Native within Alaska, or to a registered agent for resale or transfer to an Alaska Native within the state. Only authentic Native processed ivory articles of handicrafts or clothing may be sold or transferred to a non-Native, or sold in interstate commerce.

Beach ivory, which is found on the beach within one-fourth mile of the ocean, may, however, be kept by anyone. This ivory must be registered by all non-Natives with the U.S. Fish and Wildlife Service or the National Marine Fisheries Service within 30 days of discovery. Beach-found ivory must remain in the possession of the finder even if carved or scrimshawed.

Carved or scrimshawed walrus ivory (authentic Native handicraft) or other marine mammal parts made into clothing or other authentic Native handicrafts may be exported from the United States to a foreign country, but the exporter must first obtain an export permit from the USFWS. Even visitors from the Lower 48 simply traveling through, or stopping in Canada on their way home, are required to have a USFWS export and/or transit permit. Cost is $25. Mailing the carved ivory home will avoid the need for an export/transit permit. Importation of walrus or other marine mammals is illegal except for scientific research purposes or for public display once a permit is granted.

For further information contact: Special Agent-in-Charge, U.S. Fish and Wildlife Service, 1011 East Tudor Road, Anchorage 99503, phone (907) 786-3311; or Senior Resident, U.S. Fish and Wildlife Service, 1412 Airport Way, Fairbanks 99701, phone (907) 456-0239.

Jade

Most Alaskan jade is found near the Dall, Shungnak and Kobuk rivers and Jade Mountain, all north of the Arctic Circle. The stones occur in various shades of green, brown, black, yellow, white and even red. The most valuable are those that are marbled black, white and green. Gem-quality jade, about one-fourth of the total mined, is used in jewelry making. Fractured jade is used for clock faces, table tops, book ends and other items. Jade is the Alaska state gem.

Kuspuk

Eskimo woman's parka, often made with a loosely cut back so that an infant may be carried piggyback-style. Parkas are made from rabbit or fox skins; traditionally, the fur lining faces inward. The ruffs are generally wolverine or wolf fur. An outer shell, called a *qaspeg*, is worn over a fur parka to keep it clean and prevent wearing. This outer shell is usually made of brightly colored corduroy, cotton print or velveteenlike material, and may be trimmed with rickrack.

Labor and Employer Organizations

The Alaska Department of Labor directory *Labor Unions and Employer Groups* lists the following organizations:

ANCHORAGE
Alaska Public Employees Association
Alaska State District Council of Laborers
American Federation of Government Employees Council 121
Anchorage Independent Longshore Union Local No.1
Anchorage Musicians Association Local No. 650
Anchorage Typographical Union Local No. 823
Asbestos Workers Local No. 97
Associated General Contractors of America
Bartenders' International Union Local No. 883
Bricklayers and Allied Craftsmen Local No. 1
Brotherhood of Railroad Trainmen Local No. 999
Construction and General Laborers Local No. 341
Hotel, Motel, Restaurant and Construction Camp Employees Local No. 878.
International Alliance of Theatrical Stage Employees and Motion Picture Machine Operators Local No. 770
International Association of Bridge, Structural and Ornamental workers Local No. 751
International Association of Firefighters Local No. 1264
International Association of Machinists and Aerospace Workers Local No. 601
International Brotherhood of Boilermakers, Iron Ship Builders, Blacksmiths, Forgers and Helpers Local No. 498
International Brotherhood of Teamsters, Chauffeurs, Warehousemen and Helpers Local No. 959
International Brotherhood of Painters and Allied Trades Local No. 1140
Laundry and Dry Cleaning International Union Local No. 333
National Electrical Contractors Association
Operative Plasterers' and Cement Masons' International Association Local No. 867
Piledrivers, Bridge, Dock Builders and Drivers Local No. 2520
Public Employees Local No. 71
Retail Clerks Union Local No. 1496
Roofers Union Local No. 190
Sheet Metal Workers' International Association Local No. 23
United Association of Plumbers and Steamfitters Local No. 367
United Brotherhood of Carpenters and Joiners Local No. 1281
Western Alaska Building and Construction Trades Council

CORDOVA
Copper River and Prince William Sound Cannery Workers' Union
Cordova District Fisheries Union
International Longshoremen's and Warehousemen's Union Local No. 66

DILLINGHAM
Western Alaska Cooperative Marketing Association

DUTCH HARBOR
International Longshoremen's and Warehousemen's Union

FAIRBANKS
Alaska Public Employees Association
Construction and General Laborers Local No. 942
Fairbanks Central Labor Council
Fairbanks Joint Crafts Council
Hotel, Motel, Restaurant, Construction Camp Employees and Bartenders Local No. 879
International Association of Firefighters Local No. 1324
International Brotherhood of Electrical Workers Local No. 1547
International Brotherhood of Teamsters, Chauffeurs, Warehousemen and Helpers Local No. 959
International Printing and Graphic Communications Union Local No. 704
International Union of Operating Engineers Local No. 302
Musicians' Protective Union Local No. 481
NEA-Alaska (Fairbanks Education Association)
Operative Plasterers' and Cement Masons' International Association Local No. 867

Public Employees Local No. 71
Retail Clerks International Association Local No. 1689
Sheet Metal Workers' International Association Local No. 72
Technical Engineers Local No. 959
United Association of Journeymen and Apprentices of the Plumbing and Pipefitting Industry Local No. 375
United Brotherhood of Carpenters and Joiners Local No. 1243

HAINES
International Longshoremen's and Warehousemen's Union Local No. 65

JUNEAU
Alaska Public Employees Association
Associated General Contractors of America
Bartenders' International Union Local No. 869
Hotel and Restaurant Employees' Union Local No. 871
Inland Boatmen's Union of the Pacific
International Brotherhood of Electrical Workers Local No. 1547
International Brotherhood of Teamsters, Chauffeurs, Warehousemen and Helpers Local No. 959
International Longshoremen's and Warehousemen's Union Local No. 16
International Longshoremen's and *Warehousemen's* Union Local No. 41
International Union of Operating Engineers Local No. 302

Juneau Central Labor Council
Juneau and Vicinity Building and Construction Trades Council
Laborers International Union Local No. 942
Musicians' Protective Union
NEA-Alaska
National Federation of Federal Employees Local No. 251
Public Employees Local No. 71
United Association of Journeymen and Apprentices of the Plumbing and Pipefitting Industry Local No. 262
United Brotherhood of Carpenters and Joiners Local No. 2247

KETCHIKAN
Alaska Loggers Association
Association of Western Pulp and Paper Workers Local No. 783
Bartenders and Culinary Workers Union Local No. 867
International Brotherhood of Electrical Workers Local No. 1547
International Brotherhood of Teamsters, Chauffeurs, Warehousemen and Helpers Local No. 959
International *Longshoremen's* and Warehousemen's Union Local No. 62
International Longshoremen's and *Warehousemen's* Union Local No. 61
International Woodworkers of America Local No. 3-193
Ketchikan Central Labor Council
United Brotherhood of Carpenters and Joiners Local No. 1501

KODIAK
United Brotherhood of Carpenters and Joiners Local No. 2161
Inland Boatmen's Union of the Pacific

PALMER
United Mineworkers Local No. 7901
Wood, Wire and Metal Lathers International Union Local No. 529

PELICAN
International Longshoremen's and Warehousemen's Union Local No. 83

PETERSBURG
International Longshoremen's and *Warehousemen's* Union Local No. 85
Petersburg Fishermen's Union
United Industrial Workers

SELDOVIA
United Cannery Workers of Lower Cook Inlet

SEWARD
International Longshoremen's and Warehousemen's Union Local No. 60

SITKA
Hotel, Motel and Culinary Workers' and Bartenders' Union Local No. 873
International Longshoremen's and Warehousemen's Union Local No. 84
International Union, United Paperworkers Local No. 962
Retail Clerks International Association Local No. 1394
United Brotherhood of Carpenters and Joiners Local No. 466

SKAGWAY
United Transportation Union Local No. 1787

WRANGELL
International Longshoremen's and Warehousemen's Union Local No. 87
United Paperworkers' International Union Local No. 1341

Lakes

There are 94 lakes with surface areas of more than 10 square miles among Alaska's more than 3 million lakes. According to the U.S. Geological Survey, the 10 largest (larger than 20 acres) natural freshwater lakes are:

Lakes	Square Miles
Iliamna	1,000
Becharof	458
Teshekpuk	315
Naknek	242
Tustumena	117
Clark	110
Dall	100
Upper Ugashik	75
Lower Ugashik	72
Kukaklek	72

Land

At first glance it seems odd that such a huge area as Alaska has not been more heavily settled. Thousands of acres of forest and tundra, miles and miles of rivers and streams, hidden valleys, bays, coves and mountains, are spread across an area so vast that it staggers the imagination. Yet, over two-thirds of the population of Alaska remains clustered around two major centers of commerce and survival. Compared to the settlement of the western Lower 48, Alaska is not settled at all.

Visitors flying over the state are impressed by immense areas showing no sign of humanity. Current assessments indicate that approximately 160,000 acres of Alaska have been cleared, built on or otherwise directly altered by man, either by settlement or resource development, including mining, pipeline construction and agriculture. In comparison to the 365 million acres of land which comprise the total of the state, the settled or altered area currently amounts to less than 1/20th of a percent.

There are significant reasons for this lack of development in Alaska. Frozen for long periods in the dark of the Arctic, much of the land cannot support quantities of people or industry. Where the winters are "warm," the mountains, glaciers, rivers and oceans prevent easy access for commerce and trade.

The status of land, especially in Alaska, is constantly changing. In most places, the free market affects patterns of land ownership, but in Alaska, all land ownership patterns until recently were the result of a century-long process of a single landowner, the United States government.

The Statehood Act signaled the beginning of a dramatic shift in land ownership patterns. It authorized the state to select a total of 104 million of the 365 million acres of land and inland waters in Alaska. Under the Submerged Lands Act, the state also has title to submerged lands under navigable inland waters. In passing the Statehood Act, Congress cited economic independence and the need to open Alaska to economic development as the primary purposes for large Alaska land grants.

The issue of the Native claims in Alaska was cleared up with the passage of the Alaska Native Claims Settlement Act (ANCSA) on December 18, 1971. This act of Congress provided for creation of Alaska Native village and regional corporations, and gave the

Alaska Eskimos, Aleuts and Indians nearly $1 billion and the right to select 44 million acres from a land "pool" of some 115 million acres.

Immediately after the passage of the settlement act, the state filed for the selection of an additional 77 million acres of land before the creation of some Native withdrawals and withdrawals for study as National Interest Lands. The Department of the Interior refused to recognize these selections. In September of 1972, the litigation initiated by the state was resolved by a settlement affirming state selection of 41 million acres.

the options that the executive branch of the federal government could take to protect federal lands in Alaska until the Ninety-sixth Congress could consider the creation of new parks, wildlife refuges, wild and scenic rivers and forests. In keeping with this objective, the secretary of the interior withdrew from most public uses about 114 million acres of land in Alaska, under provisions of the 1976 Federal Land Policy and Management Act. On December 1, 1978, the president, under the authority of the 1906 Antiquities Act, designated 56 million acres of these lands as National Monuments.

Section 17 of the settlement act, in addition to establishing a Joint Federal-State Land Use Planning Commission, directed the secretary of the interior to withdraw from public use up to 80 million acres of land in Alaska for study as possible national parks, wildlife refuges, forests, and wild and scenic rivers. These were the National Interest Lands Congress was to decide upon, as set forth in Section 17(d)(2) of the settlement act, by December 18, 1978. The U.S. House of Representatives passed a bill (HR39) which would have designated 124 million acres of national parks, forests and wildlife refuges, and designated millions of acres of these and existing parks, forests and refuges as wilderness. Although a bill was reported out of committee, it failed to pass the Senate before Congress adjourned.

In November 1978, the secretary of the interior published a draft environmental impact supplement which listed

In February, 1980, the House of Representatives passed a modified HR39. In August, 1980, the Senate passed a compromise version of the Alaska lands bill that created 106 million acres of new conservation units and affected a total of 131 million acres of land in Alaska. In November, 1980, the House accepted the Senate version of the Alaska National Interest Lands Conservation Act, which President Jimmy Carter signed into law on December 2, 1980. This is also known as the d-2 lands bill or the compromise HR39. (*See also* the following sections: National Parks, Preserves and Monuments; National Wilderness Areas; National Wildlife Refuges; National Forests; and National Wild and Scenic Rivers.)

Alaska's land will continue to be a controversial and complex subject for some time. Implementation of the d-2 issue, and distribution of land to the Native village and regional corporations, the state of Alaska and private citizens in the state will require time. Much of this work is being done by the Bureau of Land Management. Numerous land issues created by large land exchanges, conflicting land use and management policies, and overlapping resources will require constant cooperation between landowners if the issues are going to be resolved successfully.

Acquiring Land for Private Use

The easiest and fastest way to acquire land for private use is by purchase from the private sector, through real estate agencies or directly from individuals. Because of speculation, land claim conflicts and delays involving Native, state and federal groups, however, private land is considered by many people to be in short supply and often is very expensive.

Private land in Alaska, excluding land held by Native corporations, is estimated to be more than one million acres, but less than 1 percent of the state. Much of this land passed into private hands through the federal Homestead Acts and other public land laws as well as the land disposal programs of the state, boroughs or communities. Most private land is located along Alaska's small road network. Compared to other categories of land, it is highly accessible and constitutes some of the prime settlement land.

All laws related to homesteading on federal land (as opposed to state land) in Alaska, were repealed as of 1986. Federal land is not available for homesteading, or trade and manufacturing sites.

Following are programs that are, or soon will be, in effect for the sale of state land. A one-year residency is required for all but the auction program.

Auction: The state has been selling land by public auction since statehood. The state may sell full surface rights, lease of surface or subsurface rights, or restricted title at an auction. There is a minimum bid of fair market value and the high bidder is the purchaser. Participants must be 18.

Homesite: The homesite program was passed in 1977 by the state legislature. Under its provisions each Alaskan is eligible for up to five acres. The land is free, but the individual must pay the cost of the survey and platting. Persons enrolled in this program must live on the homesite for 35 months within seven years of entry and construct a permanent, single-family dwelling on the site within five years (this is called "proving up" on the land).

Remote Parcels: This remote parcel program replaced the old open-to-entry program. It permits entry upon designated areas to stake a parcel of up to 5, 20 or 40 acres, depending on the area, and to lease the area for five years with an option for a five-year renewal. Rental under the lease is $10 per acre per year. The lease is not transferable. During the lease period the lessee must survey the land. He may then apply to purchase the land at the fair market value at the time of his initial lease application. The state will finance the sale over a period of 20 years.

Remote parcels ended July 1, 1984, as the program was replaced by the 1983 homesteading bill. Alaskans leasing remote parcels, but who have not yet purchased them, may continue under the remote parcel program or opt to obtain title by meeting homesteading requirements.

Lottery: One year of residency is required to participate in the lottery program. Successful applicants are determined by a drawing and pay the appraised market value of the land. They repay the state over a period of up to 20 years, with interest set at the current federal land loan bank rate. Lotteries require a 5 percent down payment.

The state offered 100,000 acres of land to private ownership in each fiscal year from July 1, 1979, to July 1, 1982. Disposal levels from that time forward have been based on an annual assessment of the demand for state land. Sales are scheduled for fall and spring.

On April 1, 1983, the Department of Natural Resources discontinued a program that provided Alaska residents who were registered voters a 5-percent-per-year-of-residency discount (up to $25,000) on the sale of land purchased from the state. Fifteen-year veteran residents had been eligible for up to $37,500 on this one-time program.

Homestead: Under the new law, residents of at least one year, who are 18 years or older, have a chance to receive up to 40 acres of nonagricultural land or up to 160 acres of agricultural land without paying for the acreage itself. The homesteader, however, must survey, occupy and improve the land in certain ways, and within specific time frames to receive title.

The homestead act also allows homesteaders to purchase parcels at fair market value without occupying or improving the land. This option requires only that nonagricultural land be staked, brushed and surveyed, and that parcels designed for agricultural use also meet clearing requirements.

After homesteading areas have been designed, homesteaders must stake the corners and flag the boundaries of the land, pay a fee of five dollars per acre and personally file a description of the land with the state. Title then may be acquired either by purchasing the land (after brushing, surveying and clearing); brushing the boundaries within 90 days after issuance of the entry permit; completing an approved survey of the land within two years, unless a one-year extension is granted; erecting a habitable permanent dwelling on the homestead within three years; living on the parcel for not less than 25 months within five years; and clearing and either putting into production or preparing for cultivation 25 percent of the land within five years if it is classified for agricultural use.

Up-to-date information and applications for state programs are available from the Alaska Division of Land and Water Management:

Northcentral District, 4420 Airport Way, Fairbanks 99701
Southcentral District Office, 3601 C St., Anchorage 99503
Southeastern District Office, Marine View Apts., #407, 230 S. Franklin Juneau 99801

Following is the amount of Alaska land owned by various entities as of September, 1988:

Owner	Acreage (millions of acres)
U.S. Bureau of Land Management	92.4
U.S. Fish and Wildlife	75.4
State	84.7
National Park Service	50.6
Forest Service	23.2
Native	35.1
Military and other Federal	2.6
Private	1

(Source: U.S. Bureau of Land Management)

Languages

Besides English, Alaska's languages include Haida, Tlingit, Tsimshian, Aleut, several dialects of Eskimo and several dialects of Athabascan.

Mammals

LARGE LAND MAMMALS

Black bear — Highest densities found in Southeast, Prince William Sound and southcentral coastal mountains and lowlands. Also occur in interior and western Alaska. Absent from Southeast islands north of Frederick Sound (primarily Admiralty, Baranof and Chichagof) and Kodiak archipelago. Not commonly found west of about Naknek Lake on the Alaska Peninsula, in the Aleutian Islands or on the open tundra sloping into the Bering Sea and Arctic Ocean.

Brown/grizzly bear — Found in most of Alaska. Absent from Southeast islands south of Frederick Sound and from the Aleutians (except for Unimak Island).

Polar bear — There are two groups in Alaska's Arctic rim: an eastern group found largely in the Beaufort Sea and a western group found in the Chukchi Sea between Alaska and Siberia. The latter group are the largest polar bears in the world. Old males can exceed 1,500 pounds.

American bison — In 1928, 23 bison were transplanted from Montana to Delta Junction to restore Alaska's bison population which had died out some 500 years before. Today, several hundred bison graze near Delta Junction; other herds are at Farewell, Chitina and along the lower Copper River.

Barren Ground caribou — At least 13 distinct herds: Adak, Alaska Peninsula, Arctic, Beaver, Chisana, Delta, Kenai, McKinley, Mentasta, Mulchatna, Nelchina, Porcupine and Fortymile. Porcupine and Fortymile herds range into Canada.

Sitka blacktail deer — Live in coastal rain forests of southeastern Alaska; expanded by transplants to Yakutat area, Prince William Sound, and Kodiak and Afognak islands.

Roosevelt elk — Transplanted in 1928 from Olympic Peninsula, Washington, to Raspberry and Afognak islands.

Moose — Found from the Unuk River in Southeast to the Arctic slope. Most abundant in second-growth birch forests, on timberline plateaus and along major rivers of Southcentral and Interior. Not found on islands in Prince William Sound or Bering Sea, most major islands in Southeast or on Kodiak or Aleutians group.

Mountain goat — Found in mountains throughout Southeast and north and west along coastal mountains to Cook Inlet and Kenai Peninsula; successfully transplanted to Kodiak and Baranof islands.

Musk ox — First transplanted to Nunivak Island and from there to Arctic slope around Kavik, Seward Peninsula, Cape Thompson and Nelson Island.

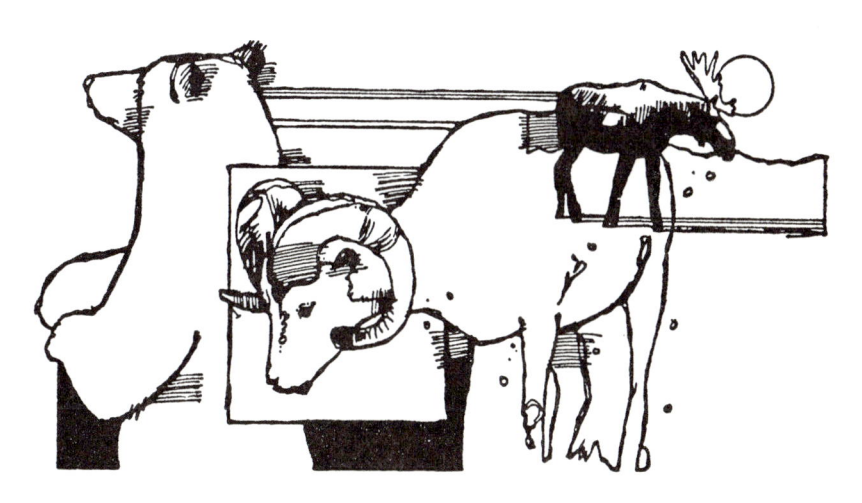

Dall sheep — Found in all major mountain ranges in Alaska except the Aleutian Range south of Iliamna Lake.

Wolf — Found throughout Alaska except Bering Sea islands, some Southeast and Prince William Sound islands, and the Aleutian Islands. Classified as big game and as fur bearer. Inhabits a variety of climates and terrains.

Wolverine — Found throughout Alaska and on some Southeast islands; abundant in the Interior and on the Alaska Peninsula. Shy, solitary creatures; not abundant in comparison with other fur bearers. Members of the weasel family. Classified as big game and as fur bearer.

FUR BEARERS

Beaver — Found in most of mainland Alaska from Brooks Range to middle of Alaska Peninsula. Abundant in some major mainland river drainages in Southeast and on Yakutat forelands. Successfully transplanted to Kodiak area. Beaver dams are sometimes destroyed to allow salmon upstream; however, the beavers can rebuild their dams quickly and usually do so on the same site.

Coyote — Relative newcomer to Alaska, showing up shortly after the turn of the century, according to old-timers and records. Not abundant on a statewide basis, but common in Tanana, Copper, Matanuska and Susitna river drainages and on Kenai Peninsula. Found as far west as Alaska Peninsula and the north side of Bristol Bay.

Fox — **Arctic** (white and blue phases): Almost entirely along the Arctic coast as far south as the northwestern shore of Bristol Bay. Introduced to Pribilof and Aleutian islands where blue color phase, most popular with fox farmers, predominates. White color phase occurs naturally on Saint Lawrence and Nunivak islands. **Red:** Found throughout Alaska except for most areas of Southeast and Prince William Sound.

Hoary marmot — Present throughout most of the mountain regions of Alaska and along the Endicott Mountains east into Canada. Does not inhabit lower elevations.

Lynx — Found throughout Alaska, except on Yukon-Kuskokwim Delta, southern Alaska Peninsula and along coastal tidelands. Relatively scarce along northern gulf coast and in southeastern Alaska.

Marten — Ranges throughout timbered Alaska, except north of the Brooks Range, on treeless sections of the Alaska Peninsula, and on the Yukon-Kuskokwim Delta. Successfully introduced to Prince of Wales, Baranof, Chichagof and Afognak islands in this century. Absent from Prince William Sound and Kodiak Island.

Muskrat — Found throughout all of mainland Alaska south of the Brooks Range except for the Alaska Peninsula west of the Ugashik lakes. Introduced to Kodiak Island, Afognak and Raspberry islands. Absent from most other Alaska islands.

River otter — Occurs throughout the state except on Aleutian Islands, Bering Sea islands and on the Arctic coastal plain east of Point Lay. Most abundant in southeastern Alaska, Prince William Sound coastal areas and on the Yukon-Kuskokwim Delta.

Raccoon — Not native to Alaska and considered an undesirable addition because of impact on native fur bearers. Found on west coast of Kodiak Island, on Japonski and Baranof islands, and other islands off Prince of Wales Island in Southeast.

Squirrel — **Northern Flying:** Occurs in interior, southcentral and southeastern Alaska where forests are sufficiently dense to provide suitable habitat. Not found in areas lacking coniferous forests. **Red:** Found in spruce forests, especially along rivers, from Southeast north to the Brooks Range. Absent from Seward Peninsula, Yukon-Kuskokwim Delta and Alaska Peninsula south of Naknek River.

Weasel — Least weasel and short-tailed weasel are found throughout Alaska, except for Bering Sea and Aleutian islands. Short-tailed weasels are brown with white underparts in summer, becoming snow-white in winter (designated ermine).

OTHER SMALL MAMMALS

Bat — There are five common bat species in Alaska.

Northern hare (Arctic hare or tundra hare) — Inhabits western and northern coastal Alaska. Weighs 12 pounds or more and measures 2½ feet long.

Snowshoe hare (or varying hare) — Occurs throughout Alaska except for lower portion of Alaska Peninsula, Arctic coast and most islands; scarce in southeastern Alaska. Cyclic population highs and lows of hares occur roughly every 10 years. Reddish brown color in summer, white in winter. Named for their big hind feet, covered with coarse hair in winter, which make for easy travel over snow.

Brown lemming — Found throughout northern Alaska and the Alaska Peninsula. Not present in Southeast, Southcentral or Kodiak archipelago. Population undergoes cyclic highs and lows.

Collared lemming — Found from Brooks Range north and from lower Kuskokwim River drainage north.

Northern bog lemming (sometimes called lemming mice) — Tiny mammals, rarely observed, occur in meadows and bogs across most of Alaska.

Deer mouse — Inhabit timber and brush in southeastern Alaska.

House mouse — Found in Alaska seaports and large communities in Southcentral.

Meadow jumping mouse — Found in southern third of Alaska from Alaska Range to Gulf of Alaska.

Collared pika — Found in central and southern Alaska; most common in Alaska Range.

Porcupine — Found in most wooded regions of mainland Alaska.

Norway rat — Came to Alaska on whaling ships to Pribilof Islands in mid-1800s; great numbers of these rats thrived in the Aleutians (the Rat Islands group is named for the Norway rats). Found in virtually all Alaska seaports and in Anchorage and Fairbanks and other population centers with open garbage dumps.

Bushy-tailed woodrat — Found along mainland coast of southeastern Alaska. Commonly named pack rats, they carry off objects such as coins, buttons or bits of broken glass, often leaving a stick or similar object in their place.

Shrew — Seven species range in Alaska.

Meadow vole (or meadow mouse) — Seven species attributed to Alaska range throughout the state.

Red-backed vole — Found throughout Alaska from Southeast to Norton Sound.

Woodchuck — Found in eastern interior between Yukon and Tanana rivers, from east of Fairbanks to Alaska-Canada border. Large, burrowing squirrels, also called ground hogs.

MARINE MAMMALS

Marine mammals found in Alaska waters are: **Dolphin** (Grampus, Pacific white-sided and Risso's); **Pacific walrus; porpoise** (Dall and harbor); **sea otter; seal** (harbor, larga, northern elephant, northern fur, Pacific bearded or *oogruk*, ribbon, ringed and spotted); **Steller sea lion;** and **whale** (Baird's beaked or giant bottlenose, beluga, narwhal, blue, bowhead, Cuvier's beaked or goosebeaked, fin or finback, gray humpback, killer, minke or little piked, northern right, pilot, sei, sperm and Stejneger's beaked or Bering Sea beaked).

The Marine Mammal Protection Act, passed by Congress on December 21,

1972, provided for a complete moratorium on the taking and importation of all marine mammals. The purpose of the act was to give protection to population stocks of marine mammals that "are, or may be, in danger of extinction or depletion as a result of man's activities." Congress further found that marine mammals have "proven themselves to be resources of great international significance, aesthetic and recreational as well as economic, and it is the sense of the Congress that they should be protected and encouraged to develop to the greatest extent feasible commensurate with sound policies of resource management and that the primary objective of their management should be to maintain the health and stability of the marine ecosystem. Whenever consistent with this primary objective, it should be the goal to obtain an optimum sustainable population keeping in mind the carrying capacity of the habitat."

At the present time, the U.S. Fish and Wildlife Service (Department of the Interior) is responsible for the management of polar bears, sea otter and walrus in Alaska. The National Marine Fisheries Service (Department of Commerce) is responsible for the management of all other marine mammals. The state of Alaska assumed management of walrus in April 1976, and relinquished it back to the USFWS in July 1979. However, an amendment to the Marine Mammal Protection Act in 1981 makes it easier for states to assume management of marine mammals and Alaska is currently going through the necessary steps to assume management of its marine mammals.

Masks

Masks have been important to the Eskimos, coastal Indians and Aleuts of Alaska.

Eskimo

The complex Eskimo masks made during the nineteenth century rank among the finest tribal art in the world. Mask-making and the ceremonialism that accompanied it were highly developed and practiced widely by the time the first Russians established trading posts in southeast Alaska in the early 1800s. By the early part of the twentieth century masks were made much less frequently and were rarely made for ceremonial use.

During certain ceremonies the shaman used masks, sometimes in conjunction with wooden puppets, in ways that frightened and entertained participants. Dancers wore religious masks in festivals that honored the spirits of animals and birds to be hunted or that needed to be appeased. Each spirit was interpreted visually in a different mask and each mask was thought to have a spirit, or *inua,* of its own. This *inua* tied the mask to the stream of spiritual beliefs present in Eskimo religion. Not all masks were benign; some were surrealistic pieces which represented angry or dangerous spirits.

Although the masks are often produced to be sold, mask-making has remained popular in some regions, notably among King Islanders, on Nunivak Island, and in other areas of southwest Alaska.

Indian

Several types of masks existed among the coastal Indians of Alaska, including simple single-face masks, occasionally having an elaborately carved totemic border; a variation of the face mask with the addition of moving parts; and transformation masks, which have several faces hidden behind the first.

Masked dances were accompanied by a chorus of tribal singers who sang songs associated with the masks and reflecting the wealth of the host. Masks were the critical element in portraying the relationship of the tribe with spirits and projecting their power to spellbind their audiences.

Masks were always created to be worn, but not all members of the tribe held sufficient status or power to wear them. Ceremonial use of masks generally took place in the fall or winter, when the spirits of the other world were said to be nearby.

Crudely carved masks created for fun were occasionally made among the Kwakiutl.

Northwest Coast Indian mask-makers primarily used alder, though red and yellow cedar were used at times.

Aleut

Examples of masks used on various islands of the Aleutian Chain for shamanistic and ceremonial purposes are reported as early as the mid-eighteenth century. Some of these early masks were described as bizarre representations of various animals, but many were apparently destroyed after use and none survive today. Aleut legends maintain that some masks were associated with ancient inhabitants of the region, a people apparently considered unrelated.

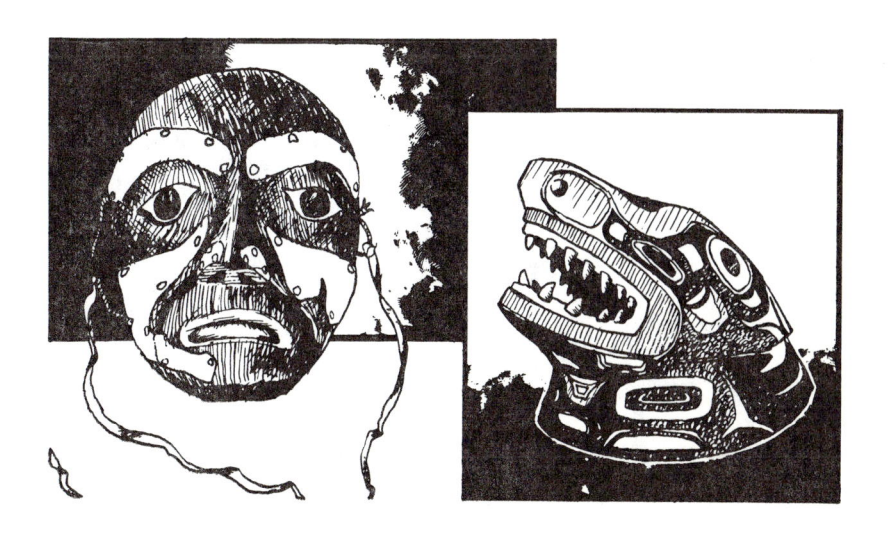

On the Shumagin Islands, a group of cavelike chambers yielded important examples of Aleut masks late in the nineteenth century. A number of well-preserved masks, apparently associated with the burials of Aleut whalers, were found. All of them had once been painted. Some of them have attached ears and pegs where tooth grips for wearing the masks would have been placed. Other pegs and holes were used for inserting feathers or carved wooden appendages similar to those of Eskimo masks of southern Alaska today. Fragments of composite masks, those decorated with feathers, appendages or movable parts, have been found on Kagamil Island with earlier remains.

Early accounts of masked Aleut dances say each dance was accompanied by special songs. Most masks were apparently hidden in caves or secret places when the ceremony ended, possibly for good luck. Bone masks worn by members of burial parties in some regions were broken and discarded at the gravesite when funeral rites were completed.

Today, no Aleut mask-makers in the old tradition survive, so further explanation of the use and significance of masks already collected depends on future archaeological investigation.

Medal of Heroism

By a law established in 1965, the Alaska governor is authorized to award, in recognition of valorous and heroic deeds, a state medal of heroism to persons who have saved a life or, at risk to their lives, have served the state or community on behalf of the health, welfare or safety of other persons. The heroism medal may be awarded posthumously. Following are recipients of the Alaska Medal of Heroism:

Albert Rothfuss (1965), Ketchikan. Rescued a child from drowning in Ketchikan Creek.

Randy Blake Prinzing (1968), Soldotna. Saved two lives at Scout Lake.

Nancy Davis (1971), Seattle. A stewardess who convinced an alleged hijacker to surrender to authorities.

Jeffrey Stone (1972), Fairbanks. Saved the lives of two youths from a burning apartment.

Gilbert Pelowook (1975), Savoonga. An Alaska state trooper who aided plane crash victims on Saint Lawrence Island.

Residents of Gambell (1975), Gambell. Provided aid and care for plane crash victims on Saint Lawrence Island.

George Jackinsky (1978), Kasilof. Rescued two persons from a burning aircraft.

Mike Hancock (1980), Lima, Ohio. In 1977, rescued a victim of a plane crash that brought down high-voltage lines.

John Stimson (1983), Cordova. A first sergeant in the Division of Fish and Wildlife Protection who died in a helicopter accident during an attempt to rescue others.

Robert Larson (1983), Anchorage. A Department of Public Safety employee who flew through hazardous conditions to rescue survivors of the crash that took John Stimson's life.

David Graham (1983), Kenai. Rescued a person from a burning car.

Darren Olanna (1984), Nome. Died while attempting to rescue a person from a burning house.

Esther Farquhar (1984), Sitka. Tried to save other members of her family from a fire in their home; lost her life in the attempt.

Billy Westlock (1986), Emmonak. Rescued a youngster from the Emmonak River.

Lt. Comm. Whiddon, Lt. Breithaupt, ASM2 Tunks, AD1 Saylor, AT3 Milne (1987), Sitka. Rescued a man and his son from their sinking boat during high seas.

Army and Air National Guard (1988), Gambell, Savoonga, Nome and Shishmaref. Searched for seven missing walrus hunters.

Metric Conversions

As in the rest of the United States, metrics are slow in coming to Alaska. These conversion formulas will help to prepare for the metric system and to understand measurements in neighboring Yukon Territory. Approximate conversions from customary to metric and vice versa:

	When you know:	You can find:	If you multiply by:
Length	Inches	millimeters	25.4
	feet	centimeters	30.5
	yards	meters	0.9
	miles	kilometers	1.6
	millimeters	inches	0.04
	centimeters	inches	0.4
	meters	yards	1.1
	kilometers	miles	0.6
Area	square inches	square centimeters	6.5
	square feet	square meters	0.09
	square yards	square meters	0.8
	square miles	square kilometers	2.6
	acres	square hectometers (hectares)	0.4
	square centimeters	square inches	0.16
	square meters	square yards	1.2
	square kilometers	square miles	0.4
	square hectometers (hectares)	acres	2.5
Weight	ounces	grams	28.4
	pounds	kilograms	0.45
	short tons	megagrams (metric tons)	0.9
	grams	ounces	0.04
	kilograms	pounds	2.2
	megagrams (metric tons)	short tons	1.1
Liquid Volume	ounces	milliliters	29.6
	pints	liters	0.47
	quarts	liters	0.95
	gallons	liters	3.8
	milliliters	ounces	0.03
	liters	pints	2.1
	liters	quarts	1.06
	liters	gallons	0.26
Temperature	degrees Fahrenheit	degrees Celsius	5/9 (after subtracting 32)
	degrees Celsius	degrees Fahrenheit	9/5 (then add 32)

Celsius

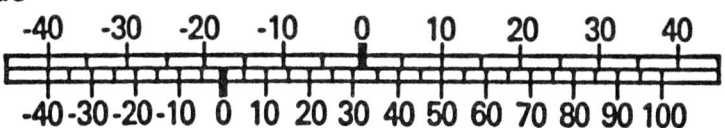

-40 -30 -20 -10 0 10 20 30 40

-40 -30 -20 -10 0 10 20 30 40 50 60 70 80 90 100

Fahrenheit

Mileage Chart

DRIVING MILEAGES BETWEEN PRINCIPAL POINTS	Anchorage, AK	Dawson City, YT	Dawson Creek, BC	Fairbanks, AK	Haines, AK	Homer, AK	Prince Rupert, BC	Seattle, WA	Skagway, AK	Valdez, AK	Whitehorse, YT
Anchorage, AK		515	1608	358	775	226	1605	2435	832	304	724
Dawson City, YT	515		1195	393	578	741	1192	2022	435	441	327
Dawson Creek, BC	1608	1195		1486	1135	1834	706	827	992	1534	884
Fairbanks, AK	358	393	1486		653	584	1483	2313	710	284	602
Haines, AK	775	578	1135	653		1001	1132	1962	359	701	251
Homer, AK	226	741	1834	584	1001		1831	2661	1058	530	950
Prince Rupert, BC	1605	1192	706	1483	1132	1831		1033	989	1531	881
Seattle, WA	2435	2022	827	2313	1962	2661	1033		1819	2361	1711
Skagway, AK	832	435	992	710	359	1058	989	1819		758	108
Valdez, AK	304	441	1534	284	701	530	1531	2361	758		650
Whitehorse, YT	724	327	884	602	251	950	881	1711	108	650	

Military

Until the rapid escalation of war in Europe in 1940-41, Congress saw little need for a strong military presence in Alaska. Spurred by World War II, and a growing realization that Alaska could shorten the route to Asia for friend and foe, the government built and now maintains units of the Air Force, Army, Navy and Coast Guard at dozens of installations across the state and on floating units in Alaskan waters. At the state level are Air National Guard and Army National Guard units. (*See* National Guard.)

The Army Corps of Engineers has three offices in Alaska: the Alaska District Office at Elmendorf Air Force Base, the Denali Area Office at Fort Richardson and the Fairbanks Resident Office at Fort Wainwright. A small number of project offices are scattered across the state at Corps construction sites. Clear, Alaska, is the site of one of three Ballistic Missile Early Warning System stations (the others are in Greenland and England). Operating since 1961, the BMEW station's three 400-foot-wide, 165-foot-high radar screens scan the skies from the North Pole to China. Designed to give the U.S. at least a 15-minute warning before the missiles hit, the BMEWS supplemented the earlier Distant Early Warning (DEW) Line, which was designed to detect bombers crossing into North American air space, but was ineffective in detecting ballistic missiles. The Alaska sector of the DEW Line System, however, is still in full operation. With facilities as shown on the map, it provides radar coverage of the North Slope and meshes with the Canadian DEW Line to provide protection from cruise-missile-carrying bombers and tactical attack at Prudhoe, and all of northern Alaska. The DEW Line is operated by a civilian contractor for the Air Force Tactical Air Command.

The 6th Infantry Division (Light) is the primary Army unit in Alaska. Headquartered at Fort Richardson near Anchorage, the division also maintains fighting forces at Fort Wainwright, near Fairbanks, and training and research facilities at Fort Greely, near Delta Junction. The division, which is under the command of a two-star (major) general, must be prepared to deploy rapidly worldwide in support of U.S. national interests and objectives, and be able to defend Alaska, including the initial defense of the Aleutian Islands.

The primary units within the division, which carry out this mission, include: The 1st and 2nd Infantry Brigades in Alaska and a third brigade, the 205th Infantry Brigade, a U.S. Army Reserve unit headquartered at Fort Snelling in St. Paul, Minnesota. In the event of a national emergency, the 205th will deploy to Alaska to "round out" the division. In addition to the three infantry brigades, major units in the division include the Aviation Brigade, Division Support Command, 6th

Signal Battalion, the 4th and 5th Battalions of the 11th Field Artillery and the 106th Military Intelligence Battalion. More Army units are scheduled to be activated in Alaska through 1989.

Primary non-divisional units and activities include the U.S. Army Information Systems Command-Alaska, which oversees all Army communications in the state, the Northern Warfare Training Center at Fort Greely, which trains soldiers, guardsmen and representatives from other services in Arctic combat and survival, and the Cold Regions Test Center, also at Fort Greely, where equipment is tested for cold weather use.

Soldiers from the division's combat units spend most of their time in training, each year culminating in a series of field training exercises. In 1987, several emergency deployment readiness exercises also were conducted, emphasizing and improving unit movement capabilities. The 6th Infantry Division (Light) is planning for its participation in Brim Frost 89, the next mid-winter, joint service exercise scheduled for January-February 1989.

In the first six months of 1988, Army aircraft were sent on 102 missions, assisting 32 soldiers and 16 civilians. The Army's High Altitude Rescue Team (HART), flying specially equipped Chinook (CH-47) helicopters, were credited with saving four and assisting one climber on Mount McKinley during the 1987 and 1988 summer climbing *(Continued on page 107)*

Total Military Expenditures in Alaska by Agency Fiscal Year 1988
(In millions of dollars)

Service	Pay	Construction	Operations & Maintenance	Other Procurement	Total
Air Force	$359.5	$ 50.4	$243.6	$132.2	$785.7
Army	298.6	57.2	127.9	46.6	530.3
Coast Guard	51.1	9.8	50.6	2.3	113.8
Corps of Engineers	22.4	0.0	23.4	.7	46.5
National Guard	52.8	7.4	19.4	8.6	88.2
Navy*	42.1	42.8	19.3	4.1	108.3
Total	$826.5	$167.6	$484.2	$194.5	$1,672.8

*Includes Marines

Military Expenditures in Alaska For Fiscal Years 1983-1988
(In millions of dollars)

	1983	1984	1985	1986	1987	1988
Military Payroll	$ 464.4	$ 469.9	$ 503.1	$ 516.0	$ 567.5	$ 595.5
Civilian Payroll	168.7	182.1	189.7	181.5	212.4	204.9
Operations & Maintenance	380.0	362.6	389.1	493.3	645.3	485.1
Construction	141.2	135.1	204.0	180.3	204.9	167.6
Subtotal Appropriated Funds	1,154.4	1,149.7	1,285.9	1,371.1	1,630.1	1,453.1
Exchange & Nonappropriated Payrolls	24.8	24.1	32.8	35.7	32.5	29.5
Other Procurement	219.0	161.0	136.9	149.5	105.4	194.5
Subtotal Other	243.8	185.1	169.7	185.2	137.9	224.0
DOD Retirement	4.0	113.1	122.3	130.4	139.5	
Total	$1,398.1	$1,338.8	$1,568.7	$1,678.6	$1,898.4	$1,816.6

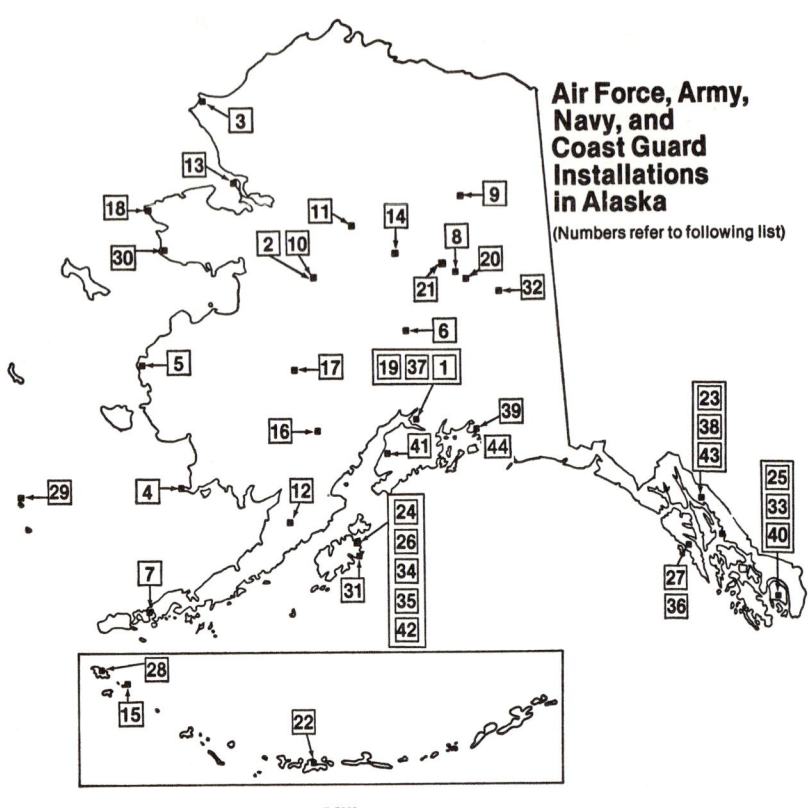

Air Force, Army, Navy, and Coast Guard Installations in Alaska
(Numbers refer to following list)

Map Key	Installation	Military Personnel
AIR FORCE		
1	Elmendorf AFB	6,751
2	Campion AFS	*
3	Cape Lisburne AFS	*
4	Cape Newenham AFS	*
5	Cape Romanzof AFS	*
6	Clear AFS	122
7	Cold Bay AFS	*
8	Eielson AFB	3,282
9	Fort Yukon AFS	*
10	Galena Airport	309
11	Indian Mountain AFS	*
12	King Salmon	275
13	Kotzebue AFS	*
14	Murphy Dome AFS	*
15	Shemya AFB	598
16	Sparrevohn AFS	*
17	Tatalina AFS	*
18	Tin City AFS	*
ARMY		
19	Fort Richardson	4,900
20	Fort Greely	600
21	Fort Wainwright	4,600
NAVY		
22	Adak	1,677
COAST GUARD		
23	17th District Office Juneau	170
24	Kodiak Support Center	287
25	Base/Group Ketchikan	101
26	Air Station Kodiak	352
27	Air Station Sitka	124
28	LORAN Station Attu	24
29	LORAN Station Saint Paul	21
30	LORAN Station Port Clarence	27
31	LORAN Station Narrow Cape	14
32	LORAN Station Tok	7
33	LORAN Station Shoal Cove	15
34	Communication Station Kodiak	94
35	LORAN Monitoring Station Kodiak	17
36	Marine Safety Detachment Sitka	1

106

37	Marine Safety Office Anchorage	25
38	Marine Safety Office Juneau	12
39	Marine Safety Office Valdez	40
40	Marine Safety Detachment Ketchikan	1
41	Marine Safety Detachment Kenai	4
42	Marine Safety Detachment Kodiak	2
43	Station Juneau	14
44	Seasonal Air Facility Cordova	

U.S. Coast Guard Cutters

Firebush	55
Ironwood	55
Planetree	55
Sedge	55
Storis	75
Sweetbrier	56
Woodrush	55
Cape Carter	14
Elderberry	6
Yocona	82
Cape Hatteras	14
Mustang	16
Naushon	16

(Continued from page 105)
seasons. One of these rescues was performed at the 18,200-foot level. It is believed to be the highest successful hoist rescue ever attempted. Between January 1987 and June 1988 M.A.S.T. (Military Assistance to Safety and Traffic) helicopters based at Fort Wainwright assisted 92 patients.

The Air Force is represented in Alaska by the Alaskan Air Command, which has headquarters at Elmendorf Air Force Base and whose mission is "Top Cover for North America." This top cover is supplied by aircraft such as the F-15 Eagles of the 43rd and 54th Tactical Fighter Squadrons, the A-10A Thunderbolt IIs of the 18th Tactical Fighter Squadron, the T-33 Shooting Stars of the 5021st Tactical Operations Squadron and the OV-10 Broncos of the 25th Tactical Air Support Squadron.

The Alaskan Air Command stands ready to train and employ combat-ready, tactical air forces to preserve the national sovereignty of United States lands, waters and air space and to provide "Top Cover for North America."

The total population of the uniformed services in Alaska on September 30, 1988 was approximately 76,560. Population figures include active duty personnel, Department of Defense Civil Service Employees, Nonappropriated Fund and Exchange personnel and dependents. Of the total, 25,647 were active duty uniformed personnel and 5,342 were Civil Service employees of the Department of Defense. The total makes up approximately 16 percent of Alaska's population.

The U.S. Coast Guard has been a part of Alaska since the mid-1800s, patrolling its enormous and notoriously unforgiving coastline with the wooden sailing and steam ships of its predecessor, the Revenue Cutter Service.

Since those early days, the service has changed names (several times, in fact) and those wooden ships have been replaced by today's modern fleet of ships, boats and aircraft, operated and maintained by Alaska's 1,900 Coast Guard men and women.

In 1986, the 17th Coast Guard District conducted 1,069 search and rescue operations, saved 262 lives and assisted in protecting $55-million worth of property. This high level of activity, combined with the state's often harsh weather and sea conditions, keeps the 17th Coast Guard District extremely active and reinforces the Coast Guard's fundamental role in the Alaskan community.

The U.S. Coast Guard's LORAN (long range navigation) stations are a system of ground stations that transmit pulsed radio signals. The 17th Coast Guard District has six LORAN sites that collectively form an umbrella of electronic aid to navigation in the North Pacific Ocean, Bering Sea and the Gulf of Alaska. Signals are used by commercial as well as Coast Guard aircraft and ships.

Minerals and Mining

(See also Coal, Gold, Oil and Gas, *and* Rocks and Gems)

In 1988, there were 1,300 people employed in mining in Alaska, according to the state Division of Geological and Geophysical Surveys. The early years of the 1970s were relatively quiet in the industry, with exploration primarily limited to geological reconnaissance. Late in 1974, restrictions on gold in the United States were lifted and the price of gold soared, spurring a revival of gold mining in the state.

By 1981, several large deposits containing minerals such as copper, chromite, molybdenum, nickel and uranium were the subject of serious exploration. Estimated exploration costs were in excess of $100 million for 1981, and more than 3,000 people were employed in the industry. In 1988, expenditures and values for exploration, development and production totaled $546 million, with 4,904 people employed in the industry.

The worth of Alaska's mineral industry in 1988 was $546 million, up from $318 million in 1987. While the production and number of small placer mines declined significantly from 1985, several larger operations continued at high or expanded production levels. The Alaska Gold Company in the Seward Peninsula saw a large increase in gold mining activity in 1987. A large-scale thawing project in 1986 allowed for the operation of the company's two dredges in 1987, which employed 125 people at the height of the mining season. The dredges processed 1.4 million cubic yards in 1987, almost doubling 1986 production.

The Usibelli Coal Mine near Healy continues as the state's commercial coal mine. Production of coal in 1988 was estimated at 1.55 million tons, with 727,000 tons burned in Interior Alaska power plants; 811,800 short tons shipped to Korea; and 13,500 tons shipped to Japan.

In June 1987, the decision was made to develop the Greens Creek mineral deposit. Located on Admiralty Island, the mine began producing 1,000 tons of ore per day in December 1988, with an estimated annual production of 84,000 tons of concentrate. The concentrate will contain approximately 6.4 million ounces of silver; 36,000 ounces of gold; 25,000 tons of zinc; and 9,000 tons of lead. At this production rate, Greens Creek Mine will become the largest silver producer in the United States. Also operating is the Red Dog Mine in northwest Alaska, whose zinc-lead-silver deposit is unusual because it includes exceptionally high grades and large tonnages of ore that are amendable to open-cut mining. Both mines experienced peak construction activity in 1988, with development expenditures totaling $270 million.

Alaska is the only state to produce platinum, the fabled metal whose rarity exceeds that of gold. More than half a million ounces of platinum have been extracted by placer operations near the village of Goodnews Bay in southwest Alaska.

The major mining effort in the state (excluding oil, gas and gold) is sand, gravel and stone. A production value of nearly $115 million was recorded in 1981, although peak levels in excess of $200 million were recorded during the oil pipeline construction period in 1975 and 1976. In 1988, however, sand, gravel and stone mining operations showed a slight increase in profits ($73.3 million) due to increased construction activity. Gold was first in metal production in 1988, and accounted for 99 percent of Alaska's total mineral production along with coal, building stone, sand and gravel. This information is according to the Alaska Division of Geological and Geophysical Surveys.

Miscellaneous Facts

State capital: Juneau.
State population: 537,800 in January 1988.
Land area: 586,412 square miles or about 365,000,000 acres — largest state in the union; one-fifth the size of the Lower 48.
Area per person: There are 1.02 square miles for each person in Alaska. New York has .003 square miles per person.
Diameter: East to west, 2,400 miles; north to south, 1,420 miles.
Coastline: 6,640 miles, point to point; as measured on the most detailed maps available, including islands, Alaska has 33,904 miles of shoreline. Estimated tidal shoreline, including islands, inlets and shoreline to head of tidewater is 47,300 miles.
Adjacent salt water: North Pacific Ocean, Bering Sea, Chukchi Sea, Arctic Ocean.
Alaska/Canada border: 1,538 miles long; length of boundary between the

Arctic Ocean and Mount Saint Elias, 647 miles; Southeast border with British Columbia and Yukon Territory, 710 miles; water boundary, 181 miles.

Geographic center: 63°50´ north, 152° west, about 60 miles northwest of Mount McKinley.

Northernmost point: Point Barrow, 71°23´ north.

Southernmost point: Tip of Amatignak Island, Aleutian Chain, 51°13´05" north.

Easternmost and westernmost points: It all depends on how you look at it. The 180th meridian — halfway around the world from the prime meridian at Greenwich, England, and the dividing line between east and west longitudes — passes through Alaska. According to one view, therefore, Alaska has both the easternmost and westernmost spots in the country! The westernmost is Amatignak Island, 179°10´ west; and the easternmost is Pochnoi Point, 179°46´ east. On the other hand, if you are facing north, east is to your right and west to your left. Therefore, the westernmost point is Cape Wrangell, Attu Island, 172°27´ east; and the easternmost is in southeastern Alaska near Camp Point, 129°59´ west.

Farthest north supermarket: In Barrow; constructed on stilts to prevent snow build-up, at a cost of $4 million.

Tallest mountain: Mount McKinley, 20,320 feet.

Largest natural freshwater lake: Iliamna, 1,150 square miles.

Longest river: Yukon, 1,400 miles in Alaska; 1,875 total.

Largest glacier: Malaspina, 850 square miles.

Largest city in population: Anchorage, population 231,492.

Largest city in area: Juneau with 3,108 square miles (also largest city in square miles in North America).

Typical Alaskan: According to 1985 census figures, 27 years old and male. (About 53 percent of Alaskans are male, the highest percentage of any state.) Median age: 27.5 years, second only to Utah as the state with the youngest population.

Oldest building: Erskine House in Kodiak, built by the Russians, probably between 1793 and 1796.

World's largest and busiest seaplane base: Lake Hood, accommodating

Alaska miscellany

more than 800 takeoffs and landings on a peak summer day.

World's largest concentration of bald eagles: Along Chilkat River, just north of Haines. More than 3,500 bald eagles gather here in fall and winter months for late salmon runs.

Median income: $46,582, seventh highest in the nation per household income.

Per capita personal income: $18,230 in 1987, fifth highest in the nation.

Miss Alaska

The legislature has declared that the young woman selected as Miss Alaska each year will be the state's official hostess. Holders of the title are selected in Anchorage each spring in a competition sponsored by the nonprofit Miss Alaska Scholarship Pageant organization.

1989 — Christine Rae McCubbins, Kenai
1988 — Launa Middaugh, Anchorage
1987 — Teresa Murton, Anchorage
1986 — Jerri Morrison, Anchorage
1985 — Kristina Christopher Taylor, Palmer
1984 — Marilin Blackburn, Anchorage
1983 — Jennifer Smith, Soldotna
1982 — Kristan Sapp, Wasilla
1981 — Laura Trollan, Juneau
1980 — Sandra Lashbrook, Chugiak-Eagle River
1979 — Lila Oberg, Matanuska Valley
1978 — Patty-Jo Gentry, Fairbanks
1977 — Lisa Granath, Kenai
1976 — Kathy Tebow, Anchorage
1975 — Cindy Suryan, Kodiak
1974 — Darby Moore, Kenai
1973 — Virginia Adams, Anchorage
1972 — Deborah Wood, Elmendorf Air Force Base
1971 — Linda Joy Smith, Elmendorf Air Force Base
1970 — Virginia Walker, Kotzebue
1969 — Gwen Gregg, Elmendorf Air Force Base
1968 — Jane Haycraft, Fairbanks
1967 — Penny Ann Thomasson, Anchorage
1966 — Nancy Lorell Wellman, Fairbanks
1965 — Mary Ruth Nidiffer, Alaska Methodist University
1964 — Karol Rae Hommon, Anchorage
1963 — Colleen Sharon Kendall, Matanuska Valley
1962 — Mary Dee Fox, Anchorage
1961 — Jean Ann Holm, Fairbanks
1960 — June Bowdish, Anchorage
1959 — Alansa Rounds Carr, Ketchikan

Mosquitoes

At least 25 species of mosquitoes are found in Alaska (the number may be as high as 40), the females of all species feeding on people, other mammals or birds. Males and females eat plant sugar, but only the females suck blood, which they use for egg production. The itch that follows the bite comes from an anticoagulant injected by the mosquito. No Alaska mosquitoes carry diseases. The insects are present from April through September in many areas of the state. Out in the Bush they are often at their worst in June, tapering off in July. The mosquito plague has usually passed by late August and September. From Cook Inlet south, they concentrate on coastal flats and forested valleys. In the Aleutian Islands, mosquitoes are absent or present only in small numbers. The most serious mosquito infestations occur in moist areas of slow-moving or standing water the type found

110

in the fields, bogs and forests of interior Alaska, from Bristol Bay eastward.

Mosquitoes are most active at dusk and dawn; low temperatures and high winds decrease their activity. Mosquitoes can be controlled by draining their breeding areas or spraying with approved insecticides. When traveling in areas of heavy mosquito infestations, it is wise to wear protective clothing, carefully screen living and camping areas, and use a good insect repellent.

Mountains

Of the 20 highest mountains in the United States, 17 are in Alaska, which has 19 peaks over 14,000 feet. The U.S. Geological Survey lists them as follows:

Map Key		Elevation
1	McKinley, South Peak*	20,320
1	McKinley, North Peak*	19,470
2	Saint Elias**	18,008
3	Foraker	17,400
4	Bona	16,500
5	Blackburn	16,390
6	Sanford	16,237
1	South Buttress	15,885
7	Vancouver**	15,700
8	Churchill	15,638
9	Fairweather**	15,300
10	Hubbard**	15,015
11	Bear	14,831
1	East Buttress	14,730
12	Hunter	14,573
13	Alverstone**	14,565
1	Browne Tower	14,530
14	Wrangell	14,163
15	Augusta**	14,070

*Note: The two peaks of Mount McKinley are known collectively as the Churchill Peaks.
**On Alaska-Canada border.

Other Well-Known Alaska Mountains	Elevation
Augustine Volcano	4,025
Deborah	12,339
Devils Paw	8,584
Devils Thumb	9,077
Doonerak	7,610
Drum	12,010
Edgecumbe	3,201
Hayes	13,832
Kates Needle	10,002
Marcus Baker	13,176
Shishaldin	9,372

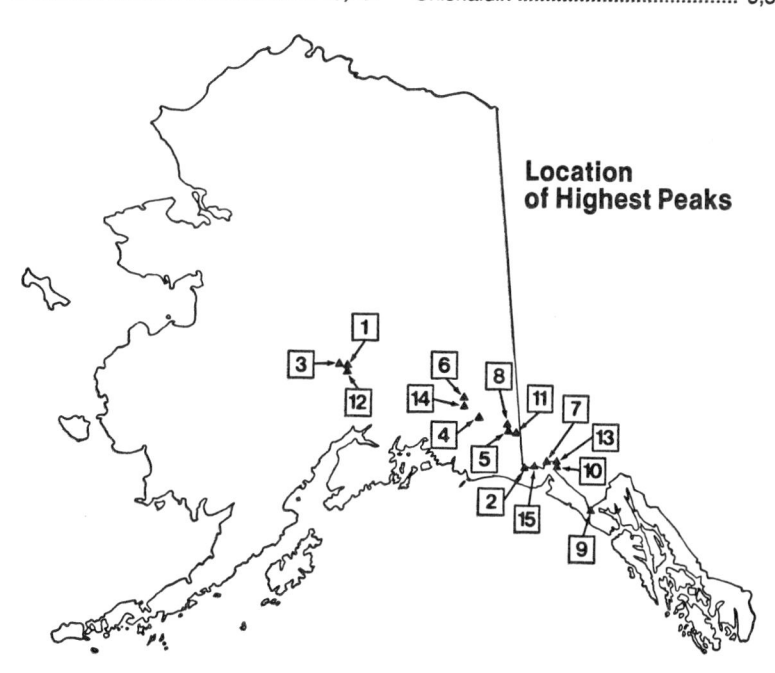

Location of Highest Peaks

Mountain Ranges	Elevation
Ahklun Mountains	1,000-3,000
Alaska Range	to 20,320
Aleutian Range	to 7,585
Askinuk Mountains	to 2,342
Baird Mountains	to 4,300
Bendeleben Mountains	to 3,730
Brabazon Range	to 5,515
Brooks Range	4,000-9,000
Chigmit Mountains	to 5,000
Chugach Mountains	to 13,176
Coast Mountains	to 18,000
Darby Mountains	to 3,083
Davidson Mountains	to 5,540
De Long Mountains	to 4,886
Endicott Mountains	to 7,000
Fairweather Range	to 15,300
Igichuk Hills	to 2,000
Kaiyuh Mountains	1,000-2,844
Kenai Mountains	to 6,000
Kiglapak Mountains	to 1,070
Kigluaik Mountains	to 4,714
Kuskokwim Mountains	to 3,973
Lookout Range	to 2,400
Mentasta Mountains	4,000-7,000
Moore Mountains	to 3,000
Nutzotin Mountains	5,000-8,000
Ray Mountains	2,500-5,500
Romanzof Mountains	to 8,700
Saint Elias Mountains	to 18,000
Schwatka Mountains	to 8,800
Shublik Mountains	to 4,500
Sischu Mountains	to 2,422
Talkeetna Mountains	6,000-8,800
Waring Mountains	to 1,800
Waxell Ridge	4,000-10,000
White Mountains	to 5,000
Wrangell Mountains	to 16,421
York Mountains	to 2,349
Zane Hills	to 4,053

Mount McKinley

Mount McKinley in the Alaska Range is the highest mountain on the North American continent. The South Peak is 20,320 feet high; the North Peak has an elevation of 19,470 feet. The mountain was named in 1896 for William McKinley of Ohio, who at the time was the Republican candidate for president. An earlier name had been Denali, a Tanaina Indian word meaning "the big one" or "the great one." The state of Alaska officially renamed the mountain Denali in 1975 and the state Geographic Names Board claims the proper name for the mountain is Denali. However, the federal Board of Geographic Names had not taken any action and congressional legislation has been introduced to retain the name McKinley in perpetuity.

Mount McKinley is within Denali National Park and Preserve (formerly Mount McKinley National Park). The park entrance is about 237 miles north of Anchorage and 121 miles south of Fairbanks via the George Parks Highway. (A 90-mile gravel road runs west from the highway through the park; vehicle traffic on the park road is restricted.) The park is also accessible via The Alaska Railroad and by aircraft. The mountain and its park are the top tourist attractions in Alaska. The finest times to see McKinley up close are on summer mornings. August is best, according to statistics based on thirteen summers of observation by park ranger Rick McIntyre. The mountain is rarely visible the entire day. The best view is from Eielson Visitor Center, located about 66 miles from the park entrance and 33 miles northeast of the summit. The center, open from early June through the second week in September, is accessible via free shuttle bus provided by the park.

A record 916 climbers attempted to reach the summit of Mount McKinley by the end of the 1988 climbing season, of which 562 were successful. This compares to only one-third of 817 climbers in 1987. Of those 916 climbers, 36 percent were from outside the U.S., with Japan leading in foreign alpinists. Also in 1988, several firsts occurred on McKinley, beginning with the solo winter ascent of Vern Tejas in March. During the summer climbing season, a 71-year-old attorney from Connecticut became the oldest person known to reach the summit, and a group of Frenchmen with artificial legs made it to the top. In 1989, the West Rib of McKinley had been successfully summited by Dave Staeheli in March, and by mid-May, six foreign alpinists had lost their lives attempting the summit.

Mukluks

Lightweight boots designed to provide warmth in extreme cold. Eskimo mukluks are traditionally made with *oogruk* (bearded seal) skin bottoms and caribou tops and trimmed with fur. (Mukluk is also another name for *oogruk*.) Athabascan mukluks are traditionally made of moose hide and trimmed with fur and beadwork.

Related reading: *Secrets of Eskimo Skin Sewing* by Edna Wilder. The complete book on the art of Eskimo skin sewing, with how-to-do-it instructions and things-to-make ideas. 125 pages, $9.95. See ALASKA NORTHWEST LIBRARY in the back of the book.

Muktuk

This Eskimo delicacy consists of the outer skin layers of whales. The two species of whales most often used for muktuk are the bowhead whale and the beluga, or white whale. The outer skin layers consist of a corky protective layer, the true skin and the blubber. In the case of beluga muktuk, the outer layer is white, the next layer is black and the blubber is pink. It may be eaten fresh, frozen, cooked or pickled.

Museums, Cultural Centers and Repositories

A visit to the following museums, historic sites, or other repositories offers a look into the rich diversity of Alaskan culture and history. For information about hours of operation and features of the collections, write to the addresses given or check with The Alaska State Division of Tourism, P.O. Box E-001, Juneau 99811; or Museums Alaska, Inc., 415 Front Street, Ketchikan 99901.

Adak Community Museum, P.O. Box 5244, NAV/STA, FPO Seattle, WA 98791
Alaska Historical & Transportation Museum, P.O. Box 920, Palmer 99645
Alaska Indian Arts, Inc., P.O. Box 271, Haines 99827 (historic site)
Alaska Resources Library, 222 W. 7th Ave., Anchorage 99513
Alaska State Archives, Pouch C-0207, Juneau 99811
Alaska State Museum, 395 Willoughby St., Juneau 99801
Alaskaland Air Museum, P.O. Box 437, Fairbanks 99707
Anaktuvuk Pass Museum, P.O. Box 21030, Anaktuvuk Pass 99721
Anchorage Museum of History & Art, 121 W. 7th Ave., Anchorage 99501
George I. Ashby Memorial Museum, P.O. Box 84, Copper Center 99573
Assumption of the Virgin Mary Church, Kenai 99611 (historic site)
Baranof Museum/Erskine House, 101 Marine Way, Kodiak 99615

Bristol Bay Historical Museum, P.O. Box 43, Naknek 99633
Circle District Historical Society, P.O. Box 1893, Central 99730
Clausen Memorial Museum, P.O. Box 708, Petersburg 99833
Cordova Museum, P.O. Box 391, Cordova 99574
Damon Memorial Museum, P.O. Box 66, Soldotna 99669
Dillingham Heritage Museum, Pouch 202, Dillingham 99576
Dinjii Zhuu Enjit Museum, P.O. Box 276, Fort Yukon 99740
Duncan Memorial Museum, P.O. Box 66, Metlakatla 99926
Eagle Historic Society, Eagle 99738
Fort Kenay Museum, P.O. Box 580, Kenai 99611
Fort Richardson Fish and Wildlife Center, Building 600, Fort Richardson 99505
Samuel K. Fox Museum, P.O. Box 3202, Dillingham 99576
Hoonah Cultural Center, P.O. Box 144, Hoonah 99829
House of Wickersham, Juneau. For information write Alaska Division of Parks, Pouch M, Juneau 99811
Charlie Hubbard Museum, P.O. Box 552, Cooper Landing 99572
Iditarod Museum, P.O. Box 870800, Wasilla 99687
Juneau Mining Museum, 490 S. Franklin St., Juneau 99801
Klawock Totem Park, P.O. Box 113, Klawock 99925 (historic site)
Matanuska Valley Museum, Greater Palmer Chamber of Commerce, Palmer 99645

Carrie M. McLain Memorial Museum, P.O. Box 281, Nome 99762
Isabel Miller Museum, 330 Harbor Drive, Sitka 99835
NANA Museum of the Arctic, P.O. Box 46, Kotzebue 99752
National Bank of Alaska Heritage Library Museum, 303 W. Northern Lights Boulevard, Anchorage 99503
Pratt Museum, 3779 Bartlett St., Homer 99603
Rasmuson Library, University of Alaska, Fairbanks 99701
Resurrection Bay Historical Society Museum, P.O. Box 871, Seward 99664
Russian Bishop's House, c/o P.O. Box 944, Sitka 99835
Saint Herman's Theological Seminary, P.O. Box 726, Kodiak 99615 (historic site)
Saxman Totem Park and Tribal House, P.O. Box 8558, Ketchikan 99901 (historic site)
Sheldon Jackson Museum, 104 College Drive, Sitka 99835
Sheldon Museum and Cultural Center, P.O. Box 236, Haines 99827
Southeast Alaska Indian Cultural Center, P.O. Box 944, Sitka 99835
Talkeetna Historical Society Museum, P.O. Box 76, Talkeetna 99676
Tanana Valley Agricultural Museum, P.O. Box 188, Fairbanks 99707
Tok Visitor Center, P.O. Box 335, Tok 99780
Tongass Historical Museum, 629 Dock St., Ketchikan 99901

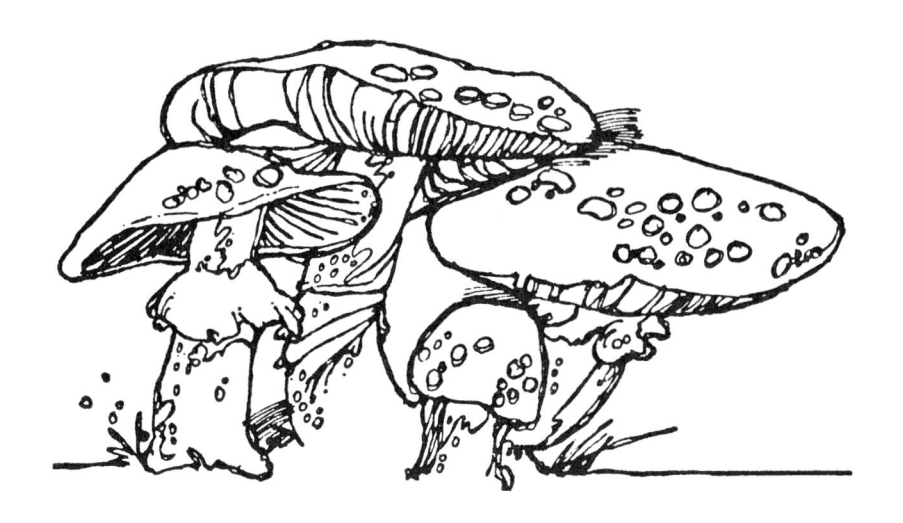

Totem Bight, Ketchikan. For information, write Alaska Division of Parks, Pouch M, Juneau 99811 (historic site)
Totem Heritage Center, 629 Dock St., Ketchikan 99901 (historic site)
Trail of '98 Museum, P.O. Box 415, Skagway 99840
Tribal House of the Bear, P.O. Box 868, Wrangell 99929 (historic site)
U.S. Historical Aircraft Preservation Museum, P.O. Box 6813, Anchorage 99502
University of Alaska Museum, P.O. Box 95351, Fairbanks 99701
Valdez Heritage Center, P.O. Box 307, Valdez 99686
Jessie Wakefield Memorial Library, P.O. Box 263, Port Lions 99550
Wales Museum, Wales 99783
Wasilla-Knik-Willow Creek Historical Society, P.O. Box 870874, Wasilla 99687
Whittier Historical Museum, P.O. Box 728, Whittier 99502
Wickersham House, P.O. Box 1794, Fairbanks 99707
Wildlife Museum, Elmendorf Air Force Base, Anchorage 99506
Wrangell Museum, P.O. Box 1050, Wrangell 99929
Yugtarvik Regional Museum, P.O. Box 388, Bethel 99559

Mushrooms

More than 500 species of mushroom grow in Alaska, and, while most are not common enough to be seen and collected readily by the amateur mycophile (mushroom hunter), many edible and choice species shoot up in any available patch of earth. Alaska's "giant arc of mushrooms" extends from Southeast's panhandle through Southcentral, the Alaska Peninsula and the Aleutian Chain and is prime mushroom habitat. Interior, western and northern Alaska also support mushrooms in abundance.

Mushroom seasons vary considerably according to temperature, humidity and available nutrients, but most occur from June through September. In a particularly cold or dry season, the crop will be scant.

A few Alaska mushroom species are considered "sickeners," and while no deadly poisonous mushrooms have been reported in the state, they may occur, especially in Southeast, which has a climate similar to Washington and northern Oregon where severely poisonous species do occur. Play it safe and be sure you know your species before foraging.

Musk Ox

Stocky, shaggy, long-haired mammals of extreme northern latitudes, musk oxen remain in the open through Alaska's long winters. Their name is misleading, for the creatures do not give musk and are more closely related to sheep and goats than to cattle. Adult males may weigh 500 to 900 pounds; females between 250 and 500 pounds. Both sexes have horns which droop down from their forehead and curve back up at the tips.

When threatened by wolves or other predators, musk oxen form circles or lines with their young in the middle. These defensive measures did not protect them from man and his gun, however.

Musk oxen were eliminated from Alaska in about 1865, when hunters shot and killed a herd of 13. The species was reintroduced to the territory in the 1930s when 34 musk oxen were purchased from Greenland and brought to the University of Alaska at Fairbanks. In 1935-36, the 31 remaining musk oxen at the university were shipped to Nunivak Island in the Bering Sea, where the herd eventually thrived. Animals from the Nunivak herd have been transplanted to areas along Alaska's western and northern coasts; at least five herds — approximately 1,200 musk oxen — now exist in the state.

Recent indications are that musk oxen from Nelson Island are spreading to the mainland and that individuals from the eastern Arctic herd have wandered west into adjacent Canada.

The soft underhair of musk oxen is called *qiviut* and grows next to the skin, protected by long guard hairs. It is shed naturally every spring. Oomingmak Musk Ox Producers' Cooperative, maintains a musk ox farm at Talkeetna, where workers gather the *qiviut* for cottage industry use. The hair is spun into yarn in Rhode Island and sent back to Alaska, where the cooperative arranges for knitters in villages in western Alaska, where jobs are scarce, to knit the yarn into clothing at their own pace.

Each village keeps its own distinct signature pattern for scarves knitted from *qiviut*. Villagers also produce stoles, tunics, hats and a smoke ring, which is a circular scarf that fits a person's head like a hood.

Permit hunts for musk oxen are allowed.

Muskeg

Deep bogs where little vegetation can grow except for sphagnum moss, black spruce, dwarf birch and a few other shrubby plants. Such swampy areas cover much of Alaska.

National Forests

Alaska contains two national forests, the Tongass and the Chugach. The Tongass occupies the panhandle or southeast portion of the state. The Chugach extends south and east of Anchorage along the southcentral Alaskan coast, encompassing most of the Prince William Sound area.

These two national forests are managed by the U.S. Forest Service for a variety of uses. They provide forest products for national and international markets; minerals; wilderness and primitive experiences; and superb scenery and views for Alaska residents and visitors.

Nearly 200 public recreation cabins are maintained on the Tongass and Chugach national forests. They receive visitors from all over the world and are a vacation bargain at $15 per night, including firewood and, on freshwater lakes, a boat. (Check with a local forest service office after January 1990, as the fee may increase slightly.)

Wildlife and fisheries are important Forest Service programs in the national forests of Alaska. The Tongass and Chugach national forests are also home to some of Alaska's most magnificent wildlife. It is here that the United States' national bird, the bald eagle and large brown (grizzly) bears may be encountered in large numbers. All five species of Pacific salmon spawn in the rivers and streams of the forests, and smaller mammals and waterfowl abound. The Forest Service is charged with the management of this rich habitat, and the Alaska Department of Fish and Game takes on the other half of the wildlife management task and manages the wildlife species that this habitat supports.

There are many recreational opportunities on the national forests of Alaska, including backpacking, fishing, hunting, photography, boating, nature study and camping to list just a few. For further information concerning recreational opportunities, contact the U.S. Forest Service office nearest the area you are visiting.

The Alaska National Interest Lands Conservation Act of 1980 — also referred to as the Alaska d-2 lands bill or lands act — increased the acreage and changed the status of certain lands in Alaska's national forests. (*See also* Land; National Parks, Preserves and Monuments; and National Wilderness Areas.)

The Alaska d-2 lands bill created approximately 5.5 million acres of wilderness (consisting of 14 units) within the 17-million-acre Tongass National Forest. It also added three new areas to the forest: the Juneau Icefield, Kates Needle and parts of the Brabazon Range, totaling more than one million acres.

The lands bill also provided extensive additions to the Chugach National Forest. These additions, totaling about two million acres, include the Nellie Juan area east of Seward, College Fiord extension, Copper/Rude rivers addition and a small extension at Controller Bay southeast of Cordova.

The following charts show the effect of the Alaska lands act on the Tongass and Chugach national forests:

	Tongass	Chugach
Total acreage before act	15,555,388	4,392,646
Total acreage after act	16,954,713	5,940,040*
Wilderness acreage created	5,453,366	none created
Wilderness Study	none created	2,019,999 acres
Wild and Scenic River Study	Situk River**	none created

*This lands act provides for additional transfers of national forest land to Native corporations, the state and the Fish and Wildlife Service of an estimated 296,000 acres on Afognak Island, and an estimated 242,000 acres to the Chugach Native Corporation.

**The lands act provides for a maximum of 640 acres on each side of the river, for each mile of river length.

Wilderness Units in Tongass National Forest (including acres)

Admiralty Island National Monument*, 937,396
Coronation Island Wilderness, 19,232
Endicott River Wilderness, 98,729
Maurelle Islands Wilderness, 4,937
Misty Fiords National Monument*, 2,142,243
Petersburg Creek-Duncan Salt Chuck Wilderness, 46,777
Russel Fiord Wilderness, 348,701
South Baranof Wilderness, 319,568
South Prince of Wales Wilderness, 90,996
Stikine-LeConte Wilderness, 448,841
Tebenkof Bay Wilderness, 66,839
Tracy Arm-Fords Terror Wilderness, 653,179
Warren Island Wilderness, 11,181
West Chichagof-Yakobi Wilderness, 264,747
Total Average, 5,453,366

*Designated monuments under d-2 bill; first areas so designated in the National Forest system.

National Guard

The Department of Military Affairs administers the Alaska Army National Guard and the Air National Guard. The guard is charged with performing military reconnaissance, surveillance and patrol operations in Alaska; providing special assistance to civil authorities during natural disasters or civil disturbances; and augmenting regular Army and Air Force in times of national emergency. About 1,086 full-time employees work for the Guard.

The Alaska Air National Guard has a headquarters unit, a composit group made up of a tactical airlift squadron, an air refueling squadron and several support squadrons and flights. The units are based at Kulis Air National Guard Base on the west side of Anchorage International Airport and at Eielson Air Force Base, in Fairbanks.

Authorized staffing is 4,565 military personnel; about 35 percent are full-time technicians. The Guard's eight C-130 Hercules cargo aircraft logged more than 4,200 hours of flight time in support of state and Air Force missions in 1986.

The major unit of the Alaska Army National Guard, with a muster of 2,300, is the 207th Infantry Group, consisting of five Scout Battalions and detachments in almost 100 communities across the state. In addition, it has an airborne element, an air traffic control detachment and an aviation detachment. The Scout Battalions are authorized one Twin Otter aircraft and two helicopters in their aviation sections. In all, the Alaska Army National Guard operates 48 aircraft.

The scout teams are a unique element in the Alaska Army National Guard, performing a full-time active mission of intelligence gathering. Many scouts are subsistence hunters and whalers who constantly comb the coastal zones, offshore waters and inland areas. Reports of Soviet naval and air activities are common since Alaska and the USSR are separated by less than 50 miles across the Bering Strait.

The Alaska Division of Emergency Services administers statewide disaster preparedness and response programs. The division is the primary contact for obtaining emergency assistance from state, federal, military and independent services. Its personnel also provide guidance and financial assistance to state and local agencies to help them prepare for and recover from disasters. The agency responds to threats or occurrences of disasters and directs disaster response in unincorporated areas where local government does not have the resources to respond adequately.

National Guard Stations in Alaska

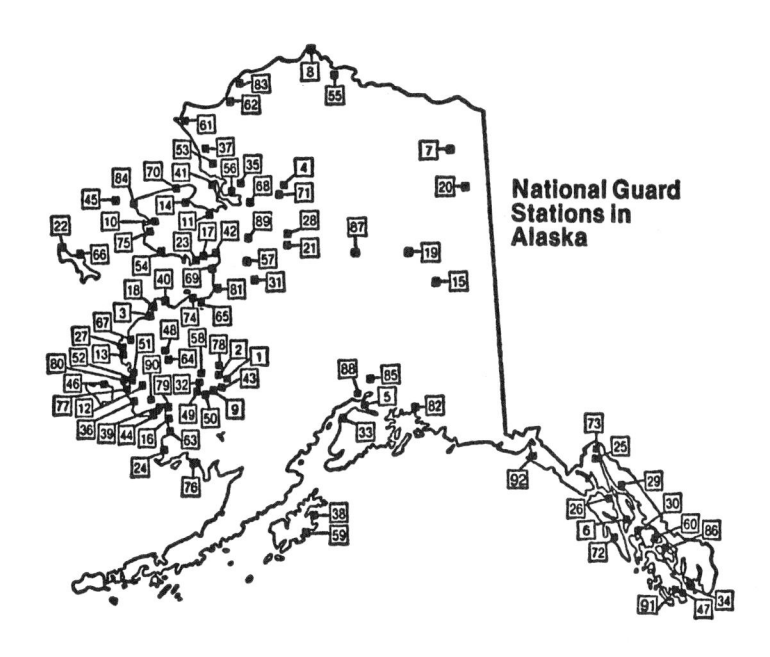

On a per capita basis, Alaska's veterans population of over 71,000 is the largest of any state. In response to increasing needs, the Division of Veterans Affairs was established in 1984. It is the state's official veterans advocate and coordinator of veterans issues and programs. It is also the liaison with federal and state agencies, veterans organizations, other states' veterans affairs organizations and the state's administration. The division ensures Alaska's veterans and their dependents are aware of every state and federal benefit available to them and assists them in taking advantage of those benefits.

National Guard Stations	Map Key
Akiachak	1
Akiak	2
Alakanuk	3
Ambler	4
Anchorage	5
Angoon	6
Arctic Village	7
Barrow	8
Bethel	9

National Guard Stations	Map Key
Brevig Mission	10
Buckland	11
Chefornak	12
Chevak	13
Craig	91
Deering	14
Delta Junction	15
Eek	16
Elim	17
Emmonak	18
Fairbanks	19
Fort Richardson	88
Fort Yukon	20
Galena	21
Gambell	22
Golovin	23
Goodnews Bay	24
Hainés	25
Hoonah	26
Hooper Bay	27
Huslia	28
Juneau	29
Kake	30
Kaltag	31
Kasigluk	32
Kenai	33
Ketchikan	34

National Guard Stations	Map Key
Kewthluk	43
Kiana	35
Kipnuk	36
Kivalina	37
Kodiak	38
Kongiganak	39
Kotlik	40
Kotzebue	41
Koyuk	42
Koyukuk	89
Kwigillingok	44
Little Diomede	45
Mekoryuk	46
Metlakatla	47
Mountain Village	48
Napakiak	49
Napaskiak	50
Newtok	51
Nightmute	52
Noatak	53
Nome	54
Noorvik	56
Nuiqsut	55
Nulato	57
Nunapitchuk	58
Old Harbor	59
Petersburg	60
Point Hope	61
Point Lay	62
Quinhagak	63
Saint Marys	64
Saint Michael	65
Savoonga	66
Scammon Bay	67
Selawik	68
Shaktoolik	69
Shishmaref	70
Shungnak	71
Sitka	72
Skagway	73
Stebbins	74
Tanana	87
Teller	75
Togiak	76
Toksook Bay	77
Tuluksak	78
Tuntutuliak	79
Tununak	80
Unalakleet	81
Valdez	82
Wainwright	83
Wales	84
Wasilla	85
White Mountain	90
Wrangell	86
Yakutat	92

National Historic Places

A "place" on the National Register of Historic Places is a district, site, building, structure or object significant to the state for its history, architecture, archaeology or culture. The national register also includes National Historic Landmarks. NHLs are properties given special status by the Secretary of the Interior for the significance to the nation, as well as to the state. The register is an official list of properties recognized by the federal government as worthy of preservation. Listing on the register begins with owner's consent and entails a nomination process with reviews by the State Historic Preservation Officer, the Alaska Historic Sites Advisory Committee and the Keeper of the National Register. Limitations are *not* placed on a listed property: the federal government does not attach restrictive covenants to the property or seek to acquire it.

Listing on the register means that a property is accorded national recognition for its significance in American history or prehistory. Other benefits include tax credits on income-producing properties and automatic qualification for federal matching funds for preservation, maintenance and restoration work when such funds are available. Listed properties are also guaranteed a full review process for potential adverse effects by federally funded, licensed or otherwise assisted projects. Such a review usually takes place while the project is in the planning stage: alternatives are sought to avoid, if at all possible, damaging or destroying the particular property in question.

SOUTHCENTRAL
Alaska Central Railroad Tunnel #1, Seward
Alaska Nellie's Homestead, Lawing vicinity
Alex (Mike) Cabin, Eklutna
American Cemetery, Kodiak
Anchorage City Hall, Anchorage
Anderson (Oscar) House, Anchorage
Ascension of Our Lord Chapel, Karluk
Ballaine House, Seward
Beluga Point Archaeological Site, North Shore, Turnagain Arm

Bering Expedition Landing Site NHL, Kayak Island
Brown & Hawkins Store, Seward
Campus Center Site, Anchorage
Cape Saint Elias Lighthouse, Kayak Island
Chilkat Oil Refinery Site, Katalla
Chisana Historic District, Chisana
Chitina Tin Shop, Chitina
Chugachik Island Archaeological Site, Kachemak Bay
Coal Village Site, Kachemak Bay
Cooper Landing Historic District, Cooper Landing
Cooper Landing Post Office, Cooper Landing
Copper River and Northwestern Railway, Chitina vicinity
Cordova Post Office and Courthouse, Cordova
Crow Creek Mine, Girdwood
Cunningham-Hall PT-6 NC692W (aircraft), Palmer
Dakah De'nin's Village Site, Chitina
David, Leopold, House, Anchorage
Diversion Tunnel, Lowell Creek, Seward
Federal Building-U.S. Courthouse (Old), Anchorage
Fort Abercrombie, Kodiak Island
Fourth Avenue Theatre, Anchorage
Gakona Roadhouse, Gakona
Government Cable House, Seward
Hirshey Mine, Hope vicinity
Holm (Victor) Cabin, Cohoe
Holy Assumption Russian Orthodox Church NHL, Kenai
Holy Resurrection Church, Kodiak
Holy Transfiguration of Our Lord Chapel, Ninilchik
Hope Historic District, Hope vicinity
Independence Mine Historic District, Hatcher Pass
KENI Radio Building, Anchorage
Kennecott Mines NHL, McCarthy vicinity
Kimball's Store, Anchorage
Knik Site, Knik vicinity
Kodiak Naval Operating Base (and Fort Greely) NHL, Kodiak Island
KOD-171 Archaeological Site, Kodiak
KOD-207 Archaeological Site, Kodiak
KOD-233 Archaeological Site, Kodiak
Lauritsen Cabin, Seward Highway
McCarthy General Store, McCarthy
McCarthy Power Plant, McCarthy
Middle Bay Brick Kiln, Kodiak
Moose River Site, Naptowne, Kenai area
Nabesna Gold Mine, Nabesna area

Nativity of Holy Theotokos Church, Afognak Island
Nativity of Our Lord Chapel, Ouzinkie
Old Eklutna Power Plant, Eklutna
Old St. Nicholas Russian Orthodox Church, Eklutna
Palmer Depot, Palmer
Palugvik Archaeological District, Hawkins Island
Pioneer School House, Anchorage
Potter Section House, Anchorage
Protection of the Theotokos Chapel, Akhiok
Rebarcheck (Raymond) Colony Farm, Palmer area
Reception Building, Cordova
Red Dragon Historic District, Cordova
Russian-American Company Magazin (Erskine House) NHL, Kodiak
St. Michael the Archangel Church, Cordova
St. Nicholas Chapel, Seldovia
St. Peter's Episcopal Church, Seward
Sts. Sergius and Herman of Valaam Chapel, Spruce Island
Sts. Sergius and Herman of Valaam Church, English Bay
Selenie Lagoon Archaeological Site, Port Graham vicinity
Seward Depot, Seward
Sourdough Lodge NHL, Gulkana vicinity
Susitna River Bridge, Alaska Railroad, Talkeetna vicinity
Swanson River Discovery Site, Kenai
Swetman House, Seward
Tangle Lakes Archaeological District, Paxson vicinity
Teeland's Store, Wasilla
Three Saints Bay Site NHL, Kodiak Island
United Protestant Church, Palmer
U.S. Bureau of Mines Safety Car #5, Palmer
Van Gilder Hotel, Seward
Wasilla Community Hall, Wasilla
Wasilla Depot, Wasilla
Wasilla Elementary School, Wasilla
Wendler Building, Anchorage
Yukon Island, Main Site NHL, Yukon Island

SOUTHEAST
Alaska Native Brotherhood Hall NHL, Sitka
Alaska Steam Laundry, Juneau
Alaska Totems, Ketchikan
Alaskan Hotel, Juneau
American Flag Raising Site NHL, Sitka
Ayson Hotel, Ketchikan

121

Bergmann Hotel, Juneau
Building No. 29 NHL, Sitka
Burkhart-Dibrell House, Ketchikan
Cable House and Station, Sitka
Cape Spencer Lighthouse NHL, Cape Spencer
Chief Shakes House, Wrangell
Chilkoot Trail and Dyea NHL, Skagway
Chilkoot Trail, Taiya River to Canadian Border, Chilkoot Pass Area
Davis, J.M., House, Juneau
Duncan, Father William, Cottage, Metlakatla
Eldred Rock Lighthouse, Lynn Canal
Emmons House, Sitka
First Lutheran Church, Ketchikan
Fort Durham NHL, Taku Harbor, Juneau vicinity
Fort William H. Seward NHL, Haines
Frances House, Juneau
Government Indian School, Haines
Old Sitka, Sitka vicinity
Russian Bishop's House, Sitka
St. John the Baptist Church, Angoon
St. Michael the Archangel Cathedral NHL, Sitka
St. Nicholas Church (Russian Orthodox), Juneau
St. Peter's Church, Sitka
St. Philip's Episcopal Church, Wrangell
Saxman Totem Park, Ketchikan
See House, Sitka
Sheldon Jackson Museum, Sitka
Sitka National Historical Park, Sitka
Sitka Naval Operating Base NHL, Sitka
Sitka Pioneers' Home, Sitka
Skagway and White Pass Historic District NHL, Skagway vicinity
Sons of Norway Hall, Petersburg
Totem Bight, Ketchikan
Twin Glacier Camps, Juneau

Governor's Mansion, Juneau
Holy Trinity Church, Juneau
Ketchikan Ranger House, Ketchikan
Klondike Gold Rush National Historic Park, Skagway area
McKay Marine Ways, Ketchikan
Mills (May) House, Sitka
Mills (W.P.) House, Sitka
New Russia Archaeological Site NHL, Yakutat
Old Sitka NHL, Sitka
Pleasant Camp, Haines Highway
Porcupine Historic District, Skagway vicinity
Redoubt St. Archangel Michael Site,
U.S. Army Corps of Engineers, Storehouse #3, Portland Canal
U.S. Army Corps of Engineers, Storehouse #4, Hyder
U.S. Coast and Geodetic Survey House, Sitka
Valentine Building, Juneau
Walker-Broderick House, Ketchikan
Wickersham, House of, Juneau
Wrangell Public School, Wrangell
Ziegler House, Ketchikan

WESTERN
Adak Army and Naval Operating Bases NHL, Adak

Anangula Site NHL, Aleutian Islands
Ananiulak Island Archaeological District, Aleutian Islands
Archaeological Site 49 Af 3, Katmai National Park and Preserve
Archaeological Site 49 MK 10, Katmai National Park and Preserve
Atka B-24 Liberator, Aleutian Islands
Attu Battlefield and U.S. Army and Navy Airfield on Attu NHL, Attu
Brooks River Archaeological District NHL, Katmai National Park and Preserve
Cape Field at Fort Glenn NHL, Aleutian Islands
Cape Krusenstern Archaeological District NHL, Kotzebue vicinity
Cape Nome Mining District Discovery Sites NHL, Nome
Cape Nome Roadhouse, Nome vicinity
Carrighar (Sally) House, Nome
Chaluka Site NHL, Umnak Island
Christ Church Mission, Anvik
Discovery Saloon, Nome
Donaldson, Lieutenant, C.V., Nome
Dutch Harbor Operating Base and Fort Mears NHL, Aleutian Islands
Elevation of the Holy Cross Church, South Naknek
Fairhaven Ditch, Imruk Lake
Fort St. Michael Site, Unalakleet vicinity
Fures Cabin, Katmai National Park and Preserve
Holy Ascension Orthodox Church NHL, Unalaska
Holy Resurrection Church, Belkofski
Iyatayet Archaeological Site NHL, Norton Sound
Japanese Occupation Site, Kiska NHL, Aleutian Islands
Kaguyak Village Site, Katmai National Park and Preserve
Kijik Historic District, Lake Clark National Park and Preserve
Kiska Japanese Occupation Site NHL, Kiska
Kolmakov Redoubt Site, Kuskokwim River, Aniak vicinity
Kukak Village, Katmai National Park and Preserve
McClain (Carrie) House, Nome
Norge Landing Site, Teller
Old Savonoski Site, Katmai National Park and Preserve
Onion Portage Archaeological District NHL, Noatak vicinity
Pilgrim Hot Springs, Seward Peninsula
Pilgrim 100B N709Y Aircraft, Dillingham

Port Moller Hot Springs Village Site, Alaska Peninsula
Presentation of Our Lord Chapel, Nikolai
Redoubt St. Michael Site, Unalakleet vicinity
St. George the Great Martyr Orthodox Church NHL, St. George Island
St. Jacob's Church, Napaskiak
St. John the Baptist Chapel, Naknek
St. John the Theologian Church, Perryville
St. Nicholas Chapel, Ekuk
St. Nicholas Chapel, Igiugig
St. Nicholas Chapel, Nondalton
St. Nicholas Chapel, Pedro Bay
St. Nicholas Church, Pilot Point
St. Nicholas Chapel, Sand Point
St. Nicholas Church, Nikolski
St. Seraphim Chapel, Lower Kalskag
St. Sergius Chapel, Chuathbaluk
Sts. Constantine and Helen Chapel, Lime Village
Sts. Peter and Paul Russian Orthodox Church NHL, St. Paul Island
Savonoski River District, Katmai National Park and Preserve
Seal Islands Historic District NHL, Pribilof Islands
Sir Alexander Nevsky Chapel, Akutan
Sitka Spruce Plantation, Amaknak Island
Solomon Roadhouse, Solomon
Takii Island Archaeological District, Katmai National Park and Preserve
TEMNAC P-38G Lightning Aircraft, Aleutian Islands
Transfiguration of Our Lord Chapel, Nushagak
Wales Archaeological District NHL, Wales vicinity

INTERIOR

Central Roadhouse, Central
Chatanika Gold Camp, Chatanika
Chena Pump House, Fairbanks
Chisana Historic District, Fairbanks
Chugwater Archaeological Site, Fairbanks
Clay Street Cemetery, Fairbanks
Creamers Dairy, Fairbanks
Davis (Mary Lee) House, Fairbanks
Dry Creek Archaeological Site NHL, Healy vicinity
Eagle Historic District NHL, Eagle
Ester Camp Historic District, Fairbanks
Fairview Inn, Talkeetna
Federal Building, U.S. Post Office, Courthouse (Old), Fairbanks

Goldstream Dredge #8, Mile 9, Old Steese Hwy.
Harding Railroad Car, Alaskaland, Fairbanks
Immaculate Conception Church, Fairbanks
Joslin (Falcon) House, Fairbanks
The Kink, Fortymile River
Ladd Field NHL (Fort Wainwright), Fairbanks
Masonic Temple, Fairbanks
Mission Church, Arctic Village
Mission House (Old), Fort Yukon
Mount McKinley National Park Headquarters, Denali National Park
Nenana Depot, Nenana
Oddfellows Hall (First Avenue Bathhouse), Fairbanks
Patrol Cabins, Denali National Park
Rainey's Cabin, Fairbanks
Rika's Landing, Big Delta
Ruby Roadhouse, Ruby
Steele Creek Roadhouse, Fortymile
Sternwheeler *Nenana,* Fairbanks
Sullivan Roadhouse, Fort Greely
Tanana Mission, Tanana
Teklanika Archaeological District, Denali National Park and Preserve
Thomas (George C.) Memorial Library NHL, Fairbanks
Wickersham House, Fairbanks
Yukon River Lifeways District, Eagle vicinity

FAR NORTH
Aluakpak Site, Wainwright vicinity
Anaktuuk Site, Wainwright vicinity
Atanik District, Wainwright vicinity
Avalitkuk Site, Wainwright vicinity
Birnirk Site, Barrow
Gallagher Flint Station Archaeological Site NHL, Sagwon
Ipiutak Archaeological District, Point Hope
Ipiutak Site NHL, Point Hope
Ivishaat Site, Wainwright vicinity
Kanitch, Wainwright vicinity
Leffingwell Camp NHL, Flaxman Island
Napanik Site, Wainwright vicinity
Negilik Site, Barrow
Point Barrow Refuge/Cape Smythe
Whaling and Trading Station, Barrow vicinity
Utkeagvik Presbyterian Church Manse, Barrow
Uyagaagruk, Wainwright vicinity
Will Rogers-Wiley Post Site, Barrow vicinity

National Parks, Preserves and Monuments

The National Park Service administers approximately 50 million acres of land in Alaska, consisting of 15 units classified as national parks, national preserves and national monuments. The Alaska National Interest Lands Conservation Act of 1980— also referred to as the Alaska d-2 land bill or lands act (*see* Land) — created 10 new National Park Service units in Alaska and changed the size and status of the three existing park service units: Mount McKinley National Park, now Denali National Park and Preserve; Glacier Bay National Monument, now a national park and preserve; and Katmai National Monument, now a national park and preserve. (See map, pages 128-129.)

Alaska's national parks, preserves and monuments registered an increase in number of visitors in 1988. The 1,117,738 visitors in 1988 was a 5 percent increase over 1987. Denali is still the most popular destination, with Glacier Bay, the second-most visited park, showing a 14 percent increase. The most dramatic growth in tourism, however, was to newer, lesser-known and less accessible parks, such as Katmai National Park and Preserve which showed a 20 percent increase in visitors in 1988.

National parks are traditionally managed to preserve scenic, wildlife and recreational values; mining, cutting of house logs, hunting and other resource exploitation are carefully regulated within park monument and preserve boundaries, and motorized access is restricted to automobile traffic on authorized roads. However, regulations for National Park Service units in Alaska recognize that these units contain lands traditionally occupied and used by Alaska Natives and rural residents for subsistence activities. Therefore, management of some parks, preserves and monuments in Alaska provides for subsistence hunting, fishing and gathering activities, and the use of such motorized vehicles as snow machines, motorboats and airplanes, where such activities are customary. In addition, the national preserves permit sport hunting.

Following is a list of National Park Service national parks, preserves and monuments. (The U.S. Forest Service manages another two national monuments: Admiralty Island National Monument, 937,000 acres; and Misty Fiords National Monument, 2.1 million acres. Both are in Southeast and part of the National Wilderness Preservation System. *See also* National Wilderness Areas and National Wild and Scenic Rivers.)

Information on the parks, preserves and monuments is available at the Alaska Public Lands Information Centers: 605 W. 4th Ave., Suite 105, Anchorage 99501; 250 Cushman St., Suite 1A, Fairbanks 99701; and P.O. Box 359, Tok 99780.

National Park Service Units	Acreage, major features, recreation
Aniakchak National Monument and Preserve Superintendent, Katmai National Park and Preserve, P.O. Box 7, King Salmon 99613	609,500 acres Aniakchak dry caldera
Bering Land Bridge National Preserve National Park Service P.O. Box 220 Nome 99762	2,509,360 acres Lava fields, archaeological sites, migratory waterfowl
Cape Krusenstern National Monument National Park Service P.O. Box 1029, Kotzebue 99752	540,000 acres Archaeological sites
Denali National Park and Preserve National Park Service P.O. Box 9 Denali Park 99755	6,000,000 acres Mount McKinley, abundant wildlife
Gates of the Arctic National Park and Preserve National Park Service P.O. Box 74680, Fairbanks 99707	8,090,000 acres Brooks Range, wild and scenic rivers, wildlife
Glacier Bay National Park and Preserve National Park Service Bartlett Cove, Gustavus 99826	3,283,168 acres Glaciers, marine wildlife
Katmai National Park and Preserve National Park Service P.O. Box 7, King Salmon 99613	3,917,618 acres Valley of Ten Thousand Smokes, brown bears
Kenai Fjords National Park National Park Service P.O. Box 1727, Seward 99664	580,000 acres Fjords, Harding Icefield, Exit Glacier
Klondike Gold Rush National Historical Park National Park Service P.O. Box 517, Skagway 99840	2,721 acres Chilkoot Trail
Kobuk Valley National Park National Park Service P.O. Box 1029 Kotzebue 99752	1,702,000 acres Archaeological sites, Great Kobuk Sand Dunes, river rafting

National Park Service Units	Acreage, major features, recreation
Lake Clark National Park and Preserve National Park Service 222 W. 7th Ave., #61 Anchorage 99513	3,661,000 acres Backcountry recreation, fishing, scenery
Noatak National Preserve National Park Service P.O. Box 1029, Kotzebue 99752	6,550,000 acres Abundant wildlife, river floating
Sitka National Historical Park National Park Service P.O. Box 738, Sitka 99752	106 acres Russian Bishop's House, trails
Wrangell-Saint Elias National Park and Preserve National Park Service P.O. Box 29, Glennallen 99588	12,400,000 acres Rugged peaks, glaciers, expansive wilderness
Yukon-Charley Rivers National Preserve National Park Service P.O. Box 64, Eagle 99738	2,211,000 acres Backcountry recreation, river floating

National Petroleum Reserve

(*See also* Oil and Gas)

In 1923, President Warren G. Harding signed an executive order creating Naval Petroleum Reserve Number 4 (NPR-4), the last of four petroleum reserves to be placed under control of the U.S. Navy. The Secretary of the Navy was charged to "explore, protect, conserve, develop, use, and operate the Naval Petroleum Reserves," including NPR-4, on Alaska's North Slope (see map in National Wild and Scenic Rivers).

The U.S. Geological Survey had begun surface exploration in the area in 1901; following creation of the 23-million acre reserve, exploration programs were conducted by the Navy. From 1944 to 1953, extensive geological and geophysical surveys were conducted and 36 test wells were drilled. Nine oil and gas fields were discovered; the largest oil field, near Umiat, contains an estimated 70-120 million barrels of recoverable oil. Active exploration was suspended in 1953.

In 1974, the Arab oil embargo, coupled with the knowledge of large petroleum reserves at nearby Prudhoe Bay, brought about renewed interest in NPR-4, and Congress directed the Navy to resume its exploration program.

In 1976, all lands within NPR-4 were redesignated the National Petroleum Reserve Alaska (NPR-A) and jurisdiction was transferred to the secretary of the interior. In 1980, Congress authorized the secretary of the interior to prescribe an expeditious program of competitive leasing of oil and gas tracts in the reserve, clearing the way for private development of the area's resources.

By mid-1983, three competitive bid lease sales, involving a total of 7.2 million acres of NPR-A, had been held. Dates of the sales and the number of acres involved are: January 1982, 1.5 million acres; May 1982, 3.5 million acres; and July 1983, 2.2 million acres. As oil prices have dropped, interest from the oil companies has lessened and leases have expired. As of mid-1989, there were 24 leases covering 558,950 acres.

The Interior Department, through USGS, continued exploration of NPR-A into the 1980s. Past naval explorations and those conducted by USGS resulted in the discovery of oil at Umiat and Cape Simpson, and several gas fields, including Walakpa, Gubic and Point Barrow. Data gathered indicates NPR-A may

126

contain recoverable reserves of 1.85 billion barrels of crude oil and 3.74 trillion cubic feet of natural gas.

National Wild and Scenic Rivers

(*See also* Rivers)

The Alaska National Interest Lands Conservation Act of December 2, 1980, gave wild and scenic river classification to 13 streams within the National Park System, 6 in the National Wildlife Refuge System and 2 in Bureau of Land Management Conservation and Recreation areas. (See map in National Parks, Preserves and Monuments.) An additional 5 rivers are located outside designated preservation units. Twelve more rivers were designated for further study and possible wild and scenic classification.

The criteria for wild and scenic river classification cover more than just float trip possibilities. Scenic features, wilderness characteristics and other recreational opportunities that would be impaired by alteration, development or impoundment are also considered.

Rivers are classified into three categories under the Wild and Scenic Rivers Act. The wild classification is most restrictive of development or incompatible uses — it stresses the wilderness aspect of the rivers. The scenic classification permits some intrusions upon the natural landscape and recreational classification is the least restrictive category. A specified amount of land back from the river's banks is also put in protected status to ensure access, use and the preservation of aesthetic values for the public.

For those desiring to float these rivers, special consideration must be given to put-in and take-out points as most of the new wild and scenic rivers are not accessible by road. This means that voyagers and their crafts have to be flown in and picked up by charter bush planes. Because Federal Aviation Administration regulations prohibit the lashing of canoes and kayaks on pontoons of floatplanes when carrying passengers, inflatable rafts and folding canvas or rubber kayaks are often more convenient and less expensive to transport.

Further information on rivers and river running can be obtained from the Alaska Public Lands Information Centers: 605 W. 4th Avenue, Suite 105, Anchorage 99501; 250 Cushman St., Suite 1A, Fairbanks 99701; and P.O. Box 359, Tok 99780; the U.S. Fish and Wildlife Service, 1011 E. Tudor Road, Anchorage 99503; and the Bureau of Land Management, 222 W. 7th Ave., #13, Anchorage 99513. (General information on rivers not listed in refuge brochures can be obtained from respective refuge offices by addressing queries to respective refuge managers. Addresses for refuges are given in the brochures.)

Rivers within National Park Areas
Alagnak — Katmai National Preserve
Alatna — Gates of the Arctic National Park
Aniakchak — Aniakchak National Monument; Aniakchak National Preserve
Charley — Yukon-Charley Rivers National Preserve
Chilikadrotna — Lake Clark National Park and Preserve
John — Gates of the Arctic National Park and Preserve
Kobuk — Gates of the Arctic National Park and Preserve
Mulchatna — Lake Clark National Park and Preserve
Noatak — Gates of the Arctic National Park and Noatak National Preserve
North Fork Koyukuk — Gates of the Arctic National Park and Preserve
Salmon — Kobuk Valley National Park
Tinayguk — Gates of the Arctic National Park and Preserve
Tlikakila — Lake Clark National Park

Rivers within National Wildlife Refuges
Andreafsky — Yukon Delta National Wildlife Refuge
Ivishak — Arctic National Wildlife Refuge
Nowitna — Nowitna National Wildlife Refuge
Selawik — Selawik National Wildlife Refuge
Sheenjek — Arctic National Wildlife Refuge
Wind — Arctic National Wildlife Refuge

Rivers within Bureau of Land Management Units
Beaver Creek — The segment of the main stem from confluence of Bear

(Continued on page 130)

NATIONAL WILDLIFE REFUGE SYSTEM
1 Alaska Maritime NWR*
  a Chuckchi Sea Unit
  b Bering Sea Unit
  c Aleutian Island Unit
  d Alaska Peninsula Unit
  e Gulf of Alaska Unit
2 Alaska Peninsula
3 Arctic
4 Becharof
5 Innoko
6 Izembek
7 Kanuti
8 Kenai
9 Kodiak
10 Koyukuk
11 Nowitna
12 Selawik
13 Tetlin
14 Togiak
15 Yukon Delta
16 Yukon Flats

NATIONAL PARK SYSTEM
17 Aniakchak Nat'l Monument and Preserve
18 Bering Land Bridge Nat'l Preserve
19 Cape Krusenstern Nat'l Monument
20 Denali Nat'l Park and Preserve
21 Gates of the Arctic Nat'l Park and Preserve
22 Glacier Bay Nat'l Park and Preserve
23 Katmai Nat'l Park and Preserve
24 Kenai Fjords Nat'l Park
25 Kobuk Valley Nat'l Park
26 Lake Clark Nat'l Park and Preserve
27 Noatak Nat'l Preserve
28 Wrangell Saint Elias Nat'l Park and Preserve
29 Yukon-Charley Rivers Nat'l Preserve
30 Klondike Gold Rush Nat'l Historical Park
31 Sitka Nat'l Historical Park

BUREAU OF LAND MANAGEMENT SYSTEM
32 Steese Nat'l Conservation Areas
33 White Mountains Nat'l Recreation Area

NATIONAL WILD AND SCENIC RIVERS SYSTEM
Rivers (25)

NATIONAL FOREST SYSTEM
34 Chugach Nat'l Forest
35 Tongass Nat'l Forest
36 Admiralty Island Nat'l Monument†
37 Misty Fiords Nat'l Monument†

Wilderness

*The Alaska Maritime National Wildlife Refuge consists of all the public lands in the coastal waters and adjacent seas of Alaska consisting of islands, islets, rocks, reefs, capes and spires.
†Admiralty Island and Misty Fiords national monument wildernesses are part of the Tongass National Forest, which includes 12 other wilderness areas as well.

National Interest Lands

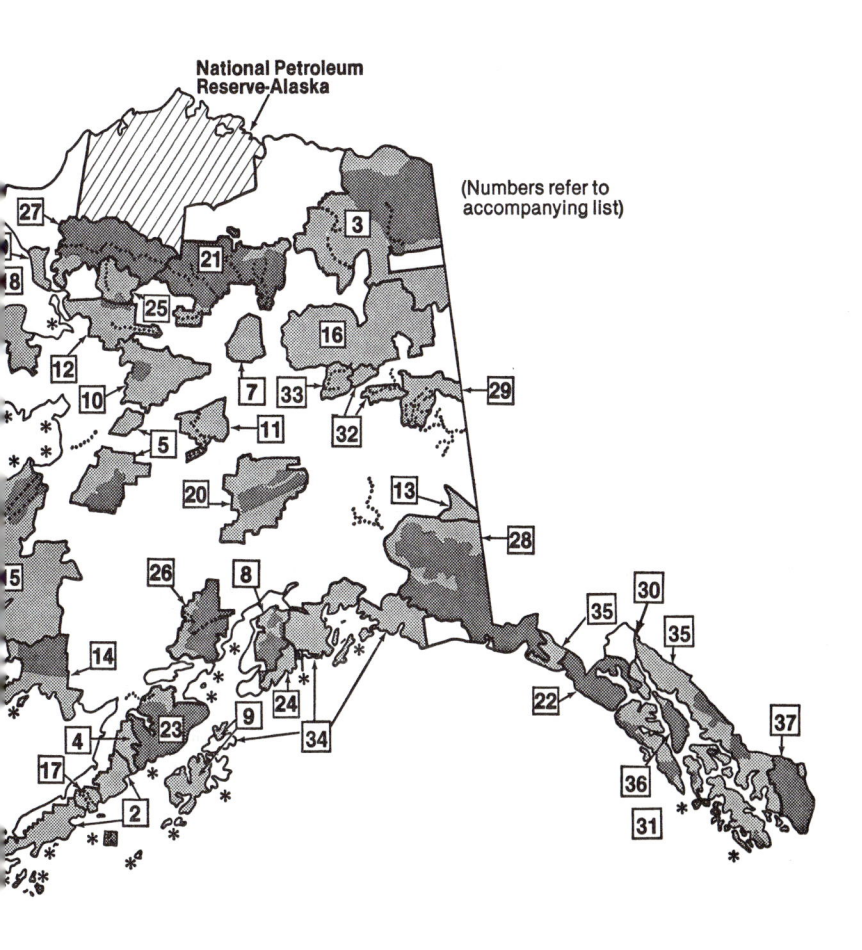

National Petroleum Reserve-Alaska

(Numbers refer to accompanying list)

(Continued from page 127)
and Champion creeks within White Mountains National Recreation Area to the Yukon Flats National Wildlife Refuge boundary.

Birch Creek — The segment of the main stem from the south side of Steese Highway downstream to the bridge at Milepost 147.

Rivers outside of designated Preservation Units

Alagnak — Those segments or portions of the main stem and Nonvianuk tributary lying outside and westward of Katmai National Park and Preserve.

Delta River — The segment from and including all of the Tangle Lakes to a point one-half mile north of Black Rapids.

Fortymile River — The main stem within the state of Alaska, plus tributaries.

Gulkana River — The main stem from the outlet of Paxson Lake to the confluence with Sourdough Creek; various segments of the west fork and middle fork.

Unalakleet River — Approximately 80 miles of the main stem.

Rivers designated for study for inclusion in Wild and Scenic Rivers System

Colville River
Etivluk-Nigu Rivers
Kanektok River
Kisaralik River
Koyuk River
Melozitna River
Porcupine River
Sheenjek River (lower segment)
Situk River
Squirrel River
Utukok River
Yukon River (Ramparts section)

National Wilderness Areas

Passage of the Alaska National Interest Lands Conservation Act on December 2, 1980, added millions of acres to the National Wilderness Preservation System. Administration of these wilderness areas is the responsibility of the agency under whose jurisdiction the land is situated. Agencies that administer wilderness areas in Alaska include the National Park Service, U.S. Fish and Wildlife Service and the U.S. Forest Service. Although the Bureau of Land Management has authority to manage wilderness in the public domain, no BLM wilderness areas exist in Alaska. (See map in National Parks, Preserves and Monuments.)

Wilderness allocations to different agencies in Alaska are:

Agency	Approximate Acreage
U.S. Forest Service	5,453,366
National Park Service	32,848,564
U.S. Fish and Wildlife Service	18,676,320

Wilderness, according to the Wilderness Act of 1964, is land sufficient in size to enable the operation of natural systems without undue influence from activities in surrounding areas and should be places in which people are visitors who do not remain. Alaska wilderness regulations follow the stipulations of the Wilderness Act as amended by the Alaska lands act. Specifically designed to allow for Alaska conditions, the rules are considerably more lenient about transportation access, human-made structures and use of mechanized vehicles. The primary objective of a wilderness area continues to be the maintenance of the wilderness character of the land. In Alaska wilderness areas, the following uses and activities are permitted:

Fishing, hunting and trapping will continue on lands within the national forests, national wildlife refuges and national park preserves. National park wilderness does not allow sport hunting, or sport or commercial trapping.

Subsistence uses, including hunting, fishing, trapping, berry gathering and use of timber for cabins and firewood will be permitted in wilderness areas by all agencies.

Public recreation or safety cabins in wilderness areas in national forests, national wildlife refuges and national park preserves will continue to be maintained and may be replaced. A limited number of new public cabins may be added if needed.

Existing special use permits and leases on all national forest wilderness lands for cabins, homesites or similar structures will continue. Use of temporary campsites, shelters and other temporary facilities and equipment related to hunting and fishing on national forest lands will continue.

Fish habitat enhancement programs, including construction of buildings, fish weirs, fishways, spawning channels and other accepted means of maintaining, enhancing, and rehabilitating fish stocks will be allowed in national forest wilderness areas. Reasonable access including use of motorized equipment will be permitted.

Special use permits for guides and outfitters operating within wilderness areas in the national forests and national wildlife refuges will be allowed to continue.

Private, state and Native lands surrounded by wilderness areas will be guaranteed access through the wilderness area.

Use of airplanes, motorboats and snow machines for *traditional* activities as a means of access into wilderness areas will be allowed to continue.

National Wildlife Refuges

There are approximately 77 million acres of National Wildlife Refuge lands in Alaska administered by the U.S. Fish and Wildlife Service. (National wildlife refuge acreage in Alaska increased nearly fourfold with the signing of the Alaska d-2 lands bill — Alaska National Interest Lands Conservation Act — in December, 1980.) Wildlife refuges are designed to protect the habitats of representative populations of land and marine mammals, other marine animals and birds. The 16 refuges vary widely in size, see map in National Parks, Preserves and Monuments.

Among the public recreational uses permitted within national wildlife refuges are sightseeing, nature observation and photography, sport hunting and fishing (under state law), boating, camping, hiking and picnicking. Trapping can be carried out under applicable state and federal laws. Commercial fishing, and related facilites (campsites, cabins, etc.), are authorized by special use permits.

Subsistence activities within national wildlife refuges are all protected under the d-2 lands bill. Use of snowmobiles, motorboats and other means of surface transportation traditionally relied upon by local rural residents for subsistence is generally permitted. Aircraft access to wildlife refuges is usually allowed, though certain areas within the Kenai National Wildlife Refuge have been closed to aircraft (a map is available from the refuge manager. Off-road vehicles may be used only on special routes or in areas designated by the refuge manager.

National Wildlife Refuge administrative addresses are followed by acreage and major features:

Alaska Maritime National Wildlife Refuge, 202 Pioneer Ave., Homer 99603 (3,548,956 acres; sea birds, sea birds, sea lions, sea otters, harbor seals).

Alaska Peninsula National Wildlife Refuge, P.O. Box 277, King Salmon 99613 (3,500,000 acres; brown bears,

131

caribou, moose, sea otters, bald eagles, peregrine falcons).

Arctic National Wildlife Refuge, Box 20, Room 226, Federal Building & Courthouse, 101 12th Ave., Fairbanks 99701 (19,351,000 acres; caribou, polar bears, grizzly bears, wolves, Dall sheep, peregrine falcons).

Becharof National Wildlife Refuge, P.O. Box 277, King Salmon 99613 (1,200,000 acres; brown bears, bald eagles, caribou, moose, salmon).

Innoko National Wildlife Refuge, P.O. Box 69, McGrath 99627 (3,850,000 acres; migratory birds, fur bearers, moose).

Izembek National Wildlife Refuge, P.O. Box 127, Cold Bay 99571 (321,000 acres; black brant, brown bears).

Kanuti National Wildlife Refuge, Box 11, Federal Building & Courthouse, 101 12th Ave., Fairbanks 99701 (1,430,000 acres; migratory birds, fur bearers, moose).

Kenai National Wildlife Refuge, 2139 Ski Hill Rd., Soldotna 99669 (1,970,000 acres; moose, salmon, mountain goats, Dall sheep, bears).

Kodiak National Wildlife Refuge, 1390 Buskin River Rd., Kodiak 99615 (1,865,000 acres; brown bears, blacktail deer, bald eagles, salmon).

Koyukuk National Wildlife Refuge, P.O. Box 287, Galena 99741 (3,550,000 acres; wolves, caribou, bear, moose).

Nowitna National Wildlife Refuge, P.O. Box 287, Galena 99741 (1,560,000 acres; migratory waterfowl, caribou, moose, bears, fur bearers).

Selawik National Wildlife Refuge, P.O. Box 270, Kotzebue 99752 (2,150,000 acres; migratory birds, caribou).

Tetlin National Wildlife Refuge, P.O. Box 155, Tok 99780 (700,000 acres; migratory waterfowl, Dall sheep, moose).

Togiak National Wildlife Refuge, P.O. Box 270, Dillingham 99576 (4,105,000 acres; nearly every major wildlife species of Alaska is represented).

Yukon Delta National Wildlife Refuge, P.O. Box 346, Bethel 99559 (19,624,458 acres; migratory birds, musk ox are found on Nunivak Island).

Yukon Flats National Wildlife Refuge, Box 14, Federal Building & Courthouse, 101 12th Ave., Fairbanks 99701 (8,630,000 acres; waterfowl).

Native People

Alaska's 64,000 Native people make up about 13 percent of the state's total population. Of those, roughly 34,000 are Eskimos, 22,000 are Indians and 8,000 are Aleuts. Although many live in widely scattered villages along the coastline and great rivers of Alaska, 9,000 Native persons lived in Anchorage in 1980, and Fairbanks had a Native population of nearly 3,000.

At the time of European discovery in 1741, the Eskimo, Indian and Aleut people lived within well-defined regions, with little mixing of ethnic groups. But they all were hunting and gathering people who did not practice agriculture.

In southeastern Alaska, the salmon, deer and other plentiful foods permitted the Tsimshian, Haida and Tlingit Indians to settle in permanent villages and develop a culture rich in art. The Athabascan Indians of the Interior took advantage of seasonal abundance of fish, waterfowl and other game. Aleuts and coastal Eskimos subsisted primarily on the rich resources of the rivers and the sea.

The Tsimshians migrated in 1887 from their former home in British Columbia to Annette Island, under Anglican minister Father William Duncan. About 1,000 now live in Metlakatla. As are most southeastern people, they are primarily fishermen.

Between 700 and 800 Haidas live in Alaska, about 200 of whom live in Hydaburg on the south end of Prince of Wales Island. They emigrated from Canada in the 1700s. Haidas excelled in the art of totem carving and are noted for precise and delicate working of wood, bone and shell.

About 10,000 Tlingits live throughout southeastern Alaska; another 1,000 live in other parts of the state, primarily in the Anchorage area. Tlingits, who arrived from Canada before the first European contact, commercially dominated the interior Canadian Indians, trading eulachon oil, copper pieces and Chilkat blankets for various furs. Like the Haidas, they are part of the totem culture; totems are used to provide a historic record of major events in the life of a family or clan.

Athabascan Indians, who occupied the vast area of interior Alaska, were nomadic people whose principal source

Traditional Native Distribution

Eskimo

Athabascan

Aleut

Tlingit

Tsimshian

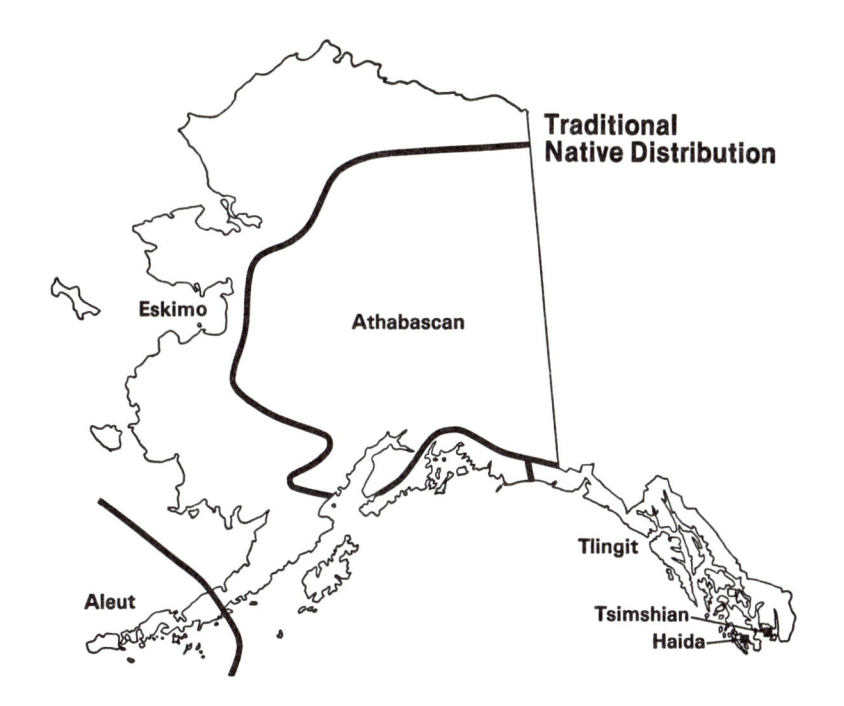

Haida

of food was land animals. Hard times and famines were frequent for all Athabascans except the Tanaina and Ahtna groups who lived along the Gulf of Alaska and could rely on salmon as their basic food.

The Aleuts have traditionally lived on the Alaska Peninsula and along the Aleutian Chain. When the Russians reached the Aleutians in the 1740s, practically every island was inhabited. Today, there are only a few permanent Aleut settlements, including two on the Pribilof Islands, where the Natives work handling seal herds for the government.

The Aleuts lived in permanent villages, taking advantage of sea life and land mammals for food. Their original dwellings were large, communal structures, housing as many as 40 families, although after Russian occupation they lived in much smaller houses, called *barabaras*. Today many Aleuts are commercial fishermen.

The Eskimos have traditionally lived in villages along the harsh Bering Sea and Arctic Ocean coastlines, and along a thin strip of the Gulf of Alaska coast, including Kodiak Island. They took salmon, waterfowl, berries, ptarmigan and a few caribou, but it was the sea and its whales, walruses and seals which provided the foundation for their existence. Houses were igloos— dwellings built partially underground and covered with sod. They did not build snow igloos.

Rapid advances in communications, transportation and other services to remote villages have altered Native life in Alaska. Economic changes, from a subsistence to a cash economy, were brought about by the passage in 1971 of the Alaska Native Claims Settlement Act. The act gave Alaska Natives $962.5 million and 44 million acres of land as compensation for the loss of lands historically occupied by their people.

NATIVE REGIONAL CORPORATIONS

Twelve regional business corporations were formed under the 1971 Alaska Native Claims Settlement Act to manage money and land received from the government. A thirteenth corporation was organized for those Natives residing outside Alaska. Following is a list of corporations and the area or region each administers (see map on page 134).

Ahtna Incorporated (Copper River Basin), Drawer G, Copper Center 99573 or 2701 Fairbanks St., Anchorage 99503.

Aleut Corporation (Aleutian Islands), 1 Aleut Plaza, 4000 Old Seward Highway, Suite 300, Anchorage 99503.

Arctic Slope Regional Corporation (Arctic Alaska), P.O. Box 129, Barrow 99723, or 313 E St., Suite 5, Anchorage 99501.

Bering Straits Native Corporation (Seward Peninsula), P.O. Box 1008, Nome 99762.

Bristol Bay Native Corporation (Bristol Bay area), P.O. Box 198, Dillingham 99576 or P.O. Box 100220, Anchorage 99510.

Calista Corporation (Yukon-Kuskokwim Delta), P.O. Box 408, Bethel 99559 or 516 Denali St., Anchorage 99501.

Chugach Alaska Corporation (Prince William Sound), 3000 A St., Suite 400, Anchorage 99503.

Cook Inlet Region, Incorporated (Cook Inlet region), 2525 C St., Anchorage 99503.

Doyon, Limited (Interior Alaska), 201 1st Ave., Suite 200, Fairbanks 99701.

Koniag, Incorporated (Kodiak area), P.O. Box 746, Kodiak 99615.

NANA Corporation (Kobuk region), P.O. Box 49, Kotzebue 99752 or 4706 Harding Dr., Anchorage 99503.

Sealaska Corporation (southeastern Alaska), One Sealaska Plaza, Juneau 99801.

Thirteenth Regional Corporation (outside Alaska), 13256 Northup Way, Suite 12, Bellevue, WA 98005.

REGIONAL NONPROFIT CORPORATIONS

Aleutian-Pribilof Islands Association, Incorporated (Aleut Corporation), 1689 C St., Anchorage 99501.

Association of Village Council Presidents (Calista Corporation), P.O. Box 219, Bethel 99559.

Bristol Bay Native Association (Bristol Bay Native Corporation), P.O. Box 237, Dillingham 99756.

Central Council of Tlingit-Haida Indian Tribes (Sealaska Corporation), One Sealaska Plaza, Suite 200, Juneau 99801.

Cook Inlet Native Association (Cook Inlet Region, Incorporated), 670 W. Fireweed Lane, Anchorage 99503.
Copper River Native Association (Ahtna Incorporated), Drawer H, Copper Center 99573.
Inupiat Community of the Arctic Slope (Arctic Slope Regional Corporation), P.O. Box 437, Barrow 99723.
Kawerak, Incorporated (Bering Straits Native Corporation), P.O. Box 948, Nome 99762.
Kodiak Area Native Association (Koniag, Incorporated), P.O. Box 172, Kodiak 99615
Maniilaq (formerly Mauneluk) Association (NANA Regional Corporation), P.O. Box 256, Kotzebue 99752.
North Pacific Rim Native Association (Chugach Alaska Corporation), 3000 A St., Suite 400, Anchorage 99503.
Tanana Chiefs Conference (Doyon, Limited), 201 1st Ave., Fairbanks 99701.

OTHER NATIVE ORGANIZATIONS
Alaska Eskimo Whaling Commission, P.O. Box 570, Barrow 99723.
Alaska Federation of Natives, 411 W. 4th Ave., Suite 1-A, Anchorage 99501.
Alaska Native Brotherhood, P.O. Box 112, Juneau 99801.
Alaska Native Commission on Alcoholism and Drug Abuse, P.O. Box 4-2463, Anchorage 99509.
Alaska Native Foundation, 411 W. 4th Ave., Suite 314, Anchorage 99501.
Alaska Native Health Board, 1135 W. 8th, Suite 2, Anchorage 99501.
Central Council of Tlingit and Haida Indian Tribes of Alaska, One Sealaska Plaza, Suite 200, Juneau 99801.
Fairbanks Native Association, Incorporated, 310 1st Ave., Fairbanks 99701.
Interior Village Association, 127-1/2 Minnie St., Fairbanks 99701.
Inuit Circumpolar Conference, Barrow 99723.
Norton Sound Health Corporation, P.O. Box 966, Nome 99762.
Southeast Alaska Regional Health Corporation, P.O. Box 2800, Juneau 99803.
Yukon-Kuskokwim Health Corporation, P.O. Box 528, Bethel 99559.
Yupiktat Bista (a branch of the Association of Village Council Presidents), Bethel 99559.

NATIVE VILLAGE CORPORATIONS
In addition to the 12 regional corporations managing money and land received as part of the Alaska Native Claims Settlement Act, eligible Native villages were required to form corporations and to choose lands made available by the settlement act by December 1974. The 203 Native villages which formed village corporations eligible for land and money benefits are listed under their regional corporation.
Ahtna Incorporated: Cantwell, Chistochina, Chitina, Copper Center, Gakona, Gulkana, Mentasta Lake, Tazlina.
Aleut Corporation: Akutan, Atka, Belkofski, False Pass, King Cove, Nelson Lagoon, Nikolski, Saint George, Saint Paul, Sand Point, Unalaska, Unga.

Arctic Slope Regional Corporation: Anaktuvuk Pass, Atkasook, Barrow, Kaktovik, Nuiqsut, Point Hope, Point Lay, Wainwright.

Bering Straits Native Corporation: Brevig Mission, Council, Golovin, Inalik/Diomede, King Island, Koyuk, Marys Igloo, Nome, Saint Michael, Shaktoolik, Shishmaref, Stebbins, Teller, Unalakleet, Wales, White Mountain.

Bristol Bay Native Corporation: Aleknagik, Chignik, Chignik Lagoon, Chignik Lake, Clarks Point, Dillingham, Egegik, Ekuk, Ekwok, Igiugig, Iliamna, Ivanof Bay, Kokhanok, Koliganek, Levelock, Manokotak, Naknek, Newhalen, New Stuyahok, Nondalton, Pedro Bay, Perryville, Pilot Point, Portage Creek, Port Heiden, South Naknek, Togiak, Twin Hills, Ugashik.

Calista Corporation: Akiachak, Akiak, Alakanuk, Andreafsky, Aniak, Atmautluak, Bethel, Bill Moores, Chefornak, Chevak, Chuathbaluk, Chuloonwick, Crooked Creek, Eek, Emmonak, Georgetown, Goodnews Bay, Hamilton, Hooper Bay, Kasigluk, Kipnuk, Kongiganak, Kotlik, Kwethluk, Kwigillingok, Lime Village, Lower Kalskag, Marshall, Mekoryuk, Mountain Village, Napaimiute, Napakiak, Napaskiak, Newtok, Nightmute, Nunapitchuk, Ohogamiut, Oscarville, Paimiut, Pilot Station, Pitkas Point, Platinum, Quinhagak, Red Devil, Russian Mission, Saint Marys, Scammon Bay, Sheldons Point, Sleetmute, Stony River, Toksook Bay, Tuluksak, Tuntutuliak, Tununak, Umkumiut, Upper Kalskag.

Chugach Natives, Incorporated: Chenaga, English Bay, Eyak, Port Graham, Tatitlek.

Cook Inlet Region, Incorporated: Chickaloon, Knik, Eklutna, Ninilchik, Seldovia, Tyonek.

Doyon, Limited: Alatna, Allakaket, Anvik, Beaver, Bettles Field, Birch Creek, Chalkyitsik, Circle, Dot Lake, Eagle, Fort Yukon, Galena, Grayling, Healy Lake, Holy Cross, Hughes, Huslia, Kaltag, Koyukuk, Manley Hot Springs, McGrath, Minto, Nenana, Nikolai, Northway, Nulato, Rampart, Ruby, Shageluk, Stevens Village, Takotna, Tanacross, Tanana, Telida.

Koniag, Incorporated: Afognak, Akhiok, Kaguyak, Karluk, Larsen Bay, Old Harbor, Ouzinkie, Port Lions, Woody Island.

NANA Regional Corporation, Incorporated: Ambler, Buckland, Deering, Kiana, Kivalina, Kobuk, Kotzebue, Noatak, Noorvik, Selawik, Shungnak.

Sealaska Corporation: Angoon, Craig, Hoonah, Hydaburg, Kake, Kasaan, Klawock, Saxman, Yakutat.

Related reading: *Roots of Ticasuk: An Eskimo Woman's Family Story.* 120 pages, $4.95. *Heroes and Heroines in Tlingit-Haida Legend.* 120 pages, $14.95. See ALASKA NORTHWEST LIBRARY in the back of the book.

Nenana Ice Classic

A gigantic betting pool offers more than $130,000 in cash prizes to the lucky winners who can guess the time, to the nearest minute, of the ice breakup on the Tanana River at the town of Nenana. Official breakup time each spring is established when the surging ice dislodges a tripod and breaks an attached line, which stops a clock set to Yukon standard time.

Tickets for the classic are sold for $2 each, entitling the holder to one guess. Ice Classic officials estimate over $7 million has been paid to lucky guessers through the years.

The primary intention of the Ice Classic was never as a fund raiser for the town, but as a statewide lottery, which was officially sanctioned by the first state legislature in one of its first actions back in 1959. But over the years the contest has benefited the town. Fifty percent of the gross proceeds goes to the winners. Nenana residents are paid salaries for ticket counting and compilation, and about 15 percent is earmarked for upkeep of the Nenana Civic Center and as donations to local groups such as the Dog Mushers, the Visitors Center and other activities or organizations.

The U.S. Internal Revenue Service also gets a large chunk of withholding taxes on the $130,000 payroll and a huge bite of each winner's share.

Another pool, the Kuskokwim Ice Classic, has been a tradition in Bethel since 1924. Initially, it was said that the

136

winner was paid 20 fish or 20 furs, but stakes are considerably higher now, with the winner receiving 40 percent of the total ticket sales.

Breakup times for the Nenana Ice Classic from 1918 through 1989, arranged in order of date and year, are:

April 20, 1940 — 3:27 p.m.
April 26, 1926 — 4:03 p.m.
28, 1969 — 12:28 p.m.
28, 1943 — 7:22 p.m.
29, 1983 — 6:37 p.m.
29, 1958 — 2:56 p.m.
29, 1953 — 3.54 p.m.
29, 1939 — 1:26 p.m.
30, 1981 — 6:44 p.m.
30, 1980 — 1:16 p.m.
30, 1979 — 6:16 p.m.
30, 1978 — 3:18 p.m.
30, 1951 — 5:54 p.m.
30, 1942 — 1.28 p.m.
30, 1936 — 12:58 p.m.
30, 1934 — 2:07 p.m.
May 1, 1956 — 11:24 a.m.
1, 1932 — 10:15 a.m.
1, 1989 — 8:14 p.m.
2, 1976 — 10:51 a.m.
2, 1960 — 7:12 p.m.
3, 1947 — 5:53 p.m.
3, 1941 — 1:50 a.m.
3, 1919 — 2:33 p.m.
4, 1973 — 11:59 a.m.
4, 1970 — 10:37 p.m.
4, 1967 — 11:55 a.m.
4, 1944 — 2:08 p.m.
5, 1963 — 6:25 p.m.
5, 1961 — 11:31 a.m.
5, 1957 — 9:30 a.m.
5, 1946 — 4:40 p.m.
5, 1929 — 3:41 p.m.
5, 1987 — 3:11 p.m.
6, 1977 — 12:46 p.m.
6, 1974 — 3:44 p.m.
6, 1954 — 6:01 p.m.
6, 1950 — 4:14 p.m.
6, 1938 — 8:14 p.m.
6, 1928 — 4:25 p.m.
7, 1965 — 7:01 p.m.
7, 1925 — 6:32 p.m.
8, 1971 — 10:50 p.m.
8, 1986 — 9:31 p.m.
8, 1968 — 9:26 p.m.
8, 1966 — 12:11 p.m.
8, 1959 — 11:26 a.m.
8, 1933 — 7:30 p.m.
8, 1930 — 7:03 p.m.
9, 1955 — 2:31 p.m.
9, 1923 — 2:00 p.m.
9, 1984 — 3:33 p.m.
10, 1982 — 5:36 p.m.
10, 1975 — 1:49 p.m.
10, 1972 — 11:56 a.m.
10, 1931 — 9:23 a.m.
11, 1985 — 2:36 p.m.
11, 1924 — 3:10 p.m.
11, 1921 — 6:42 a.m.
11, 1920 — 10:45 a.m.
11, 1918 — 9:33 a.m.
12, 1962 — 11:23 p.m.
12, 1952 — 5:04 p.m.
12, 1937 — 8:04 p.m.
12, 1927 — 5:42 a.m.
12, 1922 — 1:20 p.m.
13, 1948 — 11:13 a.m.
14, 1949 — 12:39 p.m.
15, 1935 — 1:32 p.m.
16, 1945 — 9:41 a.m.
20, 1964 — 11:41 a.m.

Newspapers and Periodicals

(Rates are subject to change)
Air Alaska, Pouch 9-9007, Anchorage 99509. Monthly. Annual rates: $15.
Air Guardian, 600 Air Guard Road, Anchorage 99502. Monthly. Annual rates: Free.
Alaska Business Monthly, P.O. Box 102696, Anchorage 99510. Monthly. Annual rates: $21.95.
Alaska Business Newsletter, 203 W. 15th Ave., Anchorage 99501. Weekly. Annual rates: $150.
Alaska Commercial Fisherman, 3933 Geneva Place, Anchorage 99508. Biweekly. Annual Rates: $30.
Alaska Construction & Oil, 360 W. Benson Blvd., Suite 208, Anchorage 99503. Monthly. Annual rates: $36 nonindustry; $10 industry.
Alaska Designs, P.O. Box 103115, Anchorage 99510. Monthly. Annual rates: Free to members.
Alaska Directory of Attorneys, 203 W. 15th Ave., Suite 102, Anchorage 99501. Semiannually. Annual rates: $20 per issue.
Alaska Fisherman's Journal, 1115 NW 46th St., Seattle, Washington 98107. Monthly. Annual rates: second class, $18; foreign, $70.
The Alaska Geographic Society, 130

137

2nd Ave. S., Edmonds, WA 98020. Quarterly. Annual rates: $39; outside the U.S., $43.

Alaska Journal of Commerce, Pouch 9-9007, Anchorage 99509. Weekly. Annual rates: $49.

ALASKA magazine, 808 E St., Suite 200, Anchorage 99501. Monthly. Annual rates: $22; outside the U.S., $26.

Alaska Media Directory, 6200 Bubbling Brook, Anchorage 99516. Annually. Annual rates: $68.

Alaska Men, 1013 E. Dimond, Suite 601, Anchorage 99515. Quarterly. Annual rates: $22.

Alaska Motorsports News, P.O. Box 140215, Anchorage 99514. Monthly. Annual rates: $29.95.

Alaska Native Magazine, P.O. Box 220230, Anchorage 99522. Quarterly. Annual rates: $18.

Alaska Oil and Industry News, Pouch 9-9007, Anchorage 99509. Monthly. Annual rates: $25.

Alaska Outdoors, P.O. Box 190324, Anchorage 99519. Monthly. Annual rates: $23.95.

Alaska Outpost, Pouch 112010, Anchorage 99511. Monthly. Annual rates: Write for information.

Alaska Public Affairs Journal, 3401 E. 42nd, #201, Anchorage 99508. Quarterly. Annual rates: $20.

Alaska Report, 241 E. 5th Ave., Suite 201, Anchorage 99501. Weekly. Annual rates: $798.

Alaska Today, U of A-Fairbanks, Dept. of Journalism and Broadcasting, Fairbanks 99775. Annually. Annual rates: $3.

Alaska Travel News, P.O. Box 202622, Anchorage 99520. May through August. Annual rates: Write for information.

Alaskan Well Being, P.O. Box 104552, Anchorage 99510. Quarterly. Annual rates: $5 by mail.

Aleutian Eagle, 3933 Geneva Place, Anchorage 99508. Weekly. Annual rates: $30; out of state, $35.

The All-Alaska Weekly, P.O. Box 970, Fairbanks 99707. Weekly. Annual rates: $20.

Anchorage Daily News, P.O. Box 149001, Anchorage 99514. Daily. Annual rates: Anchorage home delivery, $72; second-class mail, $180.

The Anchorage Times, P.O. Box 40, Anchorage 99510. Daily. Annual rates: Anchorage home delivery, $81.90.

Anchorage Visitors Guide, 201 E. 3rd Ave., Anchorage 99501. Annual rates: Free.

Arctic Soldier Magazine, Public Affairs Office, HQ, 6th Infantry Division (Light), Fort Richardson 99505. Quarterly. Annual rates: Free.

Arctic Sounder, P.O. Box 290, Kotzebue 99752. Every other week. Annual rates: $20.

Barrow Sun, 3933 Geneva Place, Anchorage 99508. Biweekly. Annual rates: $30.

Bering Straits Agluhtuk, P.O. Box 1008, Nome 99762.

Blue Water Paddler, P.O. Box 105032, Anchorage 99510. Quarterly. Annual rates: $8; $10 Canada; $12 overseas.

Borough Bugle, P.O. Box 141, Naknek 99685. Monthly. Annual rates: $13.50.

Bristol Bay Times, P.O. Box 1129, Dillingham 99576. Weekly. Annual rates: $30; first class, $60.

Capitol City Weekly, 9108 Mendenhall Mall Road, Juneau 99801. Weekly. Annual rates: Home or mail, 25¢ per week, otherwise free.

Chilkat Valley News, P.O. Box 630, Haines 99827. Weekly. Annual rates: Haines, $28; first class, $40.

Chugiak-Eagle River Star, 16941 North Eagle River Loop, Eagle River 99577. Weekly. Annual rates: $15.

Commercial Fisherman's Guide, P.O. Box 119, Port Ludlow, WA 98365. Annually. Annual rates: $9.95 per edition.

Community Blue Book, P.O. Box 91975, Anchorage 99509. Biannually. Annual rates: Write for information.

Copper River Country Journal, P.O. Box 336, Glennallen 99588. Bimonthly. Annual rates: $25.

Copper Valley Views, HC 60, Box 229, Copper Center 99573. Weekly. Annual rates: $25; first class, $45.

Cordova Times, P.O. Box 200, Cordova 99574. Weekly. Annual rates: Local, $50; first class, $90.

Daily Sitka Sentinel, P.O. Box 799, Sitka 99835. Daily except Saturday and Sunday. Annual rates: Sitka, $60. Write for mailed subscription rates.

The Delta Paper, P.O. Box 988, Delta

Junction 99737. Weekly. Annual rates: $26.

Fairbanks Daily News-Miner, P.O. Box 710, Fairbanks 99707. Daily. Annual rates: Alaska, $222. Write for rates outside Alaska.

The Frontiersman, 1261 Seward Meridian, Wasilla 99687. Semiweekly. Annual rates: Matanuska-Susitna Borough, $18.50; elsewhere, $32.

Greater Anchorage Tomorrow, 415 F St., Anchorage 99501. Monthly. Annual rates: $12.

Haines Sentinel, P.O. Box 630, Haines 99827. Annually. Annual rates: Free.

Homer News, 3482 Landings St., Homer 99603. Weekly. Annual rates: Kenai Peninsula Borough, $24; elsewhere, second class, $30; first class, $75.

Island News, P.O. Box 19430, Thorne Bay 99919. Weekly. Annual rates: $40.

Juneau Empire, 3100 Channel Drive, Juneau 99801. Daily except Saturday and Sunday. Annual rates: Juneau, $72; mailed, $104.

Kadiak Times, P.O. Box 1698, Kodiak 99615. Weekly. Annual rates: second class, $26; first class, $39.

Ketchikan Daily News, P.O. Box 7900, Ketchikan 99901. Daily except Sunday. Annual rates: $68.

Kodiak Daily Mirror, 216 W. Rezanof, Kodiak 99615. Daily except Saturday and Sunday. Annual rates: $84.

Kodiak Times, P.O. Box 1698, Kodiak 99615.

Kusko Courier, P.O. Box 224, McGrath 99627. Weekly. Annual rates: 6 months, $18.

Metro, P.O. Box 104281, Anchorage 99510. Free distribution within Anchorage.

The MILEPOST®, 22026 20th Ave. S.E. Bothell, WA 98021. Annual edition, available in March. $14.95 plus $2 for fourth-class postage; $4 for first class mail.

Mukluk News, P.O. Box 90, Tok 99780. Bimonthly. Annual rates: first class, $30; third class, $15.

Mushing, P.O. Box 149, Ester 99725. Bimonthly. Annual rates: Write for information.

New Alaskan, Rt. 1, Box 677, Ketchikan 99901. Monthly, except January. Annual rates: $7 outside of Ketchikan.

Nome Nugget, P.O. Box 610, Nome 99762. Weekly. Annual rates: Alaska, $50; Outside, $55.

Northern Adventures Magazine, 400 Denali, Wasilla 99687. Five times annually. Annual rates: Write for information.

Northland News, P.O. Box 710, Fairbanks 99707. Monthly. Annual rates: Free.

Pavlof News, P.O. Box 28, Sand Point 99661. Monthly. Annual rates: $12.

Peninsula Clarion, P.O. Box 4330, Kenai 99611. Daily except Saturday and Sunday. Annual rates: $58.

Petersburg Pilot, P.O. Box 930, Petersburg 99833. Weekly. Annual rates: Petersburg, $25; elsewhere, $28; first class, $40.

Pioneer, Public Affairs Office, HQ, 6th Infantry Brigade (Light), Fort Richardson 99505. Weekly. Annual rates: Free.

The Prudhoe Bay Journal, 4791 Bus. Park Blvd., Suite 6, Anchorage 99503. Biweekly. Annual rates: $17.50.

The River, P.O. Box 173, Aniak 99577. Biweekly. Annual rates: $10

Senior Voice, P.O. Box 102240, Anchorage 99510. Monthly. Annual rates: $15 seniors; $20, under 55.

Seward Magazine, P.O. Box 271, Seward 99664. Biannually. Annual rates: Write for information.

Seward Phoenix Log, P.O. Box 89, Seward 99664. Weekly. Annual rates: Kenai Peninsula Borough, $24; elsewhere, $30; first class, $60.

Sitka Shopper, P.O. Box 586, Sitka 99835. Biweekly. Annual rates: Free.

The Skagway News, P.O. Box 1898, Skagway 99840. Biweekly, May through October; monthly, November through April. Annual rates: $30.

Sourdough Sentinel, 21st TFW, Public Affairs, Elmendorf Air Force Base 99506. Weekly. Annual rates: Free.

Southeastern Log, P.O. Box 7900, Ketchikan 99901. Monthly. Annual rates: $12.

This Month in Fairbanks, 921 Woodway, Fairbanks 99701. June. Annual rates: $2.25.

Tundra Drums, P.O. Box 868, Bethel 99559. Weekly. Annual rates: Alaska, $20; elsewhere, $30.

Tundra Times, P.O. Box 104480, Anchorage 99510. Weekly. Annual rates: $20.

Ukpiagvik's Edgington Unedited, P.O. Box 650, Barrow 99723. Weekly. Free circulation in Barrow. Write for rates outside.

Valdez Vanguard, P.O. Box 157, Valdez 99686. Weekly. Annual rates: first class, $90; second class, $50.

Valley Sun, 1261 Seward Meridian, Wasilla 99687. Weekly. Free to Matanuska-Susitna Borough boxholders. Write for subscription rates.

Wrangell Sentinel, P.O. Box 798, Wrangell 99929. Weekly. Annual rates: $25.

Yukon Sentinel, Public Affairs Office, Bldg. 3409, Pickett Hall, Fort Wainwright 99703. Weekly. Annual rates: Free.

No-see-ums

Aptly named because, when alone, each insect is difficult to see. But in its usual swarms this tiny, gray-black, silver-winged gnat is a most persistent pest and annoys all creatures. While no-see-ums don't transmit diseases, their bites are irritating. Protective clothing, netting and a good repellent are recommended while in the bushes or near still-water ponds. Tents and recreational vehicles should be well screened.

Nuchalawoya

Nuchalawoya means "where the great waters meet"; it was originally a meeting of Athabascan chiefs held near the time of the summer solstice. Today, nuchalawoya names a festival held in June at Tanana, located at the confluence of the Tanana and Yukon rivers, and which is open to the public.

Officials

UNDER RUSSIA
Emperor Paul of Russia grants the Russian-American Company an exclusive trade charter in Alaska.
Chief Managers,
Russian-American Company
Alexander Andrevich Baranof .1799-1818
Leontil Andreanovich
    Hagemeister ....January-October 1818
Semen Ivanovich Yanovski 1818-1820
Matxei I. Muravief 1820-1825
Peter Egorovich Chistiakov ...1825-1830
Baron Ferdinand P.
    von Wrangell 1830-1835
Ivan Antonovich Kupreanof 1835-1840
Adolph Karlovich Etolin 1840-1845
Michael D. Tebenkof 1845-1850
Nikolai Y. Rosenberg...............1850-1853
Alexander Ilich Rudakof 1853-1854
Stephen Vasili Voevodski 1854-1859
Ivan V. Furuhelm 1859-1863
Prince Dmitri Maksoutoff 1863-1867

UNDER UNITED STATES
U.S. purchases Alaska from Russia in 1867; U.S. Army given jurisdiction over Department of Alaska.
Army Commanding Officers
Bvt. Maj. Gen. Jefferson C. Davis October 18, 1867-August 31, 1870
Bvt. Lt. Col. George K. Brady September 1, 1870-September 22, 1870
Maj. John C. Tidball September 23, 1870-September 19, 1871
Maj. Harvey A. Allen September 20, 1871-January 3, 1873
Maj. Joseph Stewart January 4, 1873-April 20, 1874
Capt. George R. Rodney April 21, 1874-August 16, 1874
Capt. Joseph B. Campbell August 17, 1874-June 14, 1876
(Captain E. Field was in command for one month during 1875 while Captain Campbell was out of Alaska.)
Capt. John Mendenhall June 15, 1876-March 4, 1877
Capt. Arthur Morris March 5, 1877-June 14, 1877

U.S. Army troops leave Alaska; the highest ranking federal official left in Alaska is the U.S. collector of customs. Department of Alaska is put under control of the U.S. Treasury Department.
U.S. Collectors of Customs
Montgomery P. Berry June 14, 1877-August 13, 1877
H.C. DeAhna August 14, 1877-March 26, 1878
Mottrom D. Ball March 27, 1877-June 13, 1879

U.S. Navy is given jurisdiction over the Department of Alaska.
Navy Commanding Officers

Captain L.A. Beardslee June 14, 1879-September 12, 1880
Comdr. Henry Glass September 13, 1880-August 9, 1881
Comdr. Edward Lull August 10, 1881-October 18, 1881
Comdr. Henry Glass October 19, 1881-March 12, 1882
Comdr. Frederick Pearson March 13, 1882-October 3, 1882
Comdr. Edgar C. Merriman October 4, 1882-September 13, 1883
Comdr. Joseph B. Coghlan September 15, 1883-September 13, 1884
Lt. Comdr. Henry E. Nichols September 14, 1884-September 15, 1884

Congress provides civil government for the new District of Alaska in 1884; on August 24, 1912, territorial status is given to Alaska.

Presidential Appointments

John H. Kinkead (President Arthur) July 4, 1884-May 7, 1885 (He did not reach Sitka until September 15, 1884)
Alfred P. Swineford (President Cleveland) May 7, 1885-April 20, 1889
Lyman E. Knapp (President Harrison) April 20, 1889-June 18, 1893
James Sheakley (President Cleveland) June 18, 1893-June 23, 1897
John G. Brady (President McKinley) June 23, 1897-March 2, 1906
Wilford B. Hoggatt (President Roosevelt) March 2, 1906-May 20, 1909
Walter E. Clark (President Taft) May 20, 1909-April 18, 1913
John F.A. Strong (President Wilson) April 18, 1913-April 12, 1918
Thomas Riggs, Jr. (President Wilson) April 12, 1918-June 16, 1912
Scott C. Bone (President Harding) June 16, 1921-August 16, 1925
George A. Parks (President Coolidge) June 16, 1925-April 19, 1933
John W. Troy (President Roosevelt) April 19, 1933-December 6, 1939
Ernest Gruening (President Roosevelt) December 6, 1939-April 10, 1953
B. Frank Heintzleman April 10, 1953-January 3, 1957 (President Eisenhower)
Mike Stepovich (President Eisenhower) April 8, 1957-August 9, 1958

Alaska becomes a state January 3, 1959.
Elected Governors

William A. Egan January 3, 1959-December 5, 1966
Walter J. Hickel* December 5, 1966-January 29, 1969
Keith H. Miller* January 29, 1969-December 5, 1970
William A. Egan December 5, 1970-December 5, 1974
Jay S. Hammond December 5, 1974-December 5, 1982
Bill Sheffield December 5, 1982-December 5, 1986
Steve Cowper December 5, 1986-

*Hickel resigned before completing his full term as governor in order to accept the position of secretary of the interior. He was succeeded by Miller.

Delegates to Congress

In 1906, Congress authorized Alaska to send a voteless delegate to the House of Representatives.

Frank H. Waskey 1906-1907
Thomas Cale 1907-1909
James Wickersham 1909-1917
Charles A. Sulzer .... 1917-contested election
James Wickersham .... 1918-seated ad delegate
Charles A. Sulzer .... 1919-elected; died before taking office
George Grigsby .... 1919-elected in a special election
James Wickersham .... 1921-seated as delegate, having contested election of Grigsby
Dan A. Sutherland 1921-1930
James Wickersham 1931-1933
Anthony J. Dimond 1933-1944
E.L. Bartlett 1944-1958

Unofficial delegates to Congress to promote statehood, elected under a plan first devised by Tennessee when it was seeking statehood. The Tennessee Plan delegates were not seated by Congress but did serve as lobbyists.

Senators:
Ernest Gruening 1956-1958
William Egan 1956-1958
Representative:
Ralph Rivers 1956-1958

Alaska becomes 49th state in 1959 and sends two senators and one representative to U.S. Congress.
Senators:
E.L. Bartlett 1958-1968

Ernest Gruening 1958-1968
Mike Gravel 1968-1980
Ted Stevens 1968-
Frank Murkowski 1980-

Representatives:
Ralph Rivers 1958-1966
Howard Pollock 1966-1970
Nicholas Begich 1970-1972
Don Young 1972-

Correspondence addresses for Alaska officials:

The Honorable Steve Cowper The Honorable Stephen McAlpine, Office of the Governor, P.O. Box A, Juneau, AK 99811.

The Honorable Stephen McAlpine, Office of the Lieutenant Governor, P.O. Box AA, Juneau, AK 99811

Alaska's delegation in U.S. Congress:

The Honorable Ted Stevens, United States Senate, 522 Hart Bldg., Washington, D.C. 20510

The Honorable Frank H. Murkowski, United States Senate, 709 Hart Bldg., Washington, D.C. 20510

The Honorable Donald E. Young, House of Representatives, 2331 Rayburn House Office Bldg., Washington, D.C. 20515

Alaska State Legislature

Members of the Alaska Legislature as of the end of 1986 are listed below. During sessions, members of the legislature receive mail at P.O. Box V, Juneau, Alaska 99811.

House of Representatives

District 1: Robin L. Taylor (Seat A, Republican); Cheri Davis (Seat B, Democrat).
District 2: Peter Goll (Democrat).
District 3: Ben F. Grussendorf (Democrat).
District 4: Bill Hudson (Seat A, Republican); Fran Ulmer (Seat B, Democrat).
District 5: Mike Navarre (Seat A, Democrat); C.E. Swackhammer (Seat B, Democrat).
District 6: Bette M. Cato (Democrat).
District 7: Jim Zawacki (Republican).
District 8: Fritz Pettyjohn (Seat A, Republican); Steven Rieger (Seat B, Republican).
District 9: Drue Pearce (Seat A, Republican); Alyce A. Hanley (Seat B, Republican).
District 10: H.A."Red" Boucher (Seat A, Democrat); Virginia M. Collins (Seat B, Republican).
District 11: Dave Donley (Seat A, Democrat); Max F. Gruenberg, Jr. (Seat B, Democrat).
District 12: Kay Brown (Seat A, Democrat); Johnny Ellis (Seat B, Democrat).
District 13: David Finkelstein (Seat A, Democrat); Terry Martin (Seat B, Republican).
District 14: Ramona Barnes (Seat A, Republican); Walt Furnace (Seat B, Republican).
District 15: Sam Cotten (Seat A, Democrat); Randy E. Phillips (Seat B, Republican).
District 16: Curt Menard (Seat A, Democrat); Ronald L. Larson (Seat B, Democrat).
District 17: Richard Schultz (Republican).
District 18: Mike W. Miller (Republican).
District 19: Mike Davis (Democrat).
District 20: Bert M. Sharp (Seat A, Republican); Mark Boyer (Seat B, Democrat).
District 21: Niilo Koponen (Democrat).
District 22: Eileen Panigeo MacLean (Democrat).
District 23: Richard Foster (Republican).
District 24: Kay Wallis (Democrat).
District 25: Lyman F. Hoffman (Democrat).
District 26: George G. Jacko, Jr. (Democrat).
District 27: Cliff Davidson (Democrat).

Senate

District A: Lloyd Jones (Republican).
District B: Richard I. Eliason (Republican).
District C: Jim Duncan (Democrat).
District D: Paul A. Fischer (Republican).
District E: Jalmar M. "Jay" Kerttula (Seat A, Democrat); Mike Szymanski (Seat B, Democrat).
District F: Arliss Sturgulewski (Seat A, Republican); Jan Faiks (Seat B, Republican).
District G: Mitchell E. Abood, Jr. (Seat A, Republican); Patrick M. Rodey (Seat B, Democrat).
District H: Joe Josephson (Seat A, Democrat); Rick Uehling (Seat B, Republican).
District I: Rick Halford (Seat A, Repub-

lican); Tim Kelly (Seat B, Republican).
District J: John B. "Jack" Coghill (Republican).
District K: Steve Frank (Seat A, Republican); Bettye M. Fahrenkamp (Seat B, Democrat).
District L: Al Adams (Democrat).
District M: Johne Binkley (Republican).
District N: Fred F. Zharoff (Democrat).

Oil and Gas

Alaska's first exploratory oil well was drilled in 1898 on the Iniskin Peninsula, Cook Inlet, by Alaska Petroleum Company. According to the Alaska Oil and Gas Association, oil was encountered in this first hole at about 700 feet, but a water zone beneath the oil strata cut off the oil flow. Total depth of the well was approximately 1,000 feet.

The first commercial oil discovery was made in 1902 near Katalla, near the mouth of the Bering River east of Cordova. This field produced until 1933.

As early as 1921, oil companies surveyed land north of the Brooks Range for possible drilling sites. In 1923, the federal government created Naval Petroleum Reserve Number 4 (now known as National Petroleum Reserve-Alaska, see National Petroleum Reserve) a 23-million-acre area of Alaska's North Slope. Wartime needs speeded up exploration. In 1944, the Navy began drilling operations on the petroleum reserve and continued until 1953, but made no significant oil discoveries. Since 1981, the Interior Department has leased out oil and gas tracts in the reserve.

Atlantic Richfield discovered oil in 1957 on the Kenai Peninsula, at a depth of approximately 2 miles, about 20 miles northeast of Kenai at what became known as the Swanson River Oilfield. Later, Union Oil Company found a large gas field at Kalifonsky Beach (the Kenai Gas Field) and Amoco found the first gas offshore at a location known as Middle Ground Shoals in Cook Inlet in 1962. Since 1957, the oil and gas industry has invested $45 billion in Alaska. The money has gone toward exploration, development and construction of the pipeline.

Currently, there are 15 production platforms in Cook Inlet, one of which produces only gas. Built to contend with extreme tides, siltation and ice floes, the Cook Inlet platforms are in one of three successful areas of offshore oil production in the United States. Hundreds of miles of pipeline with diameters up to 20 inches link the offshore platforms with onshore facilities at Kenai and Drift River. The deepest producing oil well in the state is in the Swanson River Oilfield on the Kenai Peninsula; total depth is 17,689 feet. Alaska had 313 active wells in 1985, including exploratory and developmental wells.

A fertilizer plant, largest of its kind on the West Coast, is located at Nikiski, near Kenai. It uses natural gas as a feed stock to manufacture ammonia and urea. Two refineries are located at Kenai; a third is at North Pole near Fairbanks. Gasoline, diesel fuel, heavy fuel oil, liquified natural gas, propane, JP-4, Jet A and asphalt are produced for use within and outside of Alaska. Crude oil topping plants located at Prudhoe Bay and at pump stations 6, 8 and 10 provide diesel oil for industrial use.

The Prudhoe Bay oil field, largest in North America, was discovered in 1968 by Atlantic Richfield Company and Exxon. Recoverable reserves were estimated to be 9.6 billion barrels of oil and 26 trillion cubic feet of natural gas. The field contains about one-quarter of the known petroleum reserves in the United States and each day produces nearly 25 percent of U.S. production and 11 percent of U.S. consumption. Peak production of 1.5 million barrels per day has begun to decline and is transported from North Slope fields via the trans-Alaska pipeline from Prudhoe Bay to Valdez (see Trans-Alaska Pipeline). In spring of 1986, it was estimated that one-half of the Prudhoe Bay recoverable oil reserve had been pumped. A $2 billion waterflood project was installed to maximize oil recovery by forcing additional oil out of the reservoir rock and into producing wells. The Central Gas Facility, recently built at Prudhoe Bay, is capable of processing 3.3 billion cubic feet of natural gas and yielding more than 40,000 barrels of natural gas liquids daily. The facility is the largest gas plant in the world with a capacity of over four billion cubic feet. Two new fields, Endicott and Lisburne, are in production with Lisburne beginning production in 1986. Endicott began production in February, 1985, and is owned by Standard Alaska (56.7 percent), Exxon (21 percent), Amoco (10.5 percent) and Union (10.5 percent). The remaining 1.3 percent is owned by ARCO, Cook Inlet Region Incorporated, Doyon Limited and Nana Regional Corporation and is the first offshore commercial development in the United States portion of the Beaufort Sea. Endicott is estimated to have 350 million barrels of oil with 37.4 million barrels produced in 1988. Milne Point, located 35 miles northwest of Prudhoe Bay, is a field operated by Conoco. Economically, this is a marginal field with estimated reserves of 100 million barrels. Conoco suspended drilling operations in February 1985, but resumed production in 1989, at the rate of 7,000 barrels per day. A new oil field is being developed by Standard near Prudhoe Bay in 1988. Niakuk is a small field, but will help overall oil production on the North Slope.

The Kuparuk River Field, 40 miles west of Prudhoe Bay, is being developed by ARCO. The eventual cost of full development is expected to be approximately $7 billion, with ARCO's share being $3.9 billion. The field went into production in mid-December 1981; approximately 303,740 barrels a day are being delivered to the trans-Alaska pipeline. In February 1989, ARCO and Exxon announced the discovery of oil at Point McIntyre adjacent to the Prudhoe Bay Field. If production proves economically feasible, oil could begin flowing in 1992.

In 1984, Shell Western discovered Oil at Seal Island, twelve miles northwest of Prudhoe Bay. Northstar Island, five miles to the west, was the site of delineation drilling in 1985 and in the same region, Sandpiper Island reported another strike in 1985. Texaco hit a strike on the Colville River Delta about eight miles northwest of the Kuparuk River field. Exploration in Navarin Basin began when Amoco drilled five wells, Exxon drilled two wells and ARCO drilled one well. The average well took 60 days to drill and the average cost per well was $20 to 30 million. Although none of the wells are considered commercially feasible, in 1986, drilling was halted by legal action. In October 1985, the 9th Circuit Court of Appeals in San Francisco ruled that drilling must stop in Navarin Basin until a lawsuit filed by the villages of Gambell and Stebbins was fully heard. In a significant decision in early 1987, the Supreme Court overturned the 9th Circuit ruling and held that the aboriginal rights of Alaska Natives were extinguished by Section 4(b) of the Alaska Native Claims Settlement Act, and that Section 810 (a) of the ANILCA, which provides protection for subsistence resources, did not extend to the Outer Continental Shelf.

The Alaska Natural Gas Transportation System — the proposed Alaska gas pipeline — was authorized by the federal government in 1977. Estimated cost was $10 billion with a completion date of 1983. A two-year delay in the northern part of the project was announced in May 1982 by Northwest Alaskan, the consortium building the project. Recent cost estimates for the gas pipeline have risen to more than $40 billion. A completion date is not set for the foreseeable future, due to problems in financing the project. Now, most industry observers feel that the proposed Trans-Alaska Gas System is the most viable idea for transporting North Slope gas to Valdez for shipment to market.

Alaska Oil and Natural Gas (Liquid) Production
(in millions of barrels)

Year	Oil*	Natural Gas**
1972	73.6	0.608
1973	73.1	0.812
1974	72.2	0.793
1975	72.0	0.765
1976	67.0	0.770
1977	171.3	0.863
1978	444.8	0.815
1979	511.3	0.635
1980	591.6	0.735
1981	587.3	0.988
1982	618.9	0.999
1983	625.6	0.692
1984	630.4	0.678
1985	666.2	0.986
1986	681.3	1.600
1987	716.0	16.500
1988	738.1	20.300

*Oil production for the years 1902-71 totaled 396,537,603 barrels; for the years 1902-82, total production amounted to 3,682,769,004 barrels.
**Natural gas (liquid) production for the years 1902-71 totaled 1,312,113 barrels; for the years 1902-83, total production was 9,218,705 barrels.
Source: *1983 Statistical Report,* Alaska Oil and Gas Conservation Commission, 3001 Porcupine Drive, Anchorage 99501.

In 1987, Alaska surpassed Texas in oil production. The top five oil-producing states, in order, were: Alaska, Texas, Louisiana, California and Oklahoma. According to the U.S. Geological Survey, Alaska provided about 20 percent of the nation's oil in 1983.

The state of Alaska receives approximately 85 percent of its general revenue from petroleum taxes and royalties, and since 1975, the state has collected more than $32 billion in oil and gas revenues. In early 1986, the price of oil dropped. Oil industry employment then declined rather than increased, and the state government was in a more tenuous fiscal situation. In 1984, petroleum-based state government revenues were $2,862 million — 78 percent of general fund revenues.

In 1984, the oil industry produced $10,675 million of crude petroleum and natural gas, mostly from the North Slope Prudhoe Bay field. Total crude oil production in the state from existing fields is still on the rise but expected to reach its peak in 1989. Meanwhile, weak world demand for crude oil has caused the production value to decline since 1981.

While crude oil produced in the North Slope cannot be exported, there are no such restrictions on natural gas. In 1987, natural gas and products derived from it (ammonia and urea) made up 13 percent of all Alaska exports. Most natural gas produced in Alaska is either locally consumed or reinjected back into oil wells.

Natural gas provides a relatively low-cost source of energy for certain Railbelt residents and businesses of Alaska. In 1983, 60 percent of power generated by Alaska utility companies used natural gas. That year the total revenues earned by the utility companies were $264 million. There are also three refineries in Alaska, which satisfy 75 percent of gasoline, diesel and jet fuel consumption in the state.

Oil and gas leasing on state land in Alaska is managed by the Department of Natural Resources, Division of Oil and Gas. The secretary of the interior is responsible for establishing oil and gas leasing on federal lands in Alaska including the outer continental shelf. In 1986, Chevron, in partnership with a native corporation, left its well at Kaktovik on the coastal plain of the Arctic National Wildlife Refuge. The land was obtained in a swap with the U.S. Department of the Interior, but Congress would have to approve any development within the boundaries of the refuge.

Parka

Pronounced *par-kee,* this over-the-head garment worn by Eskimos was made in several versions. The work parka most often came from caribou fawn skin, while the fancy parka, reserved for special occasions, used the skin of the male ground squirrel (the male offering grayer fur than the female). The rain parka, was made from *oogruk* (bearded seal) intestine. A person's wealth was judged by the quality of their best parka.

Related reading: *Secrets of Eskimo Skin Sewing* by Edna Wilder. The complete book on the art of Eskimo skin sewing, with how-to-do-it instructions and things-to-make ideas. 125 pages, $9.95. See ALASKA NORTHWEST LIBRARY in the back of the book.

Permafrost

Permafrost, perennially frozen ground, is defined as ground which remains frozen for two or more years. In its continuous form, permafrost underlies the entire arctic region to depths of 2,000 feet. In broad terms, continuous permafrost occurs north of the Brooks Range and in the alpine region of mountains (including those of the Lower 48).

Discontinuous permafrost occurs south of the Brooks Range and north of the Alaska Range. Much of the Interior and some of Southcentral are underlain by discontinuous permafrost.

Permafrost affects many man-made structures and natural bodies. It influences construction in the Arctic because building on it may cause the ground to thaw and if the ground is ice-rich, structures will sink. Arctic and subarctic rivers typically carry 55 to 65 percent of precipitation falling onto their watersheds, roughly 30 to 40 percent more than rivers of more temperate climates. Consequently, northern streams are prone to flooding and have high silt loads. Permafrost is responsible for the thousands of lakes dotting the arctic tundra because ground water is held on the surface.

A tunnel excavated in permafrost near Fox during the early 1960s is maintained cooperatively by the University of Alaska, Fairbanks and the U.S. Army Cold Regions Research and Engineering Laboratory. It is one of the few such tunnels in the world; it offers unique research opportunities on a 40,000-year-old accumulation of sediments and ice.

The tunnel is open to the general public from June 1 through August 31 each year, by appointment only, through the CRREL office.

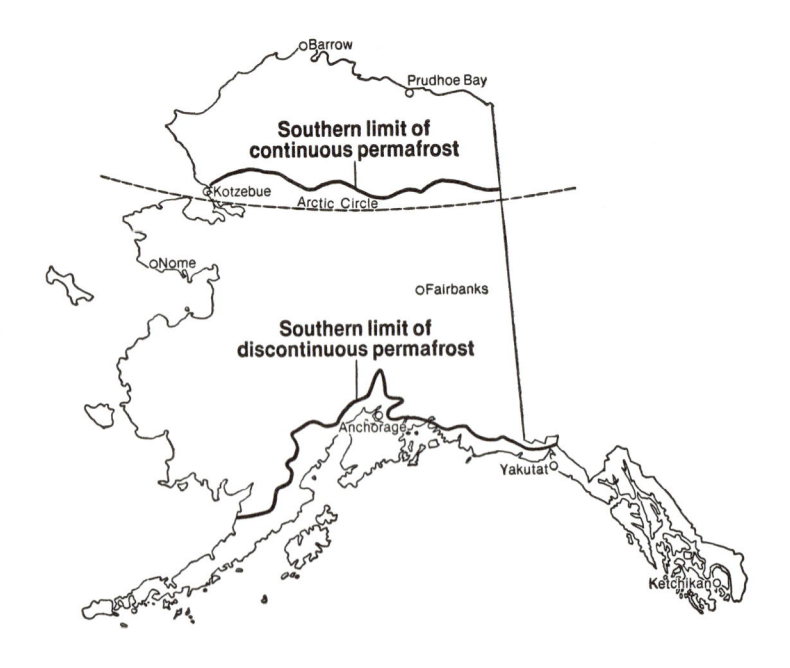

Permanent Fund

In 1976, state voters approved a constitutional amendment to establish the Alaska Permanent Fund. This provides that a percentage of all mineral lease rentals, royalties, royalty sales proceeds, federal mineral revenue sharing payments and bonuses shall be placed in a Permanent Fund. Essentially a trust fund for all Alaskans, money from the fund may be used in income-producing investments, but may not be used for state operating expenses (interest income from the Permanent Fund can go into the state's General Fund.)

In 1980, the legislature established a Permanent Fund dividend payment program, providing for distribution of the fund's earnings (interest income and capital gains on any liquidation of assets) among the people of Alaska. Eligible residents were to receive a $50 dividend for each year of residency since 1959. The U.S. Supreme Court declared the 1980 program unconstitutional on the grounds that it discriminated against short-term residents and, in 1982, a new state program was signed into law. Under the new plan, an initial $1,000 dividend was paid to applicants who had lived in the state for at least six months prior to applying. Amounts of subsequent dividend payments are computed each fiscal year by dividing one-half of the fund's earnings by the number of applicants.

If Alaska's $10 billion Permanent Fund were a foundation trust, it would be the largest in the nation, far surpassing the J. Paul Getty Trust and the Ford Foundation, according to the fund's executive director. If it were an endowment fund, it would be the largest in the nation, also. Measured on the basis of net income, the fund would rank 24th as a "Fortune 500" company.

In 1989, the dividend from the Permanent Fund may again be over $800 per Alaska resident.

Pioneers' Homes

"The state of Alaska recognizes the invaluable contributions of its older citizens and seeks to offer a place for them in which they can live in comfort and security, while remaining active members of the Alaska community. The companionship of other pioneer Alaskans whose earlier years have been spent in the exciting days of the territory is one of the advantages of living in the Pioneers' Homes." These words were taken from a state brochure describing Pioneers' Homes. The six state-supported homes offer a comfortable, secure residence for several hundred older Alaskans. The homes provide space for 355 ambulatory residents and 293 nursing spaces for bedridden and wheelchair patients.

There are two sets of criteria for admission to a Pioneers' Home. The first set of requirements are that a person be destitute and in need, be a resident of the state, and have lived continuously in Alaska for 15 years immediately preceding application for admission. Under the second set, a person must be 65 years or older, lived continuously in Alaska for 15 years immediately preceding application for admission and agree to pay the rent established by the Department of Administration. (Some exceptions are made for Alaskans who have lived in the state more than 30 years.) Race, sex, national origin and religion are not considered when determining eligibility. Some people are under the mistaken impression that to qualify for the Pioneers' Homes, one must be a member of the Pioneers of Alaska. This is not the case. Pioneers of Alaska is a private, fraternal organization and is not connected with the state-operated Pioneers' Homes.

The first Pioneers' Home was established in Sitka in 1913 for "indigent prospectors and others who have spent their years in Alaska." With the coming of statehood in 1959, the homes were officially opened to women and Alaska Natives.

For additional information about Pioneers' Homes, contact the Director of Pioneers Benefits, P.O. Box CL, Juneau 99811-0211; phone (907) 465-4400.

Following are the locations of the five homes:

Anchorage Pioneers' Home, 923 W. 11th Ave., Anchorage 99501; phone (907) 276-3414.

Fairbanks Pioneers' Home, 2221 Eagan Ave., Fairbanks 99701; phone (907) 456-4372.

Juneau Pioneers' Home, 4675 Glacier Highway, Juneau 99801.

Ketchikan Pioneers' Home, 141 Bryant, Ketchikan 99901; phone (907) 225-4111.

Palmer Pioneers' Home, 250 E. Fireweed, Palmer 99645; phone (907) 745-4241.

Sitka Pioneers' Home, 120 Katlian St., Sitka 99835; phone (907) 747-3213.

Pipeline

The trans-Alaska pipeline designer, builder and operator is the Alyeska Pipeline Service Company, a consortium of the following seven oil companies:

Sohio Alaska Pipeline Company	50.01
ARCO Pipe Line Company	21.35
Exxon Pipeline Company	20.34
Mobil Alaska Pipeline Company	4.08
Unocal Pipeline Company	1.36
Phillips Alaska Pipeline Corporation	1.36
Amerada Hess Pipeline Corporation	1.50

0.562 inch. Pipe sections before construction in lengths of 40 and 60 feet.

Cost: $8 billion, which includes terminal at Valdez, but does not include interest on money raised for construction.

Amount of oil pumped through pipeline: As of February 1988, 6 billion barrels of crude oil. On May 2, 1988, the 8,000th tanker sailed from the Marine Terminal at Valdez with a cargo of Alaska North Slope crude oil destined for U.S. markets. None of the North Slope oil is exported from the U.S.

Operations: Control center at Valdez terminal and 10 operating pump stations along line monitor and control pipeline.

Pipeline throughput: 2.1 million barrels a day, average.

Estimated crude oil reserves recoverable on the North Slope: Approximately 7 billion barrels as of February 15, 1988.

Pipeline length: 800 miles, slightly less than half that length is buried, the remainder is on 78,000 aboveground supports, located 60 feet apart, built in a flexible zigzag pattern. More than 800 river and stream crossings. Normal burial of pipe was used in stable soils and rock; aboveground pipe — insulated and jacketed — was used in thaw unstable permafrost areas. Thermal devices prevent thawing around vertical supports. 151 stop flow valves.

Pipe: Specially manufactured coated pipe with zinc anodes installed to prevent corrosion. Size is 48 inches in diameter, with thickness from 0.462 to

Terminal: 1,000-acre site at Port Valdez, northernmost ice-free harbor in the U.S., with 18 tanks providing storage capacity of 9,180,000 barrels of oil.

Valdez ship-loading capacity: 110,000 barrels per hour for each of three berths; 80,000 barrels per hour for one berth.

Length and cost of pipeline haul road built by Alyeska: 360 miles, from the Yukon River to Prudhoe Bay, $150 million.

Yukon River bridge: First bridge (2,290 feet long) spanning the Yukon in Alaska.

Important dates: July 1968, Prudhoe

Pipeline Route

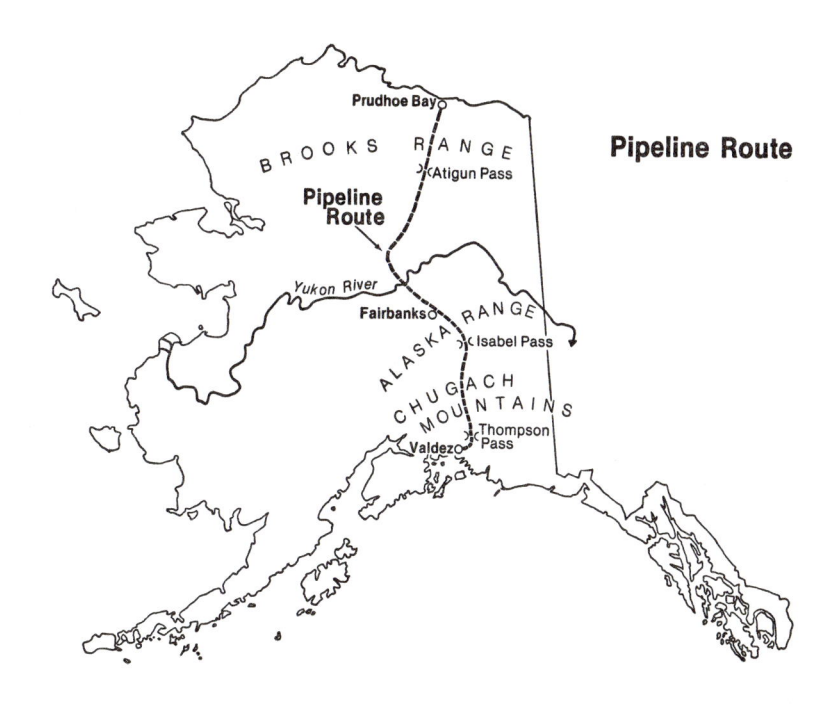

Bay oil field discovery confirmed; **1970**, suits filed to halt construction, Alyeska Pipeline Service Company formed; **November 16, 1973**, presidential approval of pipeline legislation; **April 29, 1974**, construction begins on North Slope Haul Road (now the Dalton Highway) and is completed 154 days later; **March 27, 1975**, first pipe installed at Tonsina River; **June 20, 1977**, first oil leaves Prudhoe Bay, reaches Valdez terminal July 28; **August 1, 1977**, first tanker load of oil shipped aboard the SS *ARCO Juneau*; **June 13, 1979**, tanker number 1,000 (SS *ARCO Heritage*) sails; **July 15, 1983**, 3 billionth barrel of oil leaves pump station. **September 15, 1986**, 5 billionth barrel of oil leaves pump station. **April 19, 1987**, 7,000th tanker sails from Marine Terminal with Prudhoe Bay crude oil. February 16, 1988, 6 billionth barrel arrives at the Marine Terminal. May 2, 1988, *Chevron Mississippi* is 8,000th tanker to load crude oil at Marine Terminal.

Place Names

Alaska has a rich international heritage of place names. Throughout the state names of British (Barrow), Spanish (Valdez), Russian (Kotzebue), French (La Perouse), American (Fairbanks) and Native Alaska (Sitka) origin dot the map. Some Alaska place names are quite common. There are about 70 streams called Bear Creek in Alaska (not to mention Bear Bay, Bear Bluff, Bear Canyon, Bear Cove and Bear Draw) and about 50 called Moose Creek. Many place names have an unusual history. In 1910, geologist Lawrence Martin named Sherman Glacier in the Chugach Mountains after Gen. William Tecumseh Sherman, with the explanation, "He [Sherman] said 'war is hell'; so I put him on ice, near the Sheridan Glacier."

For a comprehensive listing, description and history of Alaska's usual and unusual place names, from Aaron Creek to Zwinge Valley, see Donald Orth's *Dictionary of Alaska Place Names,* U.S.

Geological Survey Professional Paper 567.

Poisonous Plants

Alaska has few poisonous plants, considering the total number of plant species growing in the state. Baneberry *(Actaea rubra)*, water hemlock *(Cicuta douglasii* and *C. mackenzieana)* and fly agaric mushroom *(Amanita muscaria)* are the most dangerous. Be sure you have properly identified plants before harvesting for food.

Alaska has no plants poisonous to the touch, such as poison ivy and poison oak, which are found in almost all other states.

Related reading: *Plant Lore of an Alaskan Island* by Frances Kelso Graham and the Ouzinkie Botanical Society. 210 pages, $9.95. *Discovering Wild Plants, Alaska, Western Canada, The Northwest,* by Janice Schofield. 130 species are described; includes photographs and illustrations of each plant. 350 pages, $34.95. See ALASKA NORTHWEST LIBRARY in the back of the book.

Populations and Zip Codes

In the last fifteen years, population in Alaska has grown at an average annual rate of 4 percent — several times higher than the national average. In 1983, the state population grew at an unprecedented rate of 10.8 percent. Such high annual growth occurred once before in the history of Alaska, in 1975 (10.3 percent). The rush of people to Alaska did slow in 1988 with more people moving from Alaska to the Lower 48 than the reverse. Today half a million people reside in the state of Alaska.

The city of Anchorage has the highest percentage of young adults — 25 to 34 years old — in the state, with 57,592 people falling in that age range. In the five-year period from mid-1980 through mid-1985, the number of Anchorage children under 5 increased by 21,369.

The populations for cities and communities in the following lists are taken from the Alaska Department of Labor Population Estimates.

For population figures by census area, based on U.S. census figures, see the end of Population and Zip Codes category.

Community	1900	1920	1940	1950	1960	1970	1980
Anchorage	—	1,856	4,229	11,254	44,237	48,081	174,431
Barrow	—	—	—	—	—	2,104	2,207
Bethel	—	—	—	—	—	2,416	3,576
Cordova	—	955	938	1,165	1,125	1,164	1,879
Fairbanks	—	1,155	3,455	5,771	13,311	14,771	22,645
Juneau	1,864	3,058	5,729	5,956	6,797	6,050	19,528
Kenai	290	332	303	321	778	3,533	4,324
Ketchikan	459	2,458	4,695	5,305	6,483	6,994	7,198
Kodiak	341	374	864	1,710	2,628	3,798	4,756
Kotzebue	—	—	—	—	—	1,696	2,054
Nome	12,488	852	1,559	1,876	2,316	2,357	2,301
Petersburg	—	879	1,323	1,619	1,502	2,042	2,821
Seward	—	652	949	2,114	1,891	1,587	1,843
Sitka	1,396	1,175	1,987	1,985	3,237	3,370	7,803
Valdez	315	466	529	554	555	1,005	3,079
Wrangell	868	821	1,162	1,263	1,315	2,029	2,184

—Population figures unavailable
Source: Alaska Department of Labor

Community — Year Incorporated	Population	Zip
Akhiok (AH-key-ok) — 1972	123	99615
Akiachak (ACK-ee-a-chuck) — 1974	444	99551
Akiak (ACK-ee-ack) — 1970	259	99552
Akutan (ACK-oo-tan) — 1979	87	99553

Community — Year Incorporated	Population	Zip
Alakanuk (a-LACK-a-nuk) — 1969	581	99554
Aleknagik (a-LECK-nuh-gik) — 1973	182	99555
Allakaket (alla-KAK-it) — 1975	189	99720
Ambler — 1971	271	99786
Anaktuvuk Pass (an-ak-TU-vuk) — 1957	278	99721
Anchor Point	335	99556
Anchorage (Municipality) — 1920	231,492	99510
Eastchester Station	—	99501
Fort Richardson	—	99505
Elmendorf AFB	—	99506
Mountain View	—	99508
Spenard Station	—	99509
Downtown Station	—	99510
South Station	—	99511
Alyeska Pipeline Co.	—	99512
Federal Building	—	99513
Anderson — 1962	629	99744
Angoon — 1963	605	99820
Aniak (AN-ee-ack) — 1972	513	99557
Annette	176	99926
Anvik — 1969	91	99558
Arctic Village	119	99722
Atka	101	99502
Atmautluak (an-MAUT-loo-ack) — 1976	255	99559
Atqasuk — 1983	182	99791
Auke Bay	NA	99821
Barrow — 1959	3,052	99723
Beaver	101	99724
Belkofski (bel-KOF-ski)	12	99612
Bethel — 1957	4,219	99559
Bettles Field — 1985	55	99726
Big Delta	465	99737
Big Horn	401	NA
Big Lake	744	99652
Bodenburg Butte	1,396	99645
Border	NA	99780
Brevig Mission — 1969	176	99785
Buckland — 1966	259	99727
Cantwell	185	99729
Cape Yakataga	8	99574
Central	66	99730
Chalkyitsik (chawl-KIT-sik)	110	99788
Chatanika (chat-a-NEEK-a)	NA	99701
Chefornak (cha-FOR-nack) — 1974	310	99561
Chevak — 1967	548	99563
Chicken	54	99732
Chignik — 1983	155	99564
Chignik Lagoon	88	99565
Chignik Lake	146	99564
Chitina (CHIT-nah)	49	99566
Chuathbaluk (chew-ATH-ba-luck) — 1975	131	99557
Chugiak (CHOO-gee-ack)	NA	99567
Circle	107	99733
Clam Gulch	163	99568
Clarks Point — 1971	80	99569
Clear	NA	99704
Clover Pass	509	99928

Community — Year Incorporated	Population	Zip
Coffman Cove	178	99950
Cold Bay — 1982	187	99571
College	4,668	99709
Cooper Landing	404	99572
Copper Center	210	99573
Cordova — 1909	2,053	99574
Craig — 1922	961	99921
Crooked Creek	113	99575
Curry's Corner	59	99734
Deering — 1970	160	99736
Delta Junction — 1960	1,114	99737
Denali Park	59	99755
Dillingham — 1963	2,118	99576
Diomede (DY-o-mede) — 1970	168	99762
Dot Lake	90	99737
Douglas — 1902	NA	99824
Dunbar	49	NA
Dutch Harbor — 1942	1,922	99692
Eagle — 1901	185	99738
Eagle River	NA	99577
Eek — 1970	273	99578
Egegik (EEG-gah-gik)	110	99579
Ekwok (ECK-wok) — 1974	107	99580
Elfin Cove	46	99825
Elim (EE-lum) — 1970	256	99739
Emmonak (ee-MON-nuk) — 1964	660	99581
English Bay	205	99695
Ester	183	99725
Evansville	36	99726
Fairbanks — 1903	27,141	9970-
Main Office	—	99701
Eielson AFB	—	99702
Fort Wainwright	—	99703
Main Office Boxes	—	99706
Downtown Station	—	99707
College Branch	—	99708
Salcha	—	99714
False Pass	85	99583
Flat	8	99584
Fort Greely	1,650	99790
Fort Yukon — 1959	708	99740
Fox	150	99712
Fritz Creek	612	99603
Gakona (ga-KOH-na)	102	99586
Galena (ga-LEE-na) — 1971	998	99741
Gambell — 1963	511	99742
Girdwood	NA	99587
Glennallen	596	99588
Golovin (GAWL-uh-vin) — 1971	133	99762
Goodnews Bay — 1970	242	99589
Grayling — 1969	219	99590
Gulkana	122	99586
Gustavus (ga-STAY-vus)	211	99826
Haines — 1910	1,063	99827
Halibut Cove	52	99603
Harding Lake	52	99714
Healy	469	99743

Community — Year Incorporated	Population	Zip
Herring Cove	112	99928
Holy Cross — 1968	263	99602
Homer — 1964	3,706	99603
Hoonah — 1946	895	99829
Hooper Bay — 1966	776	99604
Hope	234	99605
Houston — 1966	814	99694
Hughes — 1973	97	99745
Huslia (HOOS-lee-a) — 1969	230	99746
Hydaburg — 1927	475	99922
Hyder	68	99923
Iliamna (ill-ee-YAM-nuh)	138	99606
Jakolof Bay	82	99603
Juneau — 1900	26,422	9980-
Main office	—	99801
Main office boxes	—	99802
Mendenhall Station	—	99803
State government offices	—	99811
Kachemak (CATCH-a-mack) — 1961	429	99603
Kake — 1952	665	99830
Kaktovik (kack-TOE-vik) — 1971	223	99747
Kalifonsky	340	99669
Kalskag — 1975	145	99607
Kaltag — 1969	280	99748
Karluk	107	99608
Kasaan (Ka-SAN) — 1976	62	99924
Kasigluk (ka-SEEG-luk) — 1982	413	99609
Kasilof (ka-SEE-loff)	658	99610
Kenai (KEEN-eye) — 1960	6,647	99611
Ketchikan — 1900	7,777	99901
Kiana (Ky-AN-a) — 1964	434	99749
King Cove City — 1947	552	99612
King Salmon	555	99613
Kipnuk (KIP-nuck)	435	99614
Kivalina — 1969	290	99750
Klawock (kla-WOCK) — 1929	684	99925
Klukwan	189	99827
Kobuk — 1973	86	99751
Kodiak — 1940	6,619	99615
U.S. Coast Guard Station	1,731	99619
Kokhanok (KO-ghan-ock)	121	99606
Koliganek (ko-LIG-a-neck)	149	99576
Kongiganak (kon-GIG-a-nuck)	295	99559
Kotlik — 1970	424	99620
Kotzebue (KOT-sa-bue) — 1958	2,636	99752
Koyuk — 1970	215	99753
Koyukuk (KOY-yuh-kuck) — 1973	145	99754
Kupreanof (ku-pree-AN-off) — 1975	43	99833
Kwethluk (KWEETH-luck) — 1975	518	99621
Kwigillingok (kwi-GILL-in-gock)	257	99622
Lake Minchumina (min-CHOO-min-a)	22	99757
Larsen Bay — 1974	169	99624
Levelock (LEH-vuh-lock)	126	99625
Lime Village	59	99627
Lower Kalskag — 1969	273	99626
Manley Hot Springs	127	99756
Manokotak (man-a-KO-tack) — 1970	341	99628

Community — Year Incorporated	Population	Zip
Marshall — 1970	270	99585
McGrath — 1975	460	99627
Medfra	NA	99691
Mekoryuk (ma-KOR-ee-yuk) — 1969	173	99630
Mentasta Lake	50	99780
Metlakatla — 1944	1,365	99926
Meyers Chuck	53	99903
Minto	235	99758
Montana	97	99695
Moose Creek	484	99705
Moose Pass	148	99631
Mountain Point	447	99928
Mountain Village — 1967	723	99632
Naknek (NACK-neck) — 1962	517	99633
Napakiak (NAP-uh-keey-ack) — 1970	350	99634
Napaskiak (na-PASS-kee-ack) — 1971	309	99559
Nelson Lagoon	50	99571
Nenana (nee-NA-na) — 1921	552	99760
New Stuyahok (STU-ya-hock) — 1972	360	99636
Newhalen — 1971	167	99606
Newtok — 1976	207	99559
Nightmute — 1974	145	99690
Nikishka (ni-KISH-ka)*	1,674	99635
Nikolai — 1970	126	99691
Nikolski	44	99638
Ninilchik	461	99639
Noatak	342	99761
Nome — 1901	3,208	99762
Nondalton — 1971	246	99640
Noorvik — 1964	548	99763
North Pole — 1953	1,647	99705
North Tongass Highway	2,044	99928
North Whale Pass	45	99950
Northway	116	99764
Nuiqsut (noo-IK-sut) — 1975	302	99789
Nulato — 1963	378	99765
Nunapitchuk (NU-nuh-plt-CHUCK) — 1983	363	99641
Nyac (NY-ack)	NA	99642
Old Harbor — 1966	380	99643
Oscarville	54	99695
Ouzinkie (u-ZINK-ee) — 1967	195	99644
Palmer — 1951	3,100	99645
Paxson	28	99737
Pedro Bay	71	99647
Pelican — 1943	270	99832
Pennock Island	102	99928
Perryville	127	99648
Petersburg — 1910	3,182	99833
Pilot Point	81	99649
Pilot Station — 1969	420	99650
Pitkas Point	109	99658
Platinum — 1975	62	99651
Point Baker	112	99927
Point Hope — 1966	600	99766
Point Lay	101	99759
Port Alexander — 1974	128	99836
Port Alsworth	40	99653

Community — Year Incorporated	Population	Zip
Port Graham	195	99603
Port Heiden — 1972	114	99549
Port Lions — 1966	296	99550
Portage Creek	63	99576
Prudhoe Bay	45	99734
Quinhagak (QUIN-a-gak) — 1975	462	99655
Rampart	63	99767
Red Devil	51	99656
Ruby — 1973	248	99768
Russian Mission — 1970	236	99657
Saint George — 1983	194	99591
Saint Marys — 1967	437	99658
Saint Michael — 1969	289	99659
Saint Paul — 1971	573	99660
Salamatof	755	99611
Salcha	502	99714
Sand Point — 1966	636	99661
Savoonga (suh-VOON-guh) — 1969	509	99769
Saxman — 1930	309	99901
Saxman East	464	99901
Scammon Bay — 1967	304	99662
Selawik (SELL-a-wick) — 1977	632	99770
Seldovia — 1945	552	99663
Seward — 1912	2,072	99664
Shageluk (SHAG-a-look) — 1970	167	99665
Shaktoolik (shack-TOO-lick) — 1969	185	99771
Sheldon Point — 1974	120	99666
Shishmaref (SHISH-muh-reff) — 1969	441	99772
Shungnak (SHOONG-nack) — 1967	245	99773
Sitka (City and Borough)	8,102	99835
Skagway — 1900	714	99840
Skwentna	105	99667
Slana	69	99586
Sleetmute	120	99668
Soldotna — 1967	4,021	99669
South Naknek	177	99670
Stebbins — 1969	383	99671
Sterling	1,772	99472
Stevens Village	112	99774
Stony River	79	99557
Sutton	349	99674
Takotna (Tah-KOAT-nuh)	55	99675
Talkeetna (Tal-KEET-na)	239	99676
Tanacross	118	99776
Tanana (TAN-a-nah) — 1961	420	99777
Tatitlek	108	99677
Teller — 1963	244	99778
Tenakee Springs — 1971	125	99841
Tetlin	93	99779
Thorne Bay — 1982	469	99919
Togiak (TOE-gee-yack) — 1969	623	99678
Tok (TOKE)	850	99780
Toksook Bay — 1972	396	99637
Tonsina	126	99573
Trapper Creek	NA	99683
Tuluksak (tu-LOOK-sack) — 1970	302	99679
Tuntutuliak (TUN-too-TOO-li-ack)	283	99680

Community — Year Incorporated	Population	Zip
Tununak — 1975	328	99681
Twin Hills	92	99576
Two Rivers	473	99716
Tyonek (ty-O-neck)	282	99682
Unalakleet (YOU-na-la-kleet) — 1974	802	99684
Unalaska (UN-a-LAS-ka) — 1942	1,354	99685
Upper Kalskag — 1975	144	99607
Usibelli (yoos-i-BEL-ee) Mine	104	99787
Valdez (val-DEEZ) — 1901	3,263	99686
Venetie (VEEN-a-tie)	220	99781
Wainwright — 1962	549	99782
Wales — 1964	150	99783
Ward Cove	NA	99928
Wasilla (wah-SIL-luh) — 1974	3,938	99687
White Mountain — 1969	150	99784
Whittier — 1969	260	99693
Willow	448	99688
Wrangell — 1903	2,402	99929
Yakutat (YAK-a-tat) — 1948	476	99689

Census Areas
(Numbers refer to following list)

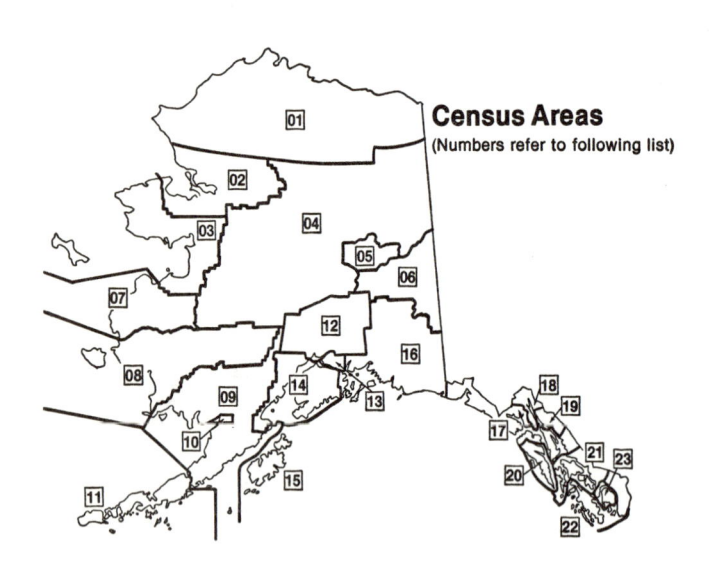

ALASKA POPULATION BY CENSUS AREA

Map Code	Census Area	1987	Population 1980	1970
	Alaska	537,800	401,851	302,583
01	North Slope Borough	5,927	4,199	NA
02	Northwest Arctic Borough	5,962	4,831	4,434
03	Nome	7,774	6,537	5,749
04	Yukon-Koyukuk	9,384	7,873	NA
05	Fairbanks North Star Borough	73,164	53,983	45,864
06	Southeast Fairbanks	6,423	5,676	NA
07	Wade Hampton	5,599	4,665	3,917
08	Bethel	13,345	10,999	NA
09	Dillingham	5,836	4,616	NA

Map Code	Census Area	1987	Population 1980	1970
10	Bristol Bay Borough	1,402	1,094	1,147
11	Aleutian Islands	9,420	7,768	NA
12	Matanuska-Susitna Borough	37,027	17,816	6,509
13	Anchorage Borough	231,492	174,431	126,385
14	Kenai Peninsula Borough	39,170	25,282	NA
15	Kodiak Island Borough	13,658	9,939	9,409
16	Valdez-Cordova	8,831	8,348	NA
17	Skagway-Yakutat-Angoon	3,684	3,478	NA
18	Haines Borough	1,850	1,680	NA
19	Juneau City & Borough	25,369	19,528	13,556
20	Sitka City & Borough	8,416	7,803	3,370
21	Wrangell-Petersburg	6,671	6,167	NA
22	Prince of Wales-Outer Ketchikan	4,964	38,223	NA
23	Ketchikan Gateway Borough	12,432	11,316	10,041

Source: July 1, 1987 estimates, Alaska Department of Labor.

Potlatch

These Native gatherings, primarily an Indian custom, are held to commemorate just about any kind of event. Traditional Native foods are served and gifts are distributed to everyone who attends. A funeral potlatch might result in the giving away of the deceased's possessions to relatives or to persons who had done favors for the deceased during his or her lifetime. Before the federal government imposed legal constraints in the nineteenth century, potlatches could take years of preparation. The host family might give away all its possessions in an attempt to demonstrate its wealth to the guests. Each guest in turn would feel an obligation to hold an even bigger potlatch.

Radio Stations

Alaska's radio stations broadcast a wide variety of music, talk shows, religious and educational programs. Many radio stations in Alaska also broadcast personal messages, long a popular and necessary form of communication in Alaska — especially in the Bush. It was in consideration of these messages — and the importance of radio stations in providing the sole source of vital weather information to fishermen and hunters — that the United States and Canada agreed to grant some Alaska radio stations international communication status. The "clear channel" status provides protection against interference from foreign broadcasters. Personal message broadcasts are heard on:

KBRW's Tundra Drums, Barrow; KYUK's Tundra Drums, Bethel; KABN's Cabin Trapline, Big Lake; KDLG's Bristol Bay Messenger, Dillingham; KIAK's Pipeline of the North, Fairbanks; KIYU's Yukon Wireless, Galena; KCAM's Caribou Clatter, Glennallen; KHNS's Listener Personals, Haines; KBBI's Bay Bush Lines, Homer; KGTL's Public Service-Line, Homer; KRBD's Muskeg Messenger, Ketchikan; KTKN's Public Service Announcements, Ketchikan; KVOK-KJJZ-FM's Highliner Crabbers, Kodiak; KSKO's KSKO Messages, McGrath; KICY's Ptarmigan Telegraph, Nome; KNOM's Hot Lines, Nome; KJNP's Trapline Chatter, North Pole; KFSK's Muskeg Messages, Petersburg; KRSA's Channel Chatters, Petersburg; KCAW-FM's Muskeg Messages, Sitka; KSRM's Tundra Tom Tom, Soldotna; and KSTK-FM's Radiograms, Wrangell.

A complete listing of Alaska's radio stations follows:

Anchorage, **KATB-FM** 89.3 MHz; P.O. Box 210389, 99521.
Anchorage, **KBYR** 700 kHz; **KNIK-FM** 105.3 MHz; P.O. Box 102200, 99510.
Anchorage, **KEAG-FM** 97 MHz; 333 W. 4th Ave., Suite 304, 99501.
Anchorage, **KENI** 550 kHz; **KENI-FM** 100.5 MHz; 1777 Forest Park Drive, 99517.

Anchorage, **KFQD** 750 kHz; **KWHL-FM** 106.5 MHz; 9200 Lake Otis Parkway, 99507.
Anchorage, **KHAR** 590 kHz; **KKLV-FM** 104.1 MHz; P.O. Box 111566, 99511.
Anchorage, **KJAM-FM** 94.5 MHz; 3605 Arctic Blvd., Suite 945, 99503.
Anchorage, **KKSD** 1080 kHz; **KASH-FM** 107.5 MHz; 1300 E. 68th, Suite 208, 99516.
Anchorage, **KLEF-FM** 98.1 MHz; 3601 C St., Suite 290, 99503.
Anchorage, **KPXR-FM** 102.1 MHz; 3700 Woodland Drive, #300, 99517.
Anchorage, **KSKA-FM** 91.1 MHz; 4101 University Drive, 99508.
Anchorage, **KXDZ-FM** 103.1 MHz; 800 E. Dimond Blvd., Suite 3-395, 99515-2028.
Anchorage, **KYAK** 650 kHz; **KGOT-FM** 101.3 MHz; 2800 E. Dowling Road, 99507.
Anchorage, **KYMG-FM** 98.9 MHz; 500 L St., Suite 200, 99501.
Barrow, **KBRW** 680 kHz; P.O. Box 109, 99723.
Bethel, **KJBA-FM** 100.1 MHz; P.O. Box 948, 99559.
Bethel, **KYUK** 640 kHz; P.O.Box 468, 99559.
Big Lake, **KABN** 830 kHz; P.O. Box 520368, 99652.
Cordova, **KLAM** 1450 kHz; P.O. Box 60, 99574.
Dillingham, **KDLG** 670 kHz; P.O. Box 670, 99576.
Eagle River, **KCFA** 1020 kHz; P.O. Box 773527, 99577
Fairbanks, **KAYY-FM** 101.1 MHz; 3504 Industrial Ave., 99701.
Fairbanks, **KCBF** 820 kHz; P.O. Box 950, 99707.
Fairbanks, **KFAR** 660 kHz; **KWLF-FM** 98.1 MHz; P.O. Box 910, 99707.
Fairbanks, **KIAK** 970 kHz; P.O. Box 73410, 99707.
Fairbanks, **KING-FM** 96 MHz; 4600 Dale Road, 99709.
Fairbanks, **KQRZ** 102.5 kHz; P.O. Box 73410, 99707.
Fairbanks, **KRKO-AM/FM**; 1028 Aurora Drive, 99708.
Fairbanks, **KSUA-FM** 103.9 MHz; P.O. Box 83831, 99708.
Fairbanks, **KUAC-FM** 104.7 MHz; University of Alaska, 99775.
Galena, **KIYU** 910 kHz; P.O. Box 165, 99741.

Glennallen, **KCAM** 790 kHz; P.O. Box 249, 99588.
Haines, **KHNS-FM** 102.3 MHz; P.O. Box 1109, 99827.
Homer, **KBBI** 890 kHz; 215 E. Main Court, 99603.
Homer, **KGTL** 620 kHz; **KWVV-FM**, 103.5 MHz; P.O. Box 103, 99603.
Juneau, **KAJD** 950 kHz; 3933 Geneva Place, Anchorage 99503.
Juneau, **KINY** 800 kHz; 1107 W. 8th St., 99801.
Juneau, **KJNO** 630 kHz; 3161 Channel Drive, Suite 2, 99801.
Juneau, **KSUP-FM** 106.3 MHz; 1107 W. 8th St., 99801.
Juneau, **KTKU-FM** 105.1 MHz; 3161 Channel Drive, Suite 2, 99801.
Juneau, **KTOO-FM** 104.3 MHz; 224 4th St., 99801.
Kenai, **KENY** 980 kHz; 6672 Kenai Spur Highway., 99611.
Kenai, **KPEN-FM** 101.7 MHz; P.O. Box 103, Homer 99603.
Ketchikan, **KRBD-FM** 105.9 MHz; 716 Totem Way, 99901.
Ketchikan, **KTKN** 930 kHz; **KGTW-FM** 105.7 MHz; P.O. Box 7700, 99901.
Kodiak, **KMXT-FM** 100.1 MHz; 718 Mill Bay Road, 99615.
Kodiak, **KVOK** 560 kHz; **KJJZ-FM** 101.1 MHz; P.O. Box 708, 99615.
Kotzebue, **KOTZ** 720 kHz; P.O. Box 78, 99752.
McGrath, **KSKO** 870 kHz; P.O. Box 70, 99627.
Naknek, **KAKN-FM** 100.9 MHz; P.O. Box O, 99633.
Nome, **KICY** 850 kHz; **KICY-FM** 100.3 MHz; P.O. Box 820, 99762.
Nome, **KNOM** 780 kHz; P.O. Box 988, 99762.
North Pole, **KJNP** 1170 kHz; **KJNP-FM** 100.3 MHz; P.O. Box 0, 99705.
Petersburg, **KFSK-FM** 100.9 MHz; P.O. Box 149, 99833.
Petersburg, **KRSA** 580 kHz; P.O. Box 650, 99833.
Seward, **KRXA** 950 kHz; P.O. Box 405, 99664.
Sitka, **KCAW-FM** 104.7 MHz; 102B Lincoln St., 99835.
Sitka, **KIFW** 1230 kHz; P.O. Box 299, 99835.
Soldotna, **KCSY** 1140 MHz; 374 Lovers Lane, 99669.
Soldotna, **KSRM** 920 kHz; **KWHQ-FM**

100.1 MHz; P.O. Box 852, Route 2, 99669.
St. Paul, **KUHB-FM** 91.9 MHz; 99660.
Valdez, **KCHU** 770 kHz; P.O. Box 467, 99686.
Valdez, **KVAK** 1230 kHz; P.O. Box 367, 99686.
Wasilla, **KNBZ-FM** 99.7 MHz; P.O. Box 871890, 99687.
Wrangell, **KSTK-FM** 101.7 MHz; P.O. Box 1141, 99929.
Yakutat, **KJFP-FM** 103.9 MHz; P.O. Box 388, 99689.

In addition to the preceding commercial and public radio stations, the Detachment 1, Air Force Broadcasting Service at Elmendorf Air Force Base (Elmendorf AFB 99506) operates the Alaskan Forces Radio Network. AFRN is the oldest broadcast network in the U.S. military. It began in January, 1942, on Kodiak Island with a volunteer crew that pieced together a low-power station from second-hand parts, borrowed records and local talent. Eventually, the servicemen generated enough interest in Hollywood and Washington, D.C., to receive "official" status. Those early efforts resulted in what is now the Armed Forces Radio and Television Service, a far-flung system of broadcast outlets serving U.S. forces around the world.

Nearly all the programming heard at AFRN locations in Alaska originates at Elmendorf AFB, although it is not broadcast in the Elmendorf vicinity. (In addition to network programming, Fort Greely originates about six hours of programming a day at their location.) Following is a list of AFRN outlets:

Fort Greely, **AFRN-FM** 90.5 MHz, 93.5 MHz
Fort Yukon, **AFRN** 1340 kHz
Galena Airport, **AFRN-FM** 90.5 MHz, 101.1 MHz
King Salmon Airport, **AFRN-FM** 90.5 MHz, 101.1 MHz
Shemya Air Force Base, **AFRN-FM** 90.5 MHz, 101.1 MHz
Tok Coast Guard Station, **AFRN-FM** 90.5 MHz, 101.1 MHz

Railroads

The Alaska Railroad is the northernmost railroad in North America and was for many years the only one owned by the United States government. Ownership now belongs to the state of Alaska. The ARR rolls on 470 miles of mainline track from the ports of Seward and Whittier to Anchorage, Cook Inlet and Fairbanks in the Interior.

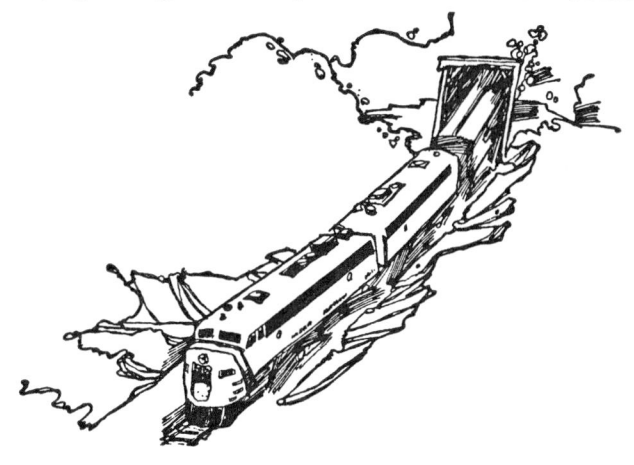

The Alaska Railroad began in 1912 with the appointment by Congress of a commission to study transportation problems in Alaska. In March 1914, the president authorized railroad lines in the territory of Alaska to connect open harbors on the southern coast of Alaska with the Interior. The Alaska Engineering Commission surveyed possible railroad routes in 1914 and, in April 1915, President Woodrow Wilson announced the selection of a route from Seward north 412 miles to the Tanana River (where Nenana is now located), with branch lines to Matanuska coal fields. The main line was later extended to Fairbanks. Construction of the railroad began in 1915. On July 15, 1923, President Warren G. Harding drove the golden spike — signifying completion of the railroad — at Nenana.

The railroad offers year-round passenger, freight and vehicle service. The ARR features flag-stop service along the Anchorage-to-Fairbanks corridor, as well as summer express trains to Denali National Park and Preserve. Passenger service is daily between mid-May and mid-September, and in winter, weekly service is available between Anchorage and Fairbanks. A one day excursion to Seward is provided five times a week. Additionally, daily service to Whittier is offered from May through September and four days a week in winter. In 1988, 361,000 passengers rode the Alaska Railroad. For more information contact The Alaska Railroad, P.O. Box 107500, Anchorage 99510.

The privately owned White Pass and Yukon Route provided a narrow-gauge link between Skagway, Alaska, and Whitehorse, Yukon Territory. At the time it was built — 1898 to 1900 — it was the farthest north any railroad had operated in North America. The railway maintained one of the steepest railroad grades in North America, climbing to 2,885 feet at White Pass in only 20 miles of track. The White Pass and Yukon Route provided both passenger and freight service until 1982, when it suspended service. In May 1988, it began operating again as an excursion train only, going from Skagway to the summit of White Pass and eight miles beyond to Fraser, British Columbia.

Regions of Alaska

SOUTHEAST

Southeast, Alaska's panhandle, stretches approximately 500 miles from Icy Bay, northwest of Yakutat, to Dixon Entrance at the United States-Canada border beyond the southern tip of Prince of Wales Island. Massive ice fields, glacier-scoured peaks and steep valleys, more than a thousand named islands, and numerous unnamed islets and reefs characterize this vertical world where few flat expanses break the steepness. Spruce, hemlock and cedar, basis for the region's timber industry, cover many of the mountain-sides.

Average temperatures range from 50°F to 60°F in July and from 20°F to 40°F in January. Average annual precipitation varies from 80 to more than 200 inches. The area receives from 30 to 200 inches of snow in the lowlands and more than 400 inches in the high mountains.

The region's economy revolves around fishing and fish processing, timber and tourism. Mining is taking on increasing importance with development of a world-class molybdenum mine near Ketchikan and a base metals mine on Admiralty Island.

Airplanes and boats provide the principal means of transportation. Only three communities in Southeast are connected to the road system: Haines via the Haines Highway to the Alaska Highway at Haines Junction; Skagway, via Klondike Highway 2 to the Alaska Highway; and Hyder, to the continental road system via the Cassiar Highway in British Columbia. Juneau, on the Southeast mainland, is the state capital; Sitka, on Baranof Island, was the capital of Russian America.

SOUTHCENTRAL/GULF COAST

The Southcentral/Gulf Coast region curves 650 miles north and west of Southeast to Kodiak Island. About two-thirds of the state's residents live in the arc between the Gulf of Alaska on the south and the Alaska Range on the north, the region commonly called Southcentral. On the region's eastern boundary, only the Copper River valley breaches the mountainous barrier of the Chugach and Saint Elias mountains. On the west rise lofty peaks of the Aleutian Range. Within this mountainous perimeter course the Susitna and Matanuska rivers.

The irregular plain of the Copper River lowland has a colder climate than the other major valley areas, with January temperatures hitting -16°F compared with average lows of 0°F in the Susitna Valley. July temperatures average 50°F to 60°F in the region.

Precipitation in the region ranges from a scant 17 inches annually in drier areas to more than 76 inches a year at Thompson Pass in the coastal mountains.

Vegetation varies from the spruce-hemlock forests of Prince William Sound to mixed spruce and birch forests in the Susitna Valley to tundra in the highlands of the Copper River-Nelchina Basin.

Alaska agriculture historically has been most thoroughly developed in the Matanuska Valley. The state's dairy industry is centered there and at a new project at Point MacKenzie across Knik Arm from Anchorage. Vegetables thrive in the area and Matanuska Valley is well known for its giant cabbages.

Hub of the state's commerce, transportation and communications is Anchorage, on a narrow plain at the foot of the Chugach Mountains, and bounded by Knik Arm and Turnagain Arm, offshoots of Cook Inlet. Population of this, Alaska's largest city, is closely tied to shifts in the state's economy.

Alaska's major banks and oil companies have their headquarters in Anchorage, as does The Alaska Railroad. The city's port handles much of the shipping in and out of the state. Anchorage International Airport saw over 1 million passengers pass through in 1987. Valdez, to the east of Anchorage on Prince Willam Sound, is the southern terminal of the trans-Alaska pipeline, which brings oil from Prudhoe Bay on the North Slope.

INTERIOR

Great rivers have forged a broad lowland, known as the Interior, in the central part of the state between the Alaska Range on the south and the Brooks Range on the north. The Yukon River carves a swath across the entire state. In the Interior, the Tanana, Porcupine, Koyukuk and several other rivers join with the Yukon to create summer and winter highways. South of the Yukon, the Kuskokwim River rises in the hills of western Interior before beginning its meandering course across the Bering Sea coast region.

Winter temperatures in the Interior commonly drop to -50°F and -60°F. Ice fog sometimes hovers over Fairbanks and other low-lying communities when the temperature falls below zero. Controlled by the extremes of a continental climate, summers usually are warmer than in any other region; high temperatures are in the 80s and 90s. The climate is semi-arid, with about 12 inches of precipitation recorded annually.

Immense forests of birch and aspen bring vibrant green and gold to the Interior's landscape. Spruce cover many of the slopes and cottonwood thrive near river lowlands. But in northern and western reaches of the Interior, the North American taiga gives way to tundra. In highlands above tree line and in marshy lowlands, grasses and shrubs replace trees.

Gold lured the first large influx of non-Natives to Alaska's Interior. Fairbanks, largest community in the region, was once a booming gold-mining camp. Now the city on the banks of Chena Slough is a transportation and supply center for eastern and northern Alaska. The main campus of the University of Alaska overlooks the city.

About 100 miles east of Fairbanks, farmers at the Delta project hope to build a foundation for agriculture based on barley. With barley for feed, Alaska farmers look for development of a beef cattle industry. At Healy, southwest of Fairbanks, the state's only operating coal mine produces coal used to generate electricity for the Interior. The rest of the Interior relies primarily on a subsistence economy, sometimes combined with a cash economy where fishing or seasonable government jobs are available.

ARCTIC

Beyond the Brooks Range, more than 80,000 square miles of tundra interlaced with meandering rivers and countless ponds spread out along the North Slope. In far northwestern Alaska, the Arctic curves south to take in Kotzebue and other villages of the Kobuk and Noatak river drainages.

Short, cool summers with temperatures usually between 30°F and 40°F allow the permanently frozen soil to thaw only a few inches. Winter temperatures range well below zero, but the Arctic Ocean moderates temperatures in coastal areas. Severe winds sweep along the coast and through mountain passes. The combination of cold and wind often drops the chill-factor temperature far below the actual temperature. Most areas receive less than 10 inches of precipitation a year, but the terrain is wet in summer because of little evaporation and frozen ground.

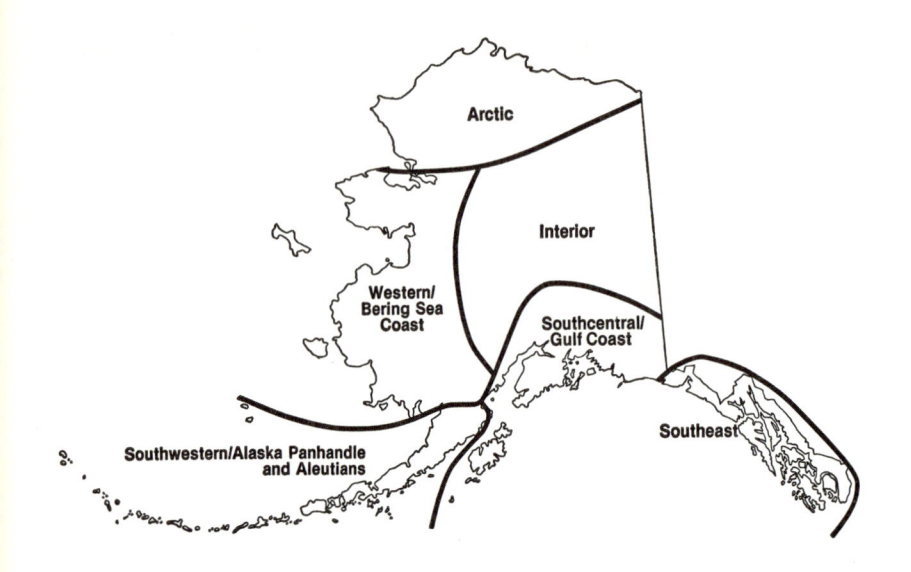

Traditionally the home of Inupiat Eskimos, the Arctic was inhabited by few non-Natives until oil was discovered at Prudhoe Bay in the 1960s. Today the region's economy is focused on Prudhoe Bay and neighboring Kuparuk oil fields. Petroleum-related jobs support most of the region's residents either directly or indirectly. Subsistence hunting and fishing fill any economic holes left by the oil industry.

Largest Inupiat Eskimo community in the world, Barrow is the center of commerce and government activity for the region. Airplanes, the major means of transportation, fan out from there to the region's far-flung villages.

The 416-mile Dalton Highway, formerly the North Slope Haul Road, connects the Arctic with the Interior. The road is open to the public only to Disaster Creek near Dietrich Camp, about 200 miles north from the junction with the Elliott Highway in the Interior. Only permit holders can travel the road north of Disaster Creek.

WESTERN/BERING SEA COAST

Western Alaska extends along the Bering Sea coast from the Arctic Circle south to where the Alaska Panhandle joins the mainland near Naknek on Bristol Bay. Home of Inupiat and Yup'ik Eskimos, the region centers around the immense Yukon-Kuskokwim river delta, the Seward Peninsula to the north and Bristol Bay to the south.

Summer temperatures range from the 30s to low 60s. Winter readings generally range from just above zero to the low 30s. Wind chill lowers temperatures considerably. Total annual precipitation is about 20 inches with northern regions drier than those to the south.

Much of the region is covered with tundra, although a band of forests covers the hills on the eastern end of the Seward Peninsula and Norton Sound. In the south near Bristol Bay, the tundra once again gives way to forests. In between, the marshy flatland of the great Yukon-Kuskokwim delta spreads out for more than 200 miles.

Gold first attracted non-Natives to the hills and creeks of the Seward Peninsula. To the south, only a few biologists studying wildlife and anthropologists entered the world of the Yup'ik Eskimos of the delta. At the extreme south, fish, including the world's largest sockeye salmon run, drew fishermen to the riches of Bristol Bay.

The villages of western Alaska are linked by air and water, dogsled and snowmachine. Commerce on the delta radiates out from Bethel, largest community in western Alaska. To the north, Nome dominates commerce on the Seward Peninsula, while several fishing communities take their livelihood from the riches of Bristol Bay.

SOUTHWESTERN/ALASKA PENINSULA AND ALEUTIANS

Southwestern Alaska includes the Alaska Peninsula and Aleutian Islands. From Naknek Lake, the peninsula curves southwest about 500 miles to the first of the Aleutian Islands; the Aleutians continue south and west more than 1,000 miles. Primarily a mountainous region with about 50 volcanic peaks, only on the Bering Sea side of the peninsula does the terrain flatten out.

The Aleutian climate is cool, with summer temperatures up to the 50s and winter readings in the 20s and lower. Winds are almost constant and fog is common. Precipitation ranges from 21 to more than 80 inches annually. The peninsula's climate is somewhat warmer in summer and cooler in winter.

More than 200 islands, roughly 5,500 square miles in area, form the narrow arc of the Aleutians, which separate the North Pacific from the Bering Sea. Nearly the entire chain is in the Alaska Maritime National Wildlife Refuge. Unimak Island, closest to the Alaska Peninsula mainland, is 1,000 miles from Attu, the most distant island. Five major island groups make up the Aleutians, all of which are treeless except for a few scattered stands that have been transplanted on the islands.

Aleuts, original inhabitants of the chain, still live at Atka, Atka Island; Nikolski, Umnak Island; Unalaska, Unalaska Island; Akutan, Akutan Island; and False Pass, Unimak Island.

The quest for furs first drew Russians to the islands and peninsula in the 1700s. The traders conquered the Aleuts and forced them to hunt marine mammals. After the United States purchased Alaska, fur traders switched their efforts to fox farming. Many foxes were turned loose on the islands, where they flourished and destroyed native wildlife. With collapse of the fur market in the 1920s and 1930s, the islands were left to themselves. This relative isolation was broken during World War II when Japanese military forces bombed Dutch Harbor and landed on Attu and Kiska islands. The United States military retook the islands, but after the war the government resettled Aleuts living in the western Aleutians to villages in the eastern Aleutians that are closer to the mainland and thus easier to defend.

Today fishing provides the main economic base for the islands and the peninsula. Many Aleuts go to Bristol Bay to fish commercially in summer.

Religion

Nearly every religion practiced in American society is found in Alaska. Following is a list of addresses for some of the major ones:

Alaska Baptist Convention, 1750 O'Malley Road, Anchorage 99516
Alaska Moravian Church, Bethel 99559

163

Assemblies of God, 1048 W. International Airport Road, Anchorage 99502
Baha'i Faith, 13501 Brayton Drive, Anchorage 99516
Chancery Orthodox Diocese of Alaska, P.O. Box 55, Kodiak 99615
Christian Science Church, 1347 L St., Anchorage 99501
Church of God, 1348 Bennington Drive, Anchorage 99508
Church of Jesus Christ of Latter Day Saints, 13111 Brayton Drive, Anchorage 99516
Congregation Beth Sholom, 7525 E. Northern Lights Blvd., Anchorage 99504
Episcopal Diocese of Alaska, 1205 Denali Way, Fairbanks 99701
Presbyterian Churches United, 616 W. 10th Ave., Anchorage 99501
Roman Catholic Archdiocese of Anchorage, 225 Cordova, Anchorage 99501
The Salvation Army, 726 E. 9th Ave., Anchorage 99501
United Methodist Church, 2300 Oak Drive, Anchorage 99508
Universal Life Church, Inc., 801 Airport Heights, Anchorage 99508

Reptiles

For all practical purposes, reptiles are not found in Alaska outside of captivity. The northern limits of North American reptilian species may be the latitude at which their embryos fail to develop during the summer. Three sightings of a species of garter snake, *Thamnophis sirtalis*, have been reported on the banks of the Taku River and Stikine River.

Rivers

(*See also* National Wild and Scenic Rivers)

There are more than 3,000 rivers in Alaska. The major navigable Alaska inland waterways are as follows:

Chilkat — Navigable by shallow-draft vessels to village of Klukwan, 25 miles above mouth.
Kobuk — Controlling channel depth is about 5 feet through Hotham Inlet, 3 feet to Ambler and 2 feet to Kobuk Village, about 210 river miles.
Koyukuk — Navigable to Allakaket by vessels drawing up to 3 feet during normally high river flow and to Bettles during occasional higher flows.
Kuskokwim — Navigable (June 1 to September 30) by 18-foot draft ocean-going vessels from mouth upriver 65 miles to Bethel. Shallow-draft (4-foot) vessels can ascend river to mile 465. McGrath is at Mile 400.
Kvichak — The river is navigable for vessels of 10-foot draft to Alaganak River, 22 miles above the mouth of Kvichak River. Remainder of this river (28 miles) navigable by craft drawing 2 to 4 feet, depending on stage of river. Drains Lake Iliamna, which is navigable an additional 70 miles.
Naknek — Navigable for vessels of 12-foot draft for 12 miles with adequate tide. Vessels with 3-foot draft can continue an additional 7.5 miles.
Noatak — Navigable (late May to mid-June) for shallow-draft barges to a point about 18 miles below Noatak

The Longest Rivers

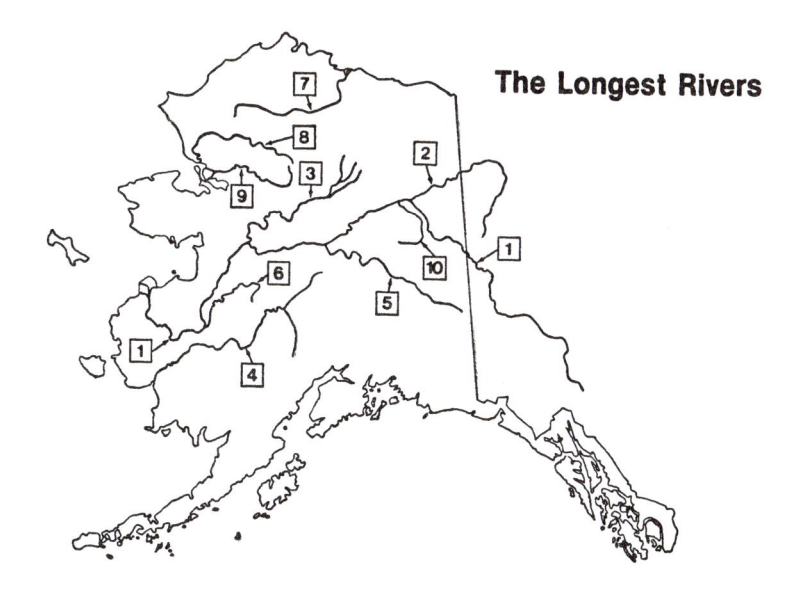

village. Shallow-draft vessels can continue on to Noatak.

Nushagak — Navigable (June 1 to August 31) by small vessels of 2½-foot draft to Nunachuak, about 100 miles above the mouth. Shallow-draft, ocean-going vessels can navigate to mouth of Wood River at mile 84.

Porcupine — Navigable to Old Crow, Yukon Territory, by vessels drawing 3 feet during spring runoff and fall rain floods.

Stikine — Navigable (May 1 to October 15) from mouth 165 miles to Telegraph Creek, British Columbia, by shallow-draft, flat-bottom river boats.

Susitna — Navigable by sternwheelers and shallow-draft, flat-bottom river boats to confluence of Talkeetna River, 75 miles upstream, but cannot cross bars at mouth of river. Not navigable by ocean-going vessels.

Tanana — Navigable by shallow-draft (4-foot), flat-bottom vessels and barges from the mouth to Nenana and by smaller river craft to the Chena River 201 miles above the mouth. Craft of 4-foot draft can navigate to Chena River on high water to University Avenue Bridge in Fairbanks.

Yukon — Navigable (June 1 to September 30) by shallow-draft, flat-bottom river boats from the mouth to near the head of Lake Bennett. It cannot be entered or navigated by ocean-going vessels. Controlling depths are 7 feet to Stevens Village and 3 to 5 feet from there to Fort Yukon.

Following are the 10 longest rivers in Alaska (see map above):

Map Key	Miles
1 Yukon*	1,875
2 Porcupine**	555
3 Koyukuk	554
4 Kuskokwim	540
5 Tanana	531
6 Innoko	463
7 Colville	428
8 Noatak	396
9 Kobuk	347
10 Birch Creek	314

*The Yukon flows about 1,400 miles in Alaska; the remainder is in Canada. It ranks fourth in North America in length (2,300 miles total), fifth in drainage area (327,600 square miles).

**About two-thirds of the Porcupine's length is in Canada.

Roadhouses

An important part of Alaska history, roadhouses were modest quarters that offered bed and board to travelers along

165

early-day Alaska trails. The majority provided accommodations for sled dog teams, as most travel occurred in winter. By 1920, there were roadhouses along every major transportation route in Alaska. Several roadhouses are included in the National Register of Historic Places. Some of these historic roadhouses house modern businesses.

Rocks and Gems

(*See also* Gold, Jade *and* Minerals and Mining)

Gemstones are not easy to find in Alaska — you have to hunt for them and often walk quite a distance. The easiest ones to collect are float-rocks that were scattered millions of years ago by glaciers. These rocks are found on ocean beaches and railroad beds, and in creeks and rivers, all over Alaska. In most rock-hunting areas, every high water, wind, heavy rain and melting patch of snow and ice uncovers a new layer, so you can hunt in the same area over and over and make new finds.

The easiest gemstones to search out are in the crypto-crystalline group of quartz minerals. These gems have crystals not visible to the naked eye. They are the jaspers, agates, cherts and flints.

Thunder eggs, geodes and agatized wood (all in the chalcedony classification) occur in Alaska. Thunder eggs have a jasper rind enclosing an agate core; harder-to-find geodes usually have an agate rind with a hollow core filled with crystals; agatized and petrified woods come in various colors and often show the plant's growth rings. Sometimes even the bark or limb structure is visible.

In addition, you might find the crystalline varieties of quartz: amethyst (purple), citrine (yellow), rose quartz (pink), rock crystal (clear) and smoky quartz (brown).

Other gems to search for in Alaska are: onyx, feldspar, porphyry, jade, serpentine, soapstone, garnet, rhodonite, sapphire, marble, amethyst, staurolite, malachite and covelite (blue copper).

School Districts

(*See also* Education)

Alaska's 55 public school districts serve approximately 101,365 kindergarten through 12th grade students. There are two types of school districts: city and borough school districts and Regional Educational Attendance Areas. The 33 city and borough school districts are located in municipalities, each contributing funds for the operation of its local schools. The 22 REAAs are located in the unorganized boroughs and have no local government to contribute funds to their schools. The REAAs are almost solely dependent upon state funds for school support. City and borough school districts are supported by about 73.6 percent state, 20.6 percent local and 5.8 percent federal funding.

The Centralized Correspondence Study program, Alaska Department of Education, P.O. Box F, Juneau 99811, provides courses by correspondence to students in grades K-12.

Following are the names and addresses of Alaska's 55 public school districts:

Adak Region Schools, Adak Naval Station, Box 34, FPO Seattle, WA 98791 (IntraAK)
Alaska Gateway Schools, Box 226, Tok 99780
Aleutian Region Schools, 1 Aleut Plaza, 4000 Old Seward Highway, Suite 301, Anchorage 99503
Anchorage Schools, 4600 DeBarr Road, Box 196614, Anchorage 99519
Annette Island Schools, Box 7, Metlakatla 99926
Bering Strait Schools, Box 225, Unalakleet 99684
Bristol Bay Borough Schools, Box 169, Naknek 99633
Chatham Schools, Box 109, Angoon 99820
Chugach Schools, 201 E. 56th Ave., Suite 210, Anchorage 99518
Copper River Schools, Box 108, Glennallen 99588
Cordova City Schools, Box 140, Cordova 99574
Craig City Schools, Box 800, Craig 99921
Delta/Greely Schools, Box 527, Delta Junction 99737
Dillingham City Schools, Box 170, Dillingham 99576
Fairbanks North Star Borough Schools, Box 1250, Fairbanks 99707

Galena City Schools, Box 299, Galena 99741
Haines Borough Schools, Box 1289, Haines 99827
Hoonah City Schools, Box 157, Hoonah 99829
Hydaburg City Schools, Box 109, Hydaburg 99922
Iditarod Area Schools, Box 90, McGrath 99627
Juneau City Schools, 10014 Crazy Horse Drive, Juneau 99801
Kake City Schools, Box 450, Kake 99830
Kashunamiut School District, 985 KSD Way, Chevak 99563
Kenai Peninsula Borough Schools, 148 N. Binkley Street, Soldotna 99669
Ketchikan Gateway Borough Schools, Pouch Z, Ketchikan 99901
King Cove City Schools, Box 6, King Cove 99612
Klawock City Schools, Box 9, Klawock 99925
Kodiak Island Borough Schools, 722 Mill Bay Road, Kodiak 99615
Kuspuk Schools, Box 108, Aniak 99557
Lake & Peninsula Schools, Box 498, King Salmon 99613
Lower Kuskokwim Schools, Box 305, Bethel 99559
Lower Yukon Schools, Box 32089, Mountain Village 99632
Matanuska-Susitna Borough Schools, Box 1688, Palmer 99645
Nenana City Schools, Box 10, Nenana 99760
Nome City Schools, Box 131, Nome 99762
North Slope Borough Schools, Box 169, Barrow 99723
Northwest Arctic Borough Schools, Box 51, Kotzebue 99752
Pelican City Schools, Box 90, Pelican 99832
Petersburg City Schools, Box 289, Petersburg 99833
Pribilof Schools, Saint Paul Island 99660
Railbelt School District, Drawer 280, Healy 99743
Saint Marys School District, Box 171, Saint Marys 99658
Sand Point School District, Box 269, Sand Point 99661
Sitka Borough Schools, Box 179, Sitka 99835
Skagway City Schools, Box 497, Skagway 99840
Southeast Island Schools, Box 8340, Ketchikan 99901
Southwest Region Schools, Box 90, Dillingham 99576
Tanana Schools, Box 89, Tanana 99777
Unalaska City Schools, Pouch 260, Unalaska 99685
Valdez City Schools, Box 398, Valdez 99686
Wrangell City Schools, Box 3319, Wrangell 99929
Yakutat City Schools, Box 427, Yakutat 99689
Yukon Flats Schools, Box 359, Fort Yukon 99740
Yukon/Koyukuk Schools, Box 309, Nenana 99760
Yupiit Schools, Box 100, Akiachak 99551

Shipping

VEHICLES

Persons shipping vehicles between Seattle and Anchorage are advised to shop around for the carrier which offers the services and rates most suited to the shipper's needs. Not all carriers offer year-round service and freight charges vary greatly depending upon the carrier, and the weight and height of the vehicle. The charge for a three-quarter-ton vehicle going south is $640. Going north, a vehicle under 66 inches in height is $1,156, and over 66 inches, but under 84 inches, the charge is $1,684. Costs for other vehicles need to be checked, as prices vary and all rates are subject to change.

Not all carriers accept rented moving trucks and trailers, and a few of those that do accept them require authorization from the rental company to carry its equipment to Alaska. Check with the carrier and your rental company before booking service.

Make your reservation at least 2 weeks in advance, and prepare to have the vehicle at the carrier's loading facility two days prior to sailing. Carriers differ on what items they allow to travel inside the vehicle, from nothing at all to goods packaged and addressed separately. Coast Guard regulations forbid the transport of vehicles holding more than one-quarter tank of gas and none of the carriers listed allow owners to accompany their vehicles in transit. *Remember to have fresh antifreeze installed in your car or truck prior to sailing.*

At a lesser rate, you can ship your vehicle aboard a state ferry to southeastern ports. However, you must accompany your vehicle or arrange for someone to drive it on and off the ferry at departure and arrival ports.

Carriers that will ship cars, truck campers, house trailers and motorhomes from Anchorage to Seattle/Tacoma include:

Wrightway Auto Carriers, 101 W. Whitney Road, Anchorage 99501, (907) 277-4549.
Sea-Land Freight Service, Inc., 1717 Tidewater Ave., Anchorage 99501, (907) 561-2899.
The Alaska Railroad, P.O. Box 107500, Anchorage 99510, (907) 265-2494.
Alaska Hydro-Train, 4300 B Street, Anchorage 99503, (907) 563-1114.
Totem Ocean Trailer Express, 619 Warehouse Ave., Suite 242, Anchorage 99501, (907) 265-7252.

In the Seattle/Tacoma area, contact:
Sea-Land Service, Inc., 3600 Port of Tacoma Road, Tacoma 98424, (206) 922-3100, 800-426-4512 (outside Washington) or 800-SEA-LAND.
Alaska Hydro-Train, P.O. Box 2287, Seattle 98111, (206) 583-8100.
Totem Ocean Trailer Express, P.O. Box 24908, Seattle 98124, (206) 628-9281 or 800-426-0074 (outside Washington, Alaska and Hawaii).
Pacific Western Lines, 5225 E. Marginal Way S., Seattle 98108, (206) 762-2960 or 800-426-2602.
Wrightway Auto Carriers or A.A.D.A. Systems, both at P.O. Box 80524, Seattle 98108, (206) 762-7840.

Vehicle shipment between southeastern Alaska and Seattle is provided by Foss Alaska Line, P.O. Box 80587, Seattle 98108, (206) 281-3915 (serves Ketchikan, Petersburg, Juneau and Sitka directly — Haines and Skagway by ferry from Juneau); and Boyer Alaska Barge Line, 7318 4th Ave. S., Seattle 98108, (206) 763-8575 (serves Ketchikan and Wrangell).

HOUSEHOLD GOODS AND PERSONAL EFFECTS

Most moving van lines have service to and from Alaska through their agency connections in most Alaska and Lower 48 cities. To initiate service, contact the van line agents nearest your starting point.

Northbound goods are shipped to Seattle and transferred through a port agent to a water-borne vessel for transportation to Alaska. Few shipments go over the road to Alaska. Southbound shipments are processed in a like manner through Alaska ports to Seattle, then on to the destination.

Haul-it-yourself companies provide service to Alaska for those who prefer to move their goods themselves. It is possible to ship a rented truck or trailer into southeastern Alaska aboard the carriers that accept privately owned vehicles (see Vehicles, preceding). A few of the carriers sailing between Seattle and Anchorage also carry rented equipment. However, shop around for this service, for it has not been common practice in the past — rates can be very high if the carrier does not yet have a specific tariff established for this type of shipment. *You will not be allowed to accompany the rented equipment.*

Sitka Slippers

Heavy-duty rubber boots, also known as Wrangell sneakers and Petersburg sneakers, worn by residents of rainy southeastern Alaska.

Skiing

Both cross-country and downhill skiing are popular forms of outdoor recreation in Alaska from November through May. There are developed ski facilities in several Alaska communities, back-country powder skiing is available by charter helicopter or ski-equipped aircraft and cross-country skiing opportunities are virtually limitless throughout the state. It is also possible to ski during the summer months by chartering a plane to reach glacier skiing spots.

ANCHORAGE

There are two major downhill ski

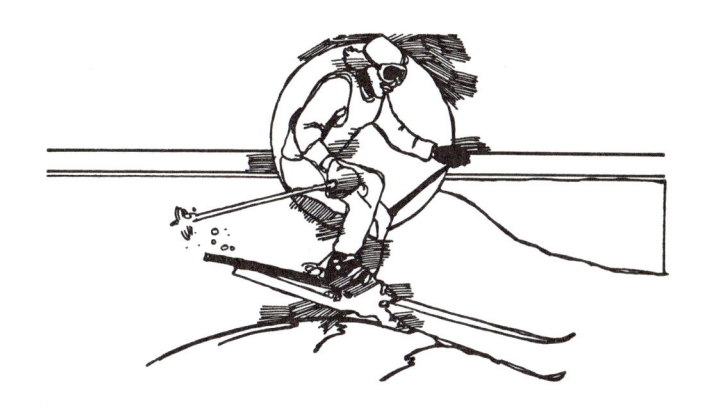

areas in the Anchorage area: Alyeska Resort and Arctic Valley. Alyeska Resort, 40 miles southeast of Anchorage, has all the amenities expected of a large ski area. Alyeska, the state's largest ski resort, offers four chairlifts with runs up to a mile long and chair No. 3 is equipped for night skiing. A fifth chairlift is reserved for racer training. The resort also has two rope tows and a Poma lift. Alyeska is open year-round, with skiing from November through April. Hours of operation depend on daylight, except for chair No. 3.

Arctic Valley, a few miles from Anchorage, is owned and operated by the Anchorage Ski Club, a nonprofit corporation. Arctic Valley is open on winter weekends and holidays. Facilities include two double chairlifts, a T-bar/Poma lift combination and three rope tows on beginner slopes.

Several smaller alpine slopes are maintained by the municipality of Anchorage, including: Centennial Park, Russian Jack Springs Park, with rope tows; and a new area at Hilltop, south of town, featuring the closest chairlift in the Anchorage area.

Popular cross-country ski trails in the Anchorage area include trails in city parks maintained by the municipality (a brochure is available): Russian Jack Springs, with nearly 5 miles of trails, 3 miles lighted; Kincaid Park, the site of the first World Cup and U.S. National men's and women's championship races in Alaska and the U.S. in March 1983, about 19 miles of trails with 4½ miles lighted and a new warm-up facility; Centennial Park with 3 miles of trails and about ½ mile lighted; Hillside Park with 5 miles of trails, 1½ miles lighted; and Chester Creek Greenbelt with 10 kilometers of trails, none lighted; ski trails in Chugach State Park; and ski trails in the Turnagain Pass area in Chugach National Forest, about 57 miles south of Anchorage.

PALMER

Hatcher Pass, site of the Independence Mine State Park, north of Palmer, is an excellent cross-country ski area with several maintained trails. The lodge has a coffee shop and warm-up area. The ski area is open from October through May.

FAIRBANKS

Fairbanks has a few small downhill ski areas, but none as large as Alyeska resort. Cleary Summit and Skiland, about 20 miles from town on the Steese Highway, both privately owned and operated, have rope tows and a chairlift at Cleary Summit; Ski Boot Hill at 4.2 mile Farmer's Loop Road has a rope tow; Birch Hill, located on Fort Wainwright, is mainly for military use; the University of Alaska has a small slope and rope tow; and Chena Hot Springs Resort at mile 57 on the Chena Hot Springs Road has a small alpine ski area which uses a tractor to transport skiers to the top of the hill.

Popular cross-country ski trails in the Fairbanks area include: Birch Hill recreation area, about 3 miles north of town on the Steese Expressway to a well-marked turnoff, then 2 miles in; the University of Alaska, Fairbanks, with 26 miles of trails that lead out to Ester Dome; Creamers Field trail near downtown; Salcha cross-country ski area, about 40 miles south of town on the Richardson Highway, with a fairly large trail system also used for ski races; Two Rivers trail area, near the elementary school at mile 10 Chena Hot Springs Road; and Chena Hot Springs Resort, offering cross-country ski trails for both novice and more experienced skiers.

JUNEAU

Eaglecrest Ski Area on Douglas Island, 12 miles from Juneau, has a 4,800-foot-long chairlift, a Platter Pull lift, a 3,000-foot-long chairlift and a day lodge. Cross-country ski trails are also available. Open from November to May. A few smaller alpine ski areas are located at Cordova, Valdez, Ketchikan and Homer. All have rope tows.

Several cross-country ski races are held each year. The largest, the Alaska Nordic Ski Cup Series, determines contestants for the Arctic Winter Games and Junior Olympic competitions. The series of five races is held in Anchorage, Homer, Salcha and Fairbanks.

Skin Sewing

(*See also* Beadwork, Mukluks *and* Parka)

The craft of sewing tanned hides and furs was a highly developed skill among Alaska's Natives. Although commercially made garments are now often worn by Eskimo villagers, women who are exceptional skin sewers still not only ensure the safety of family members who must face the harsh outdoors, but are regarded as a source of pride for the entire community.

Sewers place great importance on the use of specific materials, some of which are only available seasonally. For instance, winter-bleached sealskin can only be tanned during certain seasons. Blood, alder bark and red ochre are traditionally used for coloring on garments and footgear. Most sewers prefer sinew as thread, although in some areas sinew cannot be obtained and waxed thread or dental floss is substituted. Skins commonly used for making parkas and mukluks include seal, reindeer, caribou and polar bear. Wolf and wolverine are prized for ruffs.

Parka style, materials used and ornamentation — such as pieced calfskin or beadwork trim — vary from village to village, and between Yup'ik, Inupiat and Siberian Yup'ik sewers. The cut of parkas changes from north to south.

In most regions, mukluk style and material vary with changes in season and weather conditions. The mukluks advertise the skill of their makers and the villages where they were made.

The manufacture of children's toys, primarily clothed dolls and intricately sewn balls, still reflects the traditional ingenuity of skin sewers.

Related reading: *Secrets of Eskimo Skin Sewing* by Edna Wilder. The complete book on the art of Eskimo skin sewing, with how-to-do-it instructions and things-to-make ideas. 125 pages, $9.95. See ALASKA NORTHWEST LIBRARY in the back of the book.

Skookum

Native word meaning strong or serviceable. It originated with the Chehalis Indians of western Washington and was incorporated into the Chinook jargon, a trade language dating from the early 1800s. A skookum chuck is a narrow passage between a saltwater lagoon and the open sea. In many areas of Alaska, because of extreme tides, skookum chucks may resemble fast-flowing river rapids during changes of the tide.

Soapstone

This soft, easily worked stone is often carved into art objects by Alaskans. Most of the stone, however, is imported. Alaska soapstone is mined in the Matanuska Valley by blasting. This process gives the stone a tendency to fracture when being worked; therefore, it is not as desirable as imported soapstone.

Sourdough

This versatile, yeasty mixture was carried by many early-day pioneers and used to make bread and hot cakes. Sourdough cookery remains popular in Alaska today. Because the sourdough supply is replenished after each use, it can remain active and fresh indefinitely. A popular claim of sourdough cooks is that their batches trace back to pioneers at the turn of the century. The name also came to be applied to any Alaska or Yukon old-timer.

Related reading: *Alaska Sourdough: The Real Stuff by a Real Alaskan,* by Ruth Allman. Sourdough cookery, 190 pages, $7.95. *Cooking Alaskan,* hundreds of time-tested recipes, including a section on sourdough, 500 pages, $16.95. See ALASKA NORTHWEST LIBRARY in the back of the book.

Speed Limits

The basic speed law in Alaska states the speed limit is "no speed more than is prudent and reasonable."

The maximum speeds are 15 miles per hour in an alley, 20 miles per hour in a business district or school zone, 25 miles per hour in a residential area and 55 miles per hour on any other roadway.

Locally, municipalities and the state may, and often do, reduce or alter maximums as long as no maximum exceeds 55 miles per hour.

Squaw Candy

Salmon dried or smoked for a long time until it's very chewy. It's a staple food in winter for rural Alaskans and their dogs.

State Park System

The Alaska state park system began in July, 1959 with the transfer of federally-managed campgrounds and recreation sites from the Bureau of Land Management to the new state of Alaska. These sites were managed by the state Division of Lands until 1970; under Forestry, Parks and Recreation until 1966; then under the Parks and Recreation. The Division of Parks was created in October, 1970.

The Alaska state park system consists of approximately 111 individual units divided into 6 park management districts. There are 58 recreation sites, 16 recreation areas, 5 historic parks, 4 historic sites, 1 state trail, 7 state parks (Chugach, Denali, Chilkat, Kachemak Bay, Point Bridget, Shuyak Island and Wood-Tikchik) and 1 state preserve, the 49,000-acre Alaska Chilkat Bald Eagle Preserve.

Campsites are available on a first-come, first-served basis for $5 per night, except Eagle River in Chugach State Park and Chena River State Recreation Site in Fairbanks where the fee is $10 per night. A yearly pass is available. In addition to camping and picnicking, many units offer hiking trails and boat launching ramps; most developed campgrounds have picnic tables and toilets. General information on the state park system is available from the Division of Parks, P.O. Box 107001, Anchorage 99510.

State park units are listed by park management districts on the following pages. Designations for units of the Alaska state park system are abbreviated as follows: SP-State Park, SHP-State Historical Park, SHS-State Historic Site, SRA-State Recreation Area, SRS-State Recreation Site, ST-State Trail, SMP-State Marine Park, P-Preserve, WP-Wilderness Park. Park units designated "undeveloped" may have camping, hiking trails and limited facilities. Parks that indicate no developed campsites or picnic sites may offer fishing or river access, hiking and other activities. Numbers in the list refer to the accompanying map.

(Continued on page 174)

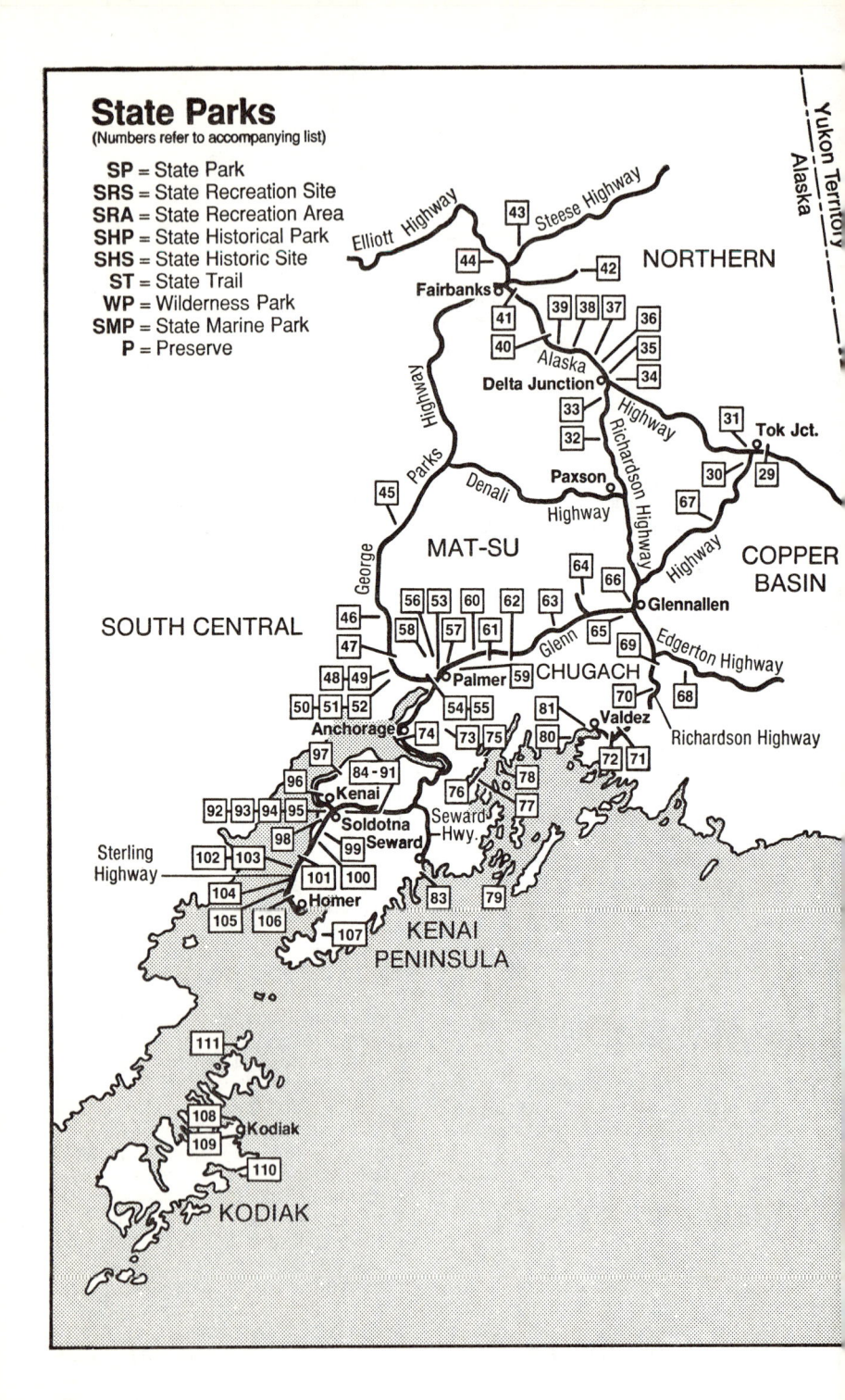

State Parks
(Numbers refer to accompanying list)

- **SP** = State Park
- **SRS** = State Recreation Site
- **SRA** = State Recreation Area
- **SHP** = State Historical Park
- **SHS** = State Historic Site
- **ST** = State Trail
- **WP** = Wilderness Park
- **SMP** = State Marine Park
- **P** = Preserve

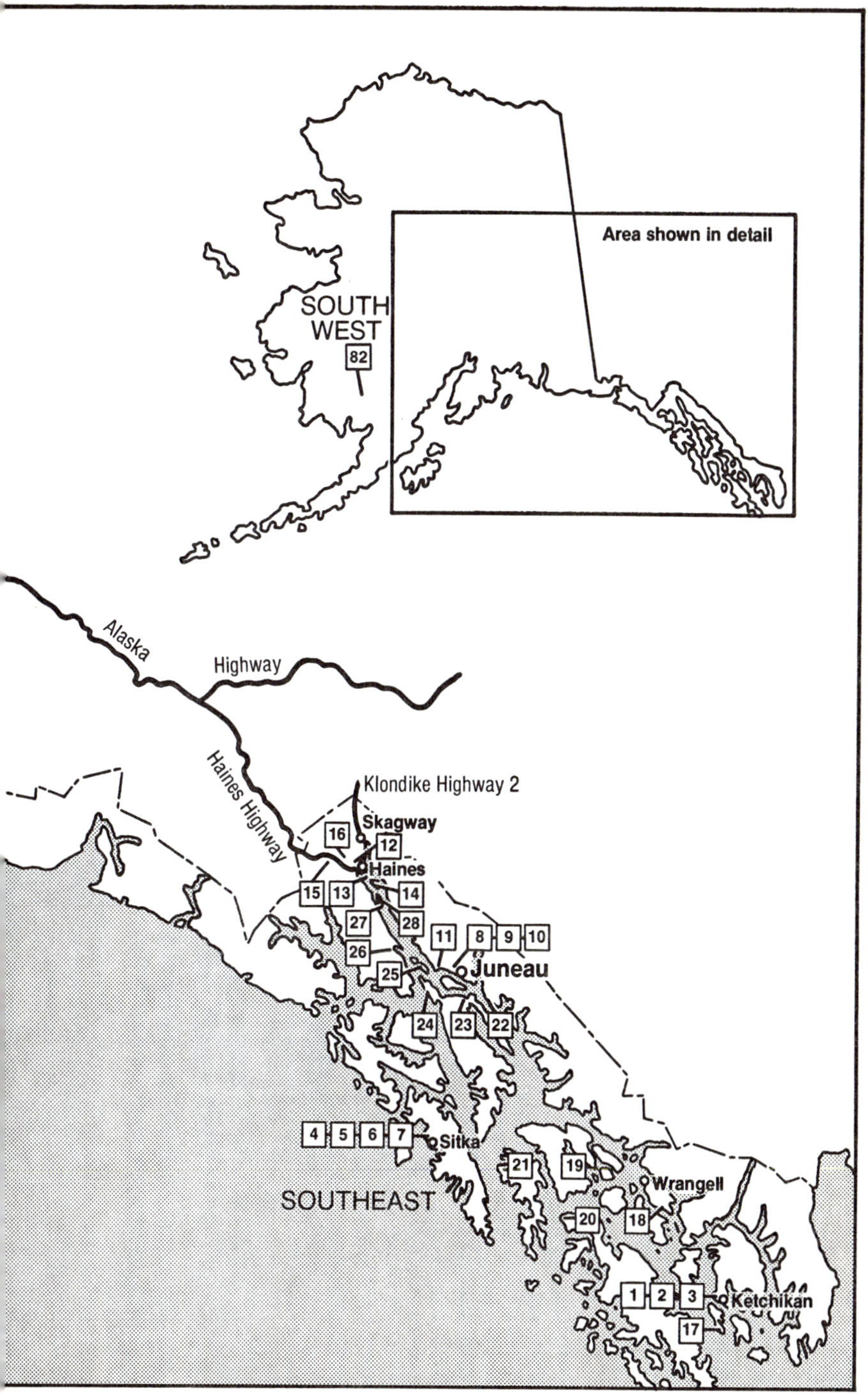
Area shown in detail
SOUTH WEST
82
Alaska Highway
Haines Highway
Klondike Highway 2
Skagway
Haines
Juneau
Sitka
Wrangell
Ketchikan
SOUTHEAST
1
2
3
4
5
6
7
8
9
10
11
12
13
14
15
16
17
18
19
20
21
22
23
24
25
26
27
28

Map Key — Acreage	Campsites	Picnic Sites	Nearest Town

SOUTHEAST DISTRICT, 400 Willoughby Bldg., Juneau 99811

#	Name — Acreage	Campsites	Picnic Sites	Nearest Town
1	Totem Bight SHP — 11	—	—	Ketchikan
2	Refuge Cove SRS — 13	—	14	Ketchikan
3	Settlers Cove SRS — 38	12	—	Ketchikan
4	Pioneer Park SRS — 3	—	—	Sitka
5	Baranof Castle SHS — 1	—	—	Sitka
6	Halibut Point SRS — 22	—	9	Sitka
7	Old Sitka SHP — 51	—	—	Sitka
8	Juneau Trail Sys. ST — 15	—	—	Juneau
9	Johnson Crk SRS — 65	—	—	Juneau
10	Wickersham SHS — 0.5	—	—	Juneau
11	Point Bridget SP — 2,800	—	—	Juneau
12	Chilkoot Lake SRS — 80	32	—	Haines
13	Portage Cove SRS — 7	9	3	Haines
14	Chilkat SP — 6,045	15	—	Haines
15	Ak-Chilkat Bald Eagle P — 49,320	—	—	Haines
16	Mosquito Lake SRS — 5	10	—	Haines
17	Dall Bay SMP — 585	—	—	Ketchikan
18	Thom's Place SMP — 1,198	—	—	Wrangell
19	Beecher Pass SMP — 660	—	—	Wrangell
20	Joe Mace Island SMP — 62	—	—	Wrangell
21	Security Bay SMP — 500	—	—	Petersburg
22	Taku Harbor SMP — 700	—	—	Juneau
23	Oliver Inlet SMP — 560	—	—	Juneau
24	Funter Bay SMP — 162	—	—	Juneau
25	Shelter Island SMP — 3,560	—	—	Juneau
26	St. James Bay SMP — 10,220	—	—	Juneau
27	Sullivan Island SMP — 2,163	—	—	Juneau
28	Chilkat Islands SMP — 6,560	—	—	Haines

NORTHERN DISTRICT, 4418 Airport Way, Fairbanks 99701

#	Name — Acreage	Campsites	Picnic Sites	Nearest Town
29	Tok River SRS — 38	50	—	Tok
30	Eagle Trail SRS — 640	40	4	Tok
31	Moon Lake SRS — 22	15	—	Tok
32	Fielding Lake SRS — 300	7	—	Delta Jct.
33	Donnelly Creek SRS — 42	12	—	Delta Jct.
34	Clearwater SRS — 27	18	—	Delta Jct.
35	Delta SRS — 7	22	6	Delta Jct.
36	Big Delta SHP — 10	—	—	Delta Jct.
37	Quartz Lake SRA — 600	16	—	Delta Jct.
38	Birch Lake SRS — 191	10	—	Delta Jct.
39	Harding Lake SRA — 169	89	52	Delta Jct.
40	Salcha River SRS — 61	25	20	Delta Jct.
41	Chena River SRS — 27	59	30	Fairbanks
42	Chena River SRA — 254,080	—	—	Fairbanks
43	Upper Chatanika River SRS — 73	25	—	Fairbanks
44	Lower Chatanika River SRA — 570	—	—	Fairbanks

MAT-SU/COPPER BASIN DISTRICT, HC 32, Box 6706, Wasilla 99687

#	Name — Acreage	Campsites	Picnic Sites	Nearest Town
45	Denali SP — 324,240	—	—	Talkeetna
46	Montana Creek SRS — 82	89	28	Talkeetna
47	Willow Creek SRS — 240	7	—	Willow
48	Nancy Lake SRA — 22,685	—	—	Willow
49	Nancy Lake SRS — 36	30	30	Willow
50	Rocky Lake SRS — 48	10	—	Wasilla
51	Big Lake North SRS — 19	60	24	Wasilla
52	Big Lake South SRS — 16	20	10	Wasilla

Map Key — Acreage	Campsites	Picnic Sites	Nearest Town
53 Kepler-Bradley Lakes SRA — 344	—	—	Palmer
54 Finger Lake SRS — 47	41	10	Palmer
55 Wolf Lake SRS — 23	4	4	Palmer
56 Independence Mine SHP — 761	—	—	Palmer
57 Summit Lake SRS — 360	—	5	Palmer
58 Moose Creek SRS — 40	12	4	Palmer
59 King Mountain SRS — 20	22	2	Palmer
60 Bonnie Lake SRS — 129	8	—	Palmer
61 Long Lake SRS — 480	9	—	Palmer
62 Matanuska Glacier SRS — 229	12	—	Palmer
63 Little Nelchina SRS — 22	11	—	Glenallen
64 Lake Louise SRA — 90	46	—	Glennallen
65 Tolsona Creek SRS — 600	10	—	Glennallen
66 Dry Creek SRS — 372	58	4	Glennallen
67 Porcupine Creek SRS — 240	—	—	Tok
68 Liberty Falls SRS — 10	8	—	Chitina
69 Squirrel Creek SRS — 350	14	—	Copper Center
70 Little Tonsina SRS — 103	8	—	Copper Center
71 Worthington Glacier SRS — 113	—	—	Valdez
72 Blueberry Lake SRS — 192	15	—	Valdez

CHUGACH/SOUTHWEST DISTRICT, P.O. Box 107001, Anchorage 99510

73 Chugach SP — 495,204	—	—	Anchorage
74 Potter Section House SHS — 0.5	—	—	Anchorage
75 Bettles Bay SMP — 680	—	—	Whittier
76 Zeigler Cove SMP — 720	—	—	Whittier
77 Surprise Cove SMP — 2,280	—	—	Whittier
78 S. Esther Island SMP — 3,360	—	—	Whittier
79 Horseshoe Bay SMP — 970	—	—	Seward
80 Sawmill Bay SMP — 2,320	—	—	Valdez
81 Shoup Bay SMP — 4,560	—	—	Valdez
82 Wood-Tikchik SP — 1,555,200	3	—	Dillingham

KENAI PENINSULA DISTRICT, P.O. Box 1247, Soldotna 99669

83 Caines Head SRA — 5,961	4	4	Seward
84 Kenai Keys SRA — 193	—	—	Sterling
85 Bings Landing SRS — 126	37	20	Sterling
86 Izaak Walton SRS — 8	38	—	Sterling
87 Morgans Landing SRA — 279	50	—	Sterling
88 Scout Lake SRS — 195	8	—	Sterling
89 Funny River SRS — 336	5	—	Sterling
90 Nilnunqa SHS — 42	—	—	Sterling
91 Kenai River Islands SRS — 69	—	—	Sterling
92 Slikok Creek SRS — 40	—	5	Soldotna
93 Big Eddy SRS — 16	—	—	Soldotna
94 Ciechanski SRS — 34	—	—	Soldotna
95 Kenai River Flats SRS — 832	—	—	Kenai
96 Bernice Lake SRS — 152	11	1	Kenai
97 Captain Cook SRA — 3,466	—	—	Kenai
98 Crooked Creek SRS — 48.5	75	5	Soldotna
99 Kasilof River SRS — 50	16	—	Soldotna
100 Johnson Lake SRA — 324	50	—	Soldotna
101 Clam Gulch SRA — 129	116	—	Soldotna
102 Ninilchik SRA — 97	165	—	Homer
103 Deep Creek SRA — 155	300	—	Homer
104 Stariski SRS — 30	13	—	Homer
105 Anchor River SRA — 213	38	—	Homer

Map Key — Acreage	Campsites	Picnic Sites	Nearest Town
106 Anchor River SRS — 53	9	—	Homer
107 Kachemak B. SP & WP — 328,290	8	1	Homer

KODIAK DISTRICT, SR Box 3800, Kodiak 99615

108 Fort Abercrombie SHP — 183	14	—	Kodiak
109 Buskin River SRS — 196	18	—	Kodiak
110 Pasagshak SRS — 20	10	—	Kodiak
111 Shuyak Island SP — 11,000	—	—	Kodiak

State Symbols

FLAG

Alaska's state flag was designed in 1926 by Benny Benson, who entered his design in a territorial flag contest for students in grades 7 through 12. The Alaska legislature adopted his design as the official flag of the territory of Alaska on May 2, 1927.

The flag consists of eight gold stars — the Big Dipper and the North Star — on a field of blue. In Benson's words, "The blue field is for the Alaska sky and the forget-me-not, an Alaska flower. The North Star is for the future state of Alaska, the most northerly of the Union. The dipper is for the Great Bear — symbolizing strength."

Benny Benson was born October 12, 1913, at Chignik, Alaska. His mother was of Aleut-Russian descent and his father was a Swedish fisherman who came to the Alaska Territory in 1904. Benson's mother died of pneumonia when Benny was four and he entered the Jesse Lee Memorial Home (then located at Unalaska).

Benny, then a seventh grade student at the Jesse Lee Home, was one of 142 students whose designs were selected for the final judging by a committee chosen by the Alaska Department of the American Legion.

Benny was awarded a $1,000 scholarship and was presented an engraved watch for winning the contest. He used the scholarship to attend the Hemphill Engineering School in Seattle in 1937. In 1963, the Alaska legislature awarded Benson an additional $2,500 as a way "of paying a small tribute to a fellow Alaskan." In November of the same year, Benson presented his award watch to the Alaska State Museum.

Benny's prophetic words, "The North Star is for the future state of Alaska, the most northerly of the Union," were realized on January 3, 1959, when Alaska was proclaimed the 49th state of the Union. The drafters of the Constitution for Alaska stipulated that the flag of the territory would be the official flag of the state of Alaska. When the flag was first flown over the capital city on July 4, 1959, Benny proudly led the parade that preceded the ceremony, carrying the flag of "eight stars on a field of blue," which he had designed 33 years before.

Benson settled in Kodiak in 1949 where he worked as a mechanic for Kodiak Airways. He was active in a movement to integrate the Elks, a white-only national organization which now has a number of Native members in Alaska. Benson had a leg amputated in 1969 and his health declined; he died of a heart attack on July 2, 1972, in Kodiak.

SEAL

The first governor of Alaska designed a seal for the then District of Alaska in 1884. In 1910, Gov. Walter E. Clark redesigned the original seal, which became a symbol for the new territory of Alaska in 1912. The constitution of Alaska adopted the territorial seal as the Seal for the State of Alaska in 1959.

Represented in the state seal are icebergs, northern lights, mining, agriculture, fisheries, fur seal rookeries and a railroad. The seal is 2-1/8 inches in diameter.

Song

Alaska's Flag

Eight stars of gold on a field of blue — Alaska's flag.
May it mean to you the blue of the sea, the evening sky,
The mountain lakes, and the flow'rs nearby;
The gold of the early sourdough's dreams,
The precious gold of the hills and streams;
The brilliant stars in the northern sky,
The "Bear" — the "Dipper" — and, shining high,
The great North Star with its steady light,
Over land and sea a beacon bright.
Alaska's flag — to Alaskans dear,
The simple flag of a last frontier.

The lyrics were written by Marie Drake as a poem that first appeared on the cover of the October 1935 *School Bulletin*, a territorial Department of Education publication which she edited while assistant commissioner of education. The music was written by Mrs. Elinor Dusenbury, whose husband, Col. Ralph Wayne Dusenbury, was commander of Chilkoot Barracks at Haines from 1933 to 1936. Mrs. Dusenbury wrote the music several years after leaving Alaska because, she was later quoted as saying, "I got so homesick for Alaska I couldn't stand it." She died October 17, 1980, in Carlsbad, California.

The territorial legislature adopted *Alaska's Flag* as the official song in 1955.

OTHER SYMBOLS

Bird: Willow ptarmigan, *Lagopus lagopus* a small Arctic grouse that lives among willows and on open tundra and muskeg. Its plumage changes from brown in summer to white in winter; feathers cover the entire lower leg and foot. Common from southwestern Alaska into the Arctic. Adopted in 1955.

Fish: King salmon, *Oncorhynchus tshawytscha,* an important part of the Native subsistence fisheries and a significant species to the state's commercial salmon fishery. This anadromous fish ranges from beyond the southern extremes of Alaska to as far north as Point Hope.

Flower: Forget-Me-Not.
Gem: Jade (*See* Jade).
Mineral: Gold (*See* Gold).
Motto: North to the Future, adopted in 1967.
Sport: Dog mushing (*See* Dog Mushing).
Tree: Sitka spruce, *Picea sitchensis,* the largest and one of the most valuable trees in Alaska. Sitka spruce grows to 160 feet in height and 3 to 5 feet in

diameter. Its long, dark green needles surround twigs that bear cones. It is found throughout Southeast and the Kenai Peninsula, along the gulf coast, and the west coast of Cook Inlet. Adopted in 1962.

Subsistence

Alaska is unique among states in that it has established the subsistence use of fish and game as the highest priority consumptive use of the resource. Alaska's legislature passed subsistence priority laws in 1978 and 1986. In addition, Congress passed a priority subsistence law in 1980 for federal lands in Alaska. Studies by the Alaska Department of Fish and Game have shown that many rural communities in Alaska depend upon subsistence hunting and fishing for a large portion of their diets.

Still a controversial issue and a difficult concept to define, subsistence is defined by Federal law as "the customary and traditional uses by rural Alaska residents of wild, renewable resources for direct personal or family consumption as food, shelter, fuel, clothing, tools or transportation, for the making and selling of handicraft articles out of nonedible byproducts of fish and wildlife resources taken for personal or family consumption, and for the customary trade, barter or sharing for personal or family consumption."

According to Alaska State Subsistence Statutes passed in 1986, only rural residents can be considered subsistence users. In addition to the rural requirement, subsistence uses can be identified by a variety of other criteria, such as long-term traditional use, local area use and frequent sharing of harvests. Subsistence also depends upon the biological status of fish and game resources, and is not authorized if harvesting will damage the resources.

Subsistence fishing regulations are available as a separate pamphlet from the Alaska Department of Fish and Game, P.O. Box 3-2000, Juneau 99802. Subsistence hunting regulations are included with the annually published state hunting regulations, also available from the ADF&G.

Sundog

"Mock suns" (parhelia) usually seen as bright spots on opposite sides of the winter sun. This optical phenomenon is created by the refraction of sunlight through tiny ice crystals suspended in the air. The ice crystals are commonly called "diamond dust."

Taiga

Taken from a Russian word that means "land of little sticks," this name is applied to the spindly white spruce and black spruce forests found in much of southcentral and interior Alaska.

Telecommunications

HISTORY

Alaska's first telecommunications project, begun in the 1860s, was designed to serve New York, San Francisco and the capitals of Europe, not particularly the residents of Nome or Fairbanks. It was part of Western Union's ambitious plan to link California to Russian America (Alaska) with an intercontinental cable that would continue under the Bering Strait to Siberia and on to Europe. Men and material were brought together on both sides of the Bering Sea, but with the first successful Atlantic cable crossing in 1867, the trans-Siberian intercontinental line was abandoned.

The first operational telegraph link in Alaska was laid in September 1900 when 25 miles of line were stretched from military headquarters in Nome to an outpost at Port Safety. It was one part of a $450,000 plan by the Army Signal Corps to connect scattered military posts in the territory with the United States. By the end of 1903, land lines linked western Alaska, Prince William Sound, the Interior and southeastern Alaska (where underwater cable was used).

Plagued by blocks of ice that repeatedly tore loose the underwater cables laid across Norton Sound, the military developed "wireless telegraphy" to span the icy water in 1903. It was the world's first application of radio-telegraph technology and marked the completion of a fragile network connecting all military stations in Alaska with the United States and each other. Sitka, Juneau, Haines and Valdez were connected by a line to Whitehorse, Yukon Territory. Nome, Fort Saint Michael, Fort Gibbon (Tanana) and Fort Egbert (Eagle) were linked with Dawson, Yukon Territory. A line from Dawson to Whitehorse continued on to Vancouver, British Columbia and Seattle.

In 1905, the 1,500 miles of land lines, 2,000 miles of submarine cables and the 107-mile wireless link became the Washington-Alaska Military Cable and Telegraph System. This, in turn, became the Alaska Communications System in 1935, reflecting a shift to greater civilian use and a system relying more heavily on wireless stations than land lines. The Alaska Communications System operated under the Department of Defense until RCA Corporation, through its division RCA Alascom, took control in 1971.

ALASCOM

Alascom, Inc., is the original long lines carrier for the state and provides a full range of modern long-distance telecommunications services to all Alaska. When Alascom purchased Alaska Communications Systems, about 5 million calls were being handled each year. Today, with more than 200 satellite communication sites in operation, Alascom handles nearly 70 million toll calls each year. To complement its satellite communications,

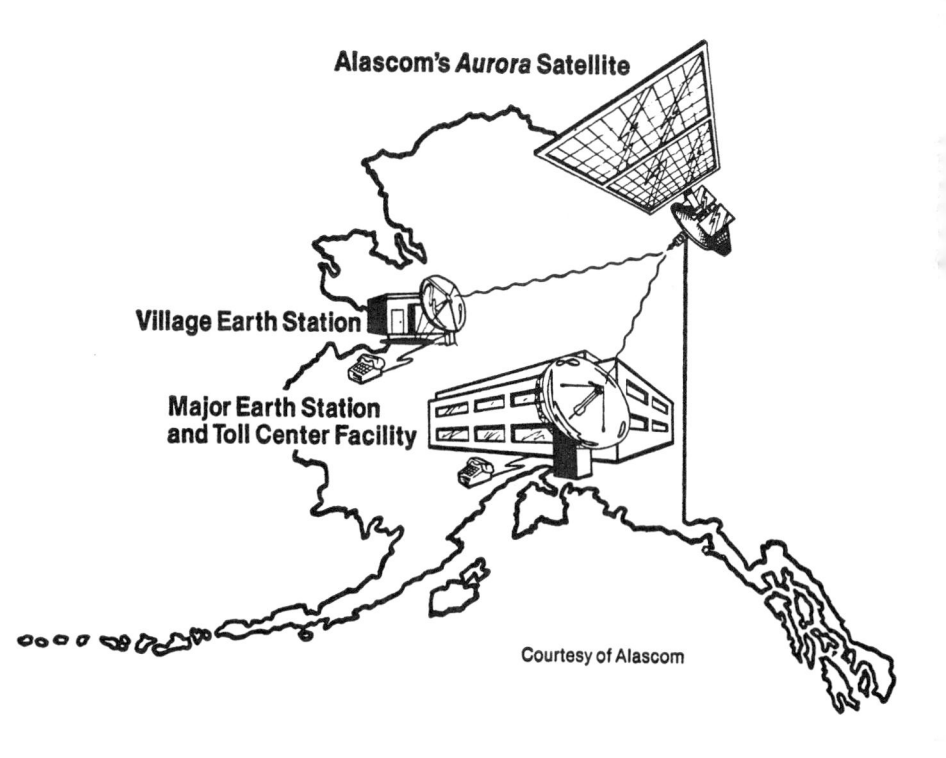

Alascom's *Aurora* Satellite

Village Earth Station

Major Earth Station and Toll Center Facility

Courtesy of Alascom

179

Alascom also maintains hundreds of miles of terrestrial microwave routes.

On October 27, 1982, Alascom launched its own telecommunications satellite, *Aurora*, into orbit from Cape Canaveral, Florida. The launching marked several firsts for Alaska: It was the first completely solid-state satellite to be placed in orbit; it was the first telecommunications satellite dedicated to a single state; and it was the first satellite to be named by a youngster in a contest. Sponsored by Alascom and the State Chamber of Commerce, the contest drew some 5,000 entries from school children across Alaska. The winner was eight-year-old Nick Francis of Eagle River, who chose *Aurora* "because it's our light in the sky to tell us we are special people."

A typical long-distance telephone call from rural Alaska to points in the Lower 48 may travel more than 100,000 miles in what engineers call a "double-hop" — a signal from a village to the satellite *Aurora*, back to toll facilities in Fairbanks, Juneau, or Anchorage, up again to *Aurora*, and finally to Lower 48 receiving stations. (The illustration on page 179 shows a single hop.) The signal is carried at speeds approaching that of light.

Improvements over the past 10 years have made long-distance telephone service available to every community of 25 persons or more in Alaska. Live or same-day television is now available to 90 percent of the state's population. In addition to message toll service and television transmissions, Alascom also provides discounted calling plans, telex, computer data transmission and access, Wide Area Telecommunications Service (WATS), Fax service, national and in-state 800 toll-free numbers, telegrams and mailgrams, dedicated line service, marine radio, foreign exchange service, and transportable satellite earth stations to the residents of Alaska. Alascom is one of the largest private employers in the state.

GENERAL COMMUNICATIONS

A relative newcomer in providing Alaska telephone service, General Communications, Inc., provides long-distance telephone service to points outside the state. GCI transmits signals via a Canadian communications satellite tying in with the AT&T national phone network in Seattle. In October 1986, GCI began long distance telephone service between Alaska and 120 countries.

Telephone Numbers in the Bush

Although most Alaskan bush communities now have full telephone service, a few villages still have only one telephone. For those villages, call the information number, 555-1212. The area code for all of Alaska is 907.

Television Stations

Television in Alaska's larger communities, such as Anchorage and Fairbanks, was available years before satellites were sent into orbit. The first satellite broadcast to the state was Neil Armstrong's moon walk in July 1969. Television reached the Bush in the late 1970s with the construction of telephone earth stations that could receive television programming via satellite transmissions. Same-day broadcasts, arriving via satellite, of news and sports events are subsidized in part by state revenues. The state also funds Satellite Television Project (TVP), which supplies general programming to over 250 rural communities. For more information about TVP, contact the Department of Administration, Division of Telecommunications Operations, 5900 East Tudor Road, Anchorage 99507.

Tapes of programming from the LearnAlaska Instructional Television Network, which is no longer on the air, are available to teachers through the state library system.

Regular network programming (ABC, CBS, NBC and PBS) from the Lower 48 reaches Alaska on a time-delayed basis. Most of the stations listed here carry a mixture of network programming, with local broadcasters specifying programming. Some stations, such as KJNP, carry locally produced programming.

Cable television is available in many communities, with the cable companies offering dozens of channels. At least one cable system offers a complete satellite earth station and 24-hour programming. Local television viewing in

Bethel, for example, includes Channel 4 (KYUK), which carries ITV programming such as PBS's "NOVA" series and "Sesame Street," and local news; cable Channel 8, which carries regular network programming; and a half-dozen other channels carrying cable programming such as movies, sports and specials.

The following list shows the commercial and public television stations in Alaska:

Anchorage, **KAKM** Channel 7 (public television); 2677 Providence Drive, 99508.
Anchorage, **KIMO** Channel 13; 2700 E. Tudor Road, 99507.
Anchorage, **KTBY** Channel 4; 1840 S. Bragaw, Suite 101, 99508.
Anchorage, **KTUU** Channel 2; P.O. Box 102880, 99510.
Anchorage, **KTVA** Channel 11; P.O. Box 102200, 99510.
Bethel, **KYUK** Channel 4 (public television); P.O. Box 468, 99559.
Fairbanks, **KATN** Channel 2; 516 Second Avenue, 99707.
Fairbanks, **KTVF** Channel 11; P.O. Box 950, 99707.
Fairbanks, **KUAC** Channel 9 (public television); University of Alaska, 99775
Juneau, **KJUD** Channel 8; 1107 W. 8th St., 99801.
Juneau, **KTOO** Channel 3 (public television); 224 4th St., 99801.
Kenai, **UHF** Channel 17; P.O. Box 4665, 99611.
North Pole, **KJNP** Channel 4; P.O. Box O, 99705.
Sitka, **KTNL** Channel 13; 520 Lake St., 99835.

Tides

In southeastern Alaska, Prince William Sound, Cook Inlet and Bristol Bay, saltwater undergoes extreme daily fluctuations, creating powerful tidal currents. Some bays may go totally dry at low tide. The second greatest tide range in North America occurs in upper Cook Inlet near Anchorage, where the maximum diurnal range during spring tides is 38.9 feet. (The greatest tide range in North America is Nova Scotia's Bay of Fundy, with spring tides to 43 feet.)

Here are diurnal ranges for some coastal communities:

	Feet
Bethel	4.0
Cold Bay	7.1
Cordova	12.4
Haines	16.8
Herschel Island	0.7
Ketchikan	15.4
Kodiak	8.5
Naknek River entrance	22.6
Nikiski	20.7
Nome	1.6
Nushagak	19.6
Point Barrow	0.4
Port Heiden	12.3
Port Moller	10.8
Sand Point	7.3
Sitka	9.9
Valdez	12.0
Whittier	12.3
Wrangell	15.7
Yakutat	10.1

Timber

According to the USDA Forest Service, Anchorage Forestry Sciences Lab, 129 million acres of Alaska's 365 million acres of land surface are forested (21 million acres of which are classified as timberland or commercial forest).

Alaska has two distinct forest ecosystems: the interior forest and the coastal rain forest. The vast interior forest covers 115 million acres, extending from the south slope of the Brooks Range to the Kenai Peninsula, and from Canada to Norton Sound. More than 13 million acres of white spruce, paper birch, quaking aspen, black cottonwood and balsam poplar stands are considered commercial forest, comparing favorably in size and growth with the forests of the lake states of Minnesota, Wisconsin and Michigan. However, 3.4 million acres of these commercial forests are unavailable for harvest because they are in designated parks or wilderness. The Interior's land management policies and remoteness from large markets have limited timber use to approximately 21 local sawmills, (many cutting less than 300,000 board feet per year) with some exports of cants and chips.

The coastal rain forests extend from Cook Inlet to the Alaska-Canada border south of Ketchikan, and they continue to provide the bulk of commercial timber volume in Alaska. Of the 13.6 million acres of forested land, 7.6 million acres support commercial stands. About 1.9 million acres of these commercial stands are in parks and wilderness and therefore are not available for harvest. Western hemlock and Sitka spruce provide most of the timber harvest for domestic and export lumber and pulp markets. Western red cedar and Alaska-cedar make up most of the balance, along with mountain hemlock and some lodgepole pine and other species. Southeastern Alaska has five major sawmills and six smaller mills, some operating intermittently.

Lands from which timber is harvested are divided into two distinct categories: privately owned by Native corporations and villages under the 1971 Native Claims Settlement Act, and publicly owned and managed federal, state and borough lands. Timber harvests from publicly owned lands are carried through short- and long-term sales offered by government agencies. Harvests on Native lands are scheduled for accelerated cutting through the early 1990s, tapering off to a lower sustained harvest in the following years.

The forest products of Alaska are also divided somewhat along the same lines as land ownership. By federal law, timber harvested from federal lands (approximately 87 percent of all timber harvested on public lands) cannot be exported without processing. Consequently, while processors dependent on federal lands produce roughly sawn lumber, pulp and chips, the Native corporations primarily produce round logs, which find more buyers in Japan. Given that the Alaska forest products industry is almost entirely dependent on the Japanese market, the processing requirement has had considerable effect on some sections of the forest industry, as it limits responsiveness to varying market conditions. Finally, pulp mills provide a market for wood chips and for lower-quality timber from both public and private lands. A market for this so-called utility wood is critical to all operators.

In 1988, more than 390 million board feet of timber were harvested from publicly owned or managed lands in Alaska (excluding Bureau of Land Management and Bureau of Indian Affairs lands). In 1988, lumber was the second most valuable product exported, with a total dollar value of over $527 million, or more than 24 percent of all the state's exports.

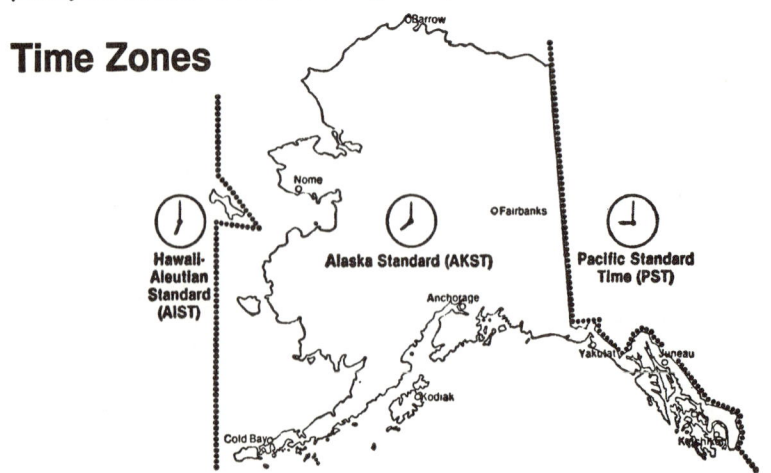

Time Zones

On September 15, 1983, transportation secretary Elizabeth Dole signed a plan to reduce the number of time zones in Alaska from four to two. The plan, which became effective October 30, 1983, when daylight saving time reverted to standard time, places 90 percent of Alaska residents on Alaska (same as Yukon) time, only one hour behind the West Coast. The far reaches of the Aleutian Islands and Saint Lawrence Island enter Hawaii-Aleutian time.

Before the change, Alaska's time zones were Pacific time (southeastern Alaska), Yukon time (Yakutat) and Alaska time (from just east of Cold Bay and west of Yakutat northward, including Nome). The shift was accomplished to facilitate doing business in Alaska, improve communications and unify residents. It had the support of the governor, the state legislature and the majority of Alaskans.

Totems

In the early days of southeastern Alaska and British Columbia, the way of life of the Indian people living there was based on the rich natural resources of the land, on respect for all living things and on a unique and complex social structure. The totemic art of the Indians reflects this rich culture. Totems are bold statements making public records of the lives and history of the people who had them carved and represent pride in clans and ancestors.

Totems, carved from yellow cedar, are a traditional art form among the Indians of British Columbia and southeastern Alaska. Although most well-known totems are tall and free standing, totemic art also was applied to houseposts and short entrance poles. The carved monuments were erected by the leading clans in each tribe in memory of their chiefs who had died. The poles also symbolized power and prestige.

Animals of the region are most often represented on the poles. Of all the crests, the frog appears most frequently, then the bear, eagle, raven, thunderbird, wolf, owl, grouse, starfish, finback whale and halibut. Also represented are figures from Indian mythology: monsters with animal features, humanlike spirits and semihistorical ancestors. Occasionally depicted are objects, devices, masks and charms, and most rarely, art illustrating plants and sky phenomena.

The poles are traditionally painted with pigments made from soil of yellow, brown and red hues, coal, cinnabar, berry juice and spruce sap. Fungus found on hemlock produces various colors: yellow when decayed, red when roasted and black when charred. Before modern paints became available, salmon eggs chewed with cedar bark formed the case, or glue, for the paint.

Totem art reached its peak after 1830, with the introduction of steel European tools acquired through fur trade, and

183

endured to about 1890. Carving activity has not been as plentiful since. Leading families competed with others, building larger and more elaborate totem poles to show their wealth and prestige.

The pole was left to stand as long as nature would permit, usually no more than 50 to 60 years. Once a pole became so rotten that it fell, it was pushed aside, left to decay naturally or used for firewood. Most totem poles still standing in parks today are 40 to 50 years old. Heavy precipitation and acid muskeg soils hasten decomposition.

Collections of totem poles may be seen in several Alaska communities, including Ketchikan, Wrangell and Sitka. Carvers may be seen practicing their art in Haines and Sitka.

Tourism

Although Alaska has been attracting tourists for nearly one hundred years, many people are surprised to learn that tourism has become the state's third-largest industry. In terms of gross sales and employment, tourism is exceeded only by the petroleum and commercial fishing industries. Historically, visitor volume has grown annually by 6 to 15 percent. In excess of 1,500 businesses in Alaska derive most of their income from sales to visitors.

State government has long recognized the value of visitor industry growth and supports this segment of the state's economy through the programs of the Alaska Division of Tourism. In fiscal year 1984-85, the division spent $8.1 million in support of the visitor industry, primarily for print and broadcast advertising, and the production and distribution of Alaska travel promotion literature.

In 1987, approximately 92.6 percent of Alaska's visitors came from the continental United States. Western Europe, Canada and Japan provide the majority of foreign arrivals. Nearly 52 percent travel on independent itineraries, with the remainder purchasing package tour programs. By transportation mode, approximately 29.5 percent of visitor arrivals are by air, 40 percent by cruise ship, 14 percent by ferry and 13 percent by auto and camper. Total arrivals for 1988 were down by 4.9 percent from summer 1987.

Alaska's scenic beauty, abundant wildlife and colorful history remain its biggest attractions. The recent, rapid growth in the adventure travel market is also evident in Alaska with increasing numbers of visitors participating in river rafting, back country trekking and a variety of wilderness experiences.

NONRESIDENT VISITOR VOLUME AND IMPACT

Year	Visitor Volume	In-State Sales* (In millions)	Primary Employment
1978	522,500	$ 270.3	6,970
1979	546,000	321.1	7,280
1980	570,600	360.4	7,925
1981	596,300	416.2	8,280
1982	623,100	480.7	8,900
1983	646,000	551.7	9,160
1984	691,200	620.0	9,875
1985	700,000	659.4	10,565
1986	787,000	700.0	10,888
1987	746,500	1,094.3	9,900
1988	709,664	NA	NA

*Excludes transportation costs to and from Alaska.
Source: State of Alaska, Division of Tourism.

Trees and Shrubs

According to the U.S. Department of Agriculture, the number of native tree species in Alaska is less than in any other state. Species of trees and shrubs in Alaska fall under the following families: yew, pine, cypress, willow, bayberry, birch, mistletoe, gooseberry, rose, maple, elaeagnus, ginseng, dogwood, crowberry, pyrola, heath, dispensia, honeysuckle and composite.

Commercial timber species include white spruce, Sitka spruce, western hemlock, mountain hemlock, western red cedar, Alaska cedar, balsam poplar, black cottonwood, quaking aspen and paper birch.

Rare tree species include the Pacific yew, Pacific silver fir, subalpine fir, silver willow and Hooker willow.

Tundra

Areas with cool temperatures, frequent winds and moisture-retaining soils. Tundra climates are harsh on plant species attempting to grow there. Mechanical stress is incurred as soils freeze around root systems and winds wear away portions exposed above rocks and snow. Consequently, the three distinct types of Alaska tundra — wet, moist and alpine — support low- growing vegetation that includes a variety of delicate flowers, mosses and lichens.

According to a report in *Alaska Science Nuggets,* every acre of Arctic tundra contains more than two tons of live fungi which survive by feeding on, thus decomposing, dead organic matter. Since the recession of North Slope ice age glaciers 12,000 years ago, a vegetative residue has accumulated a layer of peat three to six feet thick overlying the tundra.

Ulu

A traditional Eskimo woman's knife designed for scraping and chopping, this fan-shaped tool was originally made of stone with a bone handle, but today it is often shaped from an old saw blade and a wood handle is attached.

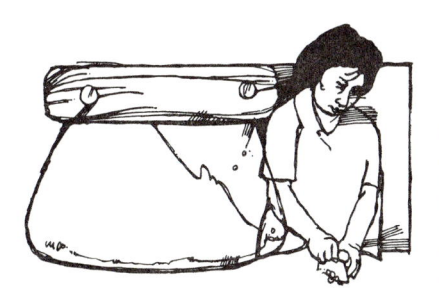

Umiak

A traditional Eskimo skin-covered boat, whose design has changed little over the centuries. Although mostly powered by outboard motors today, paddles are still used when stalking game and when ice might damage the propeller. Because the *umiaks* must often be pulled for long distances over the ice, the boats are designed to be lightweight and easily repairable. The frames are wood, often driftwood found on the beaches, and the covering can be sewn should it be punctured. The bottom is flat and the keel is bone, which prevents the skin from wearing out as it is pulled over the ice.

Female walrus skins are the preferred covering because they are the proper thickness when split (bull hides are too thick) and because it only takes two to cover a boat. However, sometimes female walrus skins are unavailable, so the Eskimos substitute skins of the bearded seal, or *oogruk*. But *oogruks* are smaller and it takes six or seven skins to cover an *umiak*.

Once the skins are stretched over the frame and lashed into place, the outside is painted with marine paint for waterproofing. Historically, the skin would have been anointed with seal oil or other fats, but the modern water proofing is now universally accepted because it does not have to be renewed after each trip.

Umiak is the Inupiat word for skin boat and is commonly used by the coastal Eskimos throughout Alaska. The Saint Lawrence Islanders, however, speak the Yup'ik dialect and their word for skin boat is *angyaq*.

Universities and Colleges

Higher education in Alaska is provided by the University of Alaska statewide system of higher education and three private institutions. The university system includes three multicampus universities, one community college and a network of service for rural Alaska. University of Alaska institutions enroll more than 30,000 people each year.

The three regional institutions of the University of Alaska are University of Alaska Anchorage, which includes Kenai Peninsula College, Kodiak College and Matanuska-Susitna College; University of Alaska Fairbanks with campuses in Bethel, Kotzebue, Valdez and Nome; and University of Alaska Southeast with campuses in Juneau, Ketchikan and Sitka. These schools offer developmental, certificate, associate, baccalaureate and graduate degree programs. Student housing is available in Bethel, Anchorage, Fairbanks and Juneau.

University of Alaska Fairbanks research facilities include the Agricultural and Forestry Experiment Station, Alaska Native Language Center, Center for Cross-Cultural Studies, Fishery Industrial Technology Center, Geophysical Institute, Juneau Center for Fisheries and Ocean Sciences, Mineral Industry Research and Petroleum Development laboratories, Museum, and institutes of Arctic Biology, Marine Science, and Northern Engineering.

The University of Alaska Anchorage is the home of the Alaska Center for International Business, Institute for Social and Economic Research, Justice Center and centers for Alcohol and Addiction Studies, High Latitude Health Research, and Economic Education.

Through the university's Cooperative Extension Service and Marine Advisory Program, research results are interpreted and transferred to people of the state.

For information on state colleges and universities, and private institutions of higher education, contact the following:

Alaska Bible College, P.O. Box 289, Glennallen 99588
Alaska Pacific University, 4101 University Drive, Anchorage 99508
Sheldon Jackson College, 801 Lincoln St., Sitka 99835

University of Alaska Anchorage, 3211 Providence Drive, Anchorage 99508:
Kenai Peninsula College, 34820 College Drive, Soldotna 99669
Kodiak College, 117 Benny Benson Drive, Kodiak 99615
Matanuska-Susitna College, P.O. Box 2899, Palmer 99645

University of Alaska Fairbanks, Fairbanks 99775:
Chukchi Campus, P.O. Box 297, Kotzebue 99752
Kuskokwim Campus, P.O. Box 368, Bethel 99559
Northwest Campus, Pouch 400, Nome 99762
Prince William Sound Community College, P.O. Box 97, Valdez 99686

University of Alaska Southeast, 11120 Glacier Highway, Juneau 99801:
Islands Campus, 1101 Sawmill Creek Boulevard, Sitka 99835
Ketchikan Campus, 7th and Madison, Ketchikan 99901

Many additional schools and institutes in Alaska offer religious, vocational and technical study. For a complete listing of these and other schools, write for the *Directory of Postsecondary Educational Institutions in Alaska,* Alaska Commission on Postsecondary Education, Pouch FP, Juneau 99811.

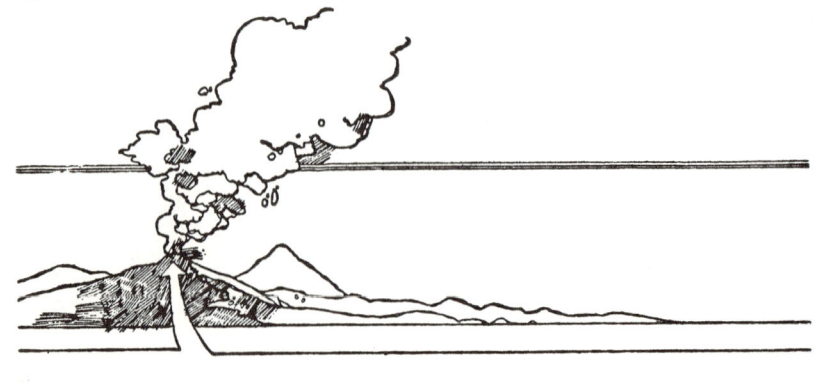

Volcanoes

The state's 10 tallest active volcanic peaks (those which have erupted during the last 10,000 years, based on information from the Smithsonian Institution) are as follows:

Map Key	Elevation
1 Mount Wrangell	14,163
2 Mount Spurr	11,070
3 Redoubt Volcano	10,197
4 Iliamna Volcano	10,016
5 Shishaldin Volcano	9,372
6 Pavlof Volcano	8,242
7 Mount Veniaminof	8,225
8 Isanotski Peaks	8,025
9 Mount Denison	7,600+
10 Mount Griggs	7,600+

Volcanoes on the Aleutian Islands, the Alaska Peninsula and in the Wrangell Mountains are part of the "Ring of Fire" that surrounds the Pacific Ocean basin. There are more than 70 potentially active volcanoes in Alaska, the majority of which have had at least one eruption since 1760, the date of earliest recorded eruptions. Pavlof Volcano is one of the most active of Alaskan volcanoes, having had more than 41 reported eruptions. One recent spectacular eruption of Pavlof in April 1986, sent ash 10 miles high, causing black snow to fall on Cold Bay. The eruption of Augustine Volcano (elev. 4,025 feet) in lower Cook Inlet on March 27, 1986, sent ash 8 miles high and disrupted air traffic in south-central Alaska for several days. Mount Veniaminof on the Alaska Peninsula most recently erupted almost continuously from June 1983 to April 1984. The most violent historical Alaskan eruption and the largest volcanic eruption in the world yet this century occurred over a 60-hour period in June 1912 from Novarupta Volcano. The eruption darkened the sky over much of the Northern Hemisphere for several days, deposited almost a foot of ash on Kodiak, 100 miles away, and filled the Valley of Ten Thousand Smokes, now contained within Katmai National Park, with more than 2.5 cubic miles of ash during its brief but extremely explosive duration.

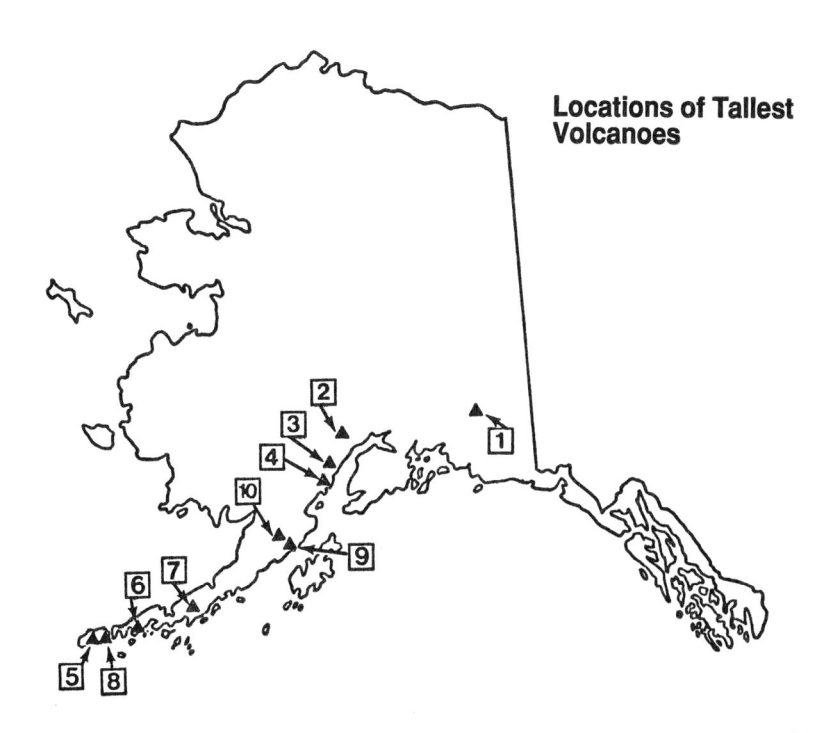

Locations of Tallest Volcanoes

Waves

According to the Alaska Tsunami Warning Center in Palmer, Alaska has had seven tsunamis which have caused fatalities in recorded history, although only for the last three have there been accurate counts of fatalities. These were of local origin and occurred between 1788 and 1964. Tsunamis originating in Alaska have caused all of the fatalities reported on the West Coast and in Alaska, and most of those in Hawaii. The most recent tsunami was in 1964 following the March 27, Good Friday earthquake. That wave completely destroyed three Alaskan villages before reaching Washington, Oregon and California, and continued to cause damage as far away as Hawaii, Chile and Japan. Tsunami is taken from the Japanese words "tsu" meaning harbor and "nami" meaning great wave. Although often erroneously called tidal waves, tides have nothing to do with them. A tidal wave is a predictable rise and fall of the sea caused by the gravitational pull of the sun and moon. In the open ocean, tides rise only a foot or two, but are higher closer to shores, particularly in Alaska. (An interesting phenomenon resulting from Alaska's tides is a tidal bore, or bore tide, a foaming wall of tidal water, caused by a flood tide surging into a constricted inlet.) Generated by earthquakes occurring on or below the sea floor, tsunamis can race across the Pacific Ocean at speeds up to 600 miles per hour. Rarely crossing the Atlantic, they cannot be seen from an airplane or felt in a ship at sea. Traveling across the open ocean, the waves are only a few feet high and can be up to 100 miles from crest to crest. Once they approach shore, however, shallower water causes the waves to grow taller by increasingly restricting their forward motion. Thus, a two-foot wave traveling 500 miles per hour in deep water becomes a 100-foot killer at 30 miles per hour as it nears the shore. The wave action of a tsunami can repeat every 15 to 30 minutes and the danger for a given area is generally not considered over until the area has been free from damaging waves for two hours.

Providing information, and timely warnings, on tsunamigenic earthquakes (those quakes measuring above 7.0 on the Richter scale) is the job of the Alaska Tsunami Warning Center, located in Palmer. Established in 1967, the ATWC now makes loss of life unnecessary for Alaska, Canada, the west coast of the United States and Hawaii, and ensures the avoidance of such tragedy as the April 1, 1946, earthquake at Scotch Cap on Unimak Island, Alaska. Within minutes after the quake struck, waves measuring 100 feet high completely destroyed the lighthouse on the island, killing five people. In less than five hours, the first wave hit Hawaii, killing 159 people. More recently, in March 1985, after an 8.1 quake in Chile, tsunami warnings were able to alert coastal Alaskans in plenty of time to take precautionary measures, though, normally, tsunamis from remote Pacific sources will not be destructive in Alaska.

Two other types of wave action which occur in Alaska are seiches and swashes. A seiche is a long, rhythmic wave in a closed or partially closed body of water. Caused by earthquakes, winds, tidal currents or atmospheric pressure, the motion of a seiche resembles the back and forth movement of a tipped bowl of water. The water moves only up and down, and can remain active from a few minutes to several hours. The highest recorded wave in Alaska, 1,740 feet, was the result of a seiche that took place in Lituya Bay on July 9, 1958. This unusually high wave was due to an earthquake-induced landslide that cleared trees from the opposite side of the bay. A swash, while sometimes confused with a seiche, is a more turbulent water action. It has no rhythmic wave motion and occurs in an area covered by shallow sea water.

Whales and Whaling

Fifteen species of both toothed and baleen whales are found in Alaskan waters. Baleen refers to the hundreds of strips of flexible bonelike material that hangs from the gum of the upper jaw. The strips are fringed and act as strainers that capture krill, tiny shrimplike organisms, upon which the whales feed. Once the baleen fills with krill, whales force water back out through the sides of their mouth, swallowing the food left behind.

Baleen whale cows are usually larger than bulls.

Baleen whales that inhabit Alaskan waters include blue, bowhead, northern right, fin or finback, humpback, sei, minke or little piked and gray. Toothed whales include sperm, beluga, killer, pilot, beaked (three species), dolphins (two species) and porpoises (two species). Rarely encountered in Alaskan waters is another toothed whale, the narwhal, a full-time resident of the Arctic. Saint Lawrence Islanders call narwhales *bousucktugutalik*, or "beluga with tusk" due to a tusk that grows from the left side of the upper jaw on bulls only. Spiraling in a left-hand direction, the tusk can reach lengths of seven to eight feet on an adult.

A few facts on three of the whales indigenous to Alaska are interesting to note. The blue whale has the distinction of being the world's largest animal, reaching lengths of 100 feet, weighing up to 200 tons and possessing a girth up to 45 feet. It is possible for an adult elephant to stand on the floor of a blue whale's mouth without touching the whale's upper jawbone. A blue whale's tongue alone can weigh four tons, its heart 1,000 pounds and its stomach can hold up to two tons of food. In 1948, a factory ship recorded taking an 89-foot blue with a liver weighing 1,000 pounds which produced 133 barrels of oil. While nursing, a blue whale cow provides 130 gallons of milk a day in 40 feedings. This allows the calf a weight gain of 8.5 pounds per hour.

The fin, or finback, is the second largest of the world's whale species, measuring up to 80 feet in length and weighing 70 tons. Hanging up to three feet from the upper jaw are 375 plates of baleen. The blow on a fin whale is 13 to 20 feet high, usually occurring once per minute between dives that vary from 2 to 28 minutes. Among the fastest swimmers of the large whales, fins can cruise at 5 or 6 knots with bursts to 20 knots when alarmed and can dive to depths of 755 feet.

The sperm whale's distinguishing feature is a huge head — one fourth to one third of the animal's total length depending upon sex (60 feet for males, 30 feet for females). The boxlike head can contain three to four tons of spermaceti, which is used as a heat resistant, high quality industrial lubricant. The deepest diving of the whales, sperm whales have been recorded at depths of 8,200 feet and once at a depth of almost two miles. They can remain submerged for 30 to 60 minutes. Valued also for their 18 to 25 ivory teeth, which measure 3 to 8 inches at sexual maturity, a sperm whale grasps prey with its teeth, then swallows it whole if possible. Its favored food is squid, cuttlefish, octopus and occasionally shark. Sperm whales reach a maximum age of 77.

WHALING

Bowhead whales have been protected from commercial whaling by the Convention for the Regulation of Whaling of 1931, the International Convention for the Regulation of Whaling of 1947, the Marine Mammal Protection Act of 1972, the Endangered Species Act of 1973 and the Convention of International Trade in Endangered Species of Wild Fauna and Flora.

Commercial whaling for gray whales has been banned by the International Convention for the Regulation of Whaling since 1947. These conventions and acts have, however, allowed for a subsistence harvest by Alaska Indians, Aleuts and Eskimos.

Since 1978, the International Whaling Commission has regulated the take of bowheads by establishing an annual catch limit for Alaska Eskimos. Also in 1978, the IWC reclassified the eastern stock of gray whales from a protected species to a sustained management stock with an annual catch limit of about 179 whales, based on the average known removals during the period 1968-77. The entire catch limit has been reserved for taking by Natives or by member governments on behalf of Natives. Other species of large baleen whales, such as minke and fin whales, are occasionally taken by Alaska Eskimos for food. The only toothed whale taken by Eskimos is the beluga and its harvest is managed by the state.

According to the National Marine Mammal Laboratory and the Alaska Department of Fish and Game, harvest figures for the years 1978-1988 (most current information available) are as follows:

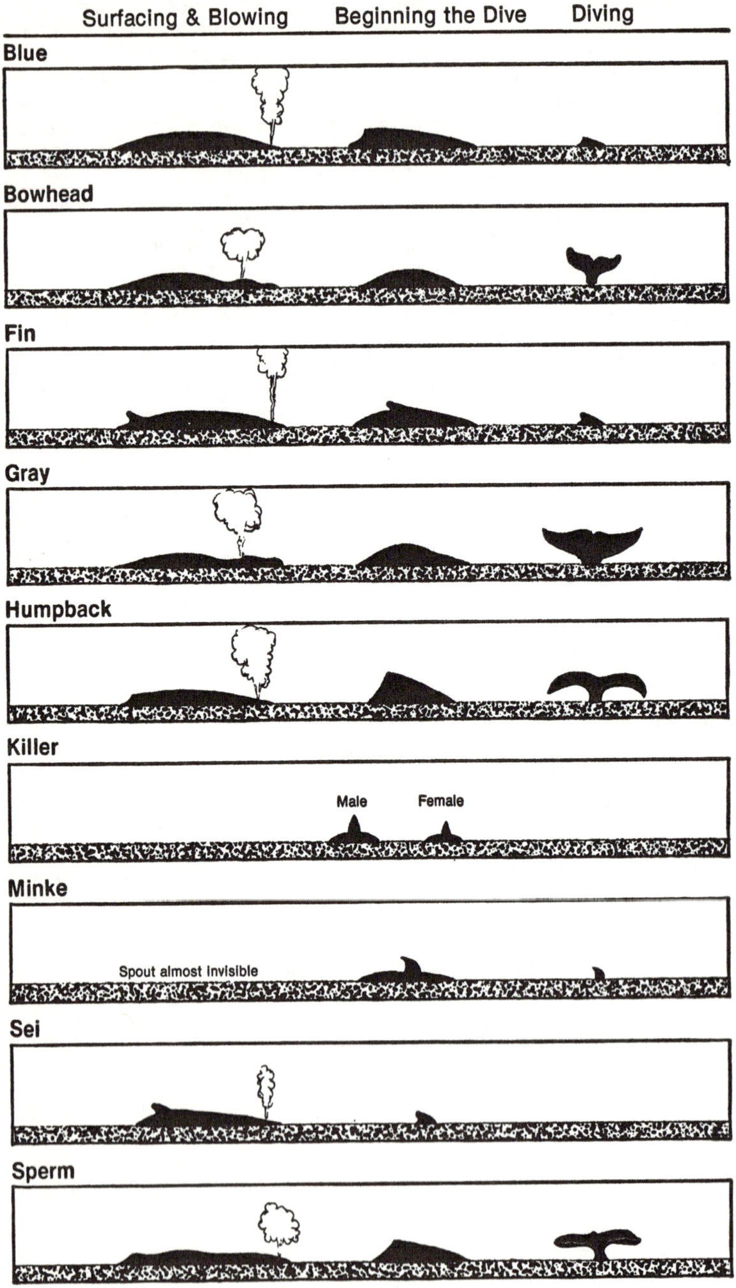

	Surfacing & Blowing	Beginning the Dive	Diving

Blue

Bowhead

Fin

Gray

Humpback

Killer — Male, Female

Minke — Spout almost invisible

Sei

Sperm

190

Year	Beluga	Gray	Minke
1979	138	3	2
1980	243-255*	3	1
1981	179-231*	NR	1
1982	307-354*	4	3
1983	226-236*	2	NR
1984	170*	NR	NR
1985	152-234*	1*	2*
1986	40-42*	NR	NR
1987	NA	NR	NR
1988	NA	NR	NR

*Approximate figures
NR= none reported
NA=not available

Wild Flowers

Wild flowers in Alaska are seldom gaudy; they are usually rather small and delicate. More than 1,500 plant species occur in the state, including trees, shrubs, ferns, grasses and sedges, as well as flowering plants.

Alpine regions are particularly rich in flora and some of the alpine species are rare. Anywhere there is tundra there is apt to be a bountiful population of flowers. The Steese Highway (Eagle Summit), Richardson Highway (Thompson Pass), Denali Highway (Maclaren Summit), Denali National Park and Preserve (Polychrome Pass), Seward Highway (Turnagain Pass), Glenn Highway just north of Anchorage (Eklutna Flats) and a locale near Wasilla (Hatcher Pass) are wonderful wildflower-viewing spots. These are all readily accessible by car. Less easily accessible floral Edens are some of the Aleutian Islands, Point Hope, Anvil Mountain and the Nome-Teller Road (both near Nome), Pribilof Islands and other remote areas.

Alaska's official flower, the forget-me-not *(Myosotis alpestris)*, is a delicate little beauty found throughout much of the state in alpine meadows and along streams. Growing to 18 inches tall, forget-me-nots are recognized by their bright blue petals surrounding a yellow "eye." A northern "cousin," the Arctic forget-me-not (*Eritrichium aretioides*), grows in sandy soil on the tundra, or in the mountains, and reaches only 4 inches in height.

Related reading: *The Alaska-Yukon Wild Flowers Guide,* edited by Helen A. White and Maxcine Williams; drawings by Virginia Howie. 218 pages, $16.95. See ALASKA NORTHWEST LIBRARY in the back of the book.

Winds

Winds abound in Alaska, from the eastern fringes of Southeast to the western islands of the Aleutian Chain, where some of the state's windiest weather has been recorded. Overall, the causes are the same as elsewhere, incorporating planet rotation and the tendency of the atmosphere to equalize the difference between high and low pressure fronts (*see also* Climate). A few winds occur often and significantly enough to be given names: chinook, taku and williwaw.

CHINOOK

Old-timers describe chinook winds as unseasonably warm winds that can cause thaw in the middle of winter. What they also cause are power outages and property damage, especially in the Anchorage bowl, where in recent years hundreds of homes have sprung up on the Chugach Mountain hillsides over which the chinook winds howl. One such wind occurred on April Fool's Day, 1980, causing $25 million in property damage and nominating the city as a disaster area. Parts of Anchorage were without power for 60 hours.

Until recently it was not possible to predict the coming of a chinook wind. Today, however, Anchorage meteorologists can tell if the winds are gathering, when they will arrive and their relative strength. It was discerned that such a warm wind could only originate in Prince William Sound and that its speed had to be at least 55 miles per hour or faster just to cross the 3,500-foot Chugach Mountains. Other factors that need to be present are a storm near Bethel and relatively stable air over Anchorage. Meteorologists predict the coming of chinook winds 55 percent of the time.

TAKU

Taku winds are the sudden, fierce gales that sweep down from the icecap behind Juneau and Douglas, and plague residents there. Takus are shivering cold winds capable of reaching 100 miles per hour. They have been known to send a two-by-four timber flying through the wall of a frame house.

WILLIWAWS

Williwaws are sudden gusts of wind that can reach 113 miles per hour after the wind "builds up" on one side of a mountain and suddenly spills over into what may appear to be a relatively protected area. Williwaws are considered the bane of Alaska mariners. The term was originally applied to a strong wind in the Strait of Magellan.

World Eskimo-Indian Olympics

An audience of thousands watches the annual spectacle of several hundred Native athletes from Alaska competing in the World Eskimo-Indian Olympics in Fairbanks. Held over four days the second to last weekend in July, the self-supporting games draw participants from all of Alaska's Native populations (Eskimo, Aleut, Athabascan, Tlingit, Haida and Tsimshian). Canadian Eskimos are invited to participate each year in the WEIO, but funding problems have prohibited their coming since 1981.

Spectators thrill to the sight of such feats as the knuckle hop and the ear-weight competition. Other traditional Native sports and competitions include the greased pole walk, fish cutting, stick pull, Indian-Eskimo dancing, men's and women's blanket toss, and the spectacular two-foot and one-foot high kicks. Each year the judges choose a Native queen to reign over the four-day Olympics. She reigns through the year, making several appearances throughout the state, representing the WEIO. The judges also pick the prettiest baby. Some of the more boisterous games include the lively white men/Native women tug of war and the muktuk eating contest.

The games will be held on Wednesday, Thursday, Friday and Saturday evenings at the Big Dipper Recreation Center in Fairbanks July 25-28, 1990. Advance tickets may be purchased from the World Eskimo-Indian Olympics Committee, P.O. Box 2433, Fairbanks 99707.

Yearly Highlights — 1989

Following is a collection of the more significant news events of the year just past . . . the high spots for a record of the times. THE ALASKA ALMANAC® wishes to credit the *Anchorage Daily News* as the primary source of information for Yearly Highlights—1989.

RECORD-BREAKING COLD SPELL COVERS ALASKA

Cold weather in Alaska doesn't usually raise eyebrows, but January's cold snap did just that. Across the state, Alaskans watched in amazement as temperatures fell, fell some more and then stayed where they fell. The official low recorded was minus 76 degrees; however, lower temperatures than that were reported at various locations within the Interior.

Caused by a massive high pressure system, the cold settled in for three weeks. It seemed much longer, though, due to temperatures dropping on the front end of the high pressure system and very slowly rising on the tail end.

The weather was also responsible for barometric pressure so high that aviation operations were curtailed or suspended altogether. This resulted in stranding travelers up to two weeks if they happened to be traveling via air taxis.

Alaska's weather was so severe that national news programs devoted major coverage to it throughout its duration. For Alaskans, the "Winter of '89" will not soon be forgotten.

SLED DOG RACES BIG ON FIRSTS

February's World Championship Sled Dog Race, held in Anchorage during Fur Rendezvous, scored two firsts in its history in 1989. It was the first time that a woman, Roxy Wright-Champaine, won, and the first time the purse reached $50,000.

Wright-Champaine went on to become the first woman to win the Fairbanks North American Sled Dog Race one month later. She also broke the record for the 30-mile final leg of that race by almost three minutes. All in all, a good year for Roxy!

STATE PARK VOLUNTEERS GROW IN NUMBERS

Requests from 45 states and 6 foreign countries came in for summer volunteer positions with Alaska state parks in 1989. In an effort to work around employee cuts, Neil Johannsen, director of Alaska's 118 parks that cover 3 million acres, began recruiting volunteers five years ago. Since then, the numbers have grown, recruiting has turned into answering requests and it has become competitive to volunteer for state park jobs. As a result, the summer of 1988 saw over 200,000 hours of work done by volunteers — more than by paid staff. Additionally, repeat volunteers have begun showing up, people who can slip right into the position and get to work. According to Johannsen, the parks will gain approximately $500,000 worth of services from volunteers in 1989 — people who have become "a major element in our ability to serve."

AND THE RUSSIAN CAME

For eight days, February 20-27, Alaska was treated to the company and talents of 90 visiting Soviets. Everything from trade fairs, receptions and journalism panel discussions to rock concerts, adopt-a-Soviet programs and student exchanges took place. The days and nights were crammed full of activities for both the Russians and Alaskans.

In the first of what is hoped will be many more such visits, the possibility for improved relations between the two countries became more reality than dream in 1989. If nothing else, a lot of talking took place, and that's a good start to improving anything.

The Soviets came with three objectives in mind: to open trade contacts, improve diplomatic efforts, and increase cultural and personal relations. While the trade and diplomatic areas may not have progressed beyond talking into anything more concrete, there was no doubt that human relations soared. How could they not when, for instance, elementary schoolchildren got personal visits from the delegates (who answered all of their questions), or when Anchorage residents extended a welcoming handshake whenever they saw the Soviets, and Anchorage homes were opened as alternatives to hotels. Goodwill overflowed.

Traveling was done by Alaskans, too. Three teachers and three schoolchildren from Soldotna left for a visit to Magadan, USSR, the same day the Soviet delegation came to Anchorage with students and teachers from Magadan. The two cities' schools had been corresponding since 1988, and as part of the new cultural awareness program, a student-teacher exchange took place — a visit that won't soon be forgotten by either city.

When it was all over, friendship, goodwill and future promise prevailed. Bridges had been built where none had been before.

BIKERS RIDE THE IDITAROD TRAIL

Four men with mountain bikes rode the Iditarod Trail from Anchorage to Nome in March. The bikers began their trek on March 3rd, the day before the start of the Iditarod Sled Dog Race, and finished on March 25th, 10 days after winner Joe Runyan and his team crossed the finish line. The men followed the same 1,100-mile trail the mushers take.

EARTHQUAKE ANNIVERSARY

Twenty-five years have passed since the 1964 Good Friday earthquake. While a rather somber anniversary for Anchorage, it does allow a look back at the progress made since March 27, 1964.

Six months after the devastation of Black Friday's disaster, Anchorage's business and political leaders decided to rebuild downtown, the area hardest hit by the 9.2 quake. Progress since then has been only up and out — a positive attitude on the one hand, and a problem on the other given the possibility of another quake. The shocks that hit Anchorage at 5:36 P.M. caused $86 million in damages and the loss of only nine lives — timing was a critical factor. A quake of equal magnitude now would cause an estimated $405.8 million in damages, and untold loss of lives depending on what time of day it struck. But Anchorage, and Alaska for that matter, has never been the type of community to wallow in pessimism over what could be. Optimism and energy are more the hallmarks of this state, and those are the traits that were dominant in the months following the quake and prevail to this day. While Anchorage residents quietly recognized the anniversary of the Black Friday disaster, they also paid tribute to the strength and resilience of their city.

MUSHER RESCUED DURING IDITAROD RACE

For some mushers the 1989 Iditarod Sled Dog Race meant more than winning, or even placing in the top 20 money, when rookie musher Mike Madden of North Pole ran into trouble. Madden was found lying in the snow beside his sled, semi-conscious and delirious, about 30 miles from the checkpoint town of Iditarod by fellow musher Jamie Nelson. Nelson had just bundled Madden into a sleeping bag when four other mushers — Jerry Austin, Mitch Brazin, Kathy Halverson and Lynwood Fiedler — stopped to render help. For nearly 18 hours the five mushers stayed with Madden until a helicopter with a doctor on board arrived.

Evacuated to Humana Hospital in Anchorage, Madden was found to be poisoned with salmonella, contaminated dog food being the probable cause. Doctors felt that without the assistance from the five who stopped to help, Madden may not have survived.

The mushers gave up valuable race time but felt they had gained far more than they lost. Referring to the historic 1925 life-saving diphtheria serum run that followed the Iditarod Trail, Fiedler said, "...that's what this race is supposed to be all about, people with dog teams helping other people."

OIL SPILL LARGEST IN U.S. HISTORY

March 24, 1989, will go down in Alaska's history as a grim day indeed. Shortly after midnight on that day, the *Exxon Valdez* tanker ran aground on Bligh Reef, resulting in the largest crude oil spill ever in the U.S.

The spill happened about 25 miles from the marine terminal in Valdez that the tanker had left the night before. Mechanical failure of the ship was ruled out immediately, and attention has since focused on human error. The tanker was under the command of Captain Joe Hazelwood at the time of the 11-million-gallon spill.

Containment of the rapidly spreading oil caused the biggest problems. By morning light on the 24th, the oil was already covering an area five miles long and one mile wide, and by sundown the effected area was eight miles long and four miles wide. As the oil continued to spread, the problems from it became more apparent, with loss of wildlife and the livelihood of commercial fishermen only two of many serious consequences to consider. According to the state Department of Environmental Conservation, damage will be widespread and long-lasting.

Future months will allow better assessments of both the destruction from the spill and the overall effects of the cleanup. Changes, if any, for the oil industry in Alaska remain to be seen.

BERING BRIDGE EXPEDITION REACHES NOME

Traveling only by dogsled and skis, the Bering Bridge Expedition reached the end of their 61-day trip on May 4, 1989. The 12-member U.S.-Soviet team began their trek in mid-March in the eastern Siberian town of Anadyr, crossed the Bering Strait and concluded their trip 1,000 miles later in Nome. Original plans had called for the group to continue on to Kotzebue, but spring snow conditions made that impossible.

This expedition was the first of several joint ventures between the U.S. and Russia, and resulted in the signing of a protocol calling for the renewal of visits between Soviet and Alaska Natives. The document was signed in April on Little Diomede Island by Gov. Steve Cowper and V.I. Kobets, the Russian equivalent of a governor from the Magadan region.

DRILLING IN THE CHUKCHI SEA

Shell Western E&P Inc. received government clearance in May to begin drilling the first of several wildcat wells in the Chukchi Sea. Drilling is scheduled to begin about July 1, 1989, in what some geologists have referred to as "the best offshore prospects in the world." Shell plans to drill one to two wells per year over the next four years, and has 16 possible drill sites in mind. The Chukchi Sea is north of Point Barrow, separating Alaska and the Soviet Union at their farthest north points.

ANOTHER GRAY WHALE STUCK IN ALASKA WATERS

Those California gray whales are at it again! In October 1988, Alaska received world-wide help with two grays that needed rescuing from the freezing waters off Point Barrow. In May 1989 another gray needed rescuing when it found its way into the fishing net of two Chignik subsistence salmon fishermen. By cutting the net, the gray was able to get free and was last seen heading toward the ocean. According to the fishermen, the net was a total loss, but the whale didn't care; he only wanted out.

ICE CLASSIC COMES TO THE BERING STRAIT

Alaska and the Soviets are teaming up again. This time, though, the results will produce not only goodwill, but dollars and rubles as well, as both sides play host to the first annual Alaska-Soviet Ice Classic in 1990. Patterned after Alaska's famed Nenana Ice Classic, the tripod — used to determine when the ice breaks — will be erected on the frozen Bering Strait between Big and Little Diomede islands. Cash winners will be drawn from both sides of the international date line, with extra proceeds going toward furthering U.S.-Soviet cultural exchanges. The ice usually breaks between mid-May and early June, with the $2 tickets going on sale in April.

KAYAKERS TAKE TO THE WATERS BETWEEN ALASKA AND USSR

In June, a kayaking expedition planned to cross the Bering Strait between Nome and the Siberian coastal town of Provideniya. The group consisted of six Alaskans and two or three Soviets who will make the 400-mile trip beginning in Nome. Plans for the expedition were formalized in February 1989 between Alaskan organizer Doug Van Etten and Soviet Minister Gennady Alfrenko, director of the Foundation for Social Innovation.

OIL SPILL PROMPTS DELAY IN DRILLING PROJECTS

Governor Steve Cowper has requested that several oil drilling projects scheduled for summer 1989 be put on the back burner for a while. This action was prompted by the March 24th oil spill in

Prince William Sound caused by the *Exxon Valdez* tanker running aground. According to Cowper, the spill showed that oil companies are not prepared to respond adequately to major oil disasters.

Several companies will be affected should Cowper's request be granted by the federal government. Shell Western E&P Inc. had planned to begin drilling the first of several wildcat wells in the Chukchi Sea, as had Amoco Production Co. in the Beaufort Sea and ARCO Alaska Inc. in Camden Bay. While the federal government is deciding this matter, the state is going over contingency plans to insure they will work as well in actuality as they do on paper.

100,000-YEAR-OLD BONE FOUND

The lower jawbone of a mastodon that lived 100,000 years ago was uncovered in June 1989. Found by dredge operators at a sand and gravel pit located just outside of Fairbanks, the 25-pound bone is believed to have come from a 20-year-old female. The upper jawbone of another mastodon was found last year in about the same location. Both pieces have been given to the University of Alaska, Fairbanks.

SOVIET BUSINESSPEOPLE COME TO TOWN

Another delegation of Soviets hit Anchorage in June. About 60 people, representing several professions, worked on developing the business contacts made earlier in 1989 when the first group of Russians came to Alaska.

Unlike February's visit, this one will not focus on social events, but will hone in on the ideas coming from that first visit. If all goes according to plan, this will be the last large group of Soviets to head this way. Instead, groups will be smaller and more focused on specific ideas. This trip is to lay the groundwork for those future trips.

SOVIETS GRANTED ASYLUM

Two Moscow journalists who defected in April 1989 were granted asylum by the U.S. government.

The defection took place in June on Little Diomede Island during a goodwill mission celebrating closer relations between Alaska and the Soviet Far East. The journalists, Alexander Genkin and Anatoly Tkachenko, forged papers to gain seats on the Diomede delegation, then sought out a National Guard scout and requested asylum.

Stating that they defected because of restrictions governing the press, Genkin and Tkachenko are the first Soviets to defect in Alaska in the past 20 years. According to Washington, D.C., 43 Soviet citizens requested asylum during the 1988-89 fiscal year.

FAIRBANKSANS MAKE MONEY ON THEIR PENNIES

Denali State Bank President Gary Roth put out a call for pennies in spring 1989, and 260,000 of them came flowing in, overwhelming the tellers and president alike.

Seems the bank has two fast-food restaurants that need lots of pennies every day. But to ship and insure a $50 bag of pennies from the federal reserve costs $18, a hefty 36 percent cost. Roth thought an appeal to the public might help and threw in a cash reward to boot — a 20 percent bonus for loose pennies, 25 percent if rolled. That meant a person could make $50 on $200 worth of rolled pennies.

Copper coins came in by the thousands, and in spite of the bonuses offered, the Fairbanks bank made money. For the $2,600 collected in pennies, the bank paid $3,198 — federal reserve pennies would have cost them $3,536.

ANCHORAGE LOSES OLYMPIC BID

An hour's debate was all it took for the U.S. Olympic Committee to choose Salt Lake City over Anchorage to host the 1998 Winter Olympic Games. Anchorage's third attempt at getting the games in 1989 was undone by Salt Lake's more central location and their ability to begin building a training center immediately.

Anchorage Olympic Committee members, as well as athletes and coaches, feel that despite the lost bid, Anchorage came to the forefront with an excellent reputation as a world-class winter sports venue. But five years and $6.5 million is enough time and money spent for now — the AOC will not try to bring the games back to Alaska anytime soon.

ALASKA NORTHWEST LIBRARY

Many North Country books are suggested as related reading throughout THE ALASKA ALMANAC®. Following is our Alaska Northwest Library — North Country books that are available in bookstores or direct from the publisher, P.O. Box 3007, Bothell, WA 98041-3007 or call toll free 1-800-331-3510. Write for our free book catalog. Mail orders require a postage and handling fee of $1.50 fourth class or $3.50 first class per book.

ALASKA: A Pictorial Geography — A full-color photographic tour of the last frontier. 64 pp., 8-1/2 x 11, $4.95 ($6.30 Canadian).

The Alaska Airlines Story — A book of adventure and aviation history. 224 pp., 8-1/2 x 11, $12.95 ($16.45 Canadian)

THE ALASKA ALMANAC®, Facts About Alaska — Annual collection of facts about Alaska, from agriculture to williwaws, with illustrations. 203 pp., 5-3/8 x 8-3/8, $6.95 ($8.95 Canadian)

Alaska Bear Tales — Encounters between bears and humans. 318 pp., 5-3/8 x 8-3/8, $10.95 ($13.90 Canadian)

Alaska Blues: A Fisherman's Journal — True account of commercial fishing in southeastern Alaska waters with 198 black-and-white photos. 236 pp., 8-3/8 x 10-3/8, cloth, $14.95 ($18.95 Canadian)

Alaska Game Trails With a Master Guide — Hunt with Master Guide Hal Waugh. 310 pp., 5-3/8 x 8-3/8, $8.95 ($11.35 Canadian)

The ALASKA JOURNAL®: A 1986 Collection — History and arts of the north marking the 100th anniversary of the publication of Hubert How Bancroft's History of Alaska 1730-1885. Limited edition, 296 pp., 8-1/2 x 11, cloth, $24.95 ($31.70 Canadian)

Alaska Sourdough — Handwritten recipes "by a real Alaskan." 190 pp., 7-3/8 x 9, $7.95 ($10.10 Canadian)

Alaska Wild Berry Guide and Cookbook — How to find and identify edible wild berries, and how to cook them. Line drawings and color photos. 216 pp., 6 x 9, $14.95 ($18.95 Canadian)

The ALASKA WILDERNESS MILEPOST®, 1990 Edition — Where the Roads End . . . The Real Alaska Begins. A guide to 250 remote towns and villages. 416 pp., 6 x 9, $14.95 ($18.95 Canadian)

The Alaskan Bird Sketches of Olaus Murie — With excerpts from his field notes, compiled and edited by Margaret E. Murie. 64 pp., 11 x 9, $11.95 ($15.15 Canadian)

The Alaskan Camp Cook — Mouth-watering recipes for wild foods. 88 pp., 6 x 9, $4.95 ($6.30 Canadian)

Alaskan Igloo Tales — Arctic oral history written down in the early twentieth century, with illustrations. 139 pp., 10 x 7, $12.95 ($16.45 Canadian)

Alaskan Mushroom Hunters Guide — Guidebook of 101 species of mushrooms found in Alaska, with illustrations and keys. 286 pp., 5-1/2 x 8-1/4, $19.95 ($25.35 Canadian)

Alaska's Saltwater Fishes — A field guide designed for quick identification of 365 species of saltwater fishes. 384 pp., 6 x 9, $19.95 ($25.35 Canadian)

Alaska's Wilderness Medicines — Use of trees, flowers and shrubs for medicinal and other purposes. 111 pp., 6 x 9, $9.95 ($12.65 Canadian)

The Alaska-Yukon Wild Flowers Guide — Large color photos and detailed drawings of 160 species. 218 pp., 5-3/8 x 8-3/8, $16.95 ($21.35 Canadian)

Baidarka — A detailed book on kayaks, with illustrations spanning 245 years. 212 pp., 11 x 8-1/2, $24.95 ($31.70 Canadian)

E.T. Barnette: The Strange Story of the Man Who Founded Fairbanks — Colorful history from gold rush days. 176 pp., 5-1/2 x 8-1/2, $7.95 ($10.10 Canadian)

Frank Barr, Bush Pilot — Story of a bush pilot in Alaska and the Yukon. 116 pp., 5-3/8 x 8-3/8, $7.95 ($10.10 Canadian)

Bits and Pieces of Alaskan History, Volume I, 1935-1959, 208 pp., and Volume II, 1960-1974, 216 pp., 11 x 14, $14.95 each volume ($18.95 Canadian)

Martha Black — The story of Martha Black from the Dawson Gold Fields to the halls of Parliament. 166 pp., 5-3/8 x 8-3/8, $9.95 ($12.65 Canadian)

Building the Alaska Log Home — Comprehensive book for the person who wants to build with logs. 178 pp., 8-1/2 x 11, $19.95 ($25.35 Canadian)

Capture of Attu — The Aleutian campaign of World War II. 80 pp., 8-1/2 x 11, $6.95 ($8.85 Canadian)

Chilkoot Pass: The Most Famous Trail in the North — Updated in 1983; a popular guide for hikers and history buffs. 214 pp., 5-3/8 x 8-3/8, $9.95 ($12.65 Canadian)

Cooking Alaskan — Hundreds of time-tested recipes including a section on sourdough. 500 pp., 8-1/2 x 11, $16.95 ($21.35 Canadian)

Dale De Armond: A First Book Collection of Her Prints — Special color sampler featuring 63 of the Juneau artist's work. 80 pp., 8-1/2 x 11, $14.95 ($18.95 Canadian)

Destination Washington — An insider's guide to the state of Washington. 196 pp., 8-3/8 x 10-3/4, $4.95 ($6.30 Canadian)

Discovering Wild Plants: Alaska, Western Canada, The Northwest — By Janice Schofield. Facts, full-color pictures and black-and-white illustrations detailing more than 130 plants. 350 pp., 8-3/8 x 10-7/8, cloth, $34.95 ($43.95 Canadian)

An Expedition to the Copper, Tanana and Koyukuk Rivers in 1885 — Adventures of Lt. Allen as he explored and mapped thousands of miles of Alaska's Interior. 96 pp., 8-1/2 x 11, $7.95 ($10.10 Canadian)

Eye of the Changer — This excellent children's book is a Northwest Indian tale. 64 pp., 8-1/2 x 11, $9.95 ($12.65 Canadian)

Fisheries of the North Pacific — Completely revised edition of the 1974 classic, with the latest on gear, processing and vessels. 432 pp., 8-3/8 x 10-3/8, $24.95 ($31.70 Canadian)

Fruits and Berries of the Pacific Northwest — Colorful story of all the varieties, the growers and the industry. 101 pp., 8-3/8 x 10 7/8, $24.95 ($31.70 Canadian)

The Gold Hustlers — Wheeling and dealing in the Klondike gold fields. 340 pp., 5-3/8 x 8-3/8, $7.95 ($10.10 Canadian)

A Guide to the Birds of Alaska — Updated and expanded; the perfect guide to species found in the 49th state. 320 pp., 6 x 9, $19.95 ($25.35 Canadian)

A Guide to the Queen Charlotte Islands — This 1989-90 revised edition provides all the maps and information needed when visiting these rugged islands. 90 pp., 5-3/8 x 8-3/8, $9.95 ($12.65 Canadian)

Handloggers — A story of adventure and romance. 250 pp., 5-1/2 x 8-1/4, $9.95 ($12.65 Canadian)

Heroes and Heroines in Tlingit-Haida Legend — Analogies between Southeast Alaska Indian legends and Greek and Roman mythology. Illustrated. 120 pp., 6 x 9, $14.95 ($18.95 Canadian)

Hibrow Cow: Even MORE Alaskan Recipes and Stories — By former Alaska State Trooper Gordon Nelson, recipes and humorous tales in Nelson's fourth cookbook. 168 pp., 7-5/16 x 9, $9.95 ($12.65 Canadian)

How to Build An Oil Barrel Stove — Practical instructions; illustrated. 24 pp., 8-1/2 x 11, $1.95 ($2.55 Canadian)

I Am Eskimo — Documentary of Eskimo life at the turn of the century, with illustrations. 86 pp., 7-3/4 x 9-1/8, $9.95 ($12.65 Canadian)

I Married A Fisherman — Warm, human story of a successful partnership in a commercial salmon-trolling enterprise in Southeast. 114 pp., 5-3/8 x 8-3/8, $7.95 ($10.10 Canadian)

Icebound in the Siberian Arctic — For ship, wireless and aircraft buffs. 164 pp., 5-3/8 x 8-3/8, $4.95 ($6.30 Canadian)

In Search of Gold — A stampeder follows the gold from the Yukon to Nome in 1898-99. 314 pp., 5-3/8 x 8-3/8, $9.95 ($12.65 Canadian)

Interior Alaska: A Journey Through Time — Explores the natural environment of interior Alaska and the evolution of its human lifeways. 260 pp., 6 x 9, $9.95 ($12.65 Canadian)

Island — Recounts a family's dream of settling on a remote island made a reality. 128 pp., 5-3/8 8-3/8, $9.95 ($12.65 Canadian)

The Islands of Hawaii: E Komo Mai! — A complete tour through the Hawaiian

Islands. 152 pp., 8-3/8 x 10-3/4, $6.95 ($8.85 Canadian)

Juneau: A Book of Woodcuts — Handsome prints by Dale De Armond; a whimsical history of Juneau. 50 pp., 8 x 10, slipcased, $12.95 ($16.45 Canadian)

Kendlers': The Story of a Pioneer Alaska Juneau Dairy — A half-century of a young German girl's love affair with Alaska. 168 pp., 5-3/8 x 8-3/8, $7.95 ($10.10 Canadian)

Land of Fur and Gold — The story of a loved and respected man, Raymond Thompson. 208 pp., 5-3/8 x 8-3/8, $5.95 (7.55 Canadian)

Land of the Fireweed — The story of a young woman who helped build the Alaska Highway. 200 pp., 5-3/8 x 8-3/8, $7.95 ($10.10 Canadian)

Land of the Ocean Mists — A look at the wild ocean coast west of Glacier Bay. 224 pp., 8-3/8 x 10-3/8, $7.95 ($10.10 Canadian)

The Lost Patrol — First book to unravel the tragedy of the Mounted Police patrol that perished in the winter of 1910-11 in the Northwest Territories. 138 pp., 5-3/8 x 8-3/8, $7.95 ($10.10 Canadian)

Lowbush Moose (And Other Alaskan Recipes) — A former Alaska State trooper adds special flavor to mouthwatering family recipes by telling the stories behind them. 198 pp., 7-3/8 x 9, $9.95 ($12.65 Canadian)

The MILEPOST® All-the-North Travel Guide® 1990 edition — All travel routes in western Canada and Alaska with photos and detailed maps. 530 pp., 8-3/8 x 10-3/8, $14.95 ($18.95 Canadian)

Nome Nuggets — A soldier of fortune's account of the 1900 Nome gold rush. 64 pp., 8-1/2 x 11, $5.95 ($7.55 Canadian)

NORTHWEST MILEPOSTS® — A complete guide to Washington, Oregon, Idaho, western Montana and southwestern Canada. 496 pp., 8 x 11, $14.95 ($18.95 Canadian)

Northwest Sportsman Almanac — Coffee-table beautiful, tackle-box informative guide to outdoor recreation. 291 pp., 8-3/8 x 10-7/8, cloth, $34.95 ($43.95 Canadian)

The Norwegian — Warm, witty and incredible story of a charming gold seeker. 128 pp., 5-3/8 x 8-3/8, $6.95 ($8.85 Canadian)

OhioPass — Complete guide for travelers going to Ohio. 96 pp., 8-3/8 x 10-3/4, $4.95 ($6.50 Canadian)

Once Upon an Eskimo Time — A one-year (1868) vignette in the 121-year life of an Eskimo woman. 185 pp., 5-3/8 x 8-3/8, $9.95 ($12.65 Canadian)

101 Simple Seafood Recipes — How to select, prepare and preserve seafood, plus some general things to know about them. 156 pp., 5-3/8 x 8-3/8, $6.95 ($8.85 Canadian)

Our Arctic Year — A young couple's year in the wilds of the Brooks Range, color photos. 160 pp., 11 x 8-1/2, $12.95 ($16.45 Canadian)

Pacific Halibut: The Resource and The Fishery — An impressive book on the history of this fish and fishery. 288 pp., 8-1/2 x 11; paper $19.95 ($25.35 Canadian), cloth $24.95 ($31.70 Canadian)

Pacific Northwest Gardener's Almanac — A master gardener tells what, where and how to grow vegetables and herbs; color photos. 162 pp., 8-3/8 x 10-7/8, $14.95 ($18.95 Canadian)

Pacific Troller: Life on the Northwest Fishing Grounds — A close-up of the fisherman's life, the frustrations, the humor, the excitement. 143 pp., 5-3/8 x 8-3/8, $5.95 ($7.55 Canadian)

Plant Lore of an Alaskan Island — Nutritional value, medicinal uses and recipes for eighty plants, with glimpses of Native and Russian heritage. 210 pp., 7-3/8 x 9, $9.95 ($12.65 Canadian)

Raven: A Collection of Woodcuts — De Armond woodcuts, Tlingit tales of Raven; signed, numbered, limited edition. 132 pp., 12 x 12, $100 ($127 Canadian)

Raven — Small format edition of Dale De Armond's woodcuts. 80 pp., 8-3/8 x 10-3/8, $13.95 ($17.75 Canadian)

Rie Munoz, Alaskan Artist — An illustrated selection of her work. A high-quality collection of limited edition prints from one of Alaska's foremost artists. 80 pp., 8-1/2 x 11, $19.95 ($25.35 Canadian)

River Rafting in Canada — Presents 22

river-rafting adventures in Canada, with information on outfitters for each trip. 110 pp., 11 x 8, $14.95 ($18.95 Canadian)

The Roots of Ticasuk: An Eskimo Woman's Family Story — Native history at its best. 120 pp., 5-1/2 x 8-1/2, $4.95 ($6.30 Canadian)

Secrets of Eskimo Skin Sewing — Guide to fashioning with fur and skin; patterns and color photos. 125 pp., 5-3/8 x 8-3/8, $9.95 ($12.95 Canadian)

Sitka Man — Six decades of an adventurous life in Alaska. 172 pp., 5-3/8 x 8-3/8, $7.95 ($10.10 Canadian)

Skagway Story — Skagway in the late 19th century. 167 pp., 8-1/4 x 5-1/2, $7.95 ($10.10 Canadian)

Skystruck: True Tales of an Alaska Bush Pilot — From early bush pilot to major airline captain, the remembrances of a lifetime of adventures. 175 pp., 6 x 9, $9.95 ($12.95 Canadian)

Smokehouse Bear — Great stories and recipes from Alaska. 180 pp., 7-3/8 x 9, $9.95 ($12.95 Canadian)

Sourdough Expedition — Stories of the pioneer Alaskans who climbed Mount McKinley in 1910. 64 pp., 8-1/2 x 11, $6.95 ($8.85 Canadian)

Sourdough Jim Pitcher — Adventures of a special breed of man. 64 pp., 8-1/2 x 11, $6.95 ($8.85 Canadian)

The Spirit of Massachusetts — A complete guidebook to Massachusetts. 196 pp., 8 3/8 x 10 3/4, $4.95 ($6.30 Canadian)

Tired Wolf — More great recipes and amusing anecdotes from this popular former state trooper. 210 pp., 7-1/4 x 9, $9.95 ($12.65 Canadian)

Toklat — A children's book about a grizzly and her three cubs. 114 pp., 6 x 9, $9.95 ($12.95 Canadian)

Trails of an Alaska Game Warden — Lively tales that entertain and inform by a wildlife professional. 192 pp., 5-3/8 x 8-3/8, $9.95 ($12.65 Canadian)

Trails of an Alaska Trapper — North country adventure in a true story that reads like a novel. 170 pp., 5-3/8 x 8-3/8, $9.95 ($12.65 Canadian)

Trapline Twins — Tales of the unique lifestyle of identical twin girls in Interior Alaska, trapping, dogsledding, canoeing and living off the land. 215 pp., 6 x 9, $12.95 ($16.45 Canadian)

Two in the Far North — Margaret Murie's classic adventure is back in print with 3 new chapters on Alaska today and 40 drawings. 385 pp., 5-3/8 x 8-3/8, $9.95 ($12.65 Canadian)

Under Alaskan Seas, The Shallow Water Marine Invertebrates — A handy guide and an excellent reference book. 224 pp., 5-3/8 x 8-3/8, $14.95 ($18.95 Canadian)

The Way It Was — Memories of the people and happenings of pioneer Fairbanks. 170 pp., 5-1/2 x 8-1/4, $9.95 ($12.65 Canadian)

We Live in the Alaskan Bush — True account of a young couple and their infant daughter. 135 pp., 8-3/8 x 9, $7.95 ($10.10 Canadian)

A Whaler and Trader in the Arctic — Absolutely true adventure at the turn of the century. 213 pp., 5-1/4 x 8-3/8, $9.95 ($12.65 Canadian)

Wheels on Ice — Tales of bicycling in the Far North. 66 pp., 8-1/2 x 11, $6.95 ($8.85 Canadian)

Whidbey Island Sketchbook — Charming watercolors and black-and-white sketches of Puget Sound's largest island, 64 pp., 11 x 8-1/2, $9.95 ($12.65 Canadian)

Wilderness Survival Guide — Rescue techniques and build-it-yourself survival gear for the wilderness traveler. 120 pp., 5-3/8 x 8-3/8, $9.95 ($12.65 Canadian)

Winter Watch — For 266 days, James Ramsey tested himself against the solitude and isolation of an Arctic winter while living in an old log cabin. 144 pp., 6 x 9, $9.95 ($12.65 Canadian)

Wolf Trail Lodge — Thirty years of adventure in Alaska. 120 pp., 5-3/8 x 8-3/8, $5.95 ($7.55 Canadian)

Index

THE ALASKA ALMANAC®, FACTS ABOUT ALASKA has subject categories organized alphabetically for easy reference. Following is an index to the many topics discussed. Boldface entries signify the pages on which they are found.

Agriculture, 1-2, 87
Air Travel, 2-4, 16
Akutak, 63
Alascom, 179-180
Alaska Highway, 4-5
Alaska Northwest Library, 197-200
Alcoholic Beverages, 6
Aleuts, 100-102, 132-136, 163
Alyeska, 6, 169
Amphibians, 6-7
Arctic Circle, 7, 25-28, 161-162
Arctic Winter Games, 7
Athabascans, 132-136
Aurora Borealis, 8-9

Baleen, 9
Barabara, 9
Baranof, Alexander, 76
Baseball, 9-10
Baskets, 10-11
Beadwork, 11
Bear, 81-82, 97
Beaver, 98
Bering, Vitus, 76
Bering Sea Coast, 162-163
Berries, 11-12
Billiken, 12
Bird, state, 177
Birds, 12-13
Bison, 97
Blanket Toss, 13-14
Boating, 14-15, 87
Books About Alaska and the North, 197-200
Bore Tide, 15
Borough addresses and contacts, 73-74
Boundary, Alaska-Canada, 22-23
Breakup, 15, 136-137
Bunny Boots, 15-16
Bus Lines, 16
Bush, 16, 180
Bush pilots, 16
Business, 87-88

Cabin Fever, 16-17
Cabins, 17-18
Cache, 18
Calendar of Events, 18-21
Camping, 21-22, 88

Canada-Alaska Boundary, 22-23
Canoeing, 87
Caribou, 97
Census data, 88, 150-157
Chambers of Commerce, 23
Cheechako, 24
Chilkat Blankets, 24
Chilkoot Trail, 24
Chill Factor, 24-25
Chinese slipper, 25
Chinook wind, 191-192
Chitons, 25
Climate, 25-28, 88
Coal, 28-29
Communities, 150-157
Congressional delegates, 141-143
Conk, 29
Constitution of Alaska, 29-40
Continental Divide, 40-41
Convention and Visitors Bureaus, 41
Coppers, 41
Cost of Living, 41-42
Courts, 42-44
Coyote, 98
Crab, 66-69
Cruises, 44-45
Cultural Centers, 113-115

Dall sheep, 98
Dalton Highway, 45
Daylight Hours, 46
Deer, 97
Denali, 112-113
Diamond Willow, 46
Dog Mushing, 46-48

Earthquakes, 48-49
Easternmost/westernmost points, 109
Education, 49-50, 88, 185-186
Elk, 97
Employment, 50-51
End of the Trail®, 51-62
Energy and Power, 62-63
Eskimo Ice Cream, 63
Eskimo-Indian Olympics, 192
Eskimos, 100-102, 132-136

Ferries, 63-65
Fires on Wild Lands, 65
Fish and Wildlife Service, 22
Fish, state, 178
Fish Wheel, 66
Fishing, 66-69
Flag, 176
Flowers, 191
Flying squirrel, 98
Forest Service, 17-18, 21-22
Forests, 181-182

Fox, 98
Furs and Trapping, 69

Game animals, 81-82
General Communications, 180
Glaciers and Ice Fields, 70-71
Gold, 71-72
Gold panning, 88
Gold Strikes and Rushes, 72
Government, 73-74
Governors, 141
Gulf Coast, 160-161
Gumboot, 25

Haida, 132-136
Health, 88
Highways, 4-5, 45, 74-75
Hiking, 75
History, 76-78
Holidays, 78
Homesteading, 95-96
Hooligan, 78
Hospitals and Health Facilities, 78-79
Hostels, 79-80
Hot Springs, 80-81
Housing, 88
Hunting, 81-82, 88
Hypothermia, 82

Ice, 83-84
Ice fields, 70-71
Ice Fog, 84
Icebergs, 83-84
Iceworm, 84
Iditarod Trail Sled Dog Race, 84-86
Igloo, 86
Imports and Exports, 86-87
Income, 87
Indians, 132-136
Industry, 87
Information Sources, 87-88
Interior, 161
International Boundary Commission, 22-23
Islands, 88-89
Ivory, 89-90

Jade, 90
Job opportunities, 88
Judicial system 42-44

Kayaking, 87
Kuspuk, 90

Labor and Employer Organizations, 91-93
Lakes, 93
Land, 93-96

Languages, 96
Legislators, 141-143
Lynx, 98

Mammals, 97-100
Marine Mammal Protection Act, 99-100
Marmot, 98
Marten, 98
Masks, 100-102
Medal of Heroism, 102
Metric Conversions, 103
Mileage Chart, 104
Military, 104-107
Minerals and Mining, 107-108
Miscellaneous Facts, 108-110
Miss Alaska, 110
Moose, 97
Mosquitoes, 110-111
Motto, 177
Mountain goat, 97
Mountains, 111-112
Mount McKinley, 112-113
Mukluks, 113
Muktuk, 113
Museums, Cultural Centers and Repositories, 113-115
Mushrooms, 115
Musk Ox, 97, 115-116
Muskeg, 116
Muskrat, 98

National Forests, 117-118
National Guard, 118-120
National Historic Places, 120-124
National Interest Lands Map, 128-129
National Park Service, 22
National Parks, Preserves and Monuments, 124-126
National Petroleum Reserve, 126-127
National Wild and Scenic Rivers, 127-130
National Wilderness Areas, 130-131
National Wildlife Refuges, 131-132
Native People, 87, 132-136
Native Regional Corporations, 134-135
Native Village Corporations, 135-136
Nenana Ice Classic, 136-137
Newspapers and Periodicals, 137-140
Northern lights, 8-9
No-see-ums, 140
Nuchalawoya, 140
Nursing homes, 79

Officials, 140-143
Oil and Gas, 143-145
Otter, 98

Parka, 90, **145-146**

Permafrost, 146
Permanent Fund, 147
Petroleum Reserve, 126-127
Pioneers' Homes, 147-148
Pipeline, 148-149
Place Names, 149-150
Poisonous Plants, 150
Populations and Zip Codes, 150-157
Potlatch, 157

Raccoon, 98
Radio Stations, 157-159
Railroads, 159-160
Regions of Alaska, 160-163
Reindeer, 1
Religion, 163-164
Reptiles, 164
River running, 88
Rivers, 127-130, 164-165
Roadhouses, 165-166
Rocks and Gems, 166
Russian-American Company, 140

Salmon, 66-69
School Districts, 166-167
Seal, state, 176-177
Shipping, 167-168
Sitka Slippers, 168
Skiing, 168-170
Skin Sewing, 170
Skookum, 170
Soapstone, 170
Song, state, 177
Sourdough, 170-171
Southcentral/Gulf Coast, 160-161
Southeast, 160
Southwestern/Alaska Peninsula, 163
Speed Limits, 171
Squaw Candy, 171
State Park System, 176
State Symbols, 176-178
Subsistence, 178
Sundog, 178

Taiga, 178
Taku wind, 192

Telecommunications, 178-180
Telephone Numbers in the Bush, 180
Television Stations, 180-181
Temperatures, 25-28
Tides, 181
Timber, 181-182
Time Zones, 182-183
Tlingits, 132-136
Totems, 183-184
Tourism, 41,184
Trade, foreign, 86-87
Trans-Alaska Pipeline, 148-149
Trapping, 69
Travel and visitor information, 88
Tree, state, 177-178
Trees and Shrubs, 184-185
Tsimshians, 132-136
Tundra, 185

Ulu, 185
Umiak, 185
Unemployment, 50-51
Universities and Colleges, 185-186

Vapor barrier boots, 15-16
Visitor and convention bureaus, 41
Volcanoes, 186-187

Walrus, 99
Waves, 188
Weasel, 98
Western/Bering Sea Coast, 162-163
Whales and Whaling, 188-191
Wild Flowers, 191
Wilderness Areas, 130-131
Wilderness Refuges, 131-132
Williwaws, 192
Winds, 191-192
Wolf, 98
Wolverine, 98
World Eskimo-Indian Olympics, 192

Yearly Highlights—1989, 193-196

Zip codes, 150-156

Many other fascinating books are available from
ALASKA NORTHWEST BOOKS™
Ask for them at your favorite bookstore,
or write us for a complete free catalog.

ALASKA NORTHWEST BOOKS™
A division of GTE Discovery Publications, Inc.
P.O. Box 3007
Bothell, WA 98041-3007

Or call toll free 1-800-331-3510